MW01621175

I STAND

IN THE CENTER

OF THE GOOD

American Indian Lives

I Stand in the Center of the Good

Interviews with Contemporary Native American Artists

EDITED BY LAWRENCE ABBOTT

University of Nebraska Press *Lincoln and London*

Manufactured in the United States of America.

Publication of this book was assisted by a grant from

The Andrew W. Mellon Foundation.

The paper in this book meets the minimum requirements of American

National Standard for Information Sciences — Permanence of Paper

for Printed Library Materials, ANSI Z39.48–1984.

Library of Congress Cataloging-in-Publication Data

I stand in the center of the good : interviews with contemporary

Native American artists / edited by Lawrence Abbott.

p. cm. — (American Indian lives)

ISBN 0-8032-1037-X

1. Indian artists — United States — Interviews — Juvenile literature.

2. Art, Indian — Juvenile literature. 3. Art, Modern — 20th century —

United States — Juvenile literature. [1. Indians of North America —

Interviews. 2. Artists.] I. Abbott, Lawrence, 1949– . II. Series.

N6538.A4I2 1994

704'.0397073'0904 — dc20

93-36892

CIP

AC

This book is

especially dedicated

to my mother, Dorothy,

and to my aunt Edith,

my cousin Joanne,

and my niece Jennifer,

who each helped see

me through it; and

to the memory of

my father, Lyman.

Contents

Plates

Acknowledgments

First of all, *I Stand in the Center of the Good* would not have been possible without the cooperation of the artists involved. They all gave willingly and generously of their time and energy. It has been an honor and privilege to work with them.

I also need to thank friends, colleagues, and others who contributed to the making of this book: Paule Anglim of the Paule Anglim Gallery, San Francisco; Sara Bates of American Indian Contemporary Arts, San Francisco; Christine Beacham; Bodo Beer; Diane Bridges of the Canadian Museum of Civilization, Ottawa, Ontario; John Elder of Middlebury College; Phil Fitzpatrick; Courtney Frisse; Elizabeth Grant; Clinton Hulse; John and Chris Klein; Mario Klimiades and his staff in the library and archives at the Heard Museum, Phoenix; Peter Klosky of the Roberson Center for the Arts and Sciences, Binghamton, New York; Robert Lardon; Carrie Lederer of the Falkirk Cultural Center, San Rafael, California; Arlene LewAllen and Geoffrey Gorman of the LewAllen Gallery, Santa Fe; Linda Linssen; Alfredo Lujan; Mary Beth Marchessault; Suzanne and Phillip Montalvan; Jarold Ramsey of the University of Rochester; David Rettig of the Rettig y Martinez Gallery, Santa Fe; Ron and Martha Savageau; the Bernice Steinbaum Gallery, New York City; Jerry Warman; Elizabeth Woody; Paul Zolbrod; and Kitty Zurko of the College of Wooster Art Museum, Wooster, Ohio. Thanks also need to go to the many other curators, photographers, and gallery personnel who were kind enough keep me on a clear path.

Part of this book was developed during a sabbatical sponsored by the National Endowment for the Humanities in 1990–91. I'd like to thank the Endowment for their support.

Introduction

Lining the high walls of the post office in Anadarko, Oklahoma, are sixteen murals depicting scenes from Southern Plains life. These murals, commissioned by the Section of Fine Arts Federal Work Agency of the Public Works Administration, were executed by a member of the Kiowa Nation in 1936, Stephen Mopope, with assistance from two other Kiowas, Spencer Asah and James Auchiah. With such titles as *Two Eagle Dancers*, *Kiowa Camp Site*, *Buffalo Skull with Crossed Arrows behind It*, and *Buffalo Hunter's Shield,* the panels are diverse in their subjects, from mundane camp scenes to ceremonial dances to more emblematic and symbolic representations. Some of the images are relatively static, while in others there is a suggestion of motion and movement.[1]

Although I didn't know it at the time, this book really began on an early summer afternoon in 1990 when I stopped at the Anadarko post office. I was going to the Kiowa Museum in Carnegie, and from there to find my own way to Rainy Mountain, but I decided to visit the post office. I took a lot of photographs of the murals, trying to make sense of the imagery on those walls, while the activities of the Anadarko post office went on around me. After an hour or two I packed up my tripod and camera and continued on my journey. But I never did find Rainy Mountain that day.

A week or so later this journey, quite accidentally, took me to Tyler, Texas. The Tyler Museum of Art was exhibiting a show of so-called traditional Indian art, so I made the trip down from Dallas. This exhibition featured a wide variety of watercolor and tempera works by such Southwestern artists as Waldo Mootzka (Hopi), Tonita Pena (San Ildefonso), Otis Polelonema (Hopi), and Velino Herrera (Zia), shown alongside . . . Stephen Mopope, James Auchiah, and Jack Hokeah. The Southwestern artists also depicted dancers and ceremonial scenes, but the colors, the regalia, the actions, were different. Yet, there was something similar about them, too, in the way the images were structured. But what surprised me most was seeing again those Kiowa artists, especially Mopope, this time, for me, in new company.

I decided to learn more about the company these artists kept. I began going to as many museums and galleries as I could. My wanderings took me beyond Oklahoma and Texas to Oregon, California, Arizona, New Mexico, the upper Midwest, and New York. I started to search out catalogs of "Indian art" exhibitions. This time, though, what I found was that in the newer art I came upon the company was decidedly different: garishly painted construction workers' hard hats, huge steel sculptures, photographs and photocollages, messages to America on the Spectacolor billboard in Times Square, delicate abstractions. These were a long way from the representational and precise images of dancers and scenes of life from a half century earlier. Could these new works also be "Indian art"? I began to wonder about the radical change in the imagery, about definitions of "Indian art," and about the artists themselves. From these wanderings and wonderings comes the substance of this book.

But the substance of this book is not historical, covering the context and the developments of Indian art since the 1930s; nor is it critical, analyzing the style, structure, and meaning of contemporary art; and it is not anthropological, assessing the art in terms of its tribal and cultural meaning. Rather, the substance of this book is the artists themselves, offering an opportunity for those interested in art to hear what a variety of artists have to say about their lives and their work, and, strangely enough, in their own words.

I say "strangely" because in the many, many books and essays on contemporary Native art, the voice of the artist, with some exceptions, is nearly inaudible, a sidebar to the pronouncements of art critics and scholars. But I suppose it is not unusual for critics to tell artists what they are doing (or what they are supposed to be doing). For example, in an otherwise excellent essay entitled "Frames of Reference: Native American Art in the Context of

Modern and Postmodern Art," by Gerhard Hoffman (in *The Arts of the North American Indian: Native Traditions in Evolution*, edited by Edwin Wade), in some two-dozen-plus pages of text the *words* of Native artists account for less than one. Certainly, Hoffman's purpose in his essay is to develop a context for a fuller understanding of contemporary Native art, but it might have been polite to invite the artist to the discussion. Too often, Native artists (as well as other artists of color), insofar as they are discussed at all, are talked about or to rather than with.

But talking with artists about their work seems, at first, to be an uncertain enterprise. After all, painters, photographers, and sculptors encode their perceptions in visual languages, with each piece speaking in its own way, releasing its meanings through paint, wood, clay, stone, light and shadow. Many artists might agree with George Longfish: "I don't like to make a statement about my art that rigidly codifies it. I feel that it is important that the observer bring his or her own sensibilities to the work and make an interpretation based on an individual act of looking."[2]

Still, there is at least one important reason for talking with artists, and for listening to artists talk, and that is to hear the stories behind the images, the personal and communal stories that drive the creation of their art and their lives.

This is not to say that all or even any contemporary Native art is narrative art as that term is commonly understood: telling a story through representational images. Some work is realistic (recalling the Plains and Southwestern styles), some symbolic, some abstract, some formal. There may not be obvious stories on the surface of the image. But at the same time, a great deal of Native art derives compelling narrative power from the visual representation of personal experience, culture, myth, and tradition. In this way, a painting, for example, has a narrative existing parallel to its imagery, and in the best works, image and story are inseparable.

Take, for instance, Frank LaPena's engraving entitled *Mt. Shasta*. On one level, it "holds a mirror up to Nature." One could go to Mount Shasta, and probably even find the exact vantage point LaPena took. One could hold the engraving up and declare, yes, there is a representational correspondence between the subject and the image. The artist, one could say, has skillfully represented that subject, and has told the story of the appearance of the mountain.

But this would be missing what I mean here by story or narrative. By approaching Native art in this way, the viewer would not seek out the stories within the image, stories that are personal within the communal. In terms of this work by LaPena, the stories have to do with the sacred dimension of Mount Shasta, with its healing properties and ceremonial functions; there are also personal stories of the artist embedded in the image, like the experience of Shasta's seasons, the taste of the air at fourteen thousand feet, the burden of carrying down a dead man. These many levels of story all coalesce in the engraving *Mt. Shasta*.

Of course, a viewer cannot be expected to know every personal detail which finds its way in some form into a work of art, and the embedded cultural references are sometimes difficult if not impossible to understand. But a viewer *can* respond to the range of meanings in contemporary Native art by realizing that even abstract works emerge from, and may in fact represent, concrete experiences.

Look at Emmi Whitehorse's canvases. At first glance her work appears decidedly abstract, with such forms as sticks, leaves, and other objects floating in pastel spaces. The casual viewer may conclude that her work is even a bit repetitious in color and form. But on closer look one notes subtle variations in color and composition, indicating changes in the artist's perception of her subjects. Whitehorse's *Mt. Taylor* series is not an abstraction, then, but is firmly grounded in her experience of one of the sacred mountains of the Dinetah. Her various *Mt. Taylor* works are as real and as representational as La Pena's engraving of Mount Shasta. This unity or similarity is based on the reality behind the image, the story, the narrative. I think Paula Gunn Allen's comment about Native literature also applies to visual art: "The symbolism in American Indian ceremonial literature, then, is not symbolic in the usual sense; the four mountains in the Mountain Chant do not stand for something else. They are those exact mountains perceived psychically, as it were, or mystically."[3]

Whitehorse's *Mt. Taylor* works are not, then, abstractions in the way that is usually thought of in art, but are concretizations of her direct experience of the "inner forms" of her subjects. Through the physicalization of these "inner forms" on her canvases Whitehorse is able to represent Mount Taylor in the same way that LaPena represents Mount Shasta. Paul Zolbrod has said that "this concept [of 'inner forms'] accounts for the animating power which Navajos believe is shared in all things—not just in people and animals, not just in the great mountains like Mt. Taylor or the San Francisco Peaks, and not just in huge monoliths like Shiprock or Window Rock, but even in the smallest, most inanimate items."[4] I am not saying that all Native art must be looked at through a Navajo lens, but that what is taken for abstract imagery in Native art may very well emerge from the artist's concrete perceptions, and that representational and abstract imagery may be linked more closely than is usually thought, linked as story.

And the stories being told in contemporary works are not more complex or multilayered than the stories told in the so-called traditional Indian art of the 1930s and '40s, or in the "experimental" art of the 1950s and '60s by Oscar Howe, Joe Herrera, or George Morrison. And the stories of contemporary art are not more complex than the stories and structures that inhere in what are considered crafts, like basketry, pottery, and the making of ceremonial regalia. Rather, the stories seen in today's art are of a piece with these other stories, both ancient and modern. Again, Paula Gunn Allen: "The aesthetic imperative requires that new experiences be woven into existing traditions in order for personal experience to be transmuted into communal experience; that is, so we can understand how today's events harmonize with communal consciousness."[5] What differs are the materials and the imagery used to embody story. Whether or not the materials include paint and canvas, videotape, Xerox machines, or computers, and whether or not the imagery comes from city streets or from ceremonies, from the reservation or from pop culture, there are no restrictions on what constitutes Indian art.

Critical discussion over the last few years or so has posited a bipolar model of "dominant" or "mainstream" and "marginal" cultures, assessing how the voices of the "other" have been devalued. These devalued others, or "ethnics," as the line goes, do not quite have what it takes to step into the mainstream, although some might walk in through a major museum or gallery's rear entrance if they lose enough of their otherness, or if some exotica are needed to round out an exhibition. Although these others may be admired for their creative energy (indeed, their energy probably comes from working upstream against the current), the "big time" (and big money) is reserved for those up to their necks in the mainstream. I wonder about the arrogance of this dichotomy, so convenient in its classification of those outside the aesthetic comfort zone.

But to come to a more accurate reading of contemporary Native art and its position in American culture and the art world, it might be helpful to discard the simple dichotomy of center and margin, valued and devalued, for a model that repositions artists and their work in terms of a multiplicity of communities. Henry Louis Gates, Jr., suggests this when he writes:

> The threat to the margin comes not from assimilation or dissolution—from any attempt to denude it of its defiant alterity—but, on the contrary, from the center's attempts to preserve that alterity, which result in the homogenization of the other as, simply, other. The margin's resistance to such homogenization, in turn, takes the form of breeding new margins within margins, circles within circles, an ever renewed process of differentiation, even fragmentation. . . . I submit, then, that the ritualized invocation of otherness is losing its capacity to engender new forms of knowledge and that the "margin" may have exhausted its strategic value as a position from which to theorize the very antinomies that produced it as an object of study.[6]

As Gates points out, the so-called margin should not be conceived of as one undifferentiated mass with no interior distinctions or trajectories, but as multivoiced, multidirectional in its own right.

What I would like to propose is that contemporary Native art be looked at not as marginal art, defined in contradistinction to a hypothetical center, but as a body of art that evidences multiple unities and represents multiple communities. Approached this way, contemporary Native art can be assessed on its own terms, as its own center, rather than for its position on some continuum of marginality, or by the degree to which it deviates from "traditional" Indian art, or by how much it integrates Euro-American techniques and styles. To fully grasp the diversity and complexity of Native art, and artists, the reader may do well to take up Allen's suggestion that criticism and analysis be "founded on the principle of inclusion rather than that of exclusion" and therefore derive "critical principles based on what is actually being rendered by the true experts"[7]—in this case, visual artists.

But there is another level of inclusiveness in Native thought and art which the late Robert Thomas (Cherokee) illustrated in a course of his in Native religion and spirituality that I was fortunate enough to attend at the University of Arizona a few years ago. In one of his lectures he explained that Indian people would not declare a personal emotion like "I am happy." Rather, there would be a connectedness between the individual and the universe, a reciprocal relation, which would be expressed, in this case, as "I stand in the center of the good." The individual is part of the greater circle. It was Bob Thomas who provided the title of this book. Rick Hill put it this way: "The circle, representing equality, sharing and unity, links all the aspects of culture together—art, religion, social organization, ritual, language, law and lifestyle."[8]

This approach to Native art opens up new avenues of critical discussion and appreciation and allows the viewer to understand that contemporary Native artists are part of an evolving tradition, one that is characterized by a receptivity to whatever influences and methods of production serve their particular visions. Contemporary artists are as influenced (in varying degrees) by, say, Kandinsky, abstract expressionism, surrealism, Coney Island, Walt Disney, and the current art scene as they are (in varying degrees) by earlier Indian art, tribal tradition, and their participation in ceremony. And one cannot discount the individuality of an artist's personal experience, whether that experience be of parenting, a university professorship, one's homosexuality, or one's mortality. Artists have many roles and realities and claim many communities as their own. George Longfish and Joan Randall have written about this multiplicity in regard to Northern California artists: "At the world and national level they are Indian; at the regional level they are Maidu, Paiute, and Karok. On the individual level they are Frank, George, Jean, Harry, Brian, Karen, and Dal."[9]

To borrow from ecology, contemporary Native art might be seen as representing the "edge effect," which leads to a "tendency for increased variety and density at community junctions. . . . Furthermore, some species [in this case, artists] require as part of the habitat, or as part of their life history, two or more adjacent communities that differ greatly in structure."[10]

This repositioning of Native art with the recognition of diversity in community, imagery, and methods can, I believe, dispel the misconceptions that have surrounded it. "Non-Indian" influences or lack of recognizable "Indian" imagery does not render the art of Native peoples invalid or inauthentic. This test of authenticity (really a "fallacy of authenticity") avers that Indian art is that which is stored in ethnology collections, is sold in curio shops, is primitive, and represents as much of the unsullied precontact culture as possible. Because of this fallacy of authenticity artists have been prevented from growing and audiences have been denied the opportunity to really look at Indian art, past *and* present. As Gerald McMaster has advised, "seeing is mandatory; conclusions are optional."[11] Unfortunately, for too long, seeing was optional, conclusions were mandatory.

There are many threads to see in the multihued weave of contemporary Indian art, as many meanings as there are artists. For example, some artists use satire, irony, and reversal of word or image (or both) to challenge viewer perceptions. Seemingly paradoxical, the reversals are meant to guide the viewer to see more clearly and to break out of habituation of thought and observation, to literally re-see. Hachivi Edgar Heap of Birds has reversed the letters in the names in his *Native Hosts* series, for example, to remind people of who walked this land first, and to propose questions about what happened to those people. Rick Glazer-Danay also reverses phrases in his personal statements and deconstructs meaning in his work by reassembling and juxtaposing the various components of his "toys." Rick Hill dissects American culture by combining his photographs with a satiric version of the pseudolanguage anthropologists use to explain Indian cultures. These artists desire to subvert the viewer's usual expectations about Indian art.

These artists wish to raise questions, through their work, about the history and the present social, political, and economic conditions of Native peoples, and, indeed, about global conditions. Other artists deal with these issues through different imagery. Peter Jemison's paper bags and even his nature works have political ramifications, while Jaune Quick-to-See Smith embeds environmental concerns in her painting, and Mario Martinez has recently made his homosexuality a central focus of *To My Lavender Siblings* (1991).

Jimmie Durham once wrote that "it would be impossible, and I think immoral, to attempt to discuss American Indian art sensibly without making the political realities central."[12] And at base it is probably true that Native art is political, if only insofar as it is a means of survival, a declaration of a people's existence, a way of maintaining in the face of the powers of extinction. That is probably the way it has always been for Indian people, certainly since contact and colonization. Beyond this, though, I would hope that a political reading of Native art is not another imposition on style and content. Some artists are clearly political in their imagery while others are not.

Some Native artists, while not denying the broad-scale political dimensions of their art, work from different sets of concerns. Frank Tuttle and Frank LaPena talk of the ways in which certain paintings are meant to have a particular efficacy in the world, symbolically enacting ceremonies or rituals. Other works keep alive memory, both personal and mythic, like Linda Lomahaftewa's and Emmi Whitehorse's. Other works bring honor to all that the dominant culture has dishonored, or forgotten. Kay WalkingStick and Nora Naranjo-Morse use their art to explore their own individual experiences and ways of seeing. But, finally, even these categories fall away when the full range of the art is looked at. No one artist's art is simply a category.

If the overall purpose of this book is to present the full range of Native artists' voices, then in order to do it properly, there would need to be hundreds of days, hundreds of interviews. Unfortunately, that was not possible, so I have sought to include emerging as well as more established artists, and have tried to select representative artists who are recognized and respected by their peers in the art world and who have a solid body of work behind them. The artists included here are between thirty and fifty-five years old, so there is a sense of continuity between two generations. The artists illustrate a range of regions and tribal affiliations, styles and visions, but the reader will note that Alaska and the Pacific Northwest, for example, are not represented. The exigencies of time and scheduling prevented me from visiting those areas and talking with many artists whose work is important and who deserve a wider audience. Other artists simply preferred to let their work speak by itself, a decision I fully understand. Of course, at the time of this writing, there are still younger artists in various graduate programs throughout the country, and yet even younger ones in high schools. Within a decade they will take their places in the art world and put their own stamp on "Indian art." Despite these lacunae, I hope that the artists here can in some measure stand for the whole of contemporary Native art. But it must also be remembered that these interviews reflect a specific time and place, and subsequent work by these artists will lead to new ideas, new visions, and still further work.

There can be no final word on Indian art, because creation is a continuing process. But if this book had its beginning in the Anadarko post office that summer afternoon in 1990, it reached its closure (symbolically, at least) one year later in Santa Fe through two incidents, both involving Allan Houser. The first occurred one hot July afternoon, when movement became a search for shade, in the courtyard of the Museum of Indian Arts and Culture. The museum was hosting a birthday party for Houser (his seventy-seventh), and the music was being provided by James "Snooky" Pryor, the seventy-one-year-old blues harp player, and his band. As the afternoon was winding down, Houser took the stage with Pryor and they jammed some blues for a few numbers. Pryor, who started playing harmonica at the age of seven in 1928, and Houser, who started painting in the mid-1920s . . . each man the essence of what he does. A few weeks later there was a street concert in downtown Santa Fe featuring Queen Ida and her Bon Temps Zydeco Band. The aromas of gumbo and *étouffée* filled the air. As I walked through the crowd, I spotted Allan Houser, moving to the Cajun beat.

This book celebrates the reality of contemporary Native visual expression, the reality that has woven itself out of stone, wood, clay, paint, paper, canvas, silver iodide crystals, and videotape, the reality of Allan Houser playing the blues and dancing to Zydeco music.

I STAND

IN THE CENTER

OF THE GOOD

Rick Glazer-Danay

Mohawk

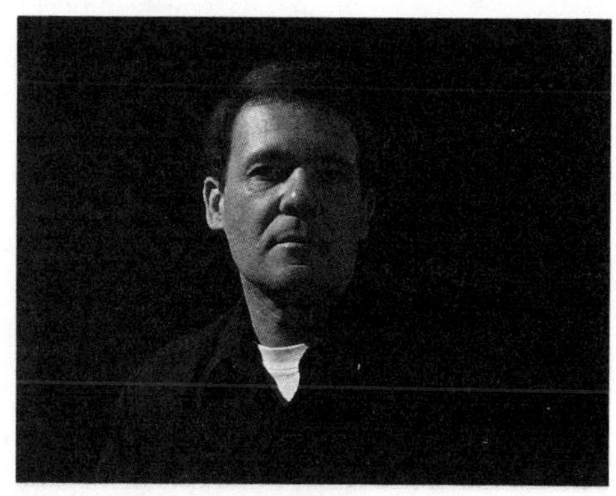

Rick Glazer-Danay is not known for understatement in his work or his comments about it. He prefers irony upon irony, juxtaposition upon juxtaposition, reversal upon reversal. His sculptures — "toys" — revel in glorious, throbbing colors, "Coney Island colors," applied to just about any object or surface he can get his hands on. In the early eighties Danay created *My Dog Spot* (1982) and *Pink Buffalo Hat* (1983), construction workers' hard hats adorned with some of his characteristic imagery: buffaloes, disembodied mouths, nude figures, Betty Boop, insects. Susan Shedd has written: "Calling to mind comic book and grafitti art, Danay creates similar worlds of seductive energy, fueled by the paradoxes of life within two cultures."[1]

In fact, this sense of paradox has evidently confused people seeking a strict and narrow definition of "Indian art." Before the Mapplethorpe controversy, Glazer-Danay had a work removed from a show. In 1986 the director of the Roberson Center for the Arts and Sciences in Binghamton, New York, made a "marketing decision" and took *Buffalo Gal with Boots* (1985) from the traveling "Art of the Seventh Generation" show, calling the work "soft core porn." Glazer-Danay even had a piece removed from an invitational show in Tulsa before the Binghamton episode. Neither situation seemed to upset him. "I disagree with the decision, but life is too short to agonize over decisions by bankers," Glazer-Danay remarked at the time of the Binghamton incident.[2]

Glazer-Danay's imagery runs from pop culture (*Punk Mohawk*, 1983) to satire (*Fry Bread Freda*, *Fry Bread Fred*, both 1983) to political commentary (*Coast to Coast and See to Sea*, 1981). Although Glazer-Danay claims to have no conscious political intention in his work, the imagery of *Coast to Coast*, especially side A, explores the complicity of religion in the exploitation of Native peoples in the "Age of Discovery" and the blissful ignorance about the condition of indigenous peoples in the contemporary world. Side B is part of an old board puzzle depicting the United States, split horizontally, with Wisconsin set off from the other states and where Ohio should be. Glazer-Danay insists that he separated Wisconsin because his experience teaching in Green Bay was alienating; yet the truncated puzzle board could also refer to the arbitrary naming and arrangement of boundaries in the fabrication of the United States.

Rick Glazer-Danay has had a varied life and career in and out of the arts. He was born in Coney Island, Brooklyn, New York, in 1942. His father was a full-blood Mohawk, his mother white. Glazer-Danay claims that he was never ashamed of being a mixed-blood, "except sometimes for the white part." He attended school at first in Coney Island and completed high school in Reseda, California, and the influences of Coney Island, Disneyland, and Hollywood inform his work. Danay has walked the high steel, served in the U.S. Army Reserve, tended bar, and worked as a bodyguard for Dean Martin.

He followed up his interest in art more formally after he witnessed an accident at a construction site in New York. He returned to California and received his B.A. degree in fine arts from California State University, Northridge, his M.A. in fine arts from California State University, Chico, and his M.F.A. from the University of California at Davis. Glazer-Danay taught at the University of Wisconsin–Green Bay from 1980 to 1985, and since 1985 has been a professor of art at

California State University at Long Beach. In the fall of 1991 he received a two-year appointment to the Rupert Costo Chair in American Indian history at the University of California at Riverside. His work is in many collections, including the permanent collections of the Philbrook Museum in Tulsa, Oklahoma, and the Department of the Interior.

In fact, Glazer-Danay now asserts that he wishes to earn his keep solely by teaching, and he has started to spread the word that he will not exhibit in galleries anymore. "Right now, I don't care who sees my work or what happens to it. I just want to work in my studio and be left alone. Maybe that will change in time, I don't know."[3] Of course, with irony not lost on Glazer-Danay, galleries and exhibits are more interested in his work than ever. On the occasion of his fiftieth birthday, Glazer-Danay circulated the following:

> HEAR ME MY COLLECTORS.
>
> "I am tired of exhibiting. Our artists are killed. Harden [*sic*] is dead. Loloma is dead. The old artists are all dead. It is the young men who say yes or no, T. C. Cannon who led the young men is dead. It is cold and we have no canvas. The collectors are freezing their funds. The artists, some of them, have run away to the hills and have no brushes, no paint; no one knows where they are — perhaps working for the B.I.A. I want to have time to work on my creations and see how many of them I can find. Maybe I shall find them among the museums. Hear me, my collectors. I am tired; my brush is worn and bent. From where the easel now stands, I will sell my creations no more forever."
>
> Richard Danay, after some of the vividest artwork ever completed, surrenders only miles from the City of Angels at the Los Angeles River, under the shadow of the Hollywood sign, upon his 50th birthday on August 12, 1992, to Rennard Strickland and Edwin Wade."[4]

We had the chance to talk during a symposium at the Heard Museum in May of 1991.

LA: In a recent essay entitled "Trickster Discourse," Gerald Vizenor writes: "The trickster . . . is imagined in narrative voices . . . which is comic liberation."[5] Can your works be considered examples of "comic liberation"?

RGD: No. I've read all that stuff. What I do is what I've always done. I've had a particular, maybe peculiar, sense of humor. I don't attribute it to anything cultural; it's just the way I think and the way I function. The work is just a natural extension of who I am in life. I don't take too much seriously—well, actually I take a lot seriously, but I turn it around to make fun of it.

LA: Humor is an unmistakable component of your work. You've titled one show "Pink Buffalos and Other Serious Notions" and you've written, "One should not take this business of art all too seriously."[6] How serious are you about humor?

RGD: Oh, very serious. For some reason, humor is neglected. Just about every artist I've met has an incredible sense of humor, but in their work they cut it off and claim that they have to be serious all the time. They treat art like something it's not. What you've got to realize is that art in America is really decorations for rich people, so if it matches their curtains they buy it and if it has the right name they buy it and if it's the right price they buy it. And when I say the right price, I mean expensive, because it's a prestige thing to show to friends and say, "Look how cultured I am. I bought a Jasper Johns" (or whatever "name" artist you want to pick). Whether they like the work or not they do those things. To me that whole scene is comical. I never take it that seriously.

LA: This seems an iconoclastic point of view in the arts in general, and also perhaps in Native American art—challenging the view that seriousness of purpose or product is equated with the worth and value of a piece.

RGD: I think that there are a lot of California artists—Billy Al Bengston, David Gilhooly, Roy deForest, William T. Wiley, for example—who have the same mentality I have, who are serious and not serious at the same time. I think artists like that have more of an impact on creative art than the decorator types or those that have Indian angst, like "How am I going to do buffaloes in a serious manner?"

LA: With the humor, though, much of your work has serious themes, political themes, like *Coast to Coast and See to Sea* [1981] or *Missionary Headrest* [1978]. Do you have a conscious, if secondary, political message in your work?

RGD: No. I don't have any political themes. I pick a subject because it strikes me as humorous or ridiculous or just not quite right. I like things that are incongruous. What I do is treat the subject as an idea, then abandon the idea and put it into an artistic context. The problem for me as an artist is how to transfer the idea immediately and work out some sort of formal context. While I'm working on it I forget the idea, like *Chief's Chair* [1987]. I never stopped after I got the initial thought, never thought about a title. All I knew was that I was going to make a chair out of all the little pieces I had lying around, and it's only afterward that I looked at it. To me, it was just a funny set of things I glued together and painted. It's hard to expect an artist to know what they're doing. *I* don't know what the hell I'm doing.

LA: Do these incongruities or things which strike you as ridiculous come from social observation?

RGD: Yeah, they just kind of seep into what I do. I don't consciously sit down and read something and then say that I'm going to make a piece about that. I kind of let things brew, for years sometimes, and all of a sudden I figure out the artistic context to put the ideas into.

LA: A strictly political reading of your work, then, is a mistake. Does it matter to you if critics, and interviewers, seek meanings you didn't intend?

RGD: No. If they think it's radical, political, what have you, that's fine. When I'm done with something I don't think about it. It surprises me, actually, when critics read all this stuff into my pieces that I never saw. But I kind of like that.

LA: On one of the panels of *Coast to Coast* there are images that could be read as a social or historical analysis of Indian-white relations.

RGD: Some of those pictures are from an old *National Geographic*. In the middle of the panel, the pictures came from an old comic book, *Thor* or *Conan the Barbarian* or something, and the third set is from a dirty magazine. And the stuff on the back I just found, old Mercury dimes and pencils, and I glued them all together. I love junk. I collect all kinds of stuff and try to make it into art.

LA: An artist's statement of a few years back seemed to be a string of non sequiturs, but is actually a well-structured series of reversals.

RGD: Yeah, I still use that.

LA: For example, you wrote, "No Sense Makes Sense," "Absurdity Saves Us from Dismal Consistency," "Paint Aint," and then reversed them as the statement progressed.[7]

RGD: Again, that's not a conscious thing. But as my work became more well-known, people started to demand a statement. So I sat down, and like in the *Reader's Digest* "Points to Ponder," I just reversed things, and I went through Wittgenstein and other things and picked out these little bits and pieces and reworded them and restructured them, and I just put them down in a stream of consciousness. Then I reversed them again and added my wife's name, and my kids' names, Coney Island, things like that.

LA: One of the phrases in that statement was "Tradition Is the Enemy of Progress," and you have a 1983 piece [*Tradition*], where those words appear on the panels. What about that work?

RGD: Jamake Highwater called me up and said he was going to make a film and would I like to be a part of it. I said no. Then he said it'd be a free week in Santa Fe, so I said yes. And since my part in the film would only take a day, I'd have a lot of free time. Anyway, he wanted a piece specially for that film. They sent me a script with his notes and said to come up with something based on the script. I had read something once about "progress is the enemy of tradition," so I reversed it. I don't always reverse things on purpose; I do it when I read, too, transpose things back and forth. So I just reversed that statement. But I think the intellectuals picked up on it more than I did. To me it was just playing word games.

LA: The piece has a sort of revolving-door effect, with a middle-class-looking white woman following a traditionally dressed Plains Indian, but he is also following her.

RGD: These were just some plastic dolls I picked up somewhere. The box was my son's microscope case. So I just put those things together in the context of what I felt about the script—it didn't make any sense to me!

LA: That piece is shown in catalogs a lot.

RGD: I think it's in the collection of the Department of the Interior.

LA: Do you work primarily with found materials, stuff that's just lying around?

RGD: They know me at all the junk stores. A lot of my art comes out of the Salvation Army. Then I repaint it. It's nice to take some junk and fix it up.

LA: Do you call your work sculpture or assemblages?

RGD: Toys. I have to keep busy, so I go into the studio and make toys. I'm just amazed that people will pay big prices for them, really amazed that people would want one in their homes. It just floors me that they buy what I make. It's really my hobby, my avocation, my life, and the way I define my existence, all in one.

LA: The toys are multisided, with two fronts or two backs, which sometimes appear unrelated, like *I'll Take Manhattan* or *Coast to Coast.* Is there some connection between these parts?

RGD: I don't know. For the *Coast to Coast* piece, it was just stuff I put together that I had lying around in the garage, an old Monopoly set, some puzzle pieces. I like puzzles. The problem is I don't work from my head. The critics will bring all these meanings up and I'll go home and say, "Oh, look what I've done."

LA: You've written that your work is from the Coney Island baroque school. Could you talk about that influence on you?

RGD: Merry-go-rounds, the roller coaster, the Steeplechase, all the colors and forms—the garishness, everything overpainted. The animated fat lady in the glass case. That's a big part of my life. It stuck with me. It really was a small community.

LA: Was that the Golden Age of Coney Island?

RGD: Well, there was always sleaze there. My family were all ironworkers, but what's interesting is that I've read where I've been born in eight places. I don't know where people get all that stuff to talk about. I lose track of it all. I was an ironworker, dishwasher, I worked at Whiskey a Go Go in L.A., I was Dean Martin's bodyguard. The sixties weren't a real big influence, more the fifties, like Hollywood Boulevard, the garishness, and the excess, the neon signs. Plus I met a lot of people when I was around fourteen. At that time I lived down the block from Ed Kienholz. He used to eat at my stepdad's restaurant on Santa Monica Boulevard, down from Barney's Beanery. He was the first one to influence me. Even then I was seriously unserious about art. I did a lot of drawing, if I wasn't beating on somebody.

LA: But it was the Golden Age of sleaze. You have a lot of recurrent images in your work: disembodied lips, naked men and women, "soft core porn," as one gallery director called it. *Buffalo Gal with Boots* was pulled from a show in New York in 1986. You've evidently upset or confused people. Do they feel your work is not appropriate Indian art?

RGD: First of all, my work is always appropriate Indian art. My work is how I define myself as an Indian person in the twentieth century. About the sex thing, it's not conscious. I've never cheated on my wife, I'm a good family man. I lead a really conservative lifestyle. My hair is short, I don't wear an earring. Maybe vicariously I'm living out some other life. Who knows?

LA: What about having a work pulled out of a show?

RGD: I don't know. In New York when they pulled the piece the Indian community got more upset than I did. They called me and I said that it didn't bother me. If I had been the director of the show I probably would have pulled it out, too. I understood the logic of the people who were upset, but I also understood the logic of the museum, where if they ask you to show something they should follow through on it, but the director runs the place, so it's his decision.

LA: Maybe we could talk about your working method or approach to making a piece.

RGD: I just sort of hop around. I usually have a bunch of different things going on at the same time. Some stuff I might put away for two to three years. It's just not working, or my wife says it's terrible. Some other things might be done in two to three days. I don't have any one set method, but I am disciplined. And I am a compulsive worker. I have a very strong work ethic and when I'm not making art I feel guilty and nervous. I must produce. I must keep busy.

LA: Do you borrow from one work to put in another?

RGD: Oh yeah. Stuff from twenty years ago I still use. As a matter of fact I make templates sometimes of images I like and I keep them and maybe five years later I'll use it again. It's sort of lazy, but I don't have to do a new design. I can just trace from the template.

LA: You work in many different materials: masonite, plastic, wood, ceramics, enamel. You mix up and combine a lot.

RGD: Anything that works.

LA: And you teach now at Cal State Long Beach?

RGD: Yeah, painting, drawing, very traditional classes. I'm the only Indian on the painting faculty. I teach egg tempera, silverpoint, encaustic. I try not to show the students my work because they'll say that I don't do in my work what I'm teaching them to do. But I was the only faculty member, outside of someone retiring, who knew these techniques. I found it amusing that none of the other faculty, who had European backgrounds and education, or who went to school at Cranbrook or Pratt, could teach these techniques. I did my M.F.A. at Cal State Davis.

LA: So it's safe to say that these materials won't show up in your pieces?

RGD: They take too long. Encaustic is smelly. Egg tempera is stinky. But I like teaching and the students. They must be given as many techniques as possible. I also teach Indian art history sometimes, but that's a three-hour lecture, and it's too much prep. I'd rather do the studio courses.

LA: You're probably most well-known, at least early in your career, for your hard hats. *Pink Buffalo Hat* has been called "a modern-day Mohawk headdress."[8] How did the hard hats come about?

RGD: My father was an ironworker, as were other family members, so hard hats were just normal to have around and look at, and in Coney Island, painting on the hat was no big deal, nothing special, just another surface to paint on. Other people said "modern," so I said, "I guess that's right."

LA: Do you still feel that your work "resacralizes daily experience"?[9]

RGD: Yeah, probably. I think deep down I'm a religious person, not in an organized-religion way, and I know that I come across as a certain type of person to many people, but basically I'm very conservative. Married twenty-one years; I've had the same car for twenty-five; I buy the same kind of Levi's every year; I only shop at Goodwill. I'm a creature of habit. And that's part of my daily thing. If my day gets turned around in any way I have to resacralize it. I need consistency in daily living.

LA: You've said, "I'm not the least inclined toward mysticism or spiritualism. I'm a cynic, and I may as well paint like a cynic."[10] Still true after nearly a decade?

RGD: Yeah. I'm still a spiritual cynic.

LA: Let's close there. Any final comments?

RGD: Are you as confused as I am?

LA: More so. But thank you.

SELECTED EXHIBITIONS

"Shared Visions" (1991–93), group traveling exhibition, Heard Museum, Phoenix, AZ.

"Pink Buffalos and Other Serious Notions: Paintings and Sculpture" (1990), solo exhibition, Lizardi/Harp Gallery, Pasadena, CA.

"Sculpture and Paintings by Richard Glazer-Danay" (1988), solo exhibition, Southern Plains Indian Museum and Crafts Center, Anadarko, OK.

"Eight Native American Artists" (1987), group exhibition, Fort Wayne Museum of Art, Fort Wayne, IN.

"Visage Transcended: Contemporary Native American Masks" (1985), group exhibition, American Indian Contemporary Arts, San Francisco, CA.

SELECTED BIBLIOGRAPHY

Sculpture and Paintings by Richard Glazer-Danay. Anadarko, OK: Southern Plains Indian Museum and Crafts Center, 1988.

Glazer-Danay, Richard. "Artist's Statement." In *Eight Native American Artists*. Fort Wayne, IN: Fort Wayne Museum of Art, 1987, p. 30.

Shan Goshorn

Cherokee

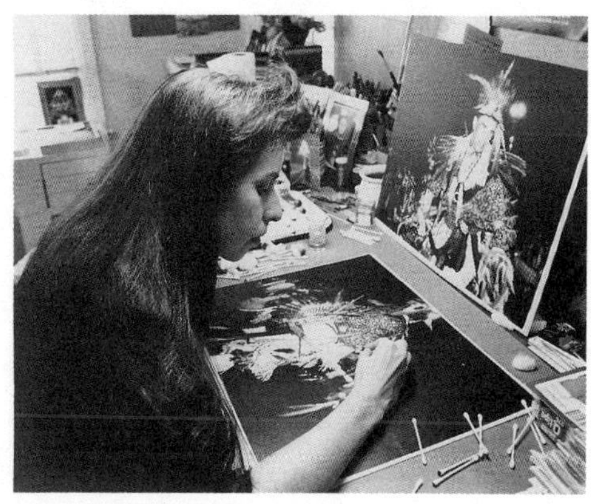

Shan Goshorn's photographs, from self-portrait to documentation, share one common characteristic: she tries to portray not only the outer reality of her subjects but their essence as well. Her series *Coming into Power* (1987) is a set of ten hand-tinted and hand-painted black and white self-portraits that visually represent her path of spiritual awakening. Each portrait depicts the artist in a kneeling, meditative position, surrounded by colors and forms. In *Recognizing the Positive Universe* the artist seems to float in a star-filled universe; in *Harmony and Balance within the Sacred Hoop of Life*, a circle of energy emanates from and envelops the artist. Its sequence of imagery "symbolizes the transition from being aware of the need for meditation and guidance to realizing power through spiritual direction, and learning how to apply this power in life to achieve good."[1]

Another series, *Honoring the Sacred Wheel* (1988), is a testimony to the endurance of Native people. In it she honors the continuity of the generations and connects their endurance to the four sacred directions and to the unending cycles of the moon.

Goshorn achieves her striking effects by tinting and painting black and white photographs with an opaque photo oil, which blocks out sections of the print. In this way, she can manipulate the image to produce the desired result. Similar (and even identical) images can be transformed and then take on new meaning in a particular series, or even in another series where the same image is used.

Goshorn, whose Wolf Clan Cherokee name is Yellow Moon, was born in Baltimore in 1957. She followed up on her childhood interest in art by first studying silversmithing at the Cleveland Institute of Art. She transferred to the Atlanta College of Art for her senior year and received her B.F.A. degree, with a double major in painting and photography, in 1980. In 1981 she moved to Tulsa, where she still lives and continues to take photographs. She is also active in Visions 37, her freelance photographic design business. Goshorn's work has been commissioned by both public and private institutions, and is held in such collections as those of Prudential Insurance, the Cherokee Heritage Center and Museum, and the Indian Arts and Crafts Board. A recent installation was completed for the Tulsa city hall. She has also done cover art and photographic illustrations for a variety of publications, including *Tales from the Cherokee Hills*, *Turtle Quarterly*, and *Tamaqua*.

Goshorn is involved in other endeavors beyond her own art. She is an accomplished storyteller and has performed in summer programs sponsored by the Tulsa County Library. She is also an Oklahoma State Arts Council artist-in-residence in rural schools, offering instruction about Native cultures through art projects, and she has worked with at-risk youth through various educational programs throughout the state.

We spoke in late June 1992 in her studio in Tulsa.

LA: You're working on a book of photographs documenting contemporary Native life?

SG: I'm working with an organization called NIIPA, the Native Indian and Inuit Photographers Association. Our project is a book that was brainstormed several years ago—our way to respond to this five-hundred-year Columbus thing. It would be a book that documents Native people by Native people, because, really, Native people have only been behind the lens for maybe two, maybe three generations, and that's even very rare. We're usually on the other side of the camera, and so hopefully we'll be able to get in and photograph more personally, more intimately, with ceremonies and family events and gatherings and things that we understand. So this book is to show how we have persevered, how we have changed, how we have adapted, and how we are still here after five hundred years.

LA: Are you doing more documentary work?

SG: Yes, but up until this year that's been very personal, because I really don't have enough images to show as a group, so it's mostly family and friends or qualified people doing something specific. For example, I photographed Daniel Drew, a Cheyenne drum maker. And, let's see, there's a Seminole woman, Betty Mae Jumper, with all of her crafts. My mother went to boarding school with her. But this year, now that I'm doing the work for the NIIPA book I mentioned, I've worked really hard with documentary. It's very different, because I usually think, "Oh, I can paint that telephone wire out." I can't do that with a straight black and white print, so composition is everything.

LA: Why do you think there's been such a growth of Native people going, as you say, behind the lens? What has led Native photographers to not only do "straight photography," documentary photography, but also, as you do, to manipulate images?

SG: Recently I think that more people are using cameras because they are accessible. You know, when they first came out, they weren't really available to Native people because they were too expensive. They were just out of the range of most Native families' income. But now we have all kinds of cameras that are inexpensive. It's easy. You can run down to the local Photomat and drop your film off. You don't have to have a whole darkroom setup.

In terms of manipulating images, I'm also a painter. I have a background in painting, and I wanted to incorporate photography into it because too often contemporary art focuses on ceremonies or events or happenings that the non-Native audience can't relate to. They have no connection to what the picture is about. I want to show people that we are here today, not stuck in the 1800s. We are part of contemporary society. We have roots that are still very strongly connected to tradition, but we are people here in the 1990s, like everyone else, and we have a voice. So when viewers see a combination of photographs with a painting, it's like, "Oh, these are photographs? These are living people?" We're not in museums with the dinosaurs and arrowheads and we're not all out on reservations, either.

LA: What's your sense of your audience? Do you seek both a Native and a non-Native audience for your work?

SG: Most definitely. It's really important to me that Native people see and respond to my work, but most of our collectors, unfortunately, are non-Natives and universities and institutions and such. A lot of my work is in Native collections, but it's because it belongs there, not necessarily because they had money to purchase it.

LA: What has been the evolution and the development of your photography? How did you come to combine painting with photography?

SG: In school [the Cleveland Institute of Art] I started out as a silversmithing major, and in my third year I took a photography class because I thought it would be important to know how to photograph all of my work. I was so impressed with how fast the medium was, and how exciting it was. You could go in and come out with, you know, ten, fifteen images in a day. And so I continued taking photographs. I changed my major to photography and painting and switched out of silversmithing. I was still painting and drawing and using a lot of color with my Native theme images, but with photography I went completely off into this commercial avenue—I moved to Atlanta and started photographing all this urban stuff. Whenever I would go home to North Carolina, I would still photograph events and people and happenings, because even in my early twenties I could see that a lot of this was not going to be around for much longer. I photographed a giveaway—a giveaway dance that my great-uncle had for his new grandson. I thought, "This is something we need to have a record of." Years later I was looking through these contact sheets and I thought, "Gosh, this would be really fun to paint." And then it was like this light went on and I saw the possibilities. It took ridiculously long for me to see how to merge these two ideas.

LA: Did your work as a silversmith have any connection at all to your painting and photography, or was that a real big transition, to go from silversmithing to visual art? I'm wondering if you shape imagery in the same way a silversmith might shape a piece, or if there was any connection with those two different ways of expression.

SG: It was a wonderful transition. I was really confined working with silver. I would love to work with metal now that I have a basic rudimentary working knowledge of it, but in school we would work all year on a necklace! And, granted, that was probably because we were learning the fundamentals of soldering and cutting and filing, but when I got into photography, it was just so exhilarating because all of a sudden all these images just opened up at once and I could do so much so quickly. It wasn't like I had to make this big transition into 2-D. Even though silversmithing was my major, I was still taking painting and drawing courses and felt very comfortable with the two-dimensional surface.

LA: So you'd been keeping the two media separate. What were the subjects of your paintings? What were your paintings like?

SG: I was still such a young artist and greatly impressed by what other Native artists were doing. I was really influenced by R. C. Gorman, T. C. Cannon, Fritz Scholder. I was interested not only in the line and the movement, but I was also intrigued by some of the political work that artists were doing as well. And so even though I began tinting and painting on photographs for commercial work in Atlanta, all that sort of changed when I moved to Oklahoma. That was in '81. Here in Tulsa I was immersed in this large tribal population. I had a chance to see all kinds of major events — dances and powwows that were happening all summer long instead of maybe three times a year.

LA: You once mentioned that you didn't consider your work to be overly political. That seems to be changing a little, with more of a political content.

SG: Right now, I don't think that you'd know that from the images. The manipulated images still appear very spiritual, I guess. But the titles would key you in to the political dimension. I just did a piece for the 1992 Red Earth competition which was called *Freedom Song for Leonard Peltier*. It would be safe to say that up until now my work has not been very political except in the fact that it deals with women's issues. Of course, that in itself is a very hot political issue right now. But in the last year, photographing for this book for NIIPA, I've become a lot more aware of issues that need to be addressed. Nineteen ninety-two has really brought up issues because we figure this is our chance to speak and we will be heard. The Leonard Peltier defense is a cause that I'm sympathetic to, and I'm doing some artwork for that, trying to get some money together to send to the defense fund.

Also, as a result of hearing tremendous speakers like Suzan Shown Harjo [president, board of directors of the Morning Star Foundation; trustee, National Museum of the American Indian, Smithsonian Institution], Tim Giago [publisher of *Indian Country Today* and the *Lakota Times*], and Michael Haney [political activist] at rallies this year, and of course friendships with Edgar Heap of Birds and Richard Ray (Whitman) [photographer of Yuchi heritage], I've become involved with trying to raise awareness of the inappropriateness of Native tribal and personal names as mascots and on buildings, vehicles, clothing, and other products. I'm scheduled to speak six or seven times in substance-abuse programs when I go home to Cherokee this fall, and I'm curious and hopeful to see how this topic will be received. The Eastern Band of the Cherokees tend to be cut off from the input of western tribes and recognizes tourism as the biggest form of industry and income to the local Native people. I have no problem with jobs and industry and even tourism, but I believe we could keep our tourists coming without selling out our tradition and heritage. Those little "war bonnets" have no place on children's heads—they represent our sacred eagle feathers, for crying out loud! All that imported junk just perpetuates the Hollywood stereotypes we're struggling to overcome. When our children grow up and see that these stereotypes are acceptable in the larger culture, that the only self-worth we as Indian people have is as a product or a label or as a child's toy, what happens to self-esteem? I really believe that this is a big contributor to our tremendous teenage alcohol-abuse problem and our disproportionately high teen suicide rate. Perhaps now is when America is ready to listen. Does anyone really think *Dances with Wolves* would have been popular twenty years ago, or when John Wayne was in his heyday?

But anyway, I've started a series called *Honest Injun*, using straight black and white photos of things like Red Man tobacco, Li'l Brave potatoes, Cherokee jeans, Washington Redskins souvenirs, Kickapoo Joy Juice, Land O' Lakes—I mean, what does that woman have to do with butter anyway? And the most offensive, Crazy Horse Malt Liquor. Crazy Horse was one of the Plains Indians' greatest spiritual leaders. He has no business being on an alcohol product. Alcohol is one of the biggest problems we have today.

As I see it, the whole issue is about ownership. No one has a right to these names, these images, but Indian people. Do you know of any other race of people used as mascots? One of my favorite posters is put out by the National Council of Christians and Jews. It shows four team pennants with names like "Pittsburgh Negroes," "Kansas City Jews," "San Diego Caucasians," and "Cleveland Indians." The bottom of the poster reads "Maybe Now You Know How Native Americans Feel."

I don't know if this new direction will be incorporated into my manipulated images or not. But I think there are people in this country that need to — and are ready to — hear the truth.

LA: Could you describe the technique that you use for creating your work? You prefer black and white photography rather than color?

SG: I work on fiber-base black and white paper, and I have a darkroom. I occasionally do some manipulative work in the darkroom, mostly with solarization and double images. But most of my work is just a straight black and white print that I tint right on the surface of the photograph. I use a product called Marshall Photo Oils, which is the same product that was used before color photography to apply color to a print. These transparent photo oils come in little tubes and you apply them with cotton balls and Q-tips, but they're transparent, so whenever you rub them on, you can still see the detail of the photograph underneath. It's like looking through sunglasses. And I'm very fortunate that I now represent the company and they support me with the work that I do. A lot of my work also uses opaque paint, whether it's gouache or acrylic or tempera. Usually I determine what in the print I want to keep and I tint that, and then I gesso out everything else and paint on the gessoed area as if it were a canvas. Each piece is an original.

LA: Do you ever take the same image and do different manipulations to the surface, use different colors, and alter it?

SG: Yes, and the image can change. The negative might be flopped, the image might be larger, I might choose to paint opaquely over more of the image. But you are working with a photograph, from a negative, so you are going to have similarities, but I make sure that all my work is original.

LA: Do you work in any particular size?

SG: I can work up to sixteen by twenty inches in my darkroom, but I'm experimenting with pieces mounted together to make them larger. I also work with a lab here in town that can go as large as four by six feet. A lot of my corporate installations are that large.

LA: What camera do you use? Any particular lenses?

SG: Most men that do photography are regular scientists, you know. They're real interested in all the numbers and all the chemical formulas, but I find that for myself I'm just real intuitive about what I do. So a lot of times I don't even know what lens size I'm working with, but I do know that you need to stop down or up. It's very intuitive, and I find that other women work this way, too. All the men who ever taught me knew all about the silver bromide crystals and how they interact and how they float to the surface when you solarize, and what happens when you do this or that. For me, it's like, "Hey, flip the light on and watch!"

LA: Could you talk about your intuitive process?

SG: I approach my work in many ways. Sometimes I actually stage models the way I want them. A good example of this is my grandmother. I knew that I wanted to illustrate her retelling some Cherokee legends because she's such a good storyteller. I wanted to paint the legend [Trail of the Sky Dog; or, How the Milky Way Came to Be] around her so people could see it happen the way that I always could when I was a child. And so she's actually telling the legend, but I knew what I wanted, and I had it all framed accordingly.

But a lot of times I don't have a clue even when I'm working on it. A good example that I like to tell of this is at the same giveaway that my great-uncle had for his grandson. It was presented at the meeting of the Native American Indian Women's Association in North Carolina, being held in a high school gymnasium. I was up on some bleachers shooting down and I knew that I would want to paint out the basketball court and all the wires for the amplifiers and everything around their feet. When I started working on that image several years later, I tinted the images that I wanted to keep, painted around them, and it looked so harsh that I began to use a toothbrush to spatter around the dancers, and the spattering just got thicker and thicker and I thought, "Whoa, where is this going?" And then all of a sudden it looked like they were moving through stars and it reminded me of a traditional belief that when we cross to the other side, when we make our spiritual transition, we cross the Milky Way. That's the path. And so it was like, "Oh, so that's what this piece is doing," and I just happened to have a mat and frame that was the right size, and I thought, "Wow, this piece came together really easy." The next day I got a phone call from Edgar Heap of Birds and he said, "Hey, there's a gallery in California and they're doing a Day of the Dead exhibition. They need some work really fast. Do you have anything new that might address that?" And I thought, "Yeah, do I ever."

LA: You have also been a storyteller for quite some time. How did you come to also be a storyteller, and is that combined in your art at all? I'm wondering, too, how much of your work has a narrative dimension to it, or might be sort of an analogue to the oral tradition.

SG: I've always been so interested in the stories of our elders. I would live with my grandmother in the summers, but since I didn't go to school there I didn't know a whole lot of people besides my relatives. So I ended up spending a lot of time with my grandmother and her friends, and that was one thing that they did. They knew I liked to hear stories and they would tell them to me. Consequently, I have illustrated a lot of the Cherokee legends, and my work does tend to have a storytelling format because a lot of times I enclose a written statement that helps to translate some of the images. I think the image should stand on its own, of course, but sometimes it helps the viewer to know that a certain image is a traditional symbol that maybe he or she wouldn't recognize.

LA: How much of your work do you consider to be autobiographical? In the *Coming into Power* series, you appear in all of the photographs, and you've used yourself as a subject in quite a bit of your other work. The series seems to have a very clear spiritual dimension.

SG: Well, I feel that most artists think that all their work is autobiographical. It's so much a part of yourself when you put it down on paper. But I run into a real interesting dilemma. As a photographer, I have to address things a little bit differently than other artists. If I go to a powwow and just snap off pictures, I've got to have permission from the participants. I can't use just anyone in my work. I talk to people that I know and often use family and friends. And so I may have a really terrific image, but until I find out who that person is and get their consent, I can't use it. The *Coming into Power* series, the self-portraits, came about because of an incident like that.

I had photographed my grandmother's best friend, and after she died, I created this series that was meant to help my grandmother ease through her mourning a little bit. It was a really cool piece, the first work that I did in a series like that. The title is *Strength, Spirit, Transition*, and it shows our friend's spiritual transition. It has eight different panels of the same image, but each panel was painted very differently. The work got a very good response from my family and from people who saw it, but to exhibit it I had to contact this woman's family and ask for their permission. They did give me permission, but their grief was still so new and the decision so difficult for them that I thought, "Man, the next piece I'm going to do is a self-portrait. No problem."

The next series came as the result of a really, really awful time in my life. Everytime that I would try to meditate or pray, all this junk was just going around in my head and I was having a hard time being grounded and focused. With all that I knew about meditation and balance, it occurred to me that nothing was available to focus on visually. I thought that if I only had visual steps, I could move ahead and think about where I was trying to go, instead of floundering around where I was stuck. So really this series was meant as sort of a self-therapy, but other people who saw it, my family and my friends, really liked it. I ended up showing it at exhibitions and such with my other work.

LA: There are ten images in this series. Is the imagery organized in a particular way?

SG: Well, this was a little bit more difficult than the other series because *Strength, Spirit, Transition* was all the same image. After the pieces were finished, I could figure out what order they should go in. But *Coming into Power* actually had a physical change or representation of enlightenment from the very beginning, a sort of an opening up. I had to really think out the process, and it was interesting because even though I might paint something, people would come and say, "That looks just like such and such," and give me their opinion, or about the second panel, "Oh, that looks like a birthing." And it was like, "Yeah! It really does." And so all of a sudden that became part of the interpretation. Or I've had people come over and say, "Oh, you do work with crystals." "No, I don't." And they'd say, "Well, that's what it looks like." It was really exciting to me that people of different religions could get something out of the series.

LA: How long did the series take you?

SG: Not as long as I think it should have because there was that great motivator—a deadline! When I was working on the piece and I started getting this great feedback, I was just working with sketches. People were saying, "Oh, yeah, this is really cool. This is really good. You should do this." And right at that time I had been asked to do a show at the Center for Exploratory and Perceptual Art [CEPA] in Buffalo, New York, and I decided that, well, for my first place to show the work, maybe CEPA would be a good place. And so I really had to scramble around and try to finish it. And although it's exhausting, I tend to work well under those kind of self-imposed deadlines.

LA: These are all sixteen by twenty inches. Do you usually sketch out a rough sense of what you want?

SG: I can work with drawings, but photography's pretty quick in itself. I can go in and crank out a couple of eight-by-tens and sketch out some ideas on them using tracing paper. It's a pretty fast medium. It's just expensive!

LA: Do you generally conceive of works in a series? Many of your most recent pieces are in series.

SG: No, I also do a lot of singular images. In fact, I've done four series, and usually the reason that I do a series is because the idea is just too complex to put in one image. Sometimes it's something that I really need to work through personally, or it's something that I want more information about. I just go on this research binge. I did the series about my grandmother's best friend passing, *Strength, Spirit, Transition*. And then the *Coming into Power* series about spiritual awakening. I did a series called *Moon Time: The Cycles of Life*, which deals with medicine wheels, the four directions, the different colors, the seasons, the everlasting hoop. And then one of my most recent series is one called *Taken to the Water*, which is about ancestors and descendants and the birth of my son and the thinking of the seventh generation.

LA: What is your ratio of what you use to what you shoot? Do you ever reuse photographs in different pieces? Of course, writers merely need to press a delete button on the word processor and start all over again. On this series, did you have a lot of false starts, or a lot of things you experimented with and said, "This just isn't working for the concept"?

SG: No, this series went amazingly smoothly. See all these boxes over there? Let's see, there's about, oh, maybe eight or nine boxes that each originally held fifty sheets of photographic paper, sixteen by twenty inches, and they're all full of images. Whenever I print, it's a lot easier to print two of something than get to the dry-mount press and have it wrinkle up, or find out that something's not working out. And so I have a bunch of extra prints that I go back to and change and do differently later. So, really, there's virtually no waste unless it's just a bad print. I mean, *black*. And even black can be used sometimes.

LA: Could you talk about how you might change an image, depending on the new context or the new intent of the work?

SG: There's a piece that I just did last month that was actually taken from the same print, the same negative actually, as a piece from the *Coming into Power* series. It wasn't meant to be a self-portrait exactly. It's meant to show a sort of Everyman, but it was a powerful piece that I got a lot of emotional responses to, and I wanted to incorporate it into the work I did to try to raise funds for the Leonard Peltier defense movement. And so the piece has been changed. The colors are different. There's also the two hand prints, both the Anglo and the Indian. But it looks like somebody's pressed up against glass or that perhaps someone is being released. But the image has changed because of the new need to bring awareness to Leonard Peltier's position. This piece will be included in a show now called "Recovery from Discovery" [1992] through the University of Maryland, and is for sale. Half of the profit has been pledged to the Leonard Peltier Defense Fund.

LA: It's interesting how the imagery can be recombined into a new context and create a new piece. You're doing different things to it and you have a different intent or meaning behind it. Even though it's the same image, the context might make one print spiritual and another print political.

SG: When I was up in Canada visiting a friend of mine, we had gone to the longhouse for a ceremony and she was dressed appropriately in her traditional clothes and she came home and was burning sweet grass. And I said, "Oh, let me take a picture," and she was smudging with her feather and we caught this movement of her feather that was so beautiful. I sent her the prints with an idea of what I was going to do to them, but she said, "Wow, did you see? Look on the wall. It's my dad's photograph right behind us. He was there with us when we were doing it." And so that all of a sudden gave me insight into a new way to do that piece. I emphasized her father because he had passed away several years earlier.

LA: Maybe we could switch gears a little bit to talk about your background and academic training. You were born in Bel Air outside of Baltimore and studied in Cleveland and Atlanta? You spent the summers in North Carolina in traditional Cherokee country?

SG: Yes, and I spent the summers growing up with my grandmother there. And I hesitate to say whether she was traditional or not. I mean, she grew up in a traditional home until she was six, and then she was carted off by the government and went to an institutional boarding school. There she was taught how wrong and how bad it was to be Indian. There's still a lot of emotion when she talks about that. Consequently, she didn't teach my mother or her other children about the traditions; they didn't grow up speaking the language. There was this great pressure among the Cherokee people in North Carolina not to be Indian. But there are still pockets where some of the old people still remember. The language is now in the school curriculum, but what the western Indians need to remember is that in North Carolina we had an additional two hundred years of [white] influence, and so we really have lost a lot of our traditional heritage and our ways. We also assimilated very easily because so many of our ideas were so similar to the colonists' when they arrived. We worshiped one Great Spirit, so it was real easy to convert to Christianity. We were farmers and hunters, so we weren't nomadic. We were agricultural. We were used to being in one place and we knew how to tend crops. We really have had to struggle to reclaim our ways.

I guess we would relate more closely to stomp dances than we would with powwows; our dances and festivals were more seasonal, based on crop harvests, the moon, and the like. We do have people that respect and practice traditional planting of seeds, and hunting and everything. And really, that *was* the religion—the respect for the Earth Mother and the Sky Father, and Sunday didn't matter. It was just an all-encompassing belief in respect for the animals and other creatures. We do have churches in North Carolina that are still conducted in the traditional language, in the Cherokee language, but they are Christian-based.

LA: In some of your visual works and written pieces you incorporate Cherokee language.

SG: I'm not fluent with the language, but living with my grandmother when I was growing up in the summers, I did pick up a lot. So I can understand certain phrases, certain manners. I know how to ask for food. But whenever I need a title translated, I send it home and ask someone to do that for me.

LA: You've written, "I see my work as a connecting force combining painting to photography, tradition to contemporary, joining male-female, Indian–non-Indian."[2] Could you explain how your work tries to make that connection and tries to create that balance?

SG: Well, my first impulse was to say that that is probably more evident with the *Coming into Power* series and *Moontime*, but I guess that it really comes out, too, with *Taken to the Water*. I use the whole idea of a medicine wheel to show characteristics from all directions, but not to lean too much in one direction. You want to have characteristics of balance; you want to have harmony. You don't want to see things too much like a man or too much like a woman. You want to respect both sides of yourself so that you can see things clearly. I mean, the traditional way is all about clarity, about how to see more clearly and how to think more clearly so that we can be better human beings.

I think all Native people, all Indian people, sort of see themselves as doing a juggling act because if you respect, or if you even show any awareness of, your tradition and your heritage, it's very difficult to assimilate that into the dominant white society that we live in. And so there's always that juggling act. Go to the stomp ground Saturday but don't tell church people on Sunday, you know? I feel that in a different way because my mother is Indian, my father is not, but I was as comfortable sitting on either grandparent's knee, whether it was white or Indian. I really feel that my path is to try to connect the two peoples, whether it's through my artwork or whatever. And also I think that women innately have that role anyway because we're such nurturers. We connect ourselves with procreation and we carry the children in.

LA: The *Moontime* series is very involved in terms of the imagery and structure that you created in terms of direction and color and translating images. Could you describe what you were trying to do in that series and what some of the imagery was all about?

SG: Once again, I was trying hard not to just make this a Cherokee or Cheyenne or Apache statement. I wanted this to encompass the ideas of a lot of Native people. I tried to assimilate and process some of the thinking and the ideas that came up most prevalently when I talked to people. I tempered a great deal of traditional knowledge. There were just layers upon layers of meaning. I guess the whole reason I was trying to do this was so I could understand it better, and I felt that doing this was a way that helped me to retain the knowledge and really understand it. And so one wheel has the directions and the different animals that are associated with those directions and some of the different symbols of the colors that are represented. And then the other one shows time passing, with the seasons, the moons, the elements, the time of day. I found that the way that helped me to apply it to my life the best was to show how thoughts fell into this cycle. In the east you would have the conception of an idea; in the south you would have the zenith, the summertime, the way that this idea had reached maturation, the way that it had reached its height. And then moving up into the west, it would be the full moon; that's the place of harvest, where you get rid of any idea that didn't apply any more—any idea that you realized was not applicable to your life at that time. Then you move up into the north to the resting period, like winter or night where you're actually preparing and waiting for the new seeds of ideas and new growth.

The term *Moontime* actually refers to the reproductive cycle, but unlike Anglo thinking, Native people see the reproductive cycle as meaning the life cycle because you have day, you have night. You have spring, summer, fall, winter. You have all these cycles that actually determine our transition into this life path and our transition out. So *Moon Time* also refers to a much broader spectrum than just a woman's cycle for having babies.

LA: And how many images were in that show?

SG: There are four images for each medicine wheel. There's two wheels, so that's eight sixteen-by-twenty-inch pieces, plus the large centerpiece that's three by three feet. These are all hand-tinted photographs that were structured with a certain meaning. If I have any kind of control over the exhibition space, I ask that they're installed two up and two down, like a circle within a rectangle shape, because they're meant to show the different directions. And then it's also mounted with my statement so that the viewer will have an idea of the different symbolic layers that are involved in the image.

LA: Apart from the photography for the NIIPA book, what other projects are you working on now?

SG: I'm very active with exhibiting. My work will be included in a show that will be going to the Franco-American Institute in

Rennes, France, this October [1992]. In December of '92 I'll have the largest solo exhibition of my career at Ursuline College, just outside of Cleveland. And I'm just finishing up a commission for a public building, doing eight twenty-by-fifty-inch panels for permanent installation in the Tulsa city hall. I keep trying to stretch and experiment.

LA: To finish up, could you talk about the *Taken to the Water* series? It seems very personal while at the same time it connects to aspects of Cherokee traditions.

SG: I found after I started working on this piece that it is very common for women artists to do a piece about the birth of their children, whether they're Indian or not. It's such a profound experience. And so I began to ask for clarification and I asked for more information about some of our traditional ceremonies. One of the ceremonies was the Water Ceremony. Once a woman felt life, the medicine person would take her down to the water and perform ceremonies that would help foresee the pregnancy, the birth, and sometimes even the life of the child. I did this series in six panels that are actually self-portraits throughout my pregnancy and then after the birth of my child. The first piece I happened to photograph right when I got pregnant, but I didn't realize I was pregnant. It was a self-portrait looking in a mirror. The next piece shows the Water Ceremony, which is centered in water but also shows stars and celestial beings. Then there's a piece about the sweat lodge. Part of our belief is that at the sweat lodge you enter on your hands and knees and you exit the same way because it's like a rebirthing. And then, let's see, the fourth piece is the star gift piece, which honors the traditional belief that we descended from the stars, but it shows the Earth Mother receiving the gift of the people. But it also goes the other way and shows the way that all mothers have to release their children to become the people that they're meant to be. And then the last piece illustrates our sacred spiral. I think that this is an interesting concept for non-Indians, because whenever non-Indian people think of a time line they think of this long line that goes clear into next Tuesday, you know, and another line where there's no relationship between the past and the future. The Native people see things on a spiral so that the things that happen here directly interlock and relate the things that are happening now and the things that will happen later. There's also the fifth piece of myself and my son with the spiral of sacred smoke around us, with a powwow circling around my legs because that's so much the heartbeat of the people. That's one of our strengths, our gatherings and our tradition. The last piece is a multiple image that shows my grandmother with her mother, my grandmother with my mother as a baby, my mother with my sister and myself, and then myself with my stepdaughter, and in the center, myself with my son, to show the continuum of the seventh generation.

SELECTED EXHIBITIONS

"Keepers of the Western Door" (1993), group exhibition, CEPA Gallery, Buffalo, NY.

"Indian Territory Artwork" (1992), group exhibition, Franco-American Institute, Rennes, France.

"Receiving Star Gift" (1992), solo exhibition, Florence O'Donnell Wasmer Gallery, Ursuline College, Pepper Pike, OH.

"Recovery from Discovery" (1992), group exhibition, Parents Association Gallery, University of Maryland, College Park, MD.

"Taken to the Water" (1991), solo exhibition, NIIPA Gallery, Hamilton, Ontario.

"Birth and Rebirth, Ancestors and Descendants" (1989), Plains Indian and Pioneer Museum, Woodward, OK.

"Song of Honor" (1988), solo exhibition, International Photography Hall of Fame, Oklahoma City, OK.

"Coming into Power" (1987), solo exhibition, NIIPA Gallery, Hamilton, Ontario, and CEPA Gallery, Buffalo, NY.

"Moontime: The Cycles of Life" (1987), solo exhibition, Southern Plains Indian Arts and Crafts Center, Anadarko, OK.

"Makers" (1986), group exhibition, Oklahoma City University, Oklahoma City, OK.

SELECTED BIBLIOGRAPHY

Goshorn, Shan. "Native View: The Indian Arts and Crafts Act, 1990." *Cross Currents* 4, 2 (March–April 1991): 4–5.

Women's Traditional Cloth [cover art], *Sequoyah: The Legend of the White Butterfly*, and *Buffalo Dancer*. *Tamaqua* 2, 2 (Winter–Spring 1991): 18, 228.

Harmony for Our Seventh Generation [cover art collage]. *Turtle Quarterly* 3, 2 (Spring–Summer, 1989).

Firebringer [cover art]. In *Tales from the Cherokee Hills*, by Jean Starr. Winston-Salem, NC: Blair Publishers, 1988.

Goshorn, Shan. "Moontime: The Cycles of Life." In *Makers*, edited by Hachivi Edgar Heap of Birds. Norman, OK: Point Riders Press, Cottonwood Arts Foundation, 1988, pp. 5–9.

Hachivi Edgar Heap of Birds

Cheyenne-Arapaho

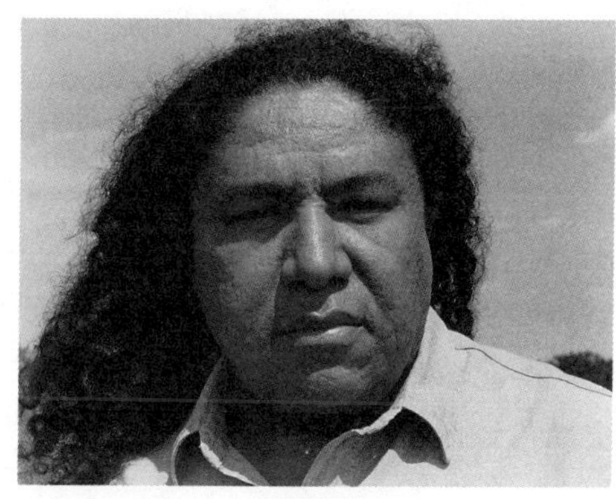

Hachivi Edgar Heap of Birds and his family live a few miles outside of Geary, Oklahoma, in a house once lived in by his grandmother. The house sits high and solitary, with sweeping views of the mostly undeveloped land. From the front yard one can see how the land breaks down and away into the reds, greens, and browns of the surrounding canyons. The air here in summer is hot and has the feel, in Scott Momaday's words, of the "anvil's edge."[1]

Heap of Birds was born in Wichita, Kansas, in 1954 and attended high school there. His formal art training began at the California College of Arts and Crafts in Oakland, California, in 1975. This was followed by a B.F.A. degree (University of Kansas, 1976) and an M.F.A. (Tyler School of Art, Temple University, 1979), both in painting. He also completed graduate work in painting at the Royal College of Art in London in 1977. He is currently an associate professor in the Department of Art at the University of Oklahoma, where he teaches painting, drawing, and a workshop in conceptual art.

In addition to his teaching, Heap of Birds has lectured on art in Europe and throughout the United States. He has also curated a number of exhibitions, including "Modern Native American Abstraction" (Philadelphia Art Alliance, 1983) and "No Beads—No

Trinkets" (Geneva, Switzerland, 1984). Heap of Birds articulated the philosophy of the Philadelphia show: "Allowing Native Americans to interpret their future with a totally open perspective shall have a great constructive outcome."[2]

Heap of Birds has been exhibiting in both group and solo shows since 1977. His "canvases" have included the side panels of commuter buses, park and freeway signs, and the Spectacolor Light billboard in Times Square. About these public-media works he has written: "We find it effective to challenge the white man through our use of the mass media. . . . the survival of our people is based upon our use of expressive forms of modern communication. The insurgent messages within these forms must serve as our present-day combative tactics."[3] The clear political dimension of Heap of Birds's work is further evident in the way he unifies language and image in many pieces. His complete message synthesizes both these ways of apprehending the world. As Lowery Stokes Sims has pointed out, "the ambition to modify linguistic habits that are deeply encoded in our collective psyche is no mean task. But artists such as Hachivi Edgar Heap of Birds have realized that there is little choice in the matter for them, so crucial is this task to the psychic and emotional survival of their communities."[4]

Heap of Birds has been the recipient of a number of commissions and awards for his work. *Building Minnesota* was sponsored by the Walker Art Center of Minneapolis and was installed from March 10 to August 20, 1990. *Mission Gifts,* sponsored by the San Jose Museum of Art, ran from November 15, 1990, to January 15, 1991. His most recent commission was *Day/Night*, an enamel porcelain sculpture sponsored by Art in Public Places of Seattle in June 1991. In 1989 Heap of Birds received the National Art Award from the Tiffany Foundation.

I met with Hachivi Edgar Heap of Birds at his home in Geary on the Cheyenne-Arapaho Reservation in late July 1991. We talked in his studio; the various sketches, paintings, and photographs pinned to the walls provide a history of his career, right up to the present moment. After the interview we drove down through the canyons in his pickup.

LA: I'd like to start out by discussing a statement you made for the "Sharp Rocks" exhibit. You mentioned that as you looked around your land here in Oklahoma and found arrowheads, you came to believe that past weaponry was both defensive and preservative.[5] Would you say that your work today has the same role?

HEHB: Yes. That was early on, around '86. I was finding arrowheads as I was hunting, and I mostly ate the food I hunted. And I realized that back then the people wouldn't be sport hunting. But the bow and arrow was a new weapon for them. I was affiliated with the warriors' society, so I started to think a lot about the past and the images of ceremonies. And then you are kind of brought up short by the present and start to ask yourself, "What happens now? What do I do now?"

As a society member I was involved in a lot of funerals from alcohol-related deaths, and I had to shake the hand of everyone in the grieving family. And I thought about how people just played themselves out and weren't allowed to participate in white society. The experience of all those funerals was very moving, but then I tried to understand what I could have done before I had to shake the hand of the dead person's relative. And so I started to think of the art as a way to help preserve life, or even as a way to represent Native people and try to improve the situation, you know, by making that representation.

And of course I'd have to push the work harder—harder than it's been pushed before, as the warriors would have pushed it. The Cheyenne warriors of a long time ago were very, very dangerous people and took a lot of risks all the time. And that's what I think the work has to do.

LA: Could you talk about your role in the warriors' society?

HEHB: Yes, a little bit. It basically functions as the caretaker of the ceremonial ways, things we do to renew the earth, and we also have the general welfare of our people in mind. I've been involved with it for about ten years, since the early eighties. I came to it when I was in my mid-twenties. I've tried to learn as much as I could about the ceremonies, although now I've sort of stepped back from the society because there is a lot of factionalism and I really don't want to dishonor it by having to nearly come to blows over problems that exist. But on the other hand, I say it's kind of interesting that the tribe is so powerful that it can fight itself and still thrive. So we have both of those elements—great diversity and differences of opinion, and a sense of unity.

LA: Was it a return to tradition for you, or were you brought up in traditional ways?

HEHB: I wasn't really educated in the traditions as a young person; like, my father won't even come to the ceremonies now. I mean, he lives on the reservation area, in Geary, but for him personally, he doesn't really know about that stuff and he chooses not to be involved in it, which happens, you know, with everything. People have their choices. It's like, people might think that all Cheyennes or all Indians are right in the middle of ceremonial life. But they're not. Cheyenne people are individuals, so they all have their own choices. He couldn't teach me about it, so I sort of found my own way back to it, which is actually another strength of the tribe. The people in their twenties and thirties now aren't like my father's generation, the sixty-year-olds and the seventy-year-olds today, who had to just get out there in the trenches and work in aircraft plants or on the road crews just to put food on the table so we could grow up and come back and take care of this stuff, like the ceremonies and the traditions. That's the way it's been.

LA: That's interesting how those local realities influence people. On another level, your work seems grounded in broader historical realities. You've referred to the Sand Creek massacre and to the process of Oklahoma statehood, while at the same time you utilize modern mass media. How did you come to integrate history and modernity in your work?

HEHB: Probably just from my own experience. I think that's how most artists are working, you know. However you live is how you're going to work. I grew up in Wichita, Kansas. My father worked for Beech Aircraft. My great-grandfather was the leader of the Elk Warriors' Society. So there are those dualities already. I went to the University of Kansas and the Royal College of Art in London and the Tyler School of Art in Philadelphia, you know, so I'm obviously versed in contemporary Western society.

So knowing those things and then coming back to the reservation area and being faced with all sorts of historical realities and responding to them, I've continued to work in a way that tries to unify both in some way. As I travel around the world or around Indian territories I'll make something about a particular place. But I use modern systems to talk about it.

LA: You've written: "The insurgent messages within these forms [of modern communication] must serve as our present-day combative tactics." Can art bring about political change and is Native art by definition political?

HEHB: I think so. No matter what you as the artist do with the work, it's identified as Native art. That's a problem in some ways and it's a solution in other ways. Other people's art isn't white art or necessarily Italian art or Chinese art or whatever; it's just art and then you deal with the issues within it. But with us, people bring their perceptions of Native America to bear on all the art being done and you have no choice about that; they're going to do it anyway. So it's how you as an artist react to that. It's a political reaction whether you disregard those perceptions or whether you take those perceptions and spin it back toward people, which my work tends to do. I try to turn things around and talk about them when they want to know about me. So that's how I see the tactics of what I do.

LA: A sense of reversal and bitter irony comes through in much of your public work, like *Native Hosts*, *Mission Gifts*, and *Building Minnesota*. Not only is there a reversal of letters and words or a mirror image of words, but there's also a reversal of the usual expectations about history, of how things were. *Building Minnesota* refers to the execution of some forty Native people in the 1860s and suggests that on a symbolic level, if not also on a real level, those executions continue today. Could you talk about how that work came about?

HEHB: A big part of it was from a song I heard, which was an honor song combined with a contemporary folk song by Larry Long, who is a singer from Minneapolis. And I introduced him to a cousin of mine, Mitch Walking Elk, who is a kind of a country folk singer and artist, and they got together and they created a song called "Water in the Rain." It chronicles what happened in the 1860s when Abraham Lincoln executed thirty-eight Dakota warriors; later Andrew Johnson executed two others, signed the death warrants. So there were forty all told. But the honor song Larry and Mitch wrote was particularly moving to me. In the middle of the regular folk song about what happened they added a traditional Dakota honor song of people who have died. And Mitch sings the song, but while he's singing, Amos Owen, a respected Dakota elder, reads the names, in Dakota, of the forty who were executed. And it goes on for a long time. Just hearing that song and thinking about it, you know, that was what Minnesota meant to me at that time.

Then the Walker Art Center in Minneapolis asked me to do a solo show there, which I did, called "Claim Your Color." It was a series of works — paintings and public works, drawings and stat photographs and multimedia type of work. So along with this show they also asked me if I wanted to do a commissioned piece, and I said, yeah, I'd do something.

Then I got the idea of making *Building Minnesota*. I went to Minneapolis for a site visit and gathered research about the forty who were hanged and thought about just honoring them by using my signs, either the one-by-one-and-a-half- or the one-by-three-and-a-half-foot ones. And that's what worked out down by the river, down along the Mississippi. I had the whole city to choose from, but I kept coming back to that water. When I did the piece, it was freezing, it was below zero, and I was running around really cold, but I kept coming back to one place, the granary [i.e., the area where large flour mills are situated], and it had a little plaque there. It was playing up the great shipping channel of the Mississippi, how it was the business hub of America and how the most grain in the world was shipped through there. Then I got to thinking about the land, and movement, and why the Dakotas are thought of being from South Dakota, like no one thinks they're from Minnesota. I didn't either; I thought, "Well, Sioux are in South Dakota; where else would they be?" And then you find that they got kicked out of here and all their warriors were executed.

All that clicked together as I was standing by the Pillsbury granary, and across the Mississippi was the Gold Medal Flour granary. I got to thinking about why would the government be so vicious. It was the largest mass execution in America's history; of course, no one even knows about it, or why it was done. Then I thought about the wheat and the land and shipping, the business aspect of it, and thinking about the Persian Gulf and the oil business. Commerce was always at the bottom of these situations, you know. It's not some kind of hatred or whatever; it's business, it's money.

So I got up early in the morning to put the piece in, like at 5:00

A.M. I had the contractors hired to put the posts in the ground for the signs, two posts apiece for the forty signs over a four-hundred-foot span, and it was going to be a tough job because the ground was frozen. But I had had this kind of waking dream about the project. It was strange; it was about flour. I went to an all-night grocery and bought forty pounds of flour. And I drew out a four-hundred-foot arc with Pillsbury flour, and when the crew came they just put the posts in on the same line as the flour. But it started snowing about eleven o'clock and I had to keep scribing out this arc with my foot as the crew came behind me putting these signs in the ground and making the arc — because I wanted the signs to come out at people. The first idea was to have a straight line, but then I thought that was too reserved, so I made the arc bulge out toward where the cars would drive by or where people walk.

LA: So this work and the other public works are more or less site specific, in the sense that this one came together at a particular place, even though you had the whole city to choose from?

HEHB: Yes, and it was also about the water, the renewal of the water, and the ceremonial Dakota ways. I know those warriors were probably trained like I am, you know, and they probably had to live without water for ceremonies lasting four days, you know, to renew the earth, and so I thought that they would respect being by the river, so I put them there.

But all of my pieces are very site specific, but that's really about the theme, which is addressing the people. See, why take my art and put it in New York or in London or in Northern Ireland? I want it to address what a specific place is about. And in my case, I guess I'm known as some kind of modernist or some kind of crazy thing, so I get chosen to be in these big museums. But instead of showing my work alone, I try to address the tribal nation that's in that area, who usually the museum doesn't know about; they've never shown their work, they never talk to them, you know. They never knew about the local history until I come to town. So I try to make people aware of that, so when I leave, the issue doesn't leave with me, which is usually the case. Most of the time the problems go with you and they go back to business as usual, so I try to open that up.

Recently I've been up to Mankato, Minnesota, where they were actually hanged, to locate a permanent site for the piece.

LA: *Building Minnesota* sounds like a phrase from a chamber of commerce pamphlet, but you twist that around, because Minnesota was actually built on the bodies of Native people. So the work really *was* about building Minnesota, but you have to go through some loops to get there.

HEHB: It's deeper than it appears. And I don't know how that happened. I mean my work just does that. I'm getting to where I don't even know how that happens anymore. Like a piece I just finished in Seattle has a lot of things going on in it, too. They just work out that way, and people seem to get into them.

LA: Would you say, then, that you're an intuitive artist, or becoming more intuitive, or do you tend to plan things out in a more formal way?

HEHB: I plan things out, you know, pretty well, particularly technically. I have to plan them out so that they actually work, because you always run into a lot of logistical problems in doing the site pieces. It's almost like the movie *Being There* with Peter Sellers. I think about that a lot, and "being there" is everything to me. It may sound strange, but it's also the Native way; it's like you go and sit down, you smoke your pipe or do what you have to do in a place that's specific, or you make the place specific by your presence, and then you make a choice, you make a decision. You take a reading of what that place is, you know, because I never make anything without going to the place. I never make the piece at my studio and then take it; I always go to the site first, sit, talk to people, look around, even take plants that are growing, bring them back, and then I get the idea for what to make,

LA: The sense of reversal of expectations and the grounding in history are also intrinsic to *Native Hosts*. How did the idea for that come about?

HEHB: The background to that is really interesting. A few years ago I met a Wampanoag from Massachusetts named Ohaneice. He worked at Tufts University and had two radio shows in Boston. I did a show at the Institute of Contemporary Art there and he interviewed me, and we got to be pretty good friends. He had a lot of interesting ideas and funny things he'd come up with. Like his skin was very pale and he said, "You know, people shouldn't be angry with us because" — and he was pretty pointed about it — "we've had the devil longer than anybody else, and he's in our skin, but that doesn't mean we're different from you guys. We've just had him longer than you've had him in Oklahoma."

I had a gig down at the University of Rhode Island, so we

rented a car and cruised down to Kingston, Rhode Island, my wife, my son, me, and Ohaneice. It was great, because as we drove he showed me which mountains they moved to make Boston with and he showed me what happened to the land. And I'm driving down the Interstate, and it's just a road to me, but he pointed out all these things.

But when we got down to the university, he was doing a benefit for Big Mountain with his radio program. So in the middle of my lecture I just said, "Well, maybe Ohaneice wants to talk about Big Mountain." I was the visiting artist that day, so I had the floor. What could they say?

But before he spoke he acknowledged all the tribes that were in the audience, and he named them, and he said that he felt privileged to come to this place and talk and be with the trees in Rhode Island. He didn't mention the president of the university or the governor or the mayor of Kingston. After the talk many people of these nations came up to me to tell me about their histories, and I became very aware that I was a guest in another Native country, and am a guest wherever I go in the world. Mayors or governors, wherever they are and whoever they are, it's not their place.

Sometime after that I got a commission for something for City Hall Park in New York City. I got this idea—I don't know where it came from—of telling New York who the host is, the real host. And I reversed the letters of "New York" on the signs because I asked for a history of the site of City Hall Park and I received—it's a pretty classic joke—a stack of Xeroxes maybe an inch thick which said that the history of the site goes back to 1620. That's when history began; yeah, that's when it started. And I told them that and they said, "Well, we don't know anything else about it." So I turned the name around after that. I'm doing a similar series in British Columbia in about a month. The signs will say that your host is all the tribes from that area.

LA: *Mission Gifts*, too, used that technique of reversing expectations and playing off of historical reality. Many people think that the missionization process in California was necessary to bring civilization to the primitive tribes, but then when you get into the background of that you find that it wasn't such a gift to Native people.

HEHB: That process was particularly vicious. I found it one of the most troubling events I've ever encountered in the history of this country. The treatment of the people, the diseases, the slaughter. On a smaller scale, it was similar to the calculated mistreatment of Jews in Germany in the thirties and forties. It was very, very vicious stuff. That history was the impetus for putting the show together.

LA: The show was actually on buses?

HEHB: On the sides of thirty commuter buses which ran throughout Santa Clara County for a couple of months or so. The signs said:

SYPHILIS / SMALL POX / FORCED BAPTISMS / MISSION GIFTS / ENDING NATIVE LIVES.

LA: Do you ever get responses from people about the public works?

HEHB: Oh yeah, yeah. There's always a lot of feedback. People get very upset about some of it. But mainly it just starts the discourse and I think that's what I try to do with all the public work. I mean, if it doesn't do that, I don't know why we're doing anything. If we didn't begin the discussion of what the reality of this country is . . . I mean, *Mission Gifts* was a little pointed maybe and a little editorialized, but with *Building Minnesota* or *Native Hosts*, I'm not saying that Minnesota or New York are terrible places and that they shouldn't have done this or they shouldn't have done that. I'm just giving the information, because maybe people didn't know that the missions brought syphilis to the tribes. And when I went to California, I asked people where the Indians are, and they say they don't know where they went. So I tell them that the missions killed a lot of them off. I'm sorry if it's a mystery why they're gone, but that's why.

LA: Would you say, then, that you try to have an educational dimension to your work?

HEHB: Particularly with the public work, because it's always dealing with history just about all the time, and it informs people about the Native response to that history. But I don't like to make it didactic, hit people over the head with it. There's a certain amount of seduction involved with all art and life and love or whatever, and you have to sort of give that out and let people solve what it is they think needs solving. If you just give them the slogan, that's not enough for me. People criticized my work in graduate school in Philadelphia because it *wasn't* a slogan. I'd tell them what it *was* about and they'd get upset because it didn't look like what I'd said at all. They'd tell me, "Wait a minute; you're using words and you've got to say what they mean."

I once talked to an older artist I met, Ed Ruda, he was a visiting professor from New York. We were sitting around one day and I said, "Ed, the critics and all these people are giving me hell about using text and are telling me it's got to mean what it says." And he said, "What does red mean? What does blue mean? People think they know what blue means, or red, but they don't, so who says that letters and words have to mean the same thing?"

LA: What *is* the function of color in your work, not in the public works, but in the *What Makes a Man* series or in a relatively abstract work like *Old Man Sits Calm near the Heat*, for example?

HEHB: Well, those are all from what is the *Neuf* ["four times" in Cheyenne] series, which are acrylic paintings like five by six feet or so, and they began from the canyon right outside the house. The earth color is very red here, so that came into it; and another part of the imagery is the break of the earth, how the earth washes. That's where some of the forms come from in the paintings. But the totality of the color, I don't know; I've always had those colors. I mean, I've always painted. I'm a painter, that's how I describe myself. I'm not really a conceptual artist or anything like that. I deal with the way things look. Even with the public work I'm very involved with the aesthetics of the letters and what colors they are and all that. So I've always had this color, which is really a lot of different colors, as you see in the studio now. It's like a lot of colors that might not work together, but I always put them together, and they're getting brighter now, too. But there isn't a specific association with those colors. When I do the gestural drawings, like the word drawings, those have a direct reference about the word itself.

LA: Like in the *What Makes a Man* series? There the colors have a pretty specific meaning.

HEHB: Yeah, you know, like *Sweet Sage*: the sage is green, and the color of the earth is green, so I do associate that. It's a little game I play within my work where the paintings never have an association but the words all have associations.

LA: How did the specific forms come about? Would you call them landscape paintings?

HEHB: Not really. People can sort of see land in them or leaves or a lot of things, but I think the images are more informed by the canyon and the trees but in a very vague kind of reference. It's not very direct anymore. Now they really make themselves and the way it's worked out is kind of interesting. This little eight-by-ten-inch painting was the first and only painting I did outdoors. But I had to paint one and then I brought it inside and it just suggested the next one and the next one, and that's been going on for maybe eight years to where even now I can see the difference between the earliest and the latest. The paintings are off on their own language totally.

But what happened one day, I was outside, and as you saw, from the top of our place here you can see twenty or thirty miles in every direction. You can see the horizon everywhere and the canyon breaks down into an arch. One day I was just out walking and all of a sudden I looked up and there was a circle in the sky and these clouds had made an upward arch which framed the downward arch, and there was this huge ellipse about a mile wide, and a few minutes later the top clouds moved and the ellipse was gone. And at that moment I realized that when I make these paintings I always start from the left with a shape and then I start from the right with a shape and I make it break down this way, see. And every painting I do I make that form and it's this view here, which I never knew until I saw it framed with clouds, when the clouds came.

LA: Does that framing give a sense a movement, or do you seek a sense of movement in those paintings?

HEHB: Yeah, I really do. I seek a lot of movement, and for a couple of reasons. The first one is more intuitive and it's about being in the canyons around here. I hunted and hiked down there, and there was a feeling of things being fixed and static. But then things would move fast, like quail against the trees, or coyotes or my dogs running by, moving like jackrabbits, and you have this flash of movement which I have seen all the time, and I like that. Somehow I like that passage of things, and I think back to the impressionists, who I discovered later, who were almost outlawed because their paintings moved too much. You know, the king of France didn't want anything to move; any kind of movement was radical. So I like in a political sense that these paintings are moving, and I hope that the world is moving and that Native America is moving, that it's not frozen. So movement, I think, is my friend. When things are moving there's always a chance.

LA: So even what might be seen as works about nature are operating on another level?

HEHB: Yes. People always want to stereotype them, say they

look like continents or something, but they haven't been here, they haven't walked around this land. They feel that all the work anyone does has to be taken specifically in their locale. With artists like Eric Fischl or Julian Schnabel, just as an example, or any of these people, everyone knows their intimate life stories because of the propaganda, so then you're informed about what they make. So people dwell on that particular place with them. With us, people think that we're just Native artists and we come in for a quick thing and we fill a slot, so we're not allowed as big a persona as Anglo artists like Robert Rauchenberg. He can do record covers or whatever, silverware, balloons, whatever, any kind of thing, and everyone just loves it. So I try to do that with my work, in the sense of trying to be a full person and not be pigeonholed into being only a Native artist.

LA: You use whole cities as your canvas, like in Minneapolis or San Jose. In Manhattan you used the Times Square message screen. This certainly blows away people's expectations about the narrow scope of Native art. You're doing a new piece in Seattle which makes a very broad statement, too.

HEHB: I just finished that. It's called *Day/Night*. It's porcelain enamel, which is a new thing for me. It's eight feet tall, forty-two inches wide, and two-sided. On the back side is an English translation of what's on the front, which is in Lushootseed, a technical version of Chief Seattle's language. One panel says "Chief Seattle, today the streets are our home," and then the other panel says "Far away, brothers and sisters, we still remember you."

It's all about the transient Native people who live in this park in Seattle, and how when tourists come to this park to get their pictures taken in front of this bronze bust of Chief Seattle, they have to step over the bodies of the Indians who are sleeping there. And there are totem poles in this park that were actually stolen from Alaska and British Columbia. No one in Washington makes these totem poles, but that's another representation of Seattle—totem poles.

All these discrepancies and miscommunications started to hit me. So when I got the commission to do a piece about Seattle, I hung out in the park, talked to people, went down to the wharf and saw the hookers and the drug dealers and all the things that were happening, you know, in the unofficial city. And then I went out to the official Indian center, which is at a beautiful place overlooking Puget Sound. I could have chosen to do a piece there, but the real Indian center for me was Pioneer Square, where people drink their wine or beer and panhandle and sleep and what not, so I chose to put it down there. I mean, that's where the tourists are going anyway. Those two directions of society are making the work; the society that you witness *is* the work.

LA: What makes the work interesting is that people are more focused on the bust of Chief Seattle than on the living Indians all around. But that's a perfect analogue of what's happening anyway. On one of the panels you have your leaf forms and on the other side are dollar signs and crosses. You're linking those images?

HEHB: Yes, in this way. Those streets of Chief Seattle's are our home, because he had all these great ideas that he offered people. His name was actually Sealth, and I just wanted to talk with him and tell him, "Look what's happened to us; look at where we are. Everything you said was true, and look where we are now. It all seems to be about money. And what has the white man's religion done for us?" But, too, the leaf patterns and tree forms show that we won't forget about people on the street, or even on this reservation. Like, when I talk to people on the street, they ask me where I'm from and I say Oklahoma, Cheyenne-Arapaho. They say, "Oh, I'm from South Dakota (or Yucatán or North Carolina)." No one says they're from Seattle, and maybe they've been there fifteen or twenty years. They never forget about their people, and their people don't forget about them.

LA: So physical removal or separation doesn't correspond to a spiritual removal. Your mind is with your people.

HEHB: Yeah, the value you have is still with the original place that you come from, your nation.

LA: There seem to me to be a number of strands in your work. You have your public work, which is highly politicized, and then you have the gestural drawings we've discussed, and you use words and language also. Is it accurate to split your work into separate categories? Do you prefer to show all the types of work together?

HEHB: Yeah. I like to do it all together. I like to do the paintings and then I even do these stat photo pieces that are black and white text, like *Brick Prick* and *Hard Weed*. So it's best when it's working together, you know. It's just that the art world doesn't want you to have that venue. They want to keep it clipped down so they can compare it with this other agenda they've got.

Like I just got some information about another group show that's going to happen, and it's just so tiresome to have another one with Native artists or with non-Native artists or whatever. I mean that I'm really tired of people creating communities of artists which don't really exist, which is what you do when you make a group show. You're making a facsimile of a community, because the curator has got an idea, not to mention a job, and they ask you to step into that idea with them. Like the Heard Museum, they get these ideas and I don't know what we've got to do with the ideas. We're individual people.

An example would be like here on the reservation area and in Oklahoma City there's a group I founded called Makers' Alliance. We show together, our kids play together, but we're not all from Oklahoma. We taught in Texas together and we made a sweat lodge together because we all might want to pray, not that we're getting paid to make a sweat lodge. Because we work together, it's legitimate that we show together. But all these shows that happen because someone had a notion, that seems off-track. In those cases, you're put in a position where they take a slice of your work but they don't take all the things you do, or even representative things. No one gets to know all the things you do. There's just that little bit that fits the agenda that seems to be popular at the moment. And so all that means being marginalized again. You're marginalized for everything in the country already, and then you're marginalized again by a museum. So I think the element that should be pushed is to have solo projects and shows, and I'm not speaking about myself. I have enough solo shows that are going to keep continuing, I'm sure. But for many Native artists trying to make a career, they should be allowed to speak fully and be all the things they are and be given a venue and a museum, just like you would any other prominent artist in the world.

LA: Do you find that if your work doesn't fit into preestablished categories of what Native art is, museums and galleries don't want to have anything to do with it?

HEHB: Oh yeah, yeah. That's pretty much a given. Or the flip side: they've reestablished the stereotype to be the political Native artist, so they want that work. They don't want to look at the prose work or the drawings because that doesn't fit into what they thought you were. All that stuff is just deadly. But the big problem I find, especially in New York and back east, is the trend of moving away from art and into the curatorial. Right now, the powers that be are curators. I was in a show in Boston, my work was there, I was there, and upstairs was an exhibition by Cindy Sherman. Anyway, the curators of our shows were there at the reception, and someone walked in and looked at my work and said, "Oh, that's interesting," and then asked what show was upstairs. And the curator of Cindy's show said, "Mine." And that's just indicative of what we've come to. It's the curator's show, not the artist's show. That's just so derailed. Another instance of this was on an invitation to a show. There weren't any artists on it, just the title of the show and the curator's name. The artists aren't necessary.

LA: The artist just serves the curator's function.

HEHB: Yeah. I think that's a big problem and that's why we have so many disjointed shows; someone's got some idea, some crazy idea. I was in London a while back and there was a show I went to called "Women in the Water." I don't know what that was. I mean, I don't know if any women thought about water or if they were into swimming or what they were doing. A student of mine called these shows theme parks, like Six Flags over Texas or Epcot Center. I agree with him. I think that's what we've got. We've got theme-park art and people get entertained, but I think exhibits should just be all about the artist, what the artist feels, and you don't really have to curate that; it already exists. You just have to find the artists and let them have their shot.

LA: It seems like there's no differentiation between going to a theme park and going to a museum or gallery.

HEHB: Well, if these type of shows would really reveal something, I'd be in favor of them, but I don't see them revealing any organizing intelligence or enlightening us. It seems to be misguided to me.

LA: To switch channels here, how did you come to integrate verbal and visual art? How do the two work together? Why work with words in the first place?

HEHB: It developed in graduate school, particularly in Philadelphia. And I went to London and I got totally confused about being Cheyenne and living there, and traveling throughout Europe, hanging out in Florence or Nice or the Riviera. I mean, it was great, but I got to feeling out of place, so I decided that I should go back to Oklahoma and learn more about where I'm from.

Anyway, I was searching pretty hard for what it was that I

should speak about, and where I really was from, and that lead me to reading histories about Cheyenne-Arapaho people. And you come up to the land, and the loss of land, and battles, and treaties being broken really quick, in the research. And so I'm faced with what to say about all this. Do I make a bunch of narrative paintings about Custer killing children in the Washita River? Then you become a realist painter portraying the massacres. What do you do? And so I ended up notating those things, more or less, rather than trying to develop a visual experience of those occurrences in history.

I had a wall in my studio in grad school and it was full of photographs and words, and it was really funny because New York City artists would come to the Tyler as visiting professors and they'd come and look at this wall. They'd say, "Where are the paintings?" I'd tell them that I didn't know how to make them yet. I've got pictures and I've got words, notations primarily, so that's how it began. I've continued that same process, not to play on the heartstrings of the public and depict a murdered child or something, but to create how I notate these emotions.

LA: The words have become a work of their own. But they're not narrative in the sense of sentences and paragraphs.

HEHB: They're like short bursts of words that I present as images. They do have an intrinsic connection. They might start out as sentences or referring to a larger experience, but it's edited down to be shorter.

LA: Is it like a free association or a kind of automatic writing?

HEHB: No, they come out of very direct experiences. For example, this one up on the wall is about Peru. It says "Metal bird turns." I had been traveling in South America, to the Amazon, and I was heading back home and very excited about getting a plane out. The plane was a jet, but it had to stop in two towns to get back to Lima, and land on these tiny runways. People were just running onto the plane and throwing their bags under the seats. That puzzled me. But I figured out that the runway had no lights and the plane couldn't really stop. It was dusk. As we taxied, there were kids playing soccer over by the runway. There was a woman walking by with her baby. There was no security or fence. It was a commercial Aero Peru flight—but I just thought about a metal bird. It suddenly seemed very primitive, just a big tin bird that was getting ready to get out of there and get back to Lima. So I put that experience down in three words. They don't speak about the whole experience, but they speak of mine. I just hope that in all the word works, even in the paintings, I'm combining my experiences with the viewer's experiences, my life with the viewer's life.

I don't think it's possible to give a full world to somebody; all you can do is slip something in for the viewer to engage with. Then through the art experience you enlarge the viewer's perception of the world and maybe something will emerge for him. Like when I saw that mother and baby, saw the kids playing soccer, saw people running onto the plane, and I was trying to get home — that's what made my life at that moment. It was a very direct experience. It wasn't a revelation.

LA: And you'll distill that experience, that moment, into words?

HEHB: Yeah. Hopefully the words will resonate because they are distilled from my perceptions.

LA: And the words are a sort of intermediary between your experience and the viewer's experience?

HEHB: More a focus on their own experience, in that they would make something new out of it with their own life rather than gain mine, internalize mine. Like, when you're in the tepee and the ceremony starts, the leaders don't say the whole world is right here for you, take this book home and read it. It's all sorts of elements which come together to make the world.

LA: And you present these elements through your work. And your work functions on numerous levels, from the personal, in *What Makes a Man,* to the national and the international, as you've shown in work about South Africa and Northern Ireland. What connections do you make between the personal and the global?

HEHB: Well, they kind of happen. It's hard to say, because you're not always able to make pieces that address international issues. It's not always clear that you can make those connections. For example, I went to Northern Ireland and spent a couple weeks in Derry and Belfast, and then I had the message made in Oklahoma. It said: PEACE / UNITE / RESPECT IRISH HOMELANDS / NO MORE KINGDOMS / NO MORE KINGS. And I had that message when I returned to there, but I was prepared to change it if people didn't like it, but the moment I took it out of my satchel everyone just flipped out about it. They said that it would go up on a billboard in downtown Derry, so we went with that message.

But even in the *Native Hosts* pieces, I worked in some ways that were tentative, because you're a visitor and you have to see if it's appropriate for you to speak, and if it's not you sit back down and let someone else talk. So those public works have their own built-in limits.

My paintings give me the greatest latitude. I come into the studio and turn on the Janet Jackson music and I stand here and paint. I come back and forth over a period of months, maybe an hour at a time, doing little parts of the painting. I don't spend day after day all day painting. But again, I relate to the paintings all the time. Like this painting here sat for maybe nine months without any changes. Now it's almost finished, but I had to react to it rather than come in and make it. I don't think you can do anything that way. People do, but they screw everything up. You can't just come in and pose something, even on canvas. You've got to let it talk back to you, have some sort of interplay.

But I think these paintings, like in the *Neuf* series, are the most personal because there are no inherent politics about them, in the sense that I'm not giving clues or thinking about how people are going to react or how they are going to read the work. The words and the gestural kind of drawings are kind of in between the paintings and the public works, the signs that go out in public. They're public because the text is very accessible to people. Everyone can pretty much read my simple words. They're about my experiences with my children, my marriage, my sexuality. So by doing four different kinds of things I can get at who I am, and if you present that, maybe people will know what you think, at least a little bit. But I couldn't use just one way of expressing myself.

LA: It sounds like the forms you work in are ways for you to explore yourself.

HEHB: Oh, yeah, totally. They have to be. That's what makes them. You can't make anything if you're empty. If you can't explore your own self, your own persona, I don't know what you do. You have to just sit back, take a trip or something.

LA: You work slowly?

HEHB: The paintings I do, but I do a lot of other things. I spend a lot of time with my kids, I travel and do other projects, curate things, little bursts of time on different projects.

LA: Your activities are quite diverse. You're not in the studio fifteen hours a day.

HEHB: No, no. But, you know, I feel — it's weird — unsuccessful most of the time. I wish I could do this better or that better, or make sure that my son didn't cry, or play more with him, but I don't know how you resolve that. You just keep plugging away at everything. But then I think that maybe it's a good thing to feel a little jittery, always to have fire under your feet. Even when you get money, like we have a little money now, but it's not a happy thing to have; nothing changes. It's weird. But you're sort of worried about that for a long time.

LA: You've referred to the language installations as "wall lyrics."

HEHB: Yeah, I guess in some kind of relationship to poetry, even though I don't like the word "poetry." I don't know what it means, but people link my work to poetry. But I was thinking about the lyrics more in terms of music. When I'm working in the studio doing the drawings there's a lot of music, very "up" music like contemporary black music, and so there's this pulse and I think the pulse gets into the drawings. When you see them they really jump around. They're not static at all, and even the edges and the fringes of them are very rough. But I always relate the images to the wall, because as I work I put them up on the wall and draw right there, make a fifteen-drawing installation right on the wall. So the drawings have more to do with music than poetry, because I feel a lot about music and it's a driving force within all the work.

LA: Can you trace back some of the other influences on your work?

HEHB: Well, I guess the first one I think about is Blackbear Bosin, the Kiowa-Comanche painter. He lived in Wichita, where I grew up, and he had a studio there, which I visited, and I did get to know him. We talked every now and then, but of course we were at odds, you know, about the things that I would make, because he had more traditional ideas about what Native art could be. He was really pretty much of an abstract painter, if you look at his work, but there were always figurative things in it. But anyway, that left a little void in between us, but we could talk about it. There was a time when Native artists, maybe they still do, argue about what Native art is or isn't, what it could or could not be. But for me he was an example that you could be an artist, that you could work as an artist. It was very rare to have someone like that.

He used to sell jewelry and stuff and he probably did things he didn't like to do, like working in an aircraft plant. He didn't have to do that too long, though, and he maintained his studio and his own lifestyle through art. So he was the first really major influence.

In high school I painted funny little Indian drawings or profiles of Indian heads, the typical kind of Plains Native work. I didn't do that for long, but it was a mannerism I saw. At undergrad school [the University of Kansas], I had a lot of teachers who weren't necessarily well known but they'd studied at places like Yale and RISD [the Rhode Island School of Design]. But they were in a weird sort of landlocked art world. In Kansas it's really isolated and deadly and it plays like Norman, Oklahoma, or something. It's hard to get out of there, like something keeps pulling you back. I learned about frustration from them, too, about how you got to move, you got to get going, and they gave me an agenda. They'd tell me about Berkeley or London as a place to study. They showed the students that we had to look beyond this local place. It's an international game we're playing and it's good to get versed in that, so I did. And that's when I applied to go to school in London and got accepted at the Royal College of Art. I went to London on a scholarship and traveled all around Europe. But like I was saying before, it was more or less an experience which showed me how much I was from another place.

But it was interesting in a way. Because of British colonization, the city is full of everybody but people from England. There are students from Malta, Hong Kong, you name it, so there's an incredibly diverse group of people. People must have thought I was from Saudi Arabia, because one time a bus driver started talking to me in Arabic. And one time a professor I didn't even know came into the studio and said that my work seemed to be more about a round place, not this New York–Frank Stella stuff which I'd been doing. And I took his advice and I came back home and found out what that earth awareness was.

Another powerful influence in grad school, when my work got a little more mature, was Vito Acconci. He gave a talk at Temple about his sexuality. He was a writer but he got into a lot of performance work. He did some crazy stuff and people thought he was nuts, but I thought he was great because he was really saying something with his own self about his own self. He wasn't pretending to do something, but putting himself on the line. And later, in '82, I had this show with him. I was putting up my work about the Sand Creek massacre and I backed into somebody and it was Vito. He was putting up his stuff. It was a great moment. I see him on the subways sometimes in New York and we guest lecture at the same schools.

LA: That's interesting. In a way you bridge Black Bear Bosin and Vito Acconci. Maybe that isn't so extreme if you think about it, the connection of the old and the new. You've written some about the Fort Marion artists and your great-grandfather, who was a prisoner there.[6] You mentioned the continuity of the warrior's spirit and the public messages in the work of the 1870s, which is what you're trying to do 120 years later. What is your sense of connection to the prison drawings?

HEHB: Well, there's been some controversy about that work. To me, there have been some strange readings by Native art experts, who aren't Natives at all, of course, but they are experts about us. And the reading is that when the Cheyenne warriors and chiefs went to Fort Marion, they were somehow happy about being there, in this totally horrible prison. This view comes from the absence of aggressive imagery in their work. In the Northern Plains drawings of the 1850s and '60s there were some very violent drawings. But my premise is that if you are in prison, you don't draw pictures about killing the warden and then expect to get out someday. They made pastoral paintings and the ones about war were the ones about hunting. But these guys were stone warriors — that was their job. But they were smart enough not to do that in prison, and they got let out to come home eventually.

So I guess what I meant is that from my looking at the art, that was the first time that Indian artists had to project what the white public would think of the art. Before, what you made was within your culture; you dealt with your own culture and you just worked. But now, we, Indian artists, are in a public arena, an international arena. And we've got to think about what that arena is all about and how we're going to work with that, like the Fort Marion prisoners had to work with what they had, and they beat it, because they got to come home. You've got to beat it that way, outsmart it. It's subversive, where they don't think you're doing that, they think you're just putting it out there, but no, you're spinning it around.

LA: In a lecture, "Insurgent Messages for America," you stated: "Countless times our combative measures through Art are misrepresented or corruptly undertaken by the non-Indian. Too often the white man masquerades as the native artist, creating many self serving images. Regretfully when true Native American Art is finally accepted the style turns out to be that which fulfills the comfortable fantasy held by the non-Indian. It must be understood that the dominant white culture is not in a position to instruct in the essence of the native outlook, but can only learn."[7] Could you expand on that?

HEHB: Well, yeah. In the institutionalized art world, many of the Indians aren't Indians at all. They have nothing to do with the nation or the culture; they'd rather deal with galleries and museums and collectors. I once had an older collector in an art history class I taught and he was only interested in how to be a more savvy buyer. The art world would rather deal with the white masquerading as the Indian because it just makes the business run smoother.

I do support trying to get rid of people who masquerade, and I support the law about identifying yourself and your nation. We've got to do something about these people who are not Indians passing themselves off as Indians. I regret that some people's parents didn't want to claim their tribal heritage because it was a discriminatory thing, but I guess I would forgo those people to get rid of the other ones. Nothing is a pure system. I mean, in the ceremony that we have you can't eat or drink, and if you want to leave, well, no one's going to force you to stay. Maybe you'll faint or maybe you'll get sick, but that's the breaks. That's what happens. But for the greater good, to make this renewal you have to make sacrifices. I think that the bulk of Native artists support the law, so we can get rid of these impostors. Anyway, we're not saying that you can't show; just don't claim to be an Indian.

LA: It seems as though there's a double-edged sword in that Native art has to look "Indian" in order to be accepted, while at the same time the ethnic artist is restricted to a different category. Do you find that work is judged by the ethnicity of the artist rather than the quality of the work, or can the two be separated out?

HEHB: I think it can be separated out. If you're honest in who you are and say who you are, then the work is going to be the work and it's not going to be automatically successful just because you're from somewhere or have a certain background.

LA: It's funny that Native people are the only group who have to prove who they are. You can call yourself a German artist and not have to go back generations.

HEHB: The weird part about it is that we don't have people masquerading as German artists. We don't have people saying, "I'm kind of black." Some people from southern Spain are part African, but they don't sit around claiming to be black artists or infringing on African events or exhibitions. It's a weird game.

LA: Why would that masquerading be done?

HEHB: There's the mythical model of the Native world, which on one hand people want to destroy the existence of Native people, while on the other they want to be part of it.

LA: That must make people schizophrenic, because at the same time you're being destroyed, you are being embraced.

HEHB: Yeah, yeah. The thing of it is to me, though, is that people don't want to be Native; they want to remain themselves while pretending to be Native. They don't want to come live like you or have fights and have drunks around; they don't want their kids to go to the second-class schools, have third-class health care. They don't want that. They want to stay themselves but yet think they're you. Then they can disavow any problems they've caused, because they're you. That washes them clean — and I say no. If you live in America, I want to know where so we can talk about the land your house is on. I don't care where you are, you are on Indian land and you're profiting from it. And when you make money on your investment, that's Indian profit you are taking. No one is in the clear on this.

It's the same in other ways, too. People ask me in all honesty if they can attend a ceremony and go through some of the rituals. But it's like when my grandma was a kid, they'd go in a wagon for a week to visit Kiowas and they'd take gifts; they wouldn't go empty-handed. Because they want to share what they had, they would take something. So when people ask me, I say, "Well, why don't you take some meat and some gifts and stick around for a week or two, instead of just zipping in and out for an hour?" If I go somewhere I gather up dishes of food or baskets of groceries to offer my hosts just as a courtesy, right? I mean, that's what is done. It's important to make that exchange.

LA: You've written about the role of sexuality in your work, and a good bit of your work addresses that. The IAIA [Institute of American Indian Arts] just had a show of the human figure in Native American art [summer 1991]. It had a good reception, but I sense that most people don't connect to Native artists doing nudes, or believe that the domain of Native artists should include the sexual or the sensual. Why is this an important dimension of your work?

HEHB: Well, it's all about the kind of dehumanization we face and the myths again, and they're related. If you're a myth, then you're not human anymore and you don't suffer human problems and there are no human solutions we can find for you. We don't have to do any legislation or reappropriation of taxes or decide on fishing rights. All we have to do is read about you in a book, make sure that you stay in the dead past. The white man has done that to Native people through taking away their sensuality and sexuality, which is very, very real. It's a very active, sexually active kind of culture, even in jesting and joking with old ladies and stuff. All these kinds of things are fair game for teasing, say, and the sexual energy is always there in our cultures, more so I think than in Anglo cultures. It's been absent, so therefore I tend to stir it into my work and it's revealing in some ways. It's just more of my reality. And then if you can face people as human beings, maybe you can deal with their problems in a real way. But we mythologize different groups—blacks, Asians, Latinos, what have you—misinterpret them, and then they're not real anymore. It's the usual ethnocentric, anthropological perspective.

LA: Looking ahead, you have an exhibit planned for Berkeley in the spring of '92. Could you talk about that?

HEHB: It's a piece actually commissioned by the Wexner at Ohio State, but part of it will be at Berkeley. It's called *Is What Is*, and it's stepping beyond *What Makes a Man* or *Sharp Rocks*. It will examine sexuality, tribalism, warriors, family, self, trying to make those things clear. That's the next step for me, to be even more personal and deal with some of these things. I've made a diagram of it. It's based on my travels to Peru and Mexico, and on my participation in ceremonies, and on my self. I made a lot of drawings in South America, and I'm going to make drawings about words.

It also involves the two coasts in this country, and the four directions. They are persona places where I become this individual who speaks about art. So the West Coast one will be called the "Boost" and there'll be an East Coast one. And then the north is a ceremonial position for the tribe, so the paintings will have a northern orientation. I'll install the paintings to the north on a kind of curved wall at the Wexner, and I'll have the Peru drawings facing south and other things facing east and west to make a directional kind of installation, kind of how I sit here in the middle of America in Oklahoma and things are moving around me, and how I move around my place here.

What it may really be about is spirits. An older Cheyenne ceremonial woman came into my studio and looked around one day and said, "I don't know if these are paintings or what they mean, but there are a lot of spirits in here, watching us." And I think that's one of the best interpretations of the paintings I've ever heard and I was very happy with that.

SELECTED SOLO EXHIBITIONS

"Is What Is" (1992), University of California Art Museum, Berkeley, CA.

"Dig the Mix" (1991), University of Colorado Art Galleries, Boulder, CO.

"Hard Weed" (1991), Artspeak Gallery, Vancouver, British Columbia, and Definitely Superior, Thunder Bay, Ontario.

"Claim Your Color" (1990), touring retrospective exhibition, Exit Art, New York, NY.

"American Policy" (1988), Orchard Gallery, Derry, Northern Ireland.

"Heh No Wah Maun Stun He Dun: What Makes A Man" (1987–88), touring exhibition, Gallery of the American Indian Community House, New York, NY.

"Sharp Rocks" (1985–87), CEPA Gallery, Buffalo, NY.

"In Our Language" (1983), language/video installation, C. N. Gorman Museum, University of California, Davis, CA.

"Foreign Bodies" (1982), Southern Plains Indian Museum and Crafts Center, Anadarko, OK

SELECTED BIBLIOGRAPHY

Price, Phyllis. "Native Host: Hachivi Edgar Heap of Birds." *Front* 3, 2 (November–December, 1991): 22–23 [interview].

Heap of Birds, Hachivi Edgar. "Artist's Statement." In *Artifacts for the Seventh Generation.* San Francisco, CA: American Indian Contemporary Arts Gallery, 1990, unp.

——. "In Honor of Rain Forest." *Caliban* 8 (1990): 73–81.

——, ed. *Makers.* Norman, OK: Point Riders Press, Cottonwood Arts Foundation, 1988.

——. "Artist's Statement." In *Eight Native American Artists.* Fort Wayne, IN: Fort Wayne Museum of Art, 1987, p. 32.

——. "Nah-Kev-Ho-Eyea-Zim." In *We Are Always Turning Around . . . on Purpose.* Old Westbury, NY: State University of New York, 1986, pp. 14–19.

——. *Sharp Rocks.* Buffalo, NY: CEPA, 1986.

——. "Introduction." In *Modern Native American Abstraction.* Philadelphia: Philadelphia Art Alliance, 1983, unp.

Rick Hill

Tuscarora

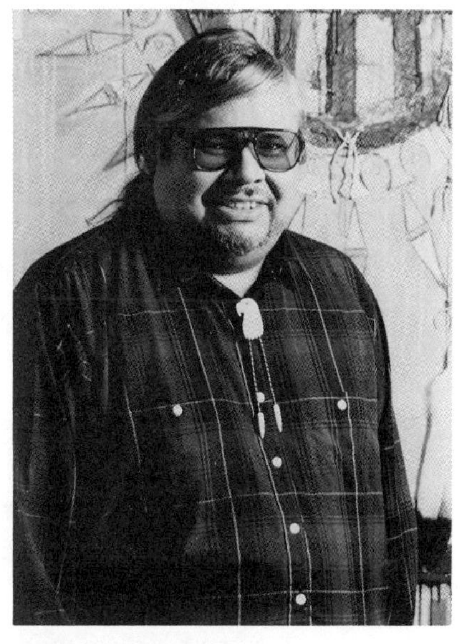

There are two distinct strands in Rick Hill's photographs and paintings: the meditative and the satirical. In the former works, Hill uses both "straight" portraiture and photo-collage, accompanied with text, to create highly personal reflections on culture, family, self, life, and death. In such works as *My Grandmother*, *My Father, My Friend*, and *My Son, Randy*, all from 1971, Hill attempts to take the measure of these lives and the meanings of those lives to him. These photographs give him the opportunity to explore the reality of his own life and to come to the realization that no one stands alone.

This realization of connectedness and endurance on both a family and a cultural level emerges powerfully in *Along the Flowered Path* (1971). The work concerns both the death of his brother and the birth of his son. Hill's brother and Hill's infant son were each borne along the same path. Hill notes about the work: "We will all follow that path sooner or later, just as our ancestors before us. Even in the afterworld, the Iroquois will walk together as one."[1] In this case, as in the other works in this series, the personal portrait encodes cultural values.

At first glance Hill's "straight" portrait photographs of real people may appear prosaic, but this is a deliberate strategy on his part to counter the pernicious legacy of Edward Curtis and the other early "Indian photographers." For Hill (and, indeed, for other Native photographers) this legacy has been the falsification of the Indian and a reification of the white conception of the Indian, actually an act of oppression. These mid- to late-nineteenth- and early-twentieth-century images have entangled the Indian in the thickets of the white imagination and prevented both Indians and whites from mutual growth and understanding. However, the "new Native photographer" "addresses directly the stilted images of the Indian in the public's mind" and is "concerned with the everyday realities" of his or her community.[2] Hill's "simple" portraits of people engaged in their daily lives take on added resonances when looked at in this broader historical and cultural frame.

Hill's photocollages more symbolically address these issues of family and culture (although his accompanying text supports the imagery). *Intermarriage* faces the problem of the gradual erosion and possible loss of identity through mixed marriages; *Transformation* and *Black Elk's Vision* (each 1971) integrate images of the past and the present to raise questions about the ways Indian people deal with their lives today. Hill does not take a romanticized view of Indian life and he sees no panacea, but says, "Our image of ourselves often outruns the reality of our daily existence. We celebrate distorted images of our past. We should quit trying to be something that we are not."[3]

The satiric paintings and photographs, though, represent another direction in Hill's work, and comment on the absurdities, and tragedies, in both Indian and mainstream cultures. Two of the most scathing paintings are *D.I.A.N.D. Dandy and Flesh-Coloured Bandaids* (1983) and *Portrait of a Whiteman* (1984). In the earlier work an Indian Affairs bureaucrat in traditionally braided hair sits for a portrait in a three-piece suit, holding a wine glass in one hand and a bottle of "Fine White Wine" in the other. The canvas around the figure is papered with Canadian currency, indicating the temptations offered by the dominant culture to sell out. This image is in turn framed by a series of flesh-colored Band-Aids. The seeming incongruity of the Band-Aids, though, is actually a quite telling comment on how the dominant society has defined "flesh-colored" to mean the color of white people's skin. Hill is suggesting that if Indians sell out for enough, and for long enough, their skin color will lighten in proportion to the loss of their cultural identity. At the end of this process, the Indians' use of "flesh-colored" Band-Aids will be quite natural. (It is interesting to note that after some African-American protests in the 1960s and '70s Johnson and Johnson began marketing dark "flesh-colored" Band-Aids for African-Americans.) In the 1984 piece Hill poses then rock star Boy George (complete with his braids) and presents him as the "archtypal Whiteman." The point Hill is making is that Boy George no more represents white people than a stoic Curtis Indian represents Indian people.

Hill's series from the 1970s, *The Whiteman in North America*, approaches its subject anthropologically, using the material objects and detritus of mainstream society as the foundation for his satirical analysis of the "true" white culture. *Cultural Icons* shows a broken piano littered with Coke bottles, while *Progress* frames a bulldozer in the foreground and a church in the background. In the introduction to the show Hill has written: "The trails of the people of the Caucasian persuasion across North America are littered with objects of their disposable culture. . . . It appears that their spiritual ways teach them that through destruction comes rebirth. Rust regenerates. Eagles regurgitate. And the dead levitate. . . . My attempt to document the Whiteman in North America has taken many years of field work and I'm proud to present this series of photographs that should prove once and for all that the Whiteman still exists."[4]

Central to Hill's art and to his writing is the concept that Native art reflects Native thought. Like the artifacts of the ancestors, contemporary art is a way of making and finding connections. In "Art as a Sovereign Act," Hill writes that art "is a way for this generation to leave evidence of cultural thought for the future generations. It is evidence that cannot be refuted by scholars or lawyers. It is evidence of the spirit of our people, alive and well. . . . We are who we think we are. Art provides the evidence of such thought."[5]

Hill is Tuscarora (Beaver Clan), and was born in 1950 near Buffalo, New York. He has had a diverse career, including stints as an ironworker. In 1968 he enrolled at the Art Institute of Chicago and studied with Robert Frank and Walker Evans. After he left Chicago he worked for the New York State Historical Society as a photographer of Iroquois artists. Following that he worked in museum positions in and around Buffalo. He holds a master's degree in American studies from the State University of New York in Buffalo and for nearly ten years taught Native art history and other courses there. In June of 1990 he was named museum director at the Institute of American Indian Arts (IAIA) in Santa Fe, and coordinated the development of the new IAIA museum space in downtown Santa Fe, which opened in June 1992. Hill stepped down from that position and returned east in the summer of 1992 to take a position at the National Museum of the American Indian in Washington, D.C., scheduled to open in the late 1990s. His work is in a variety of collections, including the Department of the Interior, the Museum of Man in Ottawa, and the Cleveland Museum of Natural History. He curated "The Alcove Show" in the summer of 1992 for the Museum of Fine Arts in Santa Fe and is one of the coordinators of *A Day in the Life of Native America*, a work in progress involving some fifty Native photographers, scheduled for publication in 1993.

We talked late one night in early August 1991. The batteries in my tape recorder ran out well before the *cerveza*.

LA: You wear many hats: writer, painter, photographer, curator, teacher, historian. How did you come to have so many different roles?

RH: The inability to hold down a job. No, I worry about that myself, why my career has taken so many turns. What happens is that there are so few Indians out there who are taking a curatorial lead that we sometimes get called upon in many different ways. I never thought that I had the ability to write, for example, but that little computer over there has turned me on and allowed me to do it. And each time you do something, you go a little bit further and you get demands to do something else, so one thing leads to another.

LA: How do you reconcile your creative energies with the bureaucratic and administrative duties you have?

RH: I'm really lucky, because my first venture in administration was in museum work, so I saw very clearly how little people understood about Indians, and at the same time I saw how big an impact what little I could do had. It became an effective way to deliver whatever message I had. I was also able to use the museum to bring in elders and other artists and to gain knowledge from them, and in turn pass that knowledge on. I found, though, that my real passion is to be the artist, but the frustration I felt in people not having access to my work led me to decide that I had to till the soil and find a way for people to have access to the Indian voice, and what I found out was that a whole lot of groundwork was needed. We had to legitimize ourselves, correct stereotypes, present our view of history, before anyone would ever *see* the art. I'm not sure we're at that point yet, either.

LA: Does your work at the Institute of American Indian Arts try to lay some of that groundwork?

RH: I'm museum director at the institute, and basically my job is to build the biggest and best museum that presents Indian art from an Indian perspective. Sounds simplistic, but that's the challenge of the job. Pete Jemison said once that he's still waiting for the Indian art catalog that will blow you away. I told Pete that he wouldn't have to wait much longer, because I plan to do that catalog [*Creativity Is Our Tradition*]. The only reason I say that is because for too long we've let other people tell us what our art is, what it means, and who are the best artists. But we have to lay claim to that, and answer those questions. So I look at my job in the overall Indian political scenario as a way of claiming our art and declaring self-determination. We are going to tell the world what that means.

LA: How will the new IAIA museum differ from the proposed Museum of the American Indian in Washington?

RH: On that point, as an Indian museum director and curator, we're not arguing if the work is anthropological, ethnographic, or fine art. We're saying that this is the work that we do, and that's what we'll present. The significance of that is that Indians make art today, that an Indian can use a computer, can do video, can photograph, or do anything they want, and still be Indian. For too long we've been measured on some kind of scale of mankind, that first we were cavemen and now we're real men. What I'm trying to say is that our art is self-validating, [that] what any generation does is valid, but also that creativity is our tradition. Tradition should not be thought of as a certain kind of style that persists throughout all history. Rather, what you see at work among Indians is this very creative and fertile mind which reenvisions the world every time an artist makes something. In one sense, then, there is a timelessness to Indian art, and it'll last forever, but you still need to see it in context. So my job is to challenge people's thinking about Indian art, especially in this town. Most people think that the only good art is the old art, like the only good Indian is a dead Indian. Indian art doesn't belong in the past; it's a part of our everyday lives. Look at how we have to live. Art is necessary.

LA: What about the contention that contemporary Indian art needs to meet mainstream standards? Or is there an "Indian aesthetic" that runs parallel to the mainstream?

RH: I don't think that there are universal standards of art which apply to every time period or to every culture. Art is a manifestation of culture, and our cultures are different, so our art is going to be different.

One thing that's beginning to bother me more and more is that Indian artists are looking for the pat on the head from the white patrons, the white curators, the white gallery owners. It's as if we somehow don't think we're good enough until the white man tells us we're really good, that we're good enough to hang in the mainstream museums and galleries. In every other area of Indian endeavor we have a policy of self-determination, but when it comes to the arts, it's like we forget the fact that we are okay. We shouldn't have to be chasing someone else's standard. You know, we've changed this in education, we've changed this in economic development, we've changed this in just about every area of Indian activity except the arts. We still let the white man set the standard. We are asked to change. It's not that the standard's bad, but until it's *our* standard of excellence we'll always be dark white people. Until we finally produce art which is meaningful to us as Indians of today, and possibly to Indians of the future, then what we do in the arts is just a shallow reflection of who we used to be.

LA: One of your goals as a museum director and curator, and as an artist, is aesthetic self-determination?

RH: I think so. It's our cultural right. It's a sovereign right. I said one time that Indian art is one of the best examples of Indian sovereignty, meaning that no one should control what we say, whether it's to cater to the curator or the patron. If you do that, you might as well sell shoes, because you remove the very legitimacy of the creative process. I mean, I'm sure that Indian artists in the 1600s didn't sit around saying, "Gee, do you think this will be in a museum someday? Maybe I better change it 'cause it's not good enough for their standards." The elders stood by what they felt was right; at the same time, change and evolution were constant. And as long as our work is sincere, and talks about a legitimate thing—personal, tribal, cultural—then it's a valid piece of art. And people need to look at the message rather than the form the message takes. It's kind of like saying good poetry can only be written in English. We know that's not true.

LA: To follow up on some of these issues, the IAIA museum recently had a show [spring 1991] of nudes in Native art. How did that show come about, and what was the response? You've also written a couple of essays about this work.

RH: I actually called it "The Human Figure in American Indian Art" because I knew if I referred to nudes there would have been more hesitancy than there was. I did the show on purpose because I knew that when I came to Santa Fe the institute was wrestling with the idea of having figure drawing in classes, and that having male and female nudes as models offended some of the staff people, some of the women artists, and it became an issue that the nude figure in art was not culturally appropriate. But then I looked at it and said, "How can you possibly teach art without teaching the human figure?" I looked at the art being done here and noticed that very few of our students had a sense of proportion, that their sense of human anatomy was grossly understated. I thought that they were not receiving the level of instruction that everyone else in art school receives, in terms of a basic approach to the arts. Then I started looking at the collection and saw that a number of works of unclothed figures never got shown. You never see these works around town in the galleries, rarely see it at any Indian art exhibitions, until maybe the artist has gained a certain amount of economic status and the art becomes socially acceptable.

I just wanted to take a look at this work and deal with some of the questions. Are reactions to the nude cultural or religious, based on some sort of moral code Indians had before contact, or is it something that's been forced on us? And I'm finding that there's a strong conservative attitude that Indians have about sex, about the human figure. Certain ideas and responses are deeply influenced by Christianity, and I was trying to raise that question. We didn't seem to have a problem with nudity before Columbus got here, so how come now all of a sudden we're saying it violates a cultural ethic? Then the other issue is, of course, the predominance of the nude female figure and the idea that Indian men always seem to make a woman who is very voluptuous, with long, flowing hair, very beautiful—you never see an ugly naked person—and I said, "Then, is that also cultural? Have we adopted the *Playboy* mentality in looking at the human figure?" Sexism is the issue, and the answer to both of those questions is maybe, probably so. There are a variety of influences on how we look at the world as Indians. At the same time, how do you legitimately create a beautiful object of art that has a naked female in it that doesn't exploit ideas about sex, about status? Does it necessarily have to be anti-female? You notice that we raised it as a question because we wanted the dialogue.

Now the reaction to the exhibition was very fascinating. People were uptight before it came out, but the artists were gung-ho, saying go for it, it's about time, and the audience was surprisingly supportive. We did this little survey form for opinions and there were very few objections. One woman vehemently objected and said that it wasn't the type of thing Indians should be doing, it wasn't Indian art, it was pornographic. But the fact is that the work exists; artists do it but they never show it. Yet the minute we mentioned that we were going to do it, the stuff started to come in. That was very important to us. There was a very conspicuous lack of naked male figures, but that's just the nature of our attitude toward that today. The show was also timely because of the controversy over Mapplethorpe. We wanted to see if there is an Indian thing that goes on here which is different from anything else. But, no, we're very much like conservative America when it comes to issues about sex.

LA: Some of the pieces were purely figurative, like Brian Nez's *Julia*, but others were abstract or symbolic, like Roger McKinney's large canvas *First Woman*, but I don't see how anyone could get uptight about that because it refers to a myth. Rick Glazer-Danay's *Buffalo Gal with Boots* raised controversy some time back and was removed from a show in Binghamton. Other pieces were ironic, like Marcus Amerman's *Blue Nude*, and then Jean LaMarr's "reclothing" of the nude female in an old photograph [by Will Soule, photographer at Fort Sill, Indian Territory, c. 1868–75] in one of her *Cover Girl* series works.

RH: The underlying thing, though, is what is Indian about the work, which challenges the very thing we've been talking about, some of the preconceptions that people bring to Indian art. What is the Indian aesthetic that our artists bring to art? And in many tribal cultures, the first human was a woman and there is this reverence toward the cultural concepts of the creation of man and woman. The historical parts I added to the exhibit, like the photographs of some petroglyphs, tried to show that works not only had a visual reference but also an obvious cultural tradition about nakedness tied to symbols of power and symbols of the earth, and I was trying to see if we shy away from it now because we know that there is something to it. But I don't think so. I think a lot of the artists are into it because it's part of their training, but also I do believe that they feel it's an area which is taboo. Artists by their very nature like to break the rules, so they try to venture in to areas that aren't socially acceptable. I was surprised to see that the diversity of the art was pretty tame, really. It wasn't all technically strong or powerful, but we were looking at the fact that it does exist. A lot of artists have worked with nudes in their studios and it does show up in portfolios, but they don't bring it out into the marketplace. Part of that shows the power of that influence. If the marketplace says a naked Indian is unacceptable and we're not going to buy that stuff, and if artists then quit doing it, we have some serious problems.

LA: To change channels a bit, what is your background and training? What did you do before you joined the institute?

RH: Ever since I started school at five years old I was told that I'd be an artist, a great artist, and that made me special, and frankly, I think that's what got me through school. Also, I was the only Indian in the class and we were the only Indian family in the community where I grew up. Because I was recognized as an artist first and an Indian second, I did drawing and all that stuff. I enjoyed it and it gave me a sense of worth. It also gave me an ego that I was better than everybody else, because that's what people told me. But somehow I imagined that the artist thing would just happen, like I'd wake up one day in a loft and be able to go over to a little café and drink wine, the typical life of an artist. I didn't realize that you really had to work at it.

But I was really raised to be an ironworker. My dad is one, my brothers are ironworkers. I started when I was sixteen, during the summers. My cultural heroes were ironworkers, not traditional people, medicine men, or artists, but people who built things. I used to go on the job and watch them work. They were Indian. I didn't have any problems with role models. I knew who we all were, growing up. I didn't have any problems. I knew that we were supposed to be good in whatever we did. And that's the way we were raised. My dad was a hard-working ironworker.

When I started studying photography, also when I was around sixteen, I just got turned on to the magic of it, the image making and the power of image making. It could be more personal than ironworking ever could be. There's a lot of personal pride in building a building—at the end of the day you can look back at what you did, at something that will stand a long time. Art became a way of building something and telling people what Indians think, so we could be admired for our brains as well as our brawn.

I had quite an emotional turmoil telling my dad that I wanted to go to art school and not become an ironworker. Actually, a misfortune turned out to be the greatest fortune in my life. My older brother fell from a building, got all busted up, and my mother said, "That's it; no more of my boys are going to be ironworkers. You're going to go to school." So I went to art school. I was afraid to tell my dad, but when I finally did, when I got up the nerve, he said, "Well, okay, be the best damn artist you can be. I'll stand by you, support you, no matter what." My high school art teacher told me to try the Art Institute of Chicago, which was good for photography. So I applied there, got accepted, and enrolled in 1968, during the Democratic national convention. There were National Guard and police on every corner. I told my brother that I thought I was going to college to get *out* of Vietnam. So that particular political battle was on. What I noticed then was that there were no Indians involved in that battle. Today we chase the Democrats like they're our heroes; back then they were bashing people's heads in. Don't forget, it wasn't that long ago. The absence of an Indian agenda surprised me.

While I was in school another brother got killed in a car wreck and my parents sort of fell apart, so I quit and went back home. I thought that I had to be near them and that they would need me there. I figured that I had learned enough at Chicago anyway. And fortunately, I did, in one sense. I had a very good art education in photography. I met all the top photographers at the time and they really encouraged me, and what they encouraged me to do was to go home and take pictures of my own people. "We can photograph Indians," they had said, "but we don't know what it's like to be an Indian. You can do that in your work." Everyone from Robert Frank to Bob Heinecken to Walker Evans said the same kind of thing. And back then it was a real oddity to be an Indian with a camera. I could use my camera to say something about Indians of today. That's what turned me on.

Then I had to get a job, so I started working for a museum, taking photographs. That developed a whole new aspect to my career. I didn't start painting until about 1973 or '74. My photography could only take me so far. I wanted to show people what Indians think when we see something, so when I take a photograph I just see more than what the negative shows. I see a long history; I see a lot of things I think go on. I did photocollages first, and then painted on the photographs, then just started painting. So to me it was a logical progression in what I wanted to say. I painted for a number of years and sort of gave up on photography. It was hard to deal with getting rejected from shows because photography was not considered an Indian art. Today I'm showing work I took twenty years ago and it's amazing that there is a bigger audience for photography than ever before. My paintings take more time; they're more thoughtful. Photography to me is more direct and you have a shorter amount of time to say what you want to say. They have more power, though, in terms of immediacy of the subject, which is us, Indians.

LA: Why the surge in Native photography? It certainly hasn't been looked as an Indian art medium.

RH: Part of the reason is that we have pushed it. We got fed up with everyone trying to have us relive their Curtis fantasy, to the point where people would visit the reservation and tell us to fold our arms and to look "stoic" or "mean." Also, the seventies didn't seem to matter to America's consciousness; the political agenda put forward by Indians didn't hit home. The TV was still there spewing out those negative stereotypes. America's kids were still afraid of us. Photography became a defensive mechanism. I always thought of Indian artists as point men in the military, going outside of the perimeter. Artists are like that, having to battle the stereotypes, battle the racism, confronting the real culture clash. That's why I think photographers said, "Enough is enough. This is who we are." They would present themselves, because at the time, the seventies, the majority of Indian painters and sculptors were still romanticizing our own past — the warrior on horseback (and most of them have never been on a horse), the Indian warrior (most have not been in war). They were trying to carry the fight on, but it wasn't dealing with where Indians are at. And photographers, writers for a while, too, were the only ones saying, "Here's who we are, here's what we look like, here's what the scene is." So legitimizing of the real Indian has captured people's imaginations. At the same time, it's the move over the last few years to want to share things Indian, like there was in the sixties. The need for photographs of Indians has brought attention to Native photographers. Frankly, people were becoming a little bored with the painting and sculpture. So we're filling a void.

LA: You've mentioned the connections between art and identity, and once wrote that "for many Native people art has been a continually changing mode to reaffirm their cultural/tribal identity."[6] How does this work?

RH: I've really been thinking about that, because we have to be careful not to put too much on the artists if that's not true. But from what I've seen, and from the artists I know who are Indians, I believe that through the personal reaffirmation, the culture is affirmed. In other words, the person has to say, "Yes, I'm an Indian." I think we're the only people who grow up and have to make such choices, like, yes, I'm going to be an Indian; yes, I will attend ceremonies; yes, I will marry an Indian; yes, I will live on the reservation; or say no to all those things. So at every point of your life you have to make these Indian decisions. Therefore, for a lot of the artists, they are trying to show the decision they made, or else make up for a lack of a decision. It's easy to celebrate the past and turn one's back on the future. And for Indians who haven't made those choices, they can be Indian in their art. It's a double-edged thing, though: my feeling is that the art should be a reaffirmation of the culture, but we have to be careful that it's not a rationalization for a lack of commitment to the perpetuation of Indians. That's a real tough area that I've been thinking about a lot lately because you just have to look at Indian lives. Like with the ironworkers — I knew they were Indian. But today you look at the art and say, "Is that guy an Indian? Does he live on the reservation? Did he grow up in his culture? Does he speak his language? Did he marry an Indian? Does he care about being an Indian?" And, unfortunately, those questions become an acid test of validity, but I think that they're very important questions. Of course, too, we don't ask those questions of other artists.

LA: One aspect of your work is satirical. In *Portrait of a Whiteman* from '84 you turn the language and imagery of anthropology around. In the 1986 exhibition of the *Whiteman in North America* series at the Thunder Bay Art Gallery in Ontario you introduce the photographs with a mockery of the scientific language of the ethnologists. How did these works come about?

RH: Both are my protests about how artists and scholars have treated Indians. I can't tell you how many museums I've walked into which had hanging from their walls a supposedly reputable piece of fine art called *Portrait of an Indian.* No name, just "an Indian." Again, we're the only race that that happens to. You don't see *Portrait of a Black Man* or *Portrait of a Chinese* or *Portrait of a White Man.* And I thought, well, maybe I'll do the first one of a white man. But look at the white man I picked — Boy George. I was saying about all these other works, they show the chiefs turned into glorious people. So I asked, "Is this a typical white man or not?" Of course, the other reason I picked Boy George was that at the time more Indians knew who he was than knew who their traditional elders were. There were Boy George fan clubs on some reservations. He was a cultural hero to a lot of Indians; more Indians could sing his songs than traditional songs. That's why I put him in a beaded frame. That painting got removed from an art show in Tennessee. Some of the white people objected to using a figure that they didn't like. I told them that was the point, because it's not the type of person I like either. But again, that's the narrowmindedness.

The *Whiteman in North America* series I started before those movies with Martin Mull [*The History of White People in America*]. I was trying to show that if I approached this as an anthropologist — now actually I have a legitimate claim to this, because J. N. B. Hewitt, the father of the Bureau of Ethnology, was my great-grandfather, and, you know, the Iroquois have had probably one of the biggest roles in the birth of ethnology, with Hewitt, Eli Parker, Arthur Parker, all those guys Lewis Henry Morgan talked to and worked with — it would be funny to judge the white man by the very same things they judge Indians by. That's why I don't have any people in the photographs. They usually judge us by things, rather than talking to us. Like Walker Evans in his WPA photographs; he had kitchens, bathrooms, bedrooms, and you were supposed to interpret the person through the objects. So I set out to photograph the things, the bathrooms, so to speak, of the white man, and I'd say, "What the hell kind of person is this, who has all of these things?" It was — I don't know how to explain it — so serious that it became ridiculous, because all of a sudden I realized that was the problem that we had to deal with. I think the only picture in the series that had someone in it was *Seafood of the Future*, which was just a piece of plastic, and I thought that was funny. Why would anybody put that in a store window to sell seafood, this plastic lobster? It didn't make any sense to me.

LA: The bitterness in the humor of the images and the mock language was so perfect in its precision. Do you think that series could be called documentary photography in any way? A critic noted once that your "goal is the redefinition of the popular image of Native peoples."[7]

RH: I think very much so. At the same time it was trying to debunk the whole concept of documentary photography, in that nobody could come out to the reservation and in two weeks, or two months, or two years, and through twenty photographs, describe who we are. People got angry with me about that exhibit, saying how could I use a few photographs to describe all of white life? But I told them, "That's the lesson. You're mad about what I'm saying about you, but the exact same is true the other way around. Nobody can come and study us, explain us, photograph us *but* us." So the show was, to me, a very direct attack on the photography of the people who, when I was going to art school, thought you could show the reality of people just by taking a week end trip. Can you take a beautiful photograph of an alcoholic lying in the street, or can you go into the ghetto and describe it and the people there? Or like the book *Bordertowns*, there's a certain legitimacy that a photographer has to deal with, more so than other artists. Again, that fantasy thing versus the reality, so when you walk into somebody's life wearing a camera, you'd better be damn sure you know what you're doing. That image has power; just like sacred power, it can be abused quicker than it can be used. That's what I was trying to get people to think about. Other people thought I was racist, anti-white.

But the other thing that inspired me was a book, *People of the First Light* or *People of the First Man,* or some such thing, talking about Indians, and that's why I wanted to call this show "People of the First Buck." Everywhere you go, you see that first dollar hanging above the white man's cash register. Indians don't have that dollar because they spent it.

LA: Is there a split between the aesthetic beauty of a photograph and the often brutal nature of the subject, so there's a beautiful presentation of a horrid scene?

RH: That was the dilemma I had in art school, because I met people like Walker Evans, Frederick Sommer, and Robert Frank. Frank, as a German, came to describe America through photographs, but in his book I think he had only two photographs of Indians. I talked about that with him. I asked him why he didn't do more with Indians, because you always hear about this German fascination with Indians. He told me, "I found Indians the hardest people to deal with." I had to tell him that maybe they found *him* the hardest to deal with. We just don't take in people and express ourselves to them, because of the long history, and it takes a long time to get to know Indians and feel comfortable with them. Take a look back at his book *The Americans*. You'll see he's riding with these two Indians in a pickup, and in another one an Indian guy is standing in front of a juke box.[8] Those two photos turned me on to show him the other side. We became pretty good friends because of that. He realized that in one sense we were both voyeurs in America, peeking over the fence, saying, "Here's how Americans live," but we're not a part of it. I think a cultural curtain exists between our people, and art can be a window, and can be a mirror.

LA: Getting back to the *White Man in America* series, how did some of the photos come about? *Christ and Color TV for Sale* and *Cultural Icons* have the feel of life found as is.

RH: It's all Columbus's fault. I really don't know. Because I was raised in photography in the social documentary mode — my high school photography teacher was a student of Harry Callahan —

there was that beautiful silvery light, and I admired Walker Evans's photographs, looking at society by what society creates. I look at the white man by what he leaves behind, and I started off taking photographs of decayed things, not saying, "This is what's wrong with white people," but saying it's fascinating to me that American culture is a dispensable society. They don't like the old houses, so they let them fall down; old cars all across America are these destroyed visions of somebody else's future. It's kind of like the Curtis Indians always lived in the past, the white man always lives in the future: everything is beautiful over the rainbow, so when the plans don't work, leave them behind and try again. This is why they bury toxic waste in the ground. Let's just cover it over and move on, sell it to somebody else. So just about everywhere I went, the city, the country, I saw these things, each one becoming a symbol of this stupid thinking. Without being prejudiced, and even though I'm not a Christian (I'm one of the few Indians I've ever met who's never been baptized), when I saw that store window with Christ all painted up right next to these used color TV's, I couldn't tell what was for sale and what wasn't. So it was the juxtaposition of the images to make my point. I didn't prearrange it. That was just like it was. That's what I found fascinating. You can find in American life any juxtaposition to rationalize any point of view. I was trying to make that point. I can be misinterpreted or read the right way, whatever the right way is. But all I did was raise the question, What does this mean? Christ is in a store window with color TV's for $55. What does that really mean?

The Eternal Question is one of my favorite ones. It sounds so glorious, but what is probably the number one question asked of most Americans: Coke or 7-Up? So that's American life. I didn't invent it; I just photographed it.

LA: There are no human figures in this series. You have storefronts, machines, busted pianos.

RH: Again, I was looking at what the white man does, what he builds, what he makes, what he leaves behind. Making that jump, can you describe a people by their surroundings? Do you need to see the faces of the people? I photographed over many years, then I put them together. One habit I have, and people criticize me, when I go to an art show, I go through all my old photographs and pull them out and put them in a certain order because to me the act of exhibiting is just as much the art as the decisive moment. I'll change titles, do all sorts of things, because here's the statement I want to make at this point in my life. Some people say, "Rick, you shouldn't show those; they're twenty years old." I say, "Well, you're over twenty; why do you still come out in public?" It's what you do with your art, not what you did. Every time I have to renew it, put it up, it has to say something new, because I change, over twenty years, over the past year. But the images can be arranged in different ways each time to make a point.

Like with the photographs, I'll recombine them. I can cut apart one of my old ones and put it together in a new collage. These are like, without being too spiritual about it, living images of my life. Every photograph I take is important because it is part of what I'm doing. When I reach back into something ten, fifteen, twenty years old and bring it back to today, I'm recharging it, trying to say that it is still valid to me. When I remake it, it carries a new life to it. Now people get pissed off when artists change the titles, but I say who cares? You have to look at why an artist would change the title. Why do we reuse the work in other ways? But that's the artist at work. Do you think that something is supposed to be put in a time capsule surrounded by Plexiglass and put in an air-tight chamber where it will never see the light of day again?—now we're talking about museums. There's a negative to the fact that we make it up as we go along; make a painting, take a photograph, you look at it and say, "Boy, that's pretty." Ten years later you say, "Yeah, that's nice, but let's try this," so I change things because I keep on living.

LA: In another series of photographs and collages you focus on your family. This is at the opposite end of the spectrum to the more satirical works.

RH: When I'm at home I'm one kind of person, when I'm on the reservation I'm another, when I go out in public I'm another, when I'm the only Indian in the crowd I'm still another, so it's like I'm a multifaceted person who reflects this situation so that they are all equally important, but that's the way Indians are in dealing with the white man or mainstream culture. We're constantly confronted with things non-Indian, and therefore to me it's only logical—and this is what bothers me about Indian art—that we should address the things that impact on our lives, instead of pretending that all Indians are in this spiritual nirvana somewhere. We have to deal with the reality that the waters are no longer clean, the skies are no longer clear, that not all Indians like being Indians, and that there is still a battle on for hearts and minds. I also see my art as a defensive mechanism to create some sort of visual legacy that will turn Indians on to wanting to remain Indian and see that we have the power of thinking.

Now some people say that satire is a perimeter defense for a weak mind. I don't believe that to be true. I believe that what I'm pointing out are the very ironic things I live with. Like me, I buy a Christmas tree but I'm not a Christian. Christmas to me should be titled "Celebration of a Dead White Man." But I celebrate it anyway. And I grew up believing that there was an Easter Bunny, Jack Frost, and all those things are part of my cultural mind, so I bring them out in the art, try to deal with them very directly; this is the world we live in. That's why I did work about ironworkers and work about my family and work about Indians and work about the white man. That's my life.

LA: Some of the collages struck me as having the theme of preserving and building while some of the other collages were sort of psychedelic.

RH: LSD had a lot to do with it. I was a child of the sixties in art school. Everything was up for grabs, and I do believe it made a difference — the threat of war, seeing a thousand guys come home dead every week — made you think differently about living and about art. I was not an advocate of war and I didn't want to go to Vietnam, so I tried to say, "What is it about living which should be celebrated? What is it about Indian life that should be kept?" The photocollages were a turning point in my life in that it was a final artistic statement at art school, summing up everything I did in the two and a half years I was there. When I did these collages it was my graduation. I no longer needed the institute. I could leave Chicago and go home. I was determined to become the Indian. I remember I brought those collages back to Buffalo and Leslie Krims was teaching there, and I went to see him and showed him the work. And we had a pretty strange conversation about it, and he suggested I photograph them as black and white photographs. I did. He was right. They took on a whole different life. The ones I keep showing are the epitome of what I was trying to say, which is basically the rebirth of Rick Hill. I finally decided that I was going to be the Indian, that those things were important to me. That when I read Black Elk's vision what struck me was that Black Elk died the very same month I was born. We're not talking about the ancient past; we're talking about my life.

When I had my son in 1971, I started thinking differently about legacy—what the hell are we working for?—and then again with my brother dying, the photocollages are a tribute to him. They call into question the overglorification of the Indian past. Here's the Indian we celebrate, we decorate him, we say he's pretty, but we don't know why. We put the Indian on the pedestal, but here's the real Indian. This, my brother, is the real Indian. But why is there no middle ground? Why do we have to live in the past and ignore who we are today? So that sort of kicked the whole thing off in my head. The purpose of art for us is to ensure the future, not just to celebrate the past.

LA: Sounds like the work has a political dimension, too. Were you politically involved at all when you were doing the collages?

RH: Not really. I got a growing Indian consciousness around Alcatraz and Wounded Knee. I had to decide if I was going to go or stay. What I did was internalize the politics, meaning I began to realize the separateness that Indian people have as nations, as citizens of our nations, and I took that tactic, rather than say, "Well, you can't fight the white man because he'll kill you." If we were fighting for the future, what were we going to build? We had all fought for hundreds of years, and I felt that all of a sudden it was placed in my hands. I said to myself, "Are you gonna cop out and just be in a darkroom or a studio or go out and do something?" And I've tried. My defense of the future is through the artwork, the museum work, the curatorial work. All that is to say that Indians are okay. We believe in ourselves. It's a fight for what we believe rather than for what the white man will give us.

A couple things turned me around when I was younger. I went to meet Ernie Smith, an Iroquois painter who painted back in the thirties. I visited his house, smaller than this room here. I went in and he said, "Are you an Indian?" I said, "Yeah," but I got kind of angry. He said, "No, you're not." "What do you mean I'm not?" He said, "You're *ongwehonweh*" our word for who we are, "you're the Haudenosaunee. Don't you ever forget that." So here's this old man teaching me a lesson, which was not to accept what the white man tells you. Find out what your people tell you. Then he started pulling these paintings out from under his bed, from his closet, from behind a dresser.

The reason I paint is because someday an Indian is going to walk into a museum and see my painting, and the story will be there, and they will be able to learn about their culture by looking at the art. That's what I needed to hear at that time. That gave art a role to play in ensuring that Indians would understand what it means to be an Indian. That's been the purpose of Rick Hill. I'm an Indian first and an artist second. Because art is an avocation, not a genetic makeup, the purpose of our art is to advance the state of Indians. So that's pretty powerful stuff.

Then another thing happened when I wanted to get politically involved. One of the old-timers told me, "Rick, you can't do everything. Some people take care of the politics, some people take care of the economics. Art and culture are your areas; you do that." I have to admit I took the lead off of one of John Lennon's songs, which says you can tear everything down, but unless you are going to build something, then you are not contributing. So that's when I decided that art is the primary building block of the Indian society of the future.

LA: The text which accompanied the photographs and collages was sort of soul-searching. You wrote: "Our visions are only directions, but our conduct is often not so glorious," and, "In my innermost visions, I am a father, but like I said, visions and reality are often worlds apart."[9] What is the tension between vision and the reality of everyday life?

RH: I think it's actually the same for everybody, as the fight over abortion points out. The dilemma is, for example, can you be a Catholic and practice birth control? Can you be a Christian and have lust in your mind? Your religious standards are almost always unattainable. There's a big difference between striving for the best and daily life. I believe that Indians say, "Let's strive for the best." We understand our earthly humanity all too well, but there is a dilemma that young Indians go through about having to make choices. One of the oppressive parts of being an Indian internally is this dimension of hypocrisy, that you know you are supposed to do something in a certain way. You know that if you don't contribute, you are part of the problem. But that's not necessarily the way you live. Like people turn to us now to fix the environment. They invite us to fly to every conference they have and invite us to drive cars and use electricity, make videotapes like everyone else, so then it raises a question of is our philosophy valid or is it like everything else? You can't judge the message by the messenger.

By the same token, I do believe it to be true that we are the generation of Indians who will decide if there will be Indians in the future. If I don't raise my kids to be the Indians, there aren't going to be any Indians. I can't tell them, "Well, sorry, you're not good enough to be an Indian because I don't plant corn or because I don't walk on the ground in bare feet." If that's not the way they live, then who's right and who's wrong? All I know is that I'm not going to impress my kids by telling them that they're wrong. During the seventies I identified a lot with T. C. Cannon even though I never met him. There was a parallel with what a lot of Indians were going through then. But we did it alone. Now it's different. Now there's a big support network among Indians and Indian artists. We're as close as a phone and we fax like everyone else. But the deeper question still exists: do we like being Indians? What are we doing to ensure there will be Indians? That's the question I raise to artists who try to represent Indian thinking to the world. Does Indian art and Indian thinking depend on Indians? Shouldn't you start with the basics: make more Indians?

LA: I've talked to a lot of artists over the last couple of months and there seems to be that split you're talking about between "Indian experience" and "American experience." *D.I.A.N.D. Dandy and Flesh-Coloured Bandaids* [1983] depicts some of the "temptations" of white society for Indians and the ease of selling out to those values. What are some of these temptations and how can they be resisted? Can art be a method of resistance?

RH: I really think so. They have to be resisted; otherwise we'll all be wearing suits and ties, having shades and braids, but having nothing upstairs. My father's from Canada and we used to go to art shows up there, especially in Ottawa, and meet these Indians there in suits and ties and they used to look down their noses at me, the artist. Then these jerks would come along and think that they were the real Indians because they had jobs. They had little gold cuff links and hung around with white people. That somehow made them more real as Indians than anybody else. The artists were just there for entertainment. I said, "I'll show these assholes." So I did this painting of this guy and the initials stand for Department of Indian Affairs and Northern Development. That's the Canadian version of the BIA. The guy in the painting works for them, but the funny part was I showed them the painting and I had these guys in mind and I knew they'd come by the show. They came by and started arguing over who it was in the painting. "It's me." "No it's not; it's me." So I said, "You're right; it's both of you." I thought I was in my satirical best and on my high horse. All of a sudden this white guy comes along with a little kid and starts looking at the painting and the kid says, "What does that mean?" The father starts describing the painting as if I wasn't there and, you know, he described everything perfectly, and finally he got to the Band-Aids. The kid said, "Daddy, what are the Band-Aids?" And I thought, "I got him now; they will never understand that." The father says, "Well, son, if you think about it, flesh-colored Band-Aids only work for white people; they don't work for Indians." Then they both walked off. So I started thinking, "Jesus, you know, he got it," but I felt bad because somebody got it. I wasn't anyone's intellectual superior anymore.

So I tried to do that in my painting at the time, to try to point out the ironies, contradictions, but at the same time it's not schizophrenic because I know where I'm coming from. And I know I am the Indian. Some of the people may criticize me, but this is the way it is. I did a painting one time of an Indian holding a beer bottle. I've always been cautious in my other work because I don't want to show negative images of Indians, as drunks, for example. When I go to these art shows all the Indians would be drinking, and at educational conferences we'd get drunk, so drinking is a part of our lives. I did a painting of an artist at an opening with shades, long hair, with two abstract paintings behind him, and I called it *The Seeker of Red Dots*. What the hell does that mean? Well, you go to an art opening and what do you wait for? The little red dots to go up, that's what you're really looking for, the sale. So the artists got a big kick out of that one. That's the way our lives are. Why should we pretend that we don't drink or that money doesn't matter to us? These are the realities of our lives. So I took, on purpose, "Here's My Life": from Boy George to this artist to the dandy — those are the people I know. I'm just trying to document my reaction to my life as an Indian.

LA: Some people would criticize you or other artists for depicting Indians in a negative light, like showing an Indian with a beer bottle, or if you show an Indian drunk, that plays into the stereotypes that white people have. Is there a subtle pressure to purify the image or not show the unsavory aspects of life? Is there an interpretive ambiguity implicit in some Native photographs that have to do with intent and product? I'm thinking specifically of Richard Ray Whitman's *Street Chiefs* series. Casual viewers might find their preconceptions about Indians solidified. In that sense could the intent be at odds with the interpretation?

RH: If we're going to live our lives by the stereotypes non-Indians have of us, we should all commit suicide, but I think you're right. Before I met Richard, I got to know his work, and I said, "What the hell is this?" Three drunken Indians standing there. I got really angry. I said to myself, "This is bad." Then I saw he exhibited with Edgar Heap of Birds and some other people, and I finally met Richard and that was going to be my question to him. But I heard a talk he gave and he explained why he does what he does, and finally he said, "My dad was a street chief. These are my dad's friends. I asked their permission." He answered any possible questions I could have in the best way. It's legitimate work. But without the explanation, the work is tough to deal with, and it reinforced one of my other premises about the interpretive moment.

We hear why the artist produced the art among Indian artists. The public has to understand that there's another dimension going on here—that it's not newspaper photography. Because what has happened in America, despite artists like Ansel Adams, people still perceive photography as magazine and newspaper pictures. So you need to hear the story of the photographs. But I also think that's true of all the art. You need to hear what people like Kay WalkingStick, Pete Jemison, or Frank LaPena have to say, because you have to understand why they do a certain thing. That doesn't mean that their work cannot stand by itself. But you need the Indian dimensions. Without Richard talking about what it was like to be the son of a street chief, his photographs would just be like my pictures of the ironworkers. People need to know that they are my father and brothers. It changes things. People say, "That's nice, that's pretty, but what's the big deal?" So that little paragraph under the photograph, or the catalog description, is absolutely essential, so that people understand we are living beings who have to deal with the realities of our lives, including the street chiefs. You're right if you would have those photographs up and not tell people that it was Indian work; they'd come in and walk out. But the minute they hear it's Indian, it's like—it's funny—there is this Rolodex of images that spins through their heads and they start reading all these things before they come to the fact that this is my dad. That changes things for us. What you're seeing is like a photo album of Indian lives and it's really strange because it's very different.

One thing that happened to me in Chicago: walking down the street, I came across a couple of these street chiefs on the sidewalk and this is what I went through. I said to myself, "Do I cross the street, because if I go straight they will pull me over?" So I said, "Oh shit, I'll cross over." But before I could, sure enough, the guy says, "Are you Indian?" I said, "Yeah." So he says, "Prove it." I figured he wanted a dollar, but he says, "If you're a real Indian, kiss me right here, on the cheek." [Pause.] The cheek near the mouth. The guy tells me that everybody looks down on him. What flashed through my mind was my dad coming home after drinking, a little stubble on his chin, smelling the same way as this guy, and saying, "Give me a kiss," as a son would kiss his father. All of a sudden, right there on the street, I realized it was an important moment. It wasn't a Kodak moment, but it was important for me to relate to another Indian I'd never met before and say, "Yes, we are both Indians." We both understood why you're here and I'm not. He just said to me, "Go do it."

And where else can you get that kind of encouragement? I don't know if that happens to other people. But here are two Indians coming together, and one telling me to make a difference, to go do something. All he wanted was a sign of affection from me that he mattered. So that's why I got upset about those photographs of Richard's at first. Now when I see them I really identify with them, because if there were just a slight change of circumstances Richard or I could be a street chief.

LA: Do you worry about intent versus interpretation? Is there an expectation of a certain meaning in Indian art, that it is limited to a fairly narrow range?

RH: I think so, and it may be the crux of the dilemma. We now have the Indian intent overshadowed by the non-Indian desire for content. We're not looking at why Indians do art but we want to see some sort of reaffirmation that the work is Indian. And suddenly when it doesn't meet the expectations — rather, false expectations — that have been laid upon us, people get upset. That's one reason why the issue is still somebody saying, "Jump this high, but if you can't jump this high, you're not an Indian." Then all kinds of issues of racism, paternalism, come into play. But the crux of Indian art is the intent, because when you take a look at what's gone on over the years, most of the Indian art has tried to say something about being an Indian. You don't see too many Indians painting a Catholic procession or talking about what it's like to be Jewish or what it would be like to be a member of a country club or to cut the grass every week. What Indians talk about, whether they were born on the reservation or whether they were baptized, is about being an Indian. Maybe it is wishful thinking for some, but that shows the strength of the intent.

It goes to my issue about reaffirmation. In one sense, art, to Indians, is cultural therapy, our way of being an Indian no matter where we are. In Santa Fe or Chicago, you can still be an Iroquois Indian. Art connects me back to my base. But I can also create other images that connect me to other Indians. People call that pan-Indianism. What we're saying is that it's important to feel Indian, to do Indian things, to think like an Indian, and the way you show that is through your art. Maybe that's the only way you can express it. It's a form of therapy, a release valve for this ironic life we lead. Like you pull up at a gas station. "How much do you want, Chief?" "I don't know; how about three dollars' worth, Pope?" They'll get the point. There is a constant pressure on us to perform as Indians. In a bar they're either scared of you or want to fight you. In a job interview they don't trust you. You walk in the stores here and security people follow you around. It's not just us; it happens to everybody. But it is a reality. On the other side, we also get wined and dined because we are Indians and we get sex because we are Indians. What a strange existence to be an Indian in America! But if you understand the other part, the obligations, a lot of people want the benefits, but not too many people are willing to pay the price—which is to assure that in the future others will not have to go through the same B.S. If we don't build the Indian society and contribute to it, then there will not be an Indian society.

So the real issue goes to who is the art intended to serve—the artist, the family, the tribe, the community, or the collector? All of the above are true, which is one reason why my work is not commercially viable. Although I sell everything I make, I'm not going to be a "success" because I don't make the pretty pictures that the white man has decided is Indian art. Those that do, I don't fault them, because you have to make a living, but then it comes down to don't claim to be an Indian prophet or try to be the next Indian art messiah. Just say, "This is my job." There's a difference between culture and commerce, and Indians understand that really clearly. They understand that the purpose of Indian Market [in Santa Fe each August] is to put as much of the white man's money into our pockets as possible. It's not to convert them about the truth of our existence, but to make an income. The non-Indian doesn't understand, because they think they are buying Indianness. They don't realize you can't buy that.

LA: You once wrote in "Photography's Next Era" about contemporary Native photographers: "The symbol is not separable from the mission they have to change people's perceptions of Natives. Their art is content-oriented. This does not mean that there has to be a sacred feather on everything in the photograph, but that there is a sacred intent to impact on the mind of the viewers. Native photography is directed right at you, the viewer—the photographer also seeks a relationship with the people who look at photographs."[10] Could you explain what you mean by this "sacred intent," and does this exist in all the contemporary Native arts?

RH: I saw that intent in the Indian photographers, a small group of people who had such passion for change about the way people look at Indians. I realized again the power of the image making that they had with a camera, and I view it very much the same way as Indians viewed treaties as sacred. We came to an agreement. We sat down and said, "Here is who we are, and here's how we are going to live together." I see photography as replicating that idea. Here's who we are, we know who you are, we're going to show you this. That's what I mean by the sacred intent, in that the response of the viewer is just as critical as the intent of the photographer. You need the viewers to respond in a way that you hoped they would. So there's a different kind of thing with the image making, the debunking of the stereotypes. That's why I say there's a sacredness of mission, but I hope we don't become cultural missionaries of the twenty-first century, where we go around the world telling everybody they're screwed up. One of my fears about Indian art is that it will become too missionizing.

LA: Given the tremendous diversity of contemporary Native fine art, not only in media, but in style and imagery—abstraction, figuration, mixed media, performance, installation—what factor or factors unify or link all of these works into what can be called "Indian art"? What do you take to be "Indian thinking"?

RH: I really believe that the underlying connection of the work is that it is not so much a fine-art aesthetic, or something just as good as the white man does, but it is the quality of the thinking that is Indian. The intellectual tradition is just as significant as the artistic tradition, and in fact may be more significant, meaning that what is distinct about Indians is our world-view and how that view pervades our thinking and our beliefs, and how it permeates the way we think of ourselves in the world. The world-view can transcend time and place, so I can feel like an Iroquois Indian, and I can identify with my ancestors and what they have done, but I can also relate to the people seven generations to come. If I can create enough of a legacy there will still be Iroquois Indians. One time a guy said to me, "In one ear you hear your ancestors whispering, telling you what to do, and in the other ear you hear the future generations crying, asking, 'What should we do?'" Our job in this generation, as it's been in all Indian generations, is to translate those whispers we hear and give them to the future. That's the logical role for the artist, to be the translator, the carrier, the transferer of knowledge so the next generation can comprehend that knowledge in its circumstances. So what Indians put in their art is how they look at the world. This then requires diversity because Indian lives are not the same; they never were and never will be. Somebody who grows up in Brooklyn as an Indian is very different from somebody who grows up in one of the pueblos. What we have to get past is that there is no acid test for being an Indian culturally. Both are valid Indian frames of reference and their art therefore represents their thinking about being Indians. We rethink and reinterpret the world as we see it through Indian eyes.

That's why even this painting on my wall shows that there is an Indian responding to the world. We still feel a passion and a compassion for the way people live. So it is the quality of Indian thinking, the decision-making process, which is the cultural mechanism, not the decision. The quality of thinking, looking, accessing information, and trying to evolve a decision is important, but the decisions will change through the generations. We've inherited patterns of thinking. That's why we can understand prehistoric Indian art, historic Indian art, and the most abstract Indian art of today. If it works, we identify with it. And if it doesn't work, maybe we are not mature enough to understand it. A few years later we may understand. Or maybe the artist needs maturity of expression to help us understand. So it's always that give and take, kind of like we're all going in the same direction, just some of us might be further ahead. The culture, then, is not the physicalness of the surroundings. It's the way we think and what we believe that makes us Indians.

When we used the flintlock we were still Indians; when we use a computer we're still Indians. We're not cultural robots. We're not in a 1491 time capsule. Our very survival is a testimony to our ability to adapt, adjust, teach, and transfer knowledge so that people quit killing us. The next thing is to assure that Indians like being Indians. We gain power through the art. Through our image making we can convince others of our strength. Indians validate Indian art first. Art by Indians will be the most powerful force for change. What will America see at the end of that process? They will see an Indian who believes in being an Indian and who likes being an Indian. People will see that we like being who we are. So many people used to say to me, "What's wrong with you people? Why don't you want to be like us?" Nothing's wrong. We like being us and want to stay us. We want to take the lead to change on our own terms, not have it forced from without.

LA: Isn't there a risk of ghettoization? Isn't there a problem if you exhibit only for Indians? Then the larger art world can really forget about you.

RH: We're already ghettoized. Name the top five works by Indians in the National Gallery, the Metropolitan, the Museum of Modern Art. I think we have to come to the reality that we're not part of that scene. Then it comes back to what are you willing to pay to become part of the club. It's like golf clubs with no blacks or Jews. Is it a victory to be the first minority in a racist club? Who the hell wants to play golf with those guys? What are the options for Indians? Tokenism? Affirmative action? A desk job? Or entrust the significance of your art to people who don't know the art or can't relate to it? When the white man first came to America they needed an Indian guide to get them through Indian country. Is the opposite now true? We don't need a white guide to get us into the white institutions. We need to stand firm with the art, and sometimes to get excluded from a place is not necessarily a bad thing. I do believe that America needs to see more art by Indians, and that we should exhibit in these institutions, but the criteria put to measure our art is off-base. It's a question of interpretation. As much as I like Lucy's effort, to me it will never ring true until the ethnics and the gays say, "Here's what it means to us," and not leave the interpretations to well-meaning people. The road to the reservation is paved with good intentions.

LA: When people hear "Indian art," they most likely think of museum artifacts, pottery, or the Santa Fe art of the 1930s. The use of video or photography renders the art impure or inauthentic. What has to be done to challenge this myth of authenticity?

RH: America loves its myths. They believe in Custer and John Wayne. If we talk about academic change, then we are "revisionists," changing history, presenting ourselves as a political maneuver. To tell you the truth, I'm not confident that America wants to change. People want to believe what they have been raised to believe through radio, TV, textbooks, and ultimately the Bible. My reaction is that it is not the job of the Indian to educate the white person, but I guess we have to. It's a real dirty job, but somebody's got to do it. Again, writers, painters, photographers, and filmmakers are doing just that. Look at us again and discover Indians for what the Indian is. There's a gluttony of punishment in America, but people are not willing to put their money where their mouths are to foster change.

People talk about authentic Indian art. What is authentic white art? Does everybody have to dress like George Washington to be an authentic American? No. But Indians have to dress like the Indians George Washington met to be real Indians. The same is true in the arts. Take jewelry. We couldn't make half the jewelry we make without the European tools and materials, yet jewelry is supposed to be a "traditional" art. The white man tells us what Indian painting is. That whole argument about traditional Indian painting amazes me, and that some Indians even adopt that position. "I'm a traditional Indian painter." What does that mean? That you paint the way a white woman told you to paint? That's traditional? The real tradition is grinding the paints and making the brushes, and painting on kiva walls, on your body, on your face. If you're really traditional you would have tattoos all over you. Why are we into this false argument about what is traditional and authentic and what is contemporary and modern? As long as the art was safe and pretty, everybody liked it, but the minute it started to have a social conscience or became political or a little aggressive, they didn't like it. America has never liked aggressive Indians. There must be a fear of seeing the liberation of Indians through art. As long as they can keep us in jail to make ledger art everything is okay. The minute we break out of jail, break out of the form, then the old-fashioned argument comes out again: "They've destroyed the character of the art. He's not a full-blood. He didn't grow up on a reservation, no wonder he's a little crazy." But those arguments don't wash. What we're doing in our art is precisely what we want to do.

SELECTED EXHIBITIONS

"A Different Vision" (1990), group exhibition, Gemini Gallery, Buffalo, NY.

"Art of the Seventh Generation: Iroquois Symbols on Canvas and Paper" (1986), group exhibition, Roberson Center for the Arts and Sciences, Binghamton, NY.

"Portraits: Paintings and Photographs by Rick Hill" (1986), solo exhibition, Thunder Bay Art Gallery, Thunder Bay, Ontario.

"Five from the Six Nations" (1983), group exhibition, Niagara County Community College Art Gallery, Sanborn, NY.

"Iroquois Art" (1982), group exhibition, C. N. Gorman Gallery, University of California, Davis, CA.

SELECTED BIBLIOGRAPHY

Hill, Rick. "Acting Like an Indian: Reflections of the Indian as Artist, and James Luna as Indian." In *James Luna: The Sacred Colors*. Sacramento, CA: La Raza/Galeria Posada, 1992, unp.

——. "Half-Indian, Half-Artist." In *The Alcove Show*. Santa Fe, NM: Museum of Fine Arts, 1992, unp.

——. "No Tourists Allowed: Only Indians with Cameras, Please!" In *No Borders*. Hamilton, Ontario: NIIPA, 1991, pp. 24–29.

——. "The Nude Human Figure in American Indian Art." *Artwinds '91* (Summer 1991): 1, 4.

——. "Savage Splendor: Sex, Lies and Stereotypes." *Turtle Quarterly* 4, 1 (Spring–Summer, 1991): 14–23.

——. "Radicals and Renegades." *Artwinds '90* (Fall 1990): 1, 4.

——. "The Rise of Neo-Native Expressionism." In *Our Land/Ourselves: American Indian Contemporary Artists*. Albany, NY: State University of New York/University Art Gallery, 1990, pp. 1–5.

——. "In Our Own Image: Stereotyped Images of Indians Lead to New Native Artform." *Muse* 6, 4 (Winter 1989): 32–43.

——. "Old Friends." *Turtle Quarterly* 2, 2 (Summer 1988): 41–47.

——. "Sacred Trust: Cultural Obligation of Museums to Native People." *Muse* 6, 3 (Fall 1988): 32–36.

——. "Iroquois Art and the Human Figure." *Turtle Quarterly* 1, 3 (Summer 1987): 2–6.

——. "Skywalkers: The Legacy of Mohawk Ironworkers." *Turtle Quarterly* 1, 4 (Fall 1987): 2–4.

——. "Indian Artists in the Twentieth Century." In *Art of the Seventh Generation: Iroquois Symbols on Canvas and Paper*. Binghamton, NY: Roberson Center for the Arts and Sciences, 1986, unp.

——. "Photography's Next Era." In *Silver Drum: Five Native Photographers*. Hamilton, Ontario: NIIPA, 1986, pp. 20–23.

——. "Seneca Art." *Turtle Quarterly* 1, 1 (1986): 4–6.

Portraits: Paintings and Photographs by Rick Hill. Thunder Bay, Ontario: Thunder Bay Art Gallery, 1986 [catalog includes brief texts by Hill on selected works].

G. Peter Jemison

Cattaraugus Seneca

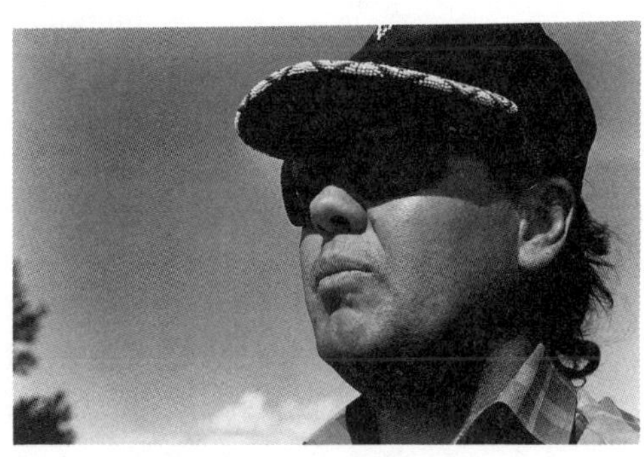

G. Peter Jemison, a member of the Heron Clan of the Seneca Nation, was born in upstate New York, in Silver Creek, in 1945, and grew up in Irving, New York, on the Cattaraugus Indian Reservation. In 1967 he received a Bachelor of Science degree in art education from the State University of New York at Buffalo. He also studied for a year at the University of Siena, Italy, in such areas as Renaissance art history, sculpture, and fresco.

Jemison balanced careers in painting, teaching art, and working as a display artist in New York and San Francisco in the early 1970s. In 1971 he was included in a group show at the Museum of the American Indian in New York City, with such artists as George Morrison (Ojibway, b. 1919), Fritz Scholder (Luiseño, b. 1937), and Neil Parsons (Blackfeet, b. 1938). From this exhibit emerged a desire to more fully understand Seneca art and cultural expression. To that end Jemison directed the Seneca Nation Education Program on the Cattaraugus Reservation from 1974 to 1978.[1]

Jemison took over as gallery director of the American Indian Community House in New York City in 1978, and in the seven years there he mounted some thirty-five exhibits of both contemporary and traditional art. Additionally, he moved the gallery to its present location in SoHo. In 1980 he began his continuing series of works done on brown paper bags and on handmade paper. The use of the "bag as canvas" came out of his direct experience in New York City and from his interest in other Native cultures: "I have been influenced by Seneca beaded bags, Lakota parfleche containers, Mimbres pottery, and Cree birchbark objects. . . . The bags afford me an opportunity for creating multiple images using juxtaposition and contrast to extend the conventional meanings of each image." About the bags Jimmie Durham has written: "They are very funny and full of irony, but they are not jokes, they are not really playing tricks."[2]

In a way Jemison's life and career have come full circle. He left New York City in 1985 to return upstate to original Seneca territory. He became director of the Ganondagan State Historic Site, a restored Seneca village in Victor, New York, just outside of Rochester. He continues to paint and exhibit his work, and in early 1992 he curated "Haudenosaunee Artists: A Common Heritage" for the State University of New York at Brockport.

Through his many moves Jemison's vision has remained steady. Combining art and activism, he responds to the challenges facing the Haudenosaunee today. *Buffalo Road III—Choices* (1990) continues his interest in juxtaposition of imagery while commenting on reservation affairs. *All Indians Don't Live West of the Mississippi* (1987) focuses on most Americans' ignorance of the living Native cultures found throughout the country. Even his drawings of nature and myth, with careful use of design and color, like *Sandburr* (1973) or *Struggle between Good and Evil* (1985), take on political resonances. As Jemison has written: "Beyond purely aesthetic concerns, I've sought to make statements about being a Seneca."[3]

Our interview took place in May 1991, during a break in the symposium at the "Shared Visions" exhibit at the Heard Museum in Phoenix.

LA: You wrote, in *This Song Remembers* (1980), that you had to "find my own way" as an Indian.[4] What did this process involve?

PJ: Well, I would say that it involved finding out what it meant to be a Seneca, and that process had to begin with finding, through people, more about the tradition. What that meant for me, the easiest way to do that, was to identify with what we call the longhouse, and to learn from the elders who are in charge of our ceremonies and so forth the basis for our thinking, which is—the short way of putting it—the code of Handsome Lake, the Seneca prophet. So that's really what I mean when I say I had to find my own way, but it also goes into the area of having to identify for me, initially, what, if anything, my art was going to look like.

LA: You were engaged in two parallel but interconnected searches?

PJ: I was. They were interconnected when I came to the conscious decision that I was going to return to our traditional way of life. Then at the same time I wanted my art to reflect something more of the understanding I was gaining through my learning. I thought it valid to learn some of our traditions, which include singing and dancing and the arts of the Seneca.

LA: So your education was with the elders and then with reestablishing ties with the traditional arts?

PJ: Yes, both at the same time, and with family members who were part of the tradition. And fortunately, they were very helpful and open about it and assisted me to return the way I wanted to.

LA: Right. I think you mentioned that you were always artistically inclined. So your education was a refinement of where you were going?

PJ: Well, I had been trained in what I would say would be the almost classical way of getting art-trained. You go and you learn, eventually, to draw, and you learn to paint and you learn to use a variety of paint, all kinds of paint. And then I went and saw the work of other artists and went to Italy to look at Renaissance art and to really look at these things that were this whole classical tradition, you know, the development of the use of figure, and all those ideas. So I had looked at that and done quite a lot of drawing and looked at a lot of art history, so I had all of those technical skills. So now the question became learning skills that I didn't have, and that was much more interesting to me, and the whole learning atmosphere with the elders and with traditional artists was completely different. We would be sitting in a room and we'd all be carving and talking about anything we wanted to talk about. We had a good time when we did it.

LA: That would also be a way of learning about the broader Seneca culture.

PJ: Yeah. That was the way, you know, and in learning to dance — that was fun. Going to hear different singers and dancers and have them and their offspring show you steps and things was great. And then going to ceremonies, and continuing to go. You must keep going.

LA: Your art education has been interesting because you studied at the University of Siena in Italy, and your training involved the "old masters."

PJ: I remember drawing from Michelangelo while I was over there, and drawing from other sculptures that I saw around. Taking the pad with me someplace and drawing and drawing. Going out into the countryside, too, in Italy, and just drawing the countryside in Italy. I learned to do fresco painting while I was there.

We painted on the walls. They had a technique where they could take the fresco off the wall and stretch it onto material on stretcher bars. They wouldn't show you the technique, but they had a way to do it in the art school — not the university. There was an art school in Siena; we went for our academics to the University of Siena, and we went to the art school for our art courses, which consisted of painting and sculpture. But we learned that classical technique of building up a fresco painting.

LA: What other influences could you point to? Is it a combination of traditional training and classical training, in Italy, and then also modernistic influences? You've mentioned Rauschenberg and Schwitters.

PJ: Schwitters, right. Well, you see, when I went to Buffalo State College in upstate New York, it was located right across the street from the Albright Knox Gallery, which is one of the better art galleries outside of New York City. I have it up there with the Walker [Art Center, Minneapolis]; it's got that level of a collection. So I haunted the halls of that place, because in those days, well, admission was free, first of all. And then, secondly, for five dollars you could join the membership library and you could look at all of the books and catalogs and invitations to the exhibits, or anything else they had in there. You could take anything off the shelf you wanted, read anything you wanted, and their only stipulation was don't put anything back, we'll put it back so it doesn't get out of order. With that kind of freedom you just looked at everything.

And during that time period I had an instructor, an abstract painter, who was a big fan of Schwitters, and so I looked at the pieces that I could find of Schwitters's work. And I think even then I kind of liked collage, and I liked Rauschenberg, always using different kinds of materials to do his work. He did some of the very first transfers — he used lighter fluid to lift images and then he did a rubbing out and always transferred it onto another surface. And he was always trying something different. At the time I guess he was considered an iconoclast. I think I liked that, too, and I probably still have a tendency to think in those terms of modifying the definitions, what have always been the definitions of what anyone thinks is art. Art can be made from all kinds of things. That to me is probably my fun in doing it, quite apart from the statement I make. I also want to keep it interesting for myself.

LA: You mentioned, in fact, today [at a discussion at the Heard Museum symposium] that you're interested in *de*-defining everything "they think about us." As for the arts, does that mean use of materials, imagery, . . .

PJ: Everything and anything. I don't mean this in the most negative way. I mean it in a way that is a positive, okay? We have been told who we are, we have had people writing who we are, writing our history, anthropologists studying our bodies, studying our human remains, studying anything they can get their hands on. And I have been in so much contact with all of that, all of this effort toward naming everything about us, that I guess I've just had it. I've really had it, and I find that when I start to talk about it, I lose it and I kind of start wanting to say that it's all invalid and that it all needs to be redefined, and that it all needs to be demystified and put into our language. I keep coming back to that point. And the only other illustration I can get is we see, through these eyes, things I'm sure are different. I can't even point to specifics and say, "This is the way it's different for me than for you. I just see this and think this." And I don't think that that's really stretching it. I think it's true that we just see things differently.

I mean, I know the reason I went home and returned to my

tradition was because I went through a whole series of things. First, I went through a white college. Then I sold art supplies and worked as a display artist in New York City and San Francisco. Then I got a teaching job and exhibited in white art galleries and learned the white art world. Okay. And I still found myself different than the people that I was associating with. I still found that I had a different sense of myself, a different sense of values, some different needs, and that I was still a little bit of a stranger out in this world. I couldn't put my hand on it, couldn't quite define what it was. And I'm not saying I was unsuccessful in that world. In fact, if you were measuring it in terms of artistic success, I was artistically successful. If you were measuring it in terms of whether you could get a job or not, I had a job. Whether you could do those things that are required of you to function in the larger world, I could do those things. But there was something missing, there really was something missing. And when I went home, I discovered what that was, what was missing. And I discovered that there was no replacement for the feelings I had had as a kid, except to go back and find those feelings. To go back and get those feelings. And that's what I did. And that's what I am doing.

LA: And those feelings, that sense of community, can be recovered?

PJ: They can be. There's something about our own sense of communication with one another, and our togetherness as a people. And I don't mean to generalize this in a way that, again, overly romanticizes anything. I'm not about romanticizing, because I work with people that are really down to earth. And yet they are some of the people who have real integrity. Integrity is very important to me. I try to be a person of integrity, and at the same time, it's nothing heavy, it's nothing that is always an intense conversation you have to have. It's not like that. It's loose, relaxed, but we get things done. It is thinking about what we have to do to get things done, like the protection of our ancestors' remains, the return of human remains from museums for proper reburial, the repatriation of sacred items for our spiritual renewal. We work at those things, and we have a certain view of why this is important to do and how this has got to be done. And we move ahead with it.

LA: So that sense of integrity and rightness is part of living, and not an add-on?

PJ: That's right.

LA: Like the Anglo sense might be "Well, today or in this particular situation I'll act with integrity," as if it's something you can select for an occasion that benefits you.

PJ: That's right. A woman explained it to me best, one of my elders. We have — those of us who follow tradition — we have the name that you will use for this interview. I have an Indian name also, another name that comes from my clan. That name has belonged to many other people. I don't even know who some of those people were that had that name. Some of them probably were some pretty important people, if you go back — I'm talking way on back and back and back — to find out where that name started. One of the guys who had that name I did know, and I did meet him. He was a very fine artist. And so you have to live up to that name. That's one of your first jobs. You're living up to that name, what that name is. You are living in a community within a family — within a family first, and then within a community — and so people have expectations of you.

LA: Do these expectations lead to a sense of freedom, or can there also be a sense of burden?

PJ: They can cut both ways. In my situation right now, I have a lot of responsibilities, a lot of responsibilities. So they're not particularly freeing, but I knew this. As an intelligent person — and we're all intelligent, and we're all expected to use our intelligence — as a person like that, I knew intuitively that I couldn't get away with just doing one thing. Because there were too many things to do. Within our community there were so many needs and so many ways that we can go. So choosing has been less of a choice. I have been more or less handed responsibilities: "this is what you will need to do; this is what we need to have done; you will do this part." The good thing about that is it gives you your sense of belonging within your community, and that is important to everyone: to know where you fit in your community. So in a certain way it's freeing. You don't have this anxiety that some people do have of "who am I?" and all that kind of stuff. Had I been raised within that very traditional framework — very traditional, like, for instance, Dick West or Allan Houser, who are still with us — I probably would never have thought through some of those questions. But I had to. And now I'm on this other path, which is a well-worn path. I'm seeing that path open before me as I go, and it's quite interesting.

LA: You've studied many different cultures, both Indian and non-Indian, traditional and modern, and you've noted an intuitive approach to form found in these arts. Do you consider yourself an intuitive artist?

PJ: Sometimes. I like the pieces that I do that are intuitive. I've found that there's a wonderful thing that happens when you are really doing work on a fairly regular basis and you are focused on your art. You're working along and you make a decision, you do something compositionally, whatever way, and at the time it's simply one more decision in the process of making this piece of work. And then at some later date you put it up — maybe it's even that evening, maybe it's a couple of days later — and you come back and take a look at it. And all of a sudden you see it and say, "Oh, wow, that's what I did! Look at that! Look how that works! Now how did I do that? How did I make that decision to do it so it would look this way, or that it would fit that way, or that it would relate to this other thing down here, or that it has that other meaning?" What it really is — and this is one idea that I know troubles some people, but I do believe it — we've been given a gift. We can use it or abuse it or lose it, but if we can use it, it's a gift that, I put it this way, we are the vehicle to make that happen. It's an energy that flows right through you when the best of everything is working, and you become the instrument of that idea. And that idea is part of our tradition, it's that the Creator is so powerful, and we are so lacking in that kind of power that the Creator has, that we have to acknowledge the help we receive from Him in everything we do. And so there is a bit of what you could call intuition and a bit of what you could call just this energy that each of us gets for doing, for being able to do, something. And it's wonderful when it kind of comes together, coalesces — whatever you want to say. That's when it's wonderful.

LA: That's not, as you apply it to artwork, dissimilar from traditional dance or traditional singing — the concept of the person being a conduit, so to speak, of a higher power.

PJ: That's right, and, you know, some of these songs are passed down generation after generation after generation, and some guys can be good singers and some guys can't be. Some guys can be good speakers and some guys can't be, and some guys can be good dancers. My son is fifteen; he's a good dancer. It's really fun to watch him dance. He's getting better and better and more fun to watch. And so it's just that: you can use [the gift] in various ways. Fortunately, we get a lot of different ways that we can use it—any of us do.

LA: You've said that returning home directly from New York City was like a redemption by nature.

PJ: Yes. My artwork was becoming more and more concerned with the natural world, and animals and birds were appearing there. I was looking for books to find good photographs of the natural world, you know, and one day I thought about that and said, "This is ridiculous. Here I am, painting the natural world out of other persons' photographs instead of experiencing it, instead of being there." And New York City is such a damn hard place to live in. At this point I was thinking to myself, "Why do I stay here?" And, well, I was locked in by a job at the time, but one day I just decided I'd had it. First of all, I was a one-man show in New York. I directed the Gallery of the American Indian Community House from 1978 to 1985. I was the curator, I was the person that hung the show, I was the person that crated and uncrated exhibits, I was the person that painted the walls, spackled the walls, wrote the press releases, put the artist up, fed the artist, you name it. So I quit the job. No sooner had I quit the job than I felt like I could stand up straight and there was this weight that came off my shoulders and chest—I could breathe. I honestly tell you, I could actually feel the difference. There was all this tense energy inside of me, holding in everything. I was containing an incredible amount of stress. I have a tendency to do that to myself because I've taken on too much, but then I was on the verge of really doing some destruction to myself. So I'm glad that I made that decision. And then, yes, a job opened up to me which took me into a situation which, as I say, if I had sat down to write a job description I would never have thought of something as good as this job. So I was handed the opportunity for directing Ganondagan.

LA: What do you do there?

PJ: I manage a seventeenth-century Seneca townsite, a historic site, in Victor, New York, which is known as Ganondagan, the town of peace, and it's where three hundred years ago maybe as many as four thousand Senecas lived, until they were attacked by a campaign of the French in 1687. The French came there with the express idea of annihilating the Senecas, and they didn't succeed. The site opened in 1987 and I've been the site manager since 1985. It's part of the New York State Office of Parks, Recreation, and Historical Preservation. We have a six-month season that runs from May 1 until the end of October, and there are 377 acres of land, with hiking trails and the visitor center. We put on special activities in the summer, very full, a whole program of things that go on there. And we try to bring together the best in whatever field that we are inviting. I mean, the best singers and dancers we can get; I bring the best traditional artists I can bring to an event. If we're going to do a storytelling program, I try to get ahold of the best storyteller. We present the highest level of the artistic expression of our people, who are dancers, singers, and storytellers, and so on.

LA: I know that you are involved in political activities. Are you involved in reservation affairs, in governance or education or any other things?

PJ: I chair a committee which is called the Haudenosaunee Standing Committee on Burial Rules and Regulations, which is all about the repatriation of our human remains and our sacred objects. It's also about the protection of our burial sites. And it shouldn't be political, but of course it is, you know. I mean, it should be a human right, but it's political because people think they've got a right to hang onto things that belong to us. So that has led to other, you might say, responsibilities, so I'm a representative for the Seneca Nation and I'm also at the same time the chair of this committee which consists of members of all six nations [of the Iroquois], Cayuga, Mohawk, Oneida, Onondaga, Seneca, and Tuscarora.

LA: In your essay in *This Song Remembers*, you wrote, "My work is not political, I'm not an activist."[5] Yet much of your work has a political implication, like *Buffalo Road III — Choices* [1990], *The Hunger Bag* [1981], and *All Indians Don't Live West of the Mississippi* [1987], for example. But other of your works are, say, pure color or pure design. Is it fair to break your work into two types of categories?

PJ: Well, in 1980 I wasn't too politically involved in issues; I was more focused on just making art. But by the mid-1980s I became more aware of what was happening, and my art started to reflect that. So today I work in both directions, and I work at them almost simultaneously. Not the same day, but I come up with these ideas and I think I really do try to not worry too much about how people are going to perceive what I've done. When I was in New York the first time around, and I was working, I remember artists telling me, "When are you going to start your series?" "Series of what?" I said. "Well, you know, a series of paintings that all look the same." Why would I do that? I thought to myself. I don't want to do that. I want to paint what I want to paint at any given time, and they're my ideas, so that's what connects them. That should be obvious; if it isn't, I can make it more obvious, but I respond to what is pushing me most, or what I'm into most. And yeah, I do want to do pieces that make a comment on events and issues. I think I've done that for a long time; actually, I know I have. And it doesn't surprise me that I said I wasn't political, but I wind up being political. The very act of showing Indian art is political.

LA: Creating itself is a political act.

PJ: It is, and people don't understand this. I've never had experiences probably as heavy as Allan Houser [Chiricahua Apache, b. 1915] has had, and probably not as heavy as even Dick West [Cheyenne, b. 1912] has had, in terms of the sort of confrontational situations they've no doubt been put in time after time simply by being Indian, and being visibly so, in the Southwest or the Plains, when it was so prejudicial toward Indians. And so we've had it easy in one way, you could say. But in another way, I chose to make it an issue. I chose that if I'm going to devote my energy in life to promoting the work of Native artists, then we're going to get some results out of this. And we're going to get them on our terms. After a while we're going to tell you, we're going to tell everyone, how it's going to be done. Because until we take control of it, it's not truly ours; it is someone else pulling strings and manipulating things. I don't mean to say even that we don't have control, because we have control of it — but when you put it out into the public arena, always an artist gives up some control. That's a given. But there's a delicate line there between what is an acceptable amount of loss of control and what is unacceptable. When it gets into the area where people start to interpret your thinking for you and start to make it something different than it is, or miss it completely, then there's a major problem.

LA: Many people seem to ignore or devalue contemporary Native art if it seems too unusual or political or not what it is supposed to look like.

PJ: Devalue it, or walk around it, or avoid the issues that are being brought to the front. And in those situations, I guess that's when I tend to get a little political and bring those concerns right out. Because I don't see any point in letting that pass, so my work might make a stronger statement. What am I saying is simply, "Look, this is the way I see things." As people we have to start changing how we're defining ourselves and how we are being defined by others.

LA: Can that be done through art?

PJ: Yeah. I think it definitely can be done through art. I still have faith that art is a way of communicating—communicating who we are. I think the paintings and sculpture of the thirties and forties and fifties by people like Dick West and Andy Tsinhnahjinnie [Navajo, b. 1916] and Fred Kabotie [Hopi, 1900–1986] and Frank Day [Maidu, 1902–76] communicate more about Indian people than all the books that could be written. It only communicates on one level, unfortunately. It communicates who we are. It does not communicate, it seems to me, all the pain that we have felt. A lot of that has been pulled out of the art and what's replaced it is the triumph of our spirit. And that's beautiful. That is extremely important, because it does say, "Look at us." Over a long time period you would think the inner spirit wouldn't have remained alive. But we've still got it.

LA: That spirit really comes out in the work of the Native "old masters."

PJ: It's really amazing. You walk up to a painting that was made in 1932, in 1954, in 1968, and it still resonates. And I have to give those guys credit. I give them a big credit, you know. I don't take anything away from those guys. They were good, they were very good, that refinement in them, and that dignity. And so that's what I'm defending. When I get up and I say, "Don't define who we are," I'm defending those traditionalists. And I know that everyone's there with the same purpose, really. They want to see Native art made public and go around the world as being an important contribution, an important manifestation of the Indian people, who are not at cross-purposes. But when we get into those slippery areas of criticism and definitions . . .

LA: It becomes like a typical art critical discussion.

PJ: Yeah, it does, and then I start to think—all of a sudden I'll catch on and I'll think, "Who is talking now? Wait a minute!" And then I think, "I've got to say something because there's a chance here that they don't get it." And must everyone leave here thinking that these people do understand it perfectly, just because they wrote a book? Just because they've been teaching for ten, twenty years, or whatever it is? That's ridiculous. That doesn't impress me. I mean, it impresses me to the extent that, hey, you're interested; that's good. That's good. But we still are the people making the art. Let us make our own art.

LA: I'd like to talk about *Buffalo Road III–Choices*, a recent piece [1990], where you juxtaposed about twenty separate images on top of a buffalo drawn in red, green, and blue. It's a fairly large work. Some images are satiric, some are of traditional people in modern scenes, some are of elders. Could you just talk about that? You've also done *Buffalo Road I* and *Buffalo Road II*.

PJ: Well, okay. To make it simple about *Buffalo Road III*. A young Mohawk man said to me, "Have you done any pieces that really relate to the current situations that are going on in our communities?" And I said to myself, I thought I *was* doing some pieces about that. Then I thought, maybe not enough. Maybe I'm not going far enough. So, with that in mind, I decided I'd do a piece which is really a commentary on the events of the last year. And so I started working on a montage. And almost as I was working on it, almost simultaneously, I think, all hell started breaking loose and all kinds of things were happening in the Mohawk territories, involving the Canadian Army, the New York State Police, involving gambling and entrepreneurs and warriors and lawyers—you name it. And I know the people involved. I have friends that live there. I had friends calling me up, asking me to help. I had a conversation with the governor of New York State on the subject. And so a lot of things happened.

So that piece is about the choices that seemed to be presented to us at this point in time. The issue of gambling casinos on our reservations versus a traditional way of life, the issue of the sovereignty of our nations, and the question of whether or not we are the generation that, in our lifetimes, are going to be the people who think the most important thing is the car you drive, the size of the house you live in, and all the material trappings that go with that. There are those who can understand that this is a critical time.

We have a wampum belt, and it's called the two-row wampum belt. And what it says, in very simple ways, is that we are traveling down this river; we are in our canoe traveling along this river. You are in your boat. You are traveling along the same river. We're traveling along together, side by side. Now, we're not going to try to get into your boat and tell you how to run your boat, and we would not want you to get into our canoe and take over our canoe. So we will be traveling, you and I, down this river, down this path of life. Now, the person who will be in the most difficult situation will be the person who tries to have a foot in the canoe and a foot in the boat, because if the course of the river shifts, that person is in the most precarious position. And in that way, we have our sovereignty and you have yours. And we have a respect for that sovereignty. I suppose that that [wampum belt] is our very earliest treaty, one that was made between the Dutch and the Haudenosaunee. And then every succeeding treaty after that was made, from our point of view, nation to nation. They recognized that they were a nation, a young fledgling nation, and we another nation, with a long, long, long history on this earth, and on this Turtle Island here too.

We're at that point in time, in our history right now, where it's testing our ability to control our destiny—and when I say "it," I should say the negative forces, the forces that are now set in motion—are testing our ability to control our destiny. Are we going to have armed thugs roaming around, controlling our reservations? Are we going to have gambling casinos that invite all types of people onto the reservation? Are we going to have armed confrontations?

LA: So it's a piece about choice and options and alternatives?

PJ: Yes.

LA: And I felt that in an earlier piece, *Salamanca Buffalo* [1984], there was a sense of freedom versus control, or a sense of a foreclosed destiny, perhaps?

PJ: Well, the fact is that the buffalo is now fenced in but protected from us, where one time he dominated the landscape in the West and he was the source of food for the people. He was their gift from the Creator, and now we can only see the herds of any size when we go watch the movie *Dances with Wolves*.

LA: If we could jump back a little bit in your career, you were known early on for your *Bag* series. You were living in New York City at the time and you have written about some of the influences on the bags: parfleches, for example. A lot of different influences were brought to bear. You made your own paper, too, I think?

PJ: I made handmade paper. I did do that. I also used ordinary paper bags and ordinary shopping bags for some of them. For some of them I went out and found different types of papers that I liked, and I folded them to resemble a paper bag. And the bags started off. I liked the fact that they were three-dimensional and you could work on different surfaces and you could create relationships that you could only understand as you moved around the bag. And sometimes you could put unrelated things on the same bag and people would make relationships, create relationships, that they saw there. The bags were very easy to work on; they're very portable. I could work on them right here on the table anytime. I don't have to have my studio, or an easel, and then set up. So, it's portable and easy to work with.

This whole notion of paper bags—I've talked about this with people. In Europe, in Italy, for example, when you went to the market you took your own bag with you if you wanted to carry stuff home. Plus they couldn't afford to hand you a paper bag; they didn't have enough trees over there. We've been throwing away paper bags like they were refuse, which people consider them. And in fact we know that it takes a lot of trees to supply this country with paper bags every day. And the trees are taken down for that reason. So I wanted to make a statement about that idea and the recycling of the bag, keeping the bag around for another use. And they become, I've said, when they get decorated, like a persona. They take on a sort of a personality and I like having them around. They go out for shows and come back. At times I think I want to get away from them, I'm going to stop doing those things. And then something will spark me again to do another one, and then they'll go out to a show and somebody will tell me how much they liked them, and they want to tell me more about it, and all this kind of stuff. The general response to them is very positive; in fact, the critics liked them, and that sort of forced me to keep on making them.

LA: You've called them "humorous and temporal," but there are, like in many of your other works, broader implications, especially in the bag *Hunger*.

PJ: *Hunger* was one where I found this bag, and the title of the maker of the bag, or the title of the bag itself, was "HomeSafe." So I cut the flap out so that you could see the word "HomeSafe." The whole title of the piece was *Hunger on Reservations While Children in Africa Starve*. This was done in 1981, before Live-Aid and everything really got going on this issue of hunger. I just got a sense of the size of the famine and I know Indian kids are hungry, and I know we could do more. And that's hard to understand, so a grocery bag is a perfect vehicle for talking about food.

LA: That piece has a lot of different levels going on.

PJ: Yeah. It has all kinds of meanings. I put on the back of it, too, a giraffe, kept in the zoo, being fed. I mean, we'll maintain a giraffe in the zoo before we'll help some hungry kids in Africa. The irony of the values of this society are the things that I like to comment on.

LA: In looking at some of the bags, they did strike me—it's interesting—as sort of a sculpture, or a three-D painting, as you mentioned, where you can *work* around it. Other bags concern Seneca traditions or things from the reservation, like *Cattaraugus Coho* [1985], because there were salmon.

PJ: Yeah, there were salmon. I always want to bring in a few things from home in my work, and beyond that, when I'm at home, I'll have some smoked fish and go with my dad to dress fish, and walk around the creek bank with him.

LA: To finish up, in Jimmie Durham's introduction to the catalog for the show "We're Always Turning Around . . . on Purpose" [1986] you are quoted as saying, "As American Indian artists, we are not fully evolved. We are still coming to terms with all the daily contradictions of our lives."[6] In the five years since that show, what's your sense of the evolutionary process? Can those resolutions to the daily contradictions ever come about in society, or in the individual?

PJ: I don't think so. No, I think not. We talk about it in this way, that when we talk about our kids, we have to talk about our kids being two hundred percent educated. They have to be one hundred percent educated about who they are, and then they have to be capable of getting an education in the white world so that they can function in that world, which is the world that they'll live in. As well, they'll go back and forth home. I have a fifteen-year-old son and it's my daily responsibility to talk with him and give him as much support for what he does as I can. And to slip in there, at every opportune moment, the story of who he is and what he's about, and what I'm about and what I do. And I try to help him to understand that, so he can be equipped for the contradictions he's going to face in his life, and perhaps be better equipped than I was, because I had to go through that experience of disillusionment and being mixed up about who I was, what I was doing, and a lot of negative things. And then I had to make my way back to what we call *ongwehonweka:a*, the Indian way of life. I came back to that, and became much better at understanding that way of life and my position and my role and my community and everything else. See, even in '86 I wouldn't have been as close to how I feel right now.

And as for the evolution of our art, I hope that never stops. I hope that continues the way it's going. This has been an eye-opener, just to come to the Heard and see the show *[Shared Visions]*, and see all these artists and hear them talking about their work. Anything they say, you know, is important. It's an interesting comment on where we are, and to have all of us sitting in the same room together, in the same hotel together, talking to one another, shows me that I made the right decision, for one thing. When I knew that it was time to turn to the tradition and find out what that was, and then let that be a force of my work, I made the right decision, as far as I'm concerned.

SELECTED EXHIBITIONS

"'For the Seventh Generation: Native American Artists Counter the Quincentenary'" (1992), group exhibition, Chenango County Council of the Arts, Norwich, NY, and Golden Artist Colors, Inc., Columbus, NY.

"The Submuloc Show/Columbus Wohs" (1992–94), group traveling exhibition, Atlatl, Phoenix, AZ.

"Our Land/Ourselves" (1991–93), group traveling exhibition, University Art Gallery, State University of New York, Albany, NY.

"Shared Visions" (1991–93), group traveling exhibition, Heard Museum, Phoenix, AZ.

"Mid-Career Retrospective: Works from 1971–1986" (1987), solo exhibition, Museum of the Plains Indian, Browning, MT.

"We Are Always Turning Around . . . on Purpose" (1986), group touring exhibition, State University of New York, Old Westbury, NY.

"Four Native American Painters" (1985), group exhibition, Wooster Art Museum, Wooster, OH.

"Contemporary Native American Art" (1983), group exhibition, Gardiner Art Gallery, Oklahoma State University, Stillwater, OK.

"Confluence of Tradition and Change" (1981), group touring exhibition, University of California, Davis, CA.

SELECTED BIBLIOGRAPHY

Jemison, G. Peter. "Curator's Statement." In *Haudenosaunee Artists: A Common Heritage*. Brockport, NY: Tower Fine Arts Gallery, State University of New York, 1992, unp.

—— (with assistance from Ansley Jemison). "For Our Land They Brought Gifts." In *The Submuloc Show/Columbus Wohs*. Phoenix, AZ: Atlatl, 1992, p. 38.

——. "Onondowagani." In *"For the Seventh Generation: Native American Artists Counter the Quincentenary, Columbus, New York."* Columbus, NY: Arts Council Gallery and Golden Artist Colors Gallery, 1992, p. 12.

——. "The Paper Bag Works." In *We Are Always Turning Around . . . on Purpose*. Old Westbury, NY: State University of New York, 1986, p. 22.

——. "Peter Jemison, Seneca Painter." In *This Song Remembers: Self-Portraits of Native Americans in the Arts*, edited by Jane Katz. Boston, MA: Houghton Mifflin, 1980, pp. 45–52.

Michael Kabotie

Hopi

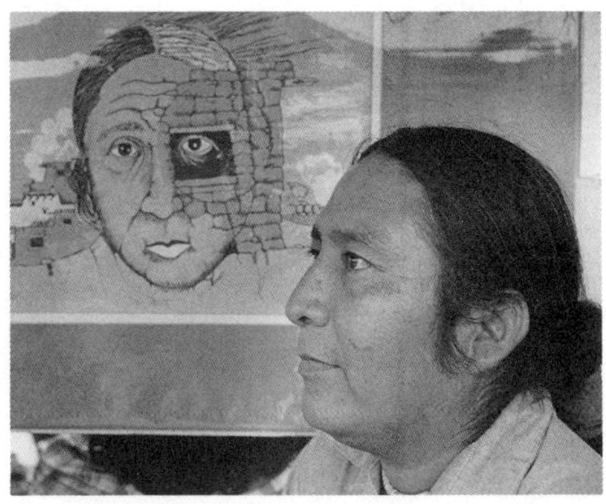

The work of Michael Kabotie (to borrow some words from Walt Whitman) "contains multitudes." His canvases are vibrant with color and usually portray images from the ceremonies and culture of the Hopis. His paintings often depict kachinas, rain spirits, and priests, and encompass corn, petroglyphs, and migration symbols, like spirals and hand- and footprints.

But while Kabotie seems to depict these traditional subjects with modernistic styles and techniques, his work should not be seen as a simple cultural grafting, resulting in "Hopi cubism." Rather, Kabotie seeks a synthesis, a wholeness, a new level of integration. His work from the late 1960s into the mid-1970s certainly shows stylistic affinities with Picasso, Braque, and Leger in pieces like *Kachina Faces* (1968), *Hopi Lovers I* (1973), and *Ceremonial Priest* (1974), but the subject matter is decidedly Hopi. As Patricia Broder has noted: "The techniques and conventions of Cubism have great appeal to modern Hopi artists." She further notes that because no one individual Hopi has complete understanding of the total culture, cubist art can reflect this limitation. Cubist forms can also show conflicts and clashes through the use of visual elements.[1]

However that may be, the so-called cubist forms as used by Kabotie, and other Hopi artists of his generation, may also be a way of both maintaining and representing the complexity of the culture itself. Instead of indicating limitation of cultural knowledge, "Hopi cubism" (for want of a better descriptive term) as a visual strategy allows the canvas to become mural-like, and to contain specific imagery of Hopi culture and also to suggest the meanings behind that imagery. The work becomes a visual analogue of the culture.

And much of Kabotie's painting transforms the Awatovi murals excavated in that abandoned Hopi village. The bands and curves of the murals are continued and extended in such pieces as *Sikyatki Hand with Bee* (1973) and *Salako the Cloud Priest* (1974). This extension of forms continues in Kabotie's work today.

This is not to say that some of his work doesn't also depict the "cultural clash" (as he himself has said),[2] but this intercultural clash comes out more explicitly in his writing. *Migration Tears* (1987), his book of poetry, covers a lot of ground, from the place of ceremony in Hopi culture to the frustrations of the artist to sometimes bemused, sometimes bitter observations. Many of his poems deal with the changes in the ways of life on the mesas. In "Nightmare" he writes, "I watched the ceremony / from the housetop / . . . The songs they mumbled / The dances, they stumbled / Faces scarred / bruised / Evergreen boughs now naked antennas / Spring blossoms hangover breath / . . . I awoke in horror " (p. 30). And "Our Land No More Forever" evokes a sense of dislocation:

Now we all stand
on mesa's edge;
aliens to our homeland,
gasping and struggling to survive
under the pollution / treads of technology,
wondering why,
Once our land no more forever?

(p. 24)

Michael Kabotie was born in 1942 in the Hopi village of Shungopavi, and went to Hopi High School and the Haskell Institute in Lawrence, Kansas, from which he graduated in 1961. He entered the College of Engineering at the University of Arizona but did not complete his study there. Instead, in the early 1960s he decided to turn his energies to art full-time. He participated in the summer programs in Tucson sponsored by the Rockefeller Foundation and there was influenced by the Cochiti artist Joe Herrera.[3] In 1966, at the Heard Museum in Phoenix, he had his first solo show. In 1973, Kabotie was also instrumental in forming Artist Hopid, a group of artists who began to experiment with traditional forms.[4] Artist Hopid exhibited throughout the United States for nearly ten years, and in 1979 works from the group were included in the South American traveling exhibition "Contemporary Amerindian Paintings/USA."

A member of the Snow-Water clan, he describes his initiation into the Hopi men's society as a significant point in his life. It was at this initiation that he received the name Lomawywesa, "Walking in Harmony."[5]

About his work Kabotie has written: "The arts have always been an integral part of my life. It is through the arts that I capture and share the values of people's spirituality, agonies, contradictions and happiness, and through the arts that I clarify my fears, passions, joys; my birth and death."[6]

We talked in May 1991 during the *Shared Visions* symposium at the Heard Museum.

LA: Your paintings are very striking, very distinctive, and you've talked about, in some of your writings, the need for new styles. How do you go about reconciling, in your visual style and approach, tradition and innovation?

MK: You know, I guess that really is not an issue. That's not much of a problem. If it's something that I need to do, like a painting, I just do it. And I don't clog up my mind about whether it's going to be the traditional way or the new way or either way. Whatever is happening, then, is what's happening.

LA: The work of your father [Fred Kabotie] developed out of the "Santa Fe style," and that style is by and large identified as "traditional Indian art." You use many of the elements which might be termed traditional, yet at the same time you've drawn on many other sources, too. How did your work develop?

MK: If I could use the 1960 Rockefeller Project as a starting point,[7] before that Rockefeller happening in Tucson, I was just into my teens, doing cartoons. That was in the mid-1950s, and before that it was a lot of descriptive drawings of kachinas and the like. But after the Rockefeller project in Tucson, I got acquainted with the Awatovi kiva murals through Joe Herrera.[8] I have talked about those murals because they've had a profound and deep impact on me. At that point I realized that our people had a long history in the arts. Then I became aware that the pottery designs, the basket designs, the kachina designs were all developed long before the coming of the white people. So I began to reflect back on those earlier art forms. Later I was in Tucson, not with the project, but in school at the University of Arizona [1961–65], and those were the times I got acquainted with European artists like Picasso, Paul Klee, Leger, all the gifted impressionists. I did a lot of looking at those people, too.

LA: You've said that sometimes when people look at your work, they say, "Oh, he's doing cubist art," but then you mentioned that Picasso may have borrowed from the Hopi people.

MK: Well, that's true, because once I began to look at the development of these European artists, I knew what they were looking at, and when I dug down, I realized that they were doing the same things as artists always do, looking into the past and picking up the energies and spirits and the work of the so-called primitive artists. I was doing the same thing when I looked back at the kiva murals.

LA: Were you aware, as a youngster, of the murals, or was it like you were a kid and didn't really pay attention to that stuff?

MK: I took a lot of those things for granted in those days because my father was an artist; those things were around all the time, and after a while you just take them for granted. It wasn't anything special. And it's sort of amazing, because my father was very well known, and I had to have an initiator who came and initiated me into another point of view, another sphere, and that was Joe Herrera.

LA: Could you talk a little about the directions he opened up?

MK: The biggest influence was planting a seed in me and opening my eyes to my people's art and to what was around me. Then there was that six-week conference in Tucson. For the first three weeks of that project I was a bad student, but for the second three weeks he worked with me. He showed me the Pueblo and Awatovi kiva murals and the reproductions. I saw them and I said, "Wow! Terrific!" Then I became more aware of this sense of history that goes further back. Then he helped me to analyze the forms I was going to use and showed me how to space things on the three canvases, how to cut the forms up spatially and how to work with them — how to solve the space, color, and design issues, and things like that.

LA: He helped you more on the technical side and didn't push you into one style or another?

MK: He introduced me to the murals and then helped me realize that I could use the murals as a foundation for my artistic development. That was the end of that aspect of our relationship. But there were other ways of communication that I really admired in this man. One July 14th I went to Cochiti to their fiesta, and there was Joe Herrera as a clown, leading the green corn dance. That had a real emotional impact on me.

LA: Other than painting and drawing, were you involved in any other arts?

MK: Yes, those other art forms — dancing, singing, composing — were all part of the Hopi teachings and the traditions that I was initiated into. I was required to do a number of things to be an active participant. You don't have any people who are specialized in certain things, like costumes, or specialized in doing the poetry and choreography. I had to do all of these things myself, and that was part of the training. So, in Hopi you pretty much have to be everything.

LA: You also write. Your book of poetry is entitled *Migration Tears*. It seems that many Native artists integrate writing, painting, and perhaps traditional singing and dancing, each one reflecting the other. Do your paintings have a storytelling or narrative dimension? I'm thinking of a painting called *Signatures of the Past* [1975] or the 1984 lithograph *Rain Spirits*. Is there a story involved in your paintings?

MK: When you say *Signatures of the Past*, that was part of my growing awareness of Hopi history when I was looking at a lot of petroglyphs. The story and inspiration for that series of paintings are clan migration stories. As the Hopi clans migrated, at every place that we visited, we'd put our signatures on the cliff walls and boulders, symbols of our totems: the clouds, corn, sun, reptiles. Then we'd move on to another place and do the same thing. Those were the signatures of the past, the clan markings on the walls, and that basically was what I was paying homage to in that series of paintings.

LA: Do you structure the paintings in such a way as to tell a story through that imagery?

MK: I think if you come from a heavy tradition, you tend to fall into telling stories of that tradition through the images of your paintings. Like my *Kachina Song Poetry* series has that kind of theme. Paintings like *Kachina Song Images* [1986], *Kachina Song Blessings* [1986], and *Rain Spirits* [1984] talk about kachinas bringing the rain, bringing blessings through songs. I try to symbolically interpret these things or capture the songs visually on paper. And so there is a story or theme behind them. But then, lately, I'm moving away from the imagery, more into shapes, curves, lines, and colors. *Kachina Elements* [1973] is one of the first in that direction. But you can still see the images of the kachinas, still see textile designs, and you'll see some petroglyphs, but they are minor in terms of the overall composition.

LA: Even with a new series of works, you still refer back to a lot of the murals?

MK: Oh, yes, the murals incorporate these various shapes like circles and corners and right angles, and every time I go back there I strip away a little bit more of the imagery and just get to the basic forms and structure of the murals. So gradually the cultural images are disappearing and just the basic forms are coming through. I'll extend a line or a circle from the mural, develop something out of it, but not really represent the mural itself.

LA: One piece of yours I especially like is *Hopi Babysitting* [1982]. It's satirical and has a cartoon aspect to it. It looks like Mickey Mouse has become a Hopi clown, and the woman in the painting has a puzzled expression. Did you have a satirical, poking-fun intent behind it?

MK: Yes, it basically had to do with the grandmother, the grandmother babysitting. When I was growing up, my grandmother was the storyteller; she would tell me the stories, and she would sing me the songs. But now we have the TV, and so the grandmother in this painting is trying to talk to the infant, but the baby is more addicted to the TV. The TV is grabbing his attention. But the imagery that looks like Mickey Mouse is a little field mouse, a Hopi story character, Tusan Homichi.

LA: Even though the TV may be a distraction, the program on the TV shows a Hopi character?

MK: Yes. If we do use the TV properly it could be an advantage to our education.

LA: You stated in *When the Rainbow Touches Down* that "we are portraying the culture clash symbolically in painting."[9] Do you think that symbolic clash is still coming out in your work?

MK: Well, I think that I'm gradually getting beyond that point. My "cartoon" era developed and continued through to *Hopi Babysitting* and things like that, but now it's beyond cartoons. Right now I'm at a point where I have taken a different journey and left those issues on the outside, and have begun to dwell deeper and deeper inside. And the further I go in my inner journey, those other things fall away. I'm coming to a point where I want to go past the cultural and ethnic aesthetic barriers, when everything is merged into oneness. There's no big and no small. There's a sense of oneness. Negatives and positives become one and you can't really distinguish them. It's a different world. But it's a beginning and it is very scary. It's new territory. It's something that I have never experienced before.

LA: That's within the last couple of years?

MK: Yes, and I think that new direction is one of the things that's reflected in my work. I showed one of the slides today [at the Heard Museum symposium in May 1991] where you see a lot of the forms with just a limited amount of things that you could recognize, like pottery and the corn. Now a lot of that imagery, material imagery, is disappearing and there is more of a concentration on form.

LA: While in the mid-1970s the cultural clash was more of a concern?

MK: I was still trying to fix the griefs.

LA: What is your process of discovery in your work?

MK: There are times I plan things out on paper and then I'll paint from that. Then there are times when I just put down an initial sort of image and things change as I go along. It works well from either side.

LA: You've talked about Joe Herrera as an artist mentor.

You've also mentioned you've had some spiritual mentors. Could you talk about that for a bit?

MK: Yes, I think the spiritual mentors are the clowns I talked about, and I see that from the point of how the Hopi clown, our clown, is symbolically born into the plaza, into the ceremonial place. The clown immediately sees that he is the only one there but then recognizes there are others that are there; at this point it's the dancer kachinas. Then he detaches himself from the spirit. The ego comes into play when he fights the spirit. The clown will say, "This is how it's going to happen." This is where he detaches his ego from his soul and continues to go berserk and does all of these insane things, until at the end, maybe at the end of the second day, the omens come to him as an owl or as a crow. An owl is that bird of prey that can see in the dark, so at that point the owl is the one that can see the dark side of the clown. And he would tell the clown that he is going away from the path, but the clown would say, "No, everything is okay." And the crow would come and say, "Well, I think you need a judgment day, a purification day." The clown says, "No, just leave us alone. Everything is just terrific." And that is denial of the insane ego that has gotten ahold of the clown.

But at the end of the day, the clown asks to be purified by the kachinas, and he symbolically confronts his insane ego. Then he makes his last desperate physical fight with those spirits who are there to help him. Then he realizes that something did happen and he goes through a transformation. Then he has to go through the process of telling the world his confession; he has to make amends to those he hurt. At the very end he shares with those people he hurt certain gifts. At the beginning of the ceremony he divided the world. Now he puts that into perspective and tells the kachinas, "Now it's your world and I'm going to work with you." It's the whole universe. This is basically a life situation that I have found in the clown adventures. Every once in a while I, too, need to cleanse out inside. This is *tsuku*.

LA: You've frequently used clowns and other kachinas as subjects, like in *Clowns and Kachinum Chanting* from '84.

MK: That shows the cloud kachina, the longhair kachina, and they come into the village early in the morning before light, before the village is awake, and the clown is there to meet them.

LA: From the top of the pueblo?

MK: No. They come in about three o'clock in the morning. And the clown sings to the kachina. He's the contrary. This is the Hopi clown. He is yellow and has a funny face, like the kachina mother. There are two sets of clowns: one is with this red across the eye, and the other half is the funny face. But then again, it's funny because clowns in the plaza consist of male and female, both at the same time.

LA: Do the dances and music of the ceremonies influence you at all?

MK: Oh, I think that my *Kachina Poetry Series* reflects this, where as a participant you do a lot of singing and dancing. Then after a while you try to capture the rhythms and imagery of the songs and try to portray them on paper, visually capture them. I try to get that spirit and sense of movement.

LA: In 1967 you were initiated into *Wuwuchim* [Hopi men's society; also spelled *Wuwtsim*] and you received your Hopi name Lomawywesa, "Walking in Harmony." Was that initiation a turning point in your life or in your artwork?

MK: Yes, I think it really had an impact on me because prior to my initiation I was going in the direction of what you'd call modern art. When I went through my initiation my approach to art changed, and that's when I began to do these large, dark Hopi designs with petroglyphs, with white petroglyphs against a dark background. That was the beginning of my spiritual journey, seeking myself through art. And I think the darkness represented that mystery, like something you know is there but you really couldn't stand to look at it. That kind of thing. And by 1970 I stopped painting because I didn't know what was happening. I didn't know what direction I was going and all of a sudden painting didn't feel right anymore. And then, after I hadn't painted for about two and a half years, there was a time when the spirit called and the murals and the artist mentors came back again, and that was a time when the formulation and the ideas about Artist Hopid began to come up, which was about the need to share, to get together to experience things. Neil David and Terrance Talaswaima [Honvantewa] thought the same about getting together. That was the beginnings of Artist Hopid.[10]

LA: You were a founding member of that group in '73. How long did Artist Hopid stay together as a formal group?

MK: I don't know if it really was a formal group. I think it's still happening, but at a different stage. It's not as intense as it was. We all shared a studio space together and started painting in one studio. As we developed, there was a lot of excitement during that time. Then I became director of the Hopi Arts and Crafts Guild because I was already directing Artist Hopid, whether I liked it or not. Inquiries came to me, so I started coordinating shows. I was pretty involved in painting and the other things of Artist Hopid. This was probably for about two years, around '75, and then I decided to take on the directorship of the guild as codirector, comanager, so that I could get some pay because I was going broke.

LA: Did you five members of Artist Hopid have a lot of influence on each other?

MK: Definitely. I remember in the third year you couldn't tell which was Mike Kabotie, which was Neil David, which was Terrance, or Delbridge [Honanie], or Milland [Lomakema] because a lot of our paintings began to look the same. You work on an idea for so long, and the other guy looks over at you, and five minutes later he's put it all together.

LA: How about use of color? Do you have symbolic use of color?

MK: My colors reflect my respect for the murals and mostly what is taught us in Hopi traditions, the four direction colors, red, green, white, black, earth colors predominantly. That's what I started doing from the beginning, mostly earth colors. Back in '67 I had a dark period when brown was dominant. But then there was a time in the eighties when my color spectrum just exploded.

LA: Do you think those colors reflected what was going on in your life at that time?

MK: I really can't analyze it all the way back. I'm sure the dark colors represented that sense of mystery I felt—the dark colors, the contrast that the petroglyphs give, which I think signifies the mystery of the past, and the search for some meaning against all those dark backgrounds.

LA: You once mentioned that "tradition doesn't mean a loss of freedom."[11] You're able to express yourself within the context of Hopi sources. I have the sense, too, that you use your art as both self-exploration and exploration of the culture.

MK: I've always identified myself as a guide. To me, I can only guide viewers through a visual experience, and then the experience is what teaches them.

LA: Maybe we can take a look at a recent work, *Kachina Still-Life* from 1990. Could you discuss the elements in the work and how they all interact? How did this particular work develop?

MK: Again, you see elements of the Awatovi murals; the bands at the bottom are the Awatovi bands. The frog, flowers, and designs are directly from the murals. The little yellow bars and circles, they're from Awatovi. The kachina in the background is contemporary, and that kachina is one of the purifiers who comes and purifies the clown. That was the beginning of a series of images on the theme of purification. And in *Kachina Still-Life* #2 [1990] you can see the same thing. Again you see the influences from Awatovi, like the corn and the feathers. The kachina is present and that's what comes to purify the people, like the Crow Mother, the scavenger. The scavenger is the one who purifies the earth, so there's a story behind it. Then with purification, you have cornfields, pottery, and your prayers. That's pretty much the message.

LA: The so-called traditional paintings of the thirties are often looked at as a cultural record or as cultural documentation. Do you feel that your work can also be seen in some way as a cultural record, even though the visual imagery is different from the work of fifty or sixty years ago?

MK: That's determined by who studies it, who puts it into a certain concept, or into their motive. It depends on how they're looking at it. All of my themes are basically very traditional. Sometimes things that were taught to me when I was a kid, the spiritual values, all those I try to conceptualize. I think that every artist reflects his or her culture and values at a certain point. Now I'm going into a different plane or sphere or consciousness or whatever you want to call it.

LA: The internal discovery?

MK: It might be a point of my artistic maturity, but I really can't answer that one.

SELECTED EXHIBITIONS

"Shared Visions" (1991–93), group traveling exhibition, Heard Museum, Phoenix, AZ.

Tempe Arts Center (1989), group exhibition, Tempe, AZ.

Lovena Ohl Gallery (1987, 1988, 1991), two-person and group exhibitions, Scottsdale, AZ.

"Celebrate the Spirits" (1985), group exhibition, Matthews Center, Arizona State University, Tempe, AZ.
"'What's in a Name?'" (1984), group exhibition, Gallery 10, Scottsdale, AZ.

SELECTED BIBLIOGRAPHY

Kabotie, Michael. *Migration Tears*. Los Angeles: American Indian Studies Center, University of California, 1987.

Frank LaPena

Nomtipom Wintu

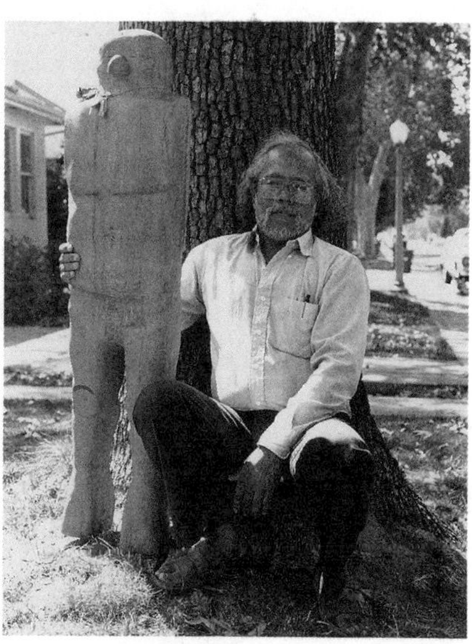

We live our lives by the turning of the seasons and the passage of the Milky Way. We direct our actions by the fullness of the moon and the need to do ceremonies, to put things at rest in winter and awaken them in the spring. With our lives and our works we create a metaphor of the universe; all things are one with us. We arrange things according to tradition and pay attention in detail. The essence of color is its power to heal. It is also a spiritual element and represents the four directions. — Frank LaPena, The World Is a Gift

Tradition. Ceremony. Color. These are the foundations of Frank LaPena's work, the generative forces out of which his paintings, drawings, and woodcuts emerge. This does not mean that LaPena's work resembles what is termed traditional Indian art, or that his work is strictly documentation. Rather, LaPena seeks to bring out the essence and meaning of ritual, to embody a level of spirituality in the image that would not otherwise be tangible. Such paintings as *Dance Spirit* (1981), *Deer Rattle/Deer Dancer* (1981), and *Bear Dancer* (1983) and such wood engravings as *Big Head Spirit* (1987) and *Wuk' Wuk* (1987) do not simply render images but also contain ritual significance. To Christopher Brown, "such images . . . [are] still enacted among many modern tribes as a way of preserving and reinvesting that heritage with contemporary meaning."[1] Frank LaPena's work makes a connection between the physical and the spiritual, between the traditional and the contemporary.

But LaPena's connection to the living tradition of the Wintu people also manifests itself in other ways. He has published two books of poems, *SUNUSA Stopped the Rain* (1979) and *The Gift of Singing* (1976), both published by Chalatien Press, Sacramento, California, and wrote the chapter on the Wintus for the Smithsonian Institution's *Handbook of North American Indians*. LaPena has also been a consultant to the Smithsonian for the new National Museum of the American Indian, the California State Indian Museum, and the Ishi Project at Berkeley. He has written the arts column for the quarterly *News from Native California* since 1987. In addition, he actively participates as a Maidu dancer and traditionalist, and is fluent in the Wintu language.

LaPena began exhibiting his work in 1960 and has shown his art in both solo and group shows steadily since then. It is in a number of permanent collections, including those of the Heard Museum, the University of Utah, the Crocker Museum (Sacramento, California), and the Indian Arts and Crafts Board in Washington, D.C.

LaPena was born in 1937 in San Francisco. He spent his early years in boarding schools in Nevada and, later, Salem, Oregon. His Wintu family held responsibility for maintaining and preserving the tribe's traditions, and his great-uncle, Grant Towendolly, was the last formally trained Wintu traditional leader. Tauhindauli, LaPena's Indian name, derives from these ancestors.

LaPena received his bachelor's degree in 1965 from the California State University at Chico and his master's in anthropology in 1978 from the California State University at Sacramento, where he is now a professor of art and ethnic studies and director of the Native American Studies Program.

About his life and work LaPena has said: "I extend myself outward and connect to being. I express myself in images to give you dance and art."[2] For LaPena, there is no separation between word, image, and movement. All express the essential unity of things.

We talked one afternoon in early May 1991 at the Heard Museum symposium on Native American art.

LA: Could we start by talking about your teaching at Cal State Sacramento?

FL: I've been there since 1971. Since 1974 I've been director of Native American Studies. At this time I teach an introduction to ethnicity in America, dealing with questions concerning immigrants and related issues. I emphasize immigration, labor, and education and focus on the black, Asian, Mexican-American, and Native American experiences. Of course, in order to talk about that in history you have to deal with other groups, too, so I deal with the Irish a lot, and obviously the idea of religion is important because of the Protestant ethic. Beyond that you have the whole question of social values. It's fun to open up the minds of the students to new information. I have a range of students — Asians, Chicanos, Native Americans, Euro-Americans, a mixture.

I try to draw some parallels in the histories of those groups. There are some mutually shared problem areas and one of them would be the fact that people of color have historically been isolated and not allowed to participate in the "American dream." And what becomes very clear is that in the colonial system the disenfranchisement that was put on the indigenous people got switched to the other people of color, and in California the major target became the Chinese, because of the exploitation of gold mines, while the Native indigenous people continued to be destroyed. We tend to forget that the missionization period of 1769 to 1833 was highly destructive to coastal and southern California tribal groups, because the missions were built through the enslavement of Native people and the taking of their land. So I think that there are lots of shared things, but they are shared negative things.

I also have an art appreciation class that I teach to nonmajors that starts with prehistoric cave painting and goes up to as far as I can get in a semester. Right now in that class I'm talking about Northern California painters, both Indian and non-Indian, and what distinguishes them as group or region. One thing that does distinguish the Indian artists is not simply that they are making art, but that they are also reaching out to the larger field of artists and being accepted. So just getting their work out there is a factor. Another thing about most of the Indian artists I know is that they have some connection to their cultures and they are also involved in the traditional aspects of their cultures. They might be singers or dancers or makers of ceremonial regalia. That's probably the major thing that distinguishes them as a group. But at the same time every artist is autonomous. Our stuff is individual and differs according to the individual. That's unlike some areas of the country where there seems to be a prevailing regional style. We believe in the autonomous involvement of people.

LA: Do you think that that autonomy exists in the Southwest?

FL: I don't think it does overall. It does in the sense that a few people may create a new style, but once it gets noted or an individual gets major recognition, then a whole bunch of people come running to that style because the market is there. In a way the market is a valuable thing because it allows people to exist and maintain some kind of livelihood with their art, and yet at the same time it may lead to an inundation of copiers. And the galleries promote that just as much as the artists.

LA: Do galleries and markets have a very strong impact on contemporary Native art? Do Native artists have to consider market forces?

FL: I think that there are two things, and one of the things I was going to say is that artists are autonomous, wherever they are. If you're an artist, you're kind of an odd person. You have some things to say and you say them, in spite of whatever goes on. If you're going into it as a young person, the tendency is that the market can manipulate you, and that's both good and bad. Sometimes it's positive, because you now have a place to show. But if you are being directed totally by the whim of the market, that particular market at that time is not going to last twenty years or thirty years. But what I like to do is look and see the people who are working and see if they come out of a certain school or a certain style, and is the market giving them access not only to selling but to maintaining, or are they falling by the wayside? The other thing that we haven't even talked about is that the market allows traditional artists and craftspeople to exist, because there is value in a market for someone working traditionally.

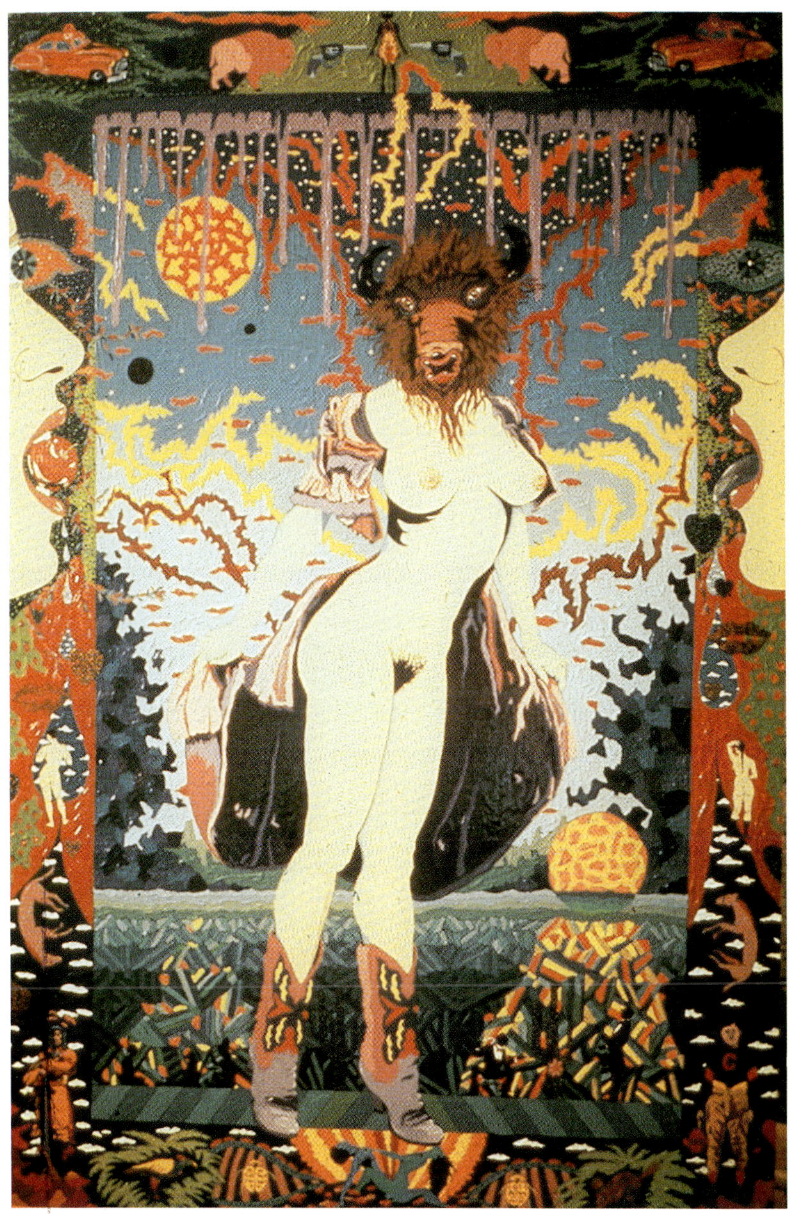

RICK GLAZER-DANAY, *Buffalo Gal with Boots*
1985, acrylic on canvas, 116.8 x 76.2 cm. Collection of the artist.
Photograph by Rick Glazer-Danay, courtesy of the artist.

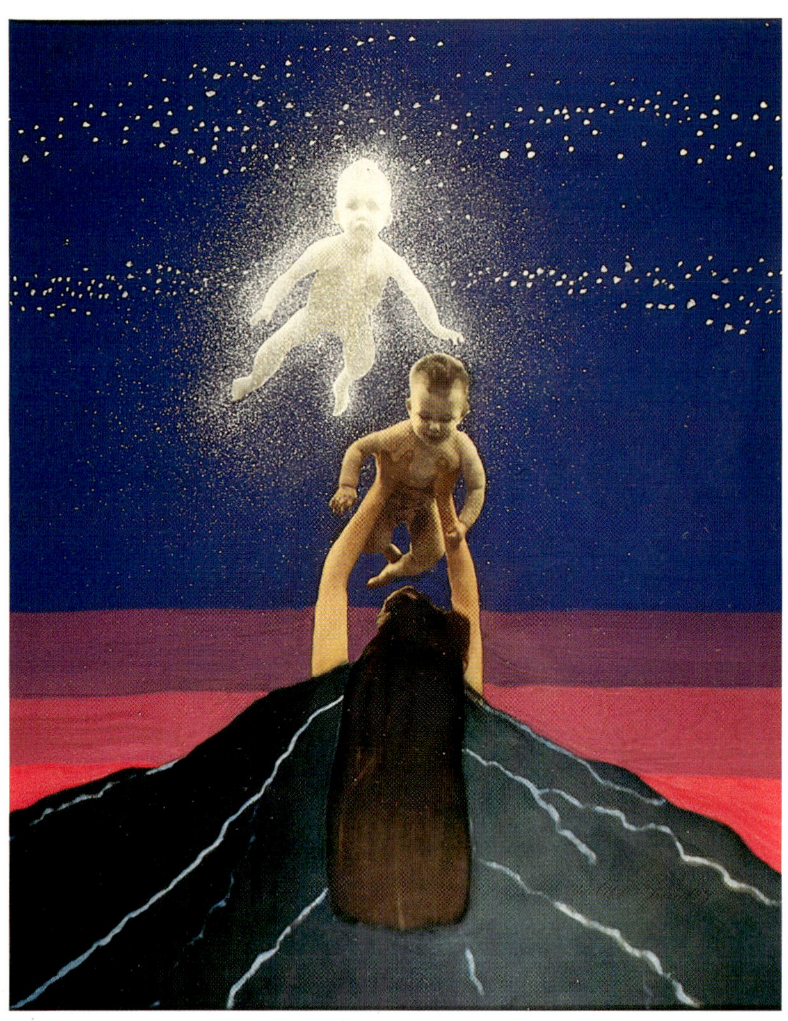

SHAN GOSHORN, *Receiving Star Gift*
1992, hand-painted photograph, 50.8 x 41.6 cm.
Collection of the artist. Photograph by Shan Goshorn,
courtesy of the artist.

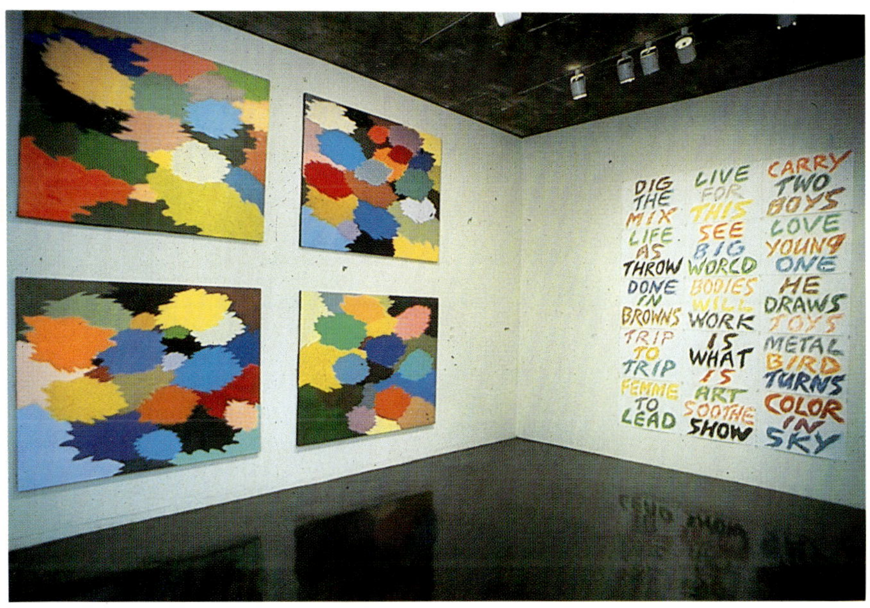

HACHIVI EDGAR HEAP OF BIRDS, *Is What Is*
1991, installation. Photograph by Hachivi Edgar Heap of Birds, courtesy of the artist.

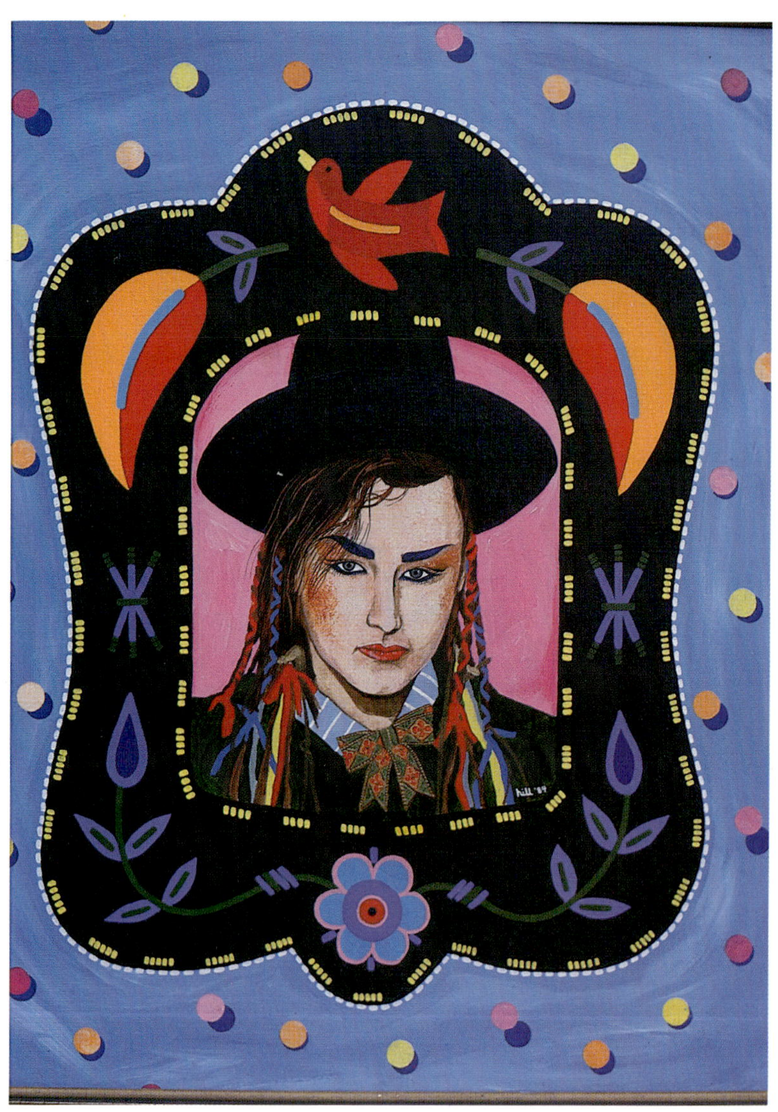

RICK HILL, *Portrait of a Whiteman*
1983, acrylic on canvas, 76 x 61.5 cm. Collection of S. Lohrey, Memphis, Tennessee. Photograph by Rick Hill, courtesy of the artist.

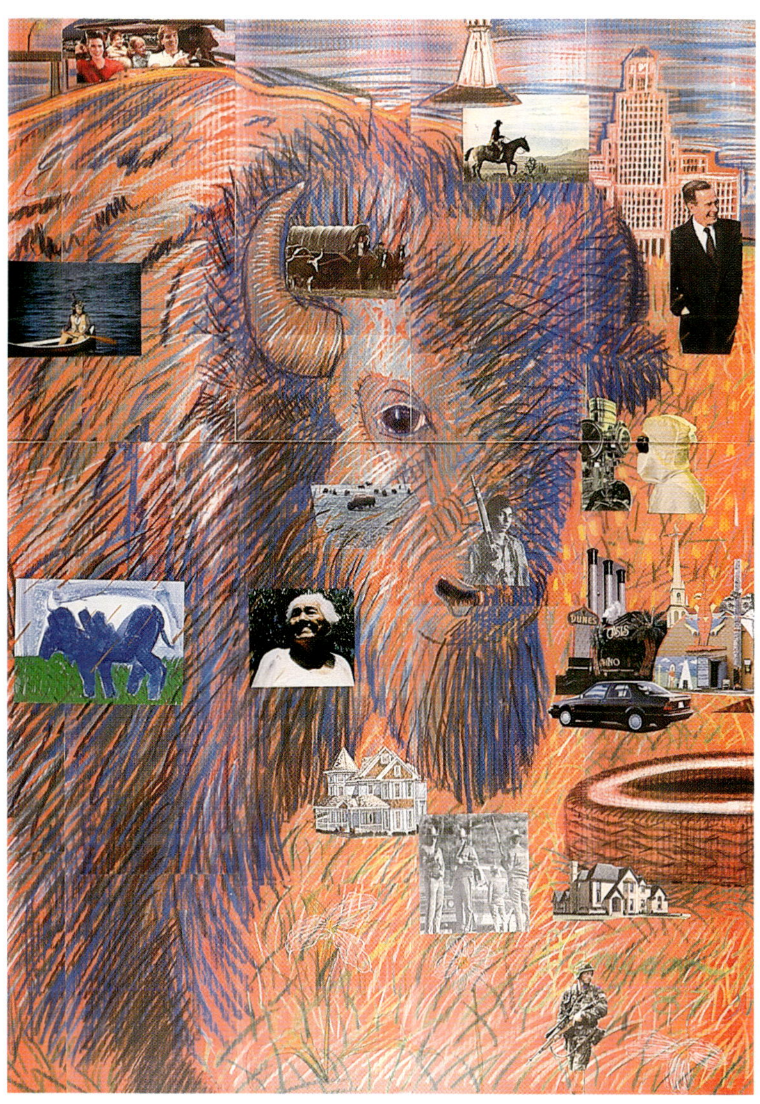

G. Peter Jemison, *Buffalo Road III—Choices*
1990, mixed media, 152.4 x 121.9 cm.
Photograph by Craig Smith, courtesy of the
Heard Museum, Phoenix, Arizona.

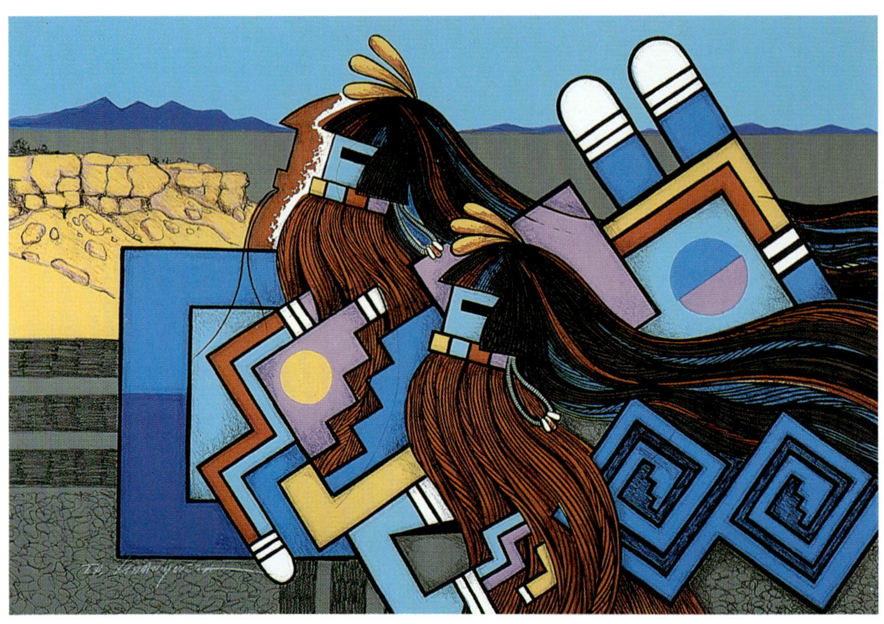

Michael Kabotie, *Rain Spirits*
1984, limited edition lithograph, 38.1 x 55.8 cm.
Photograph by Peter L. Bloomer, courtesy of the artist.

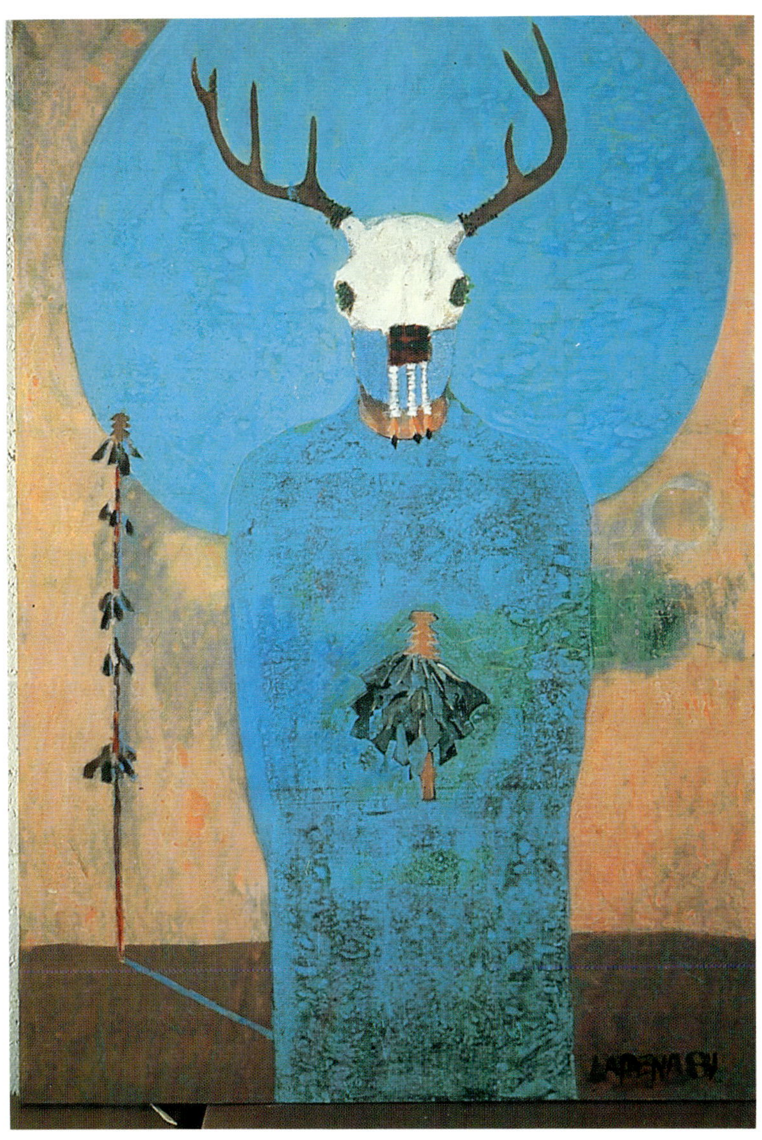

Frank LaPena, *Deer Rattle, Deer Dancer*
1981, acrylic on canvas, 121.9 x 86.3 cm. Collection of the Heard Museum. Photograph courtesy of the Heard Museum, Phoenix, Arizona.

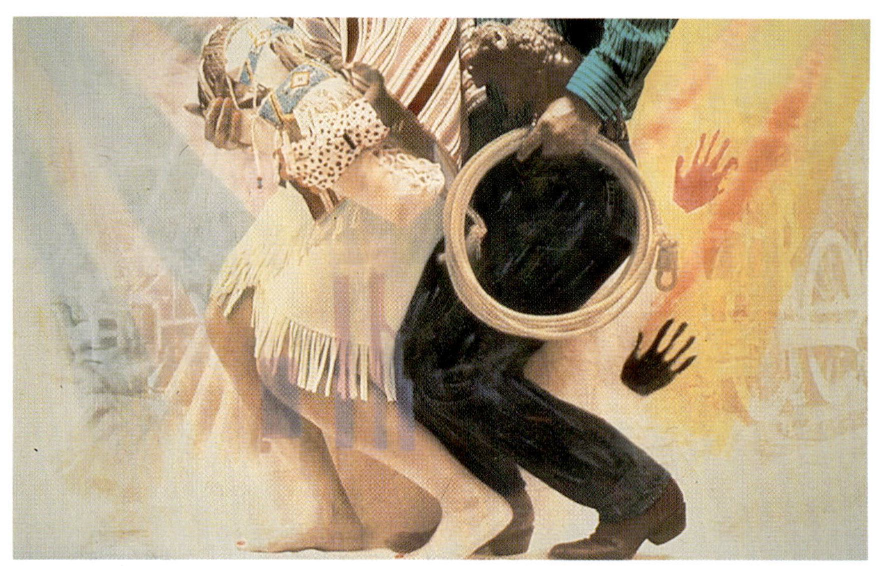

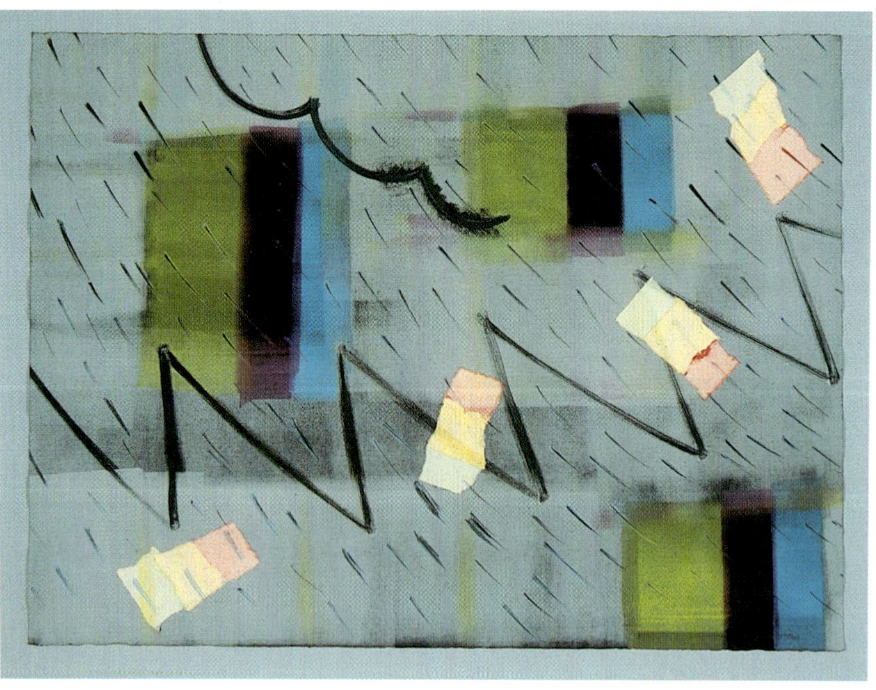

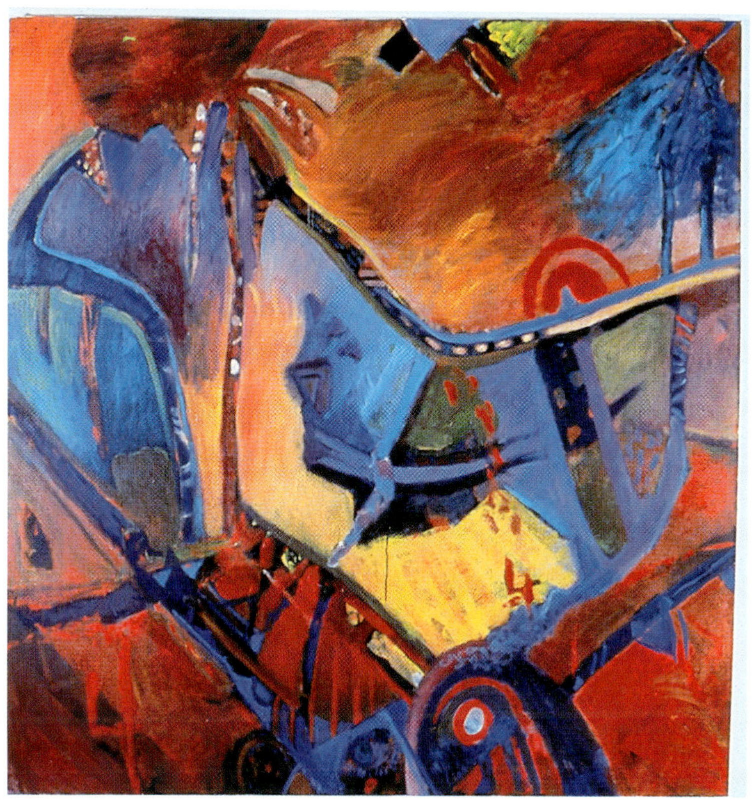

MARIO MARTINEZ, *Bleeding Earth (above)*
1987, acrylic on canvas, 182.8 x 177.8 cm. Collection of the artist. Photograph by Joe Schopplein, used by permission.

CARM LITTLE TURTLE, *Iron Horse (left above)*
1990, hand-painted photograph, 50.8 x 41.6 cm. Collections of the Center for Contemporary Photography, Tucson, Arizona, and the Heard Museum, Phoenix, Arizona. Photograph by Carm Little Turtle, courtesy of the artist.

LINDA LOMAHAFTEWA, *Prayers from Marvin (left below)*
1988, monotype, 50.8 x 76.2 cm. Collection of Terry Duffy, Santa Fe, New Mexico. Photograph by Linda Lomahaftewa, courtesy of the artist.

George Longfish, *The End of the Innocence (below)*
1991–92, acrylic on canvas, 3 panels. Collection of the artist. Left panel: "Appropriate Goods," 243.8 x 259 cm., photograph by Harry Foster, courtesy of the Canadian Museum of Civilization; center panel: "Owning Your Cultural Information," 243.8 x 213.3 cm., photograph by Sam Woo, courtesy of the artist; right panel: "History Repeating Itself," 243.8 x 259 cm., photograph by Sam Woo, courtesy of the artist.

Nora Naranjo-Morse, *Flat Fetishes (right)*
1990, Santa Clara micaceous clay (left, 30.4 x 15.2 cm; right, 35.5 x 20.3 cm.) Private collection. Photograph by Mary Fredenburgh, courtesy of the photographer.

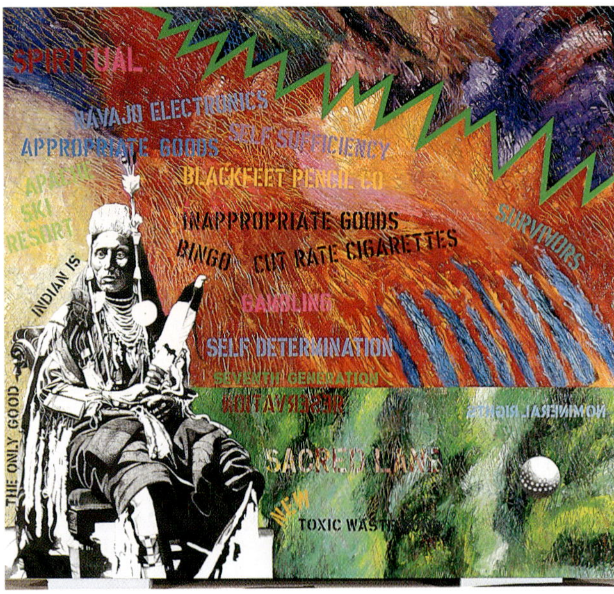

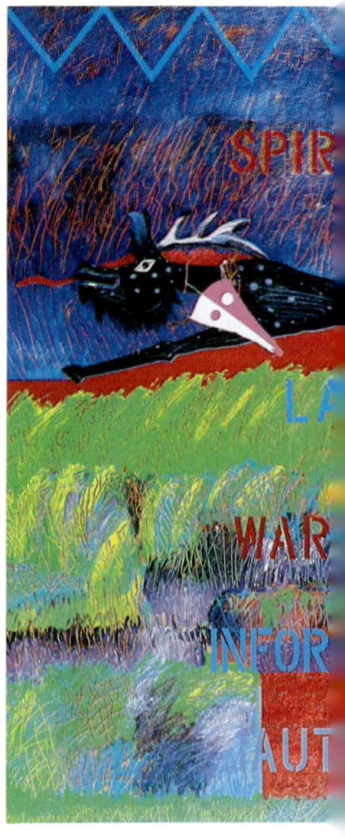

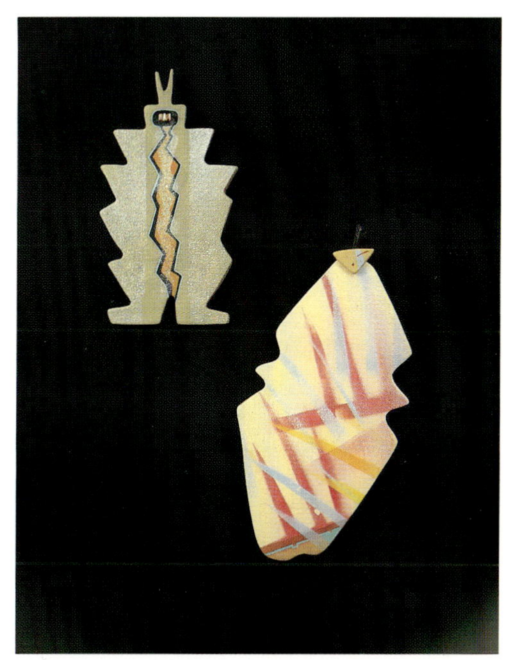

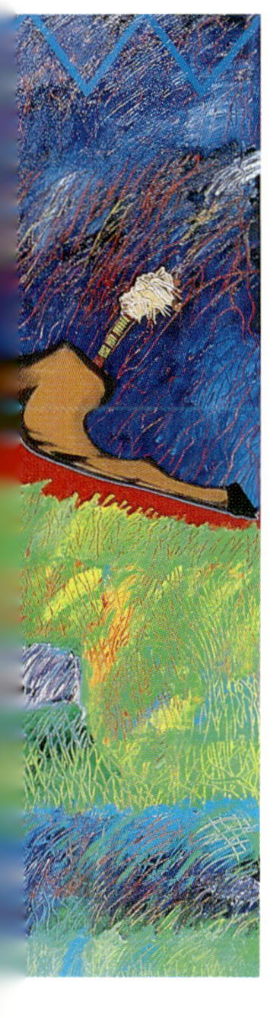

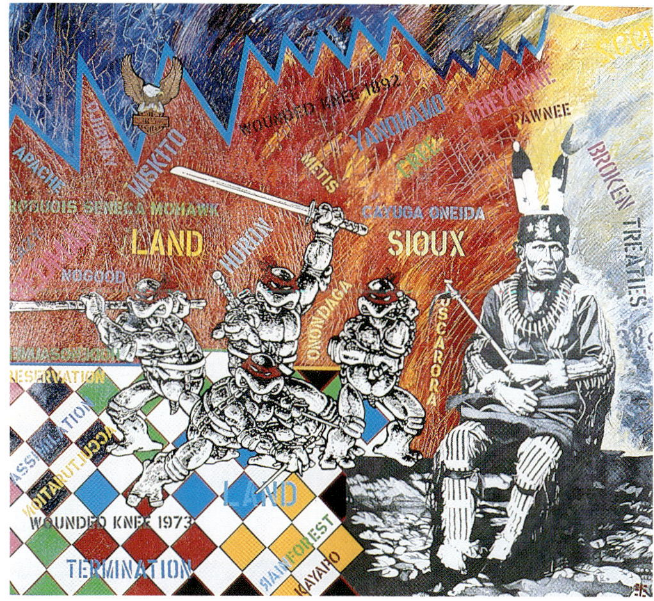
WOUNDED KNEE 1892
OJIBWAY
MISKITO
APACHE
YANOMAMO
CHEYENNE
PAWNEE
METIS
CREE
BROKEN
TREATIES
IROQUOIS SENECA MOHAWK
CAYUGA ONEIDA
LAND
SIOUX
HURON
NOGOOD
ONONDAGA
USCARORA
RESERVATION
ASSIMILATION
WOUNDED KNEE 1973
LAND
RAINFOREST
TERMINATION
KAYAPO

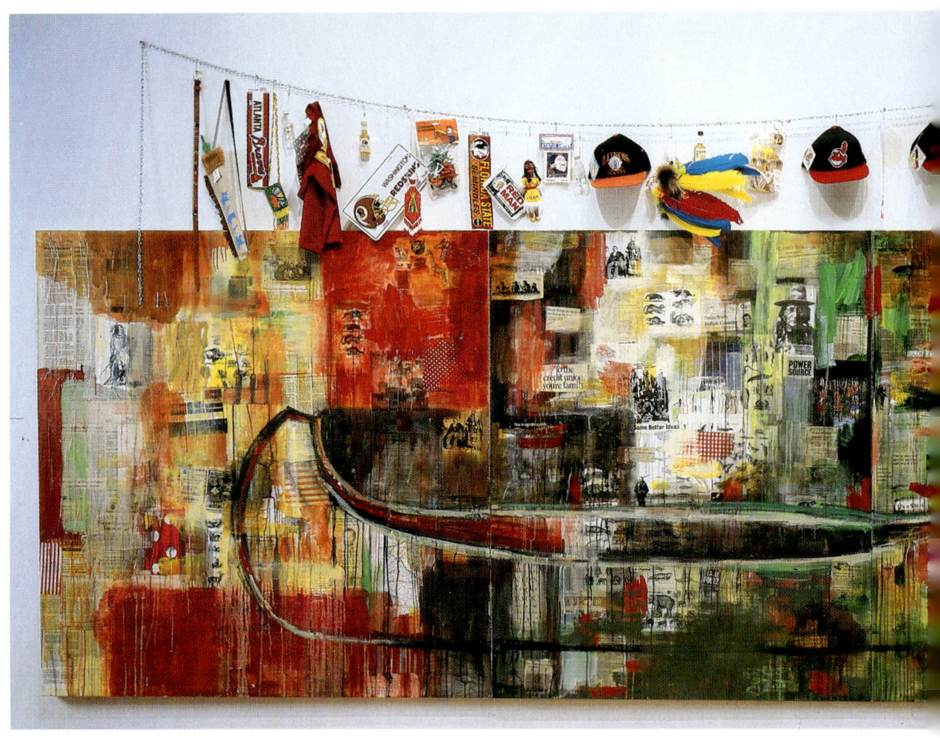

JAUNE QUICK-TO-SEE SMITH, *Trade (Gifts for Trading Land with White People)* 1992, oil, mixed media, collage on canvas, objects, 152.4 x 431.8 cm. Collection of the Chrysler Museum, Norfolk, Virginia. Photograph courtesy of the Steinbaum Krauss Gallery, New York, New York.

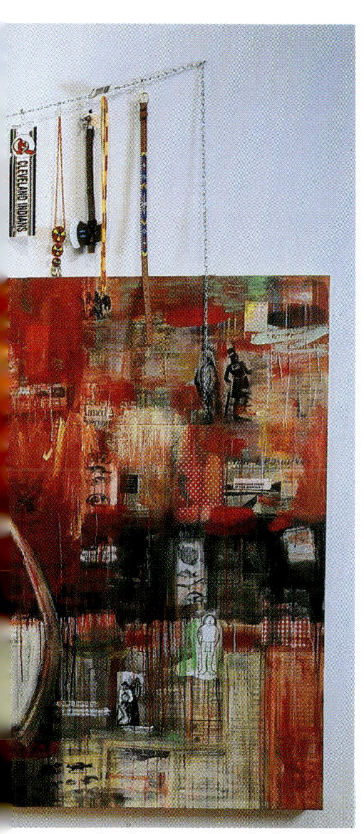

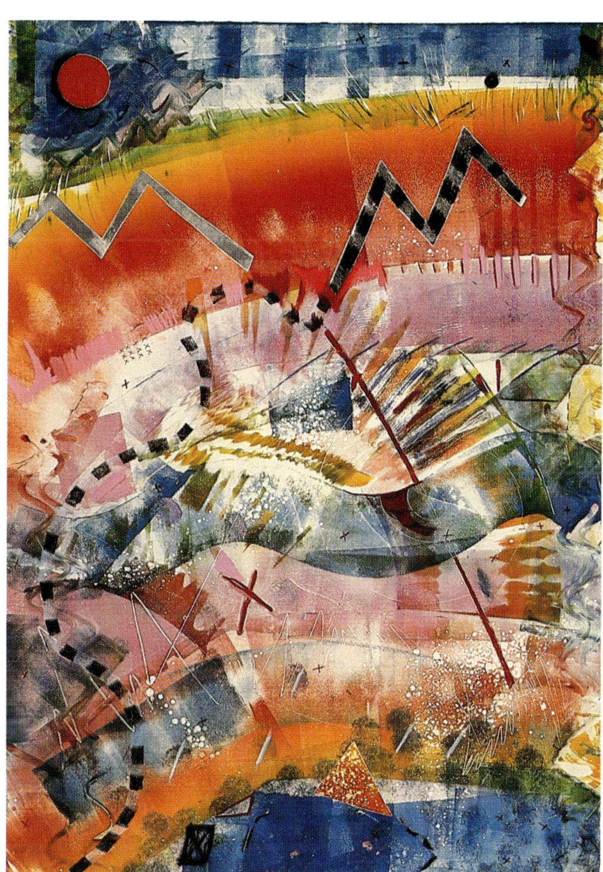

SUSAN STEWART, from the *Awé* series
1990, monotype, 105.4 x 72.6 cm. Collection of the artist. Photograph copyright 1990 Courtney Frisse; from the exhibition *Our Land/Ourselves*, University at Albany, State University of New York.

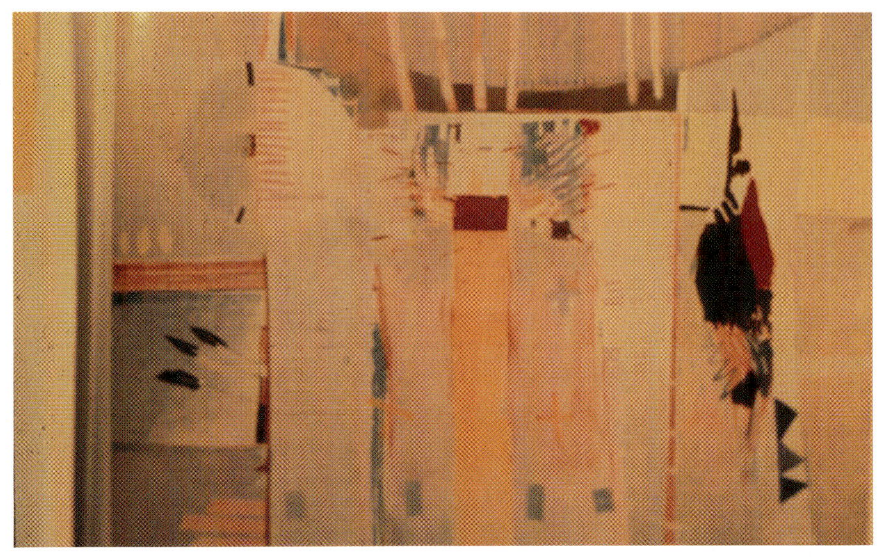

FRANK TUTTLE, *The Abundance of Things*
1984, mixed media, 81.2 x 106.6 cm. Collection of Kathleen Kelly, Sacramento, California. Photograph by Frank Tuttle, courtesy of the artist.

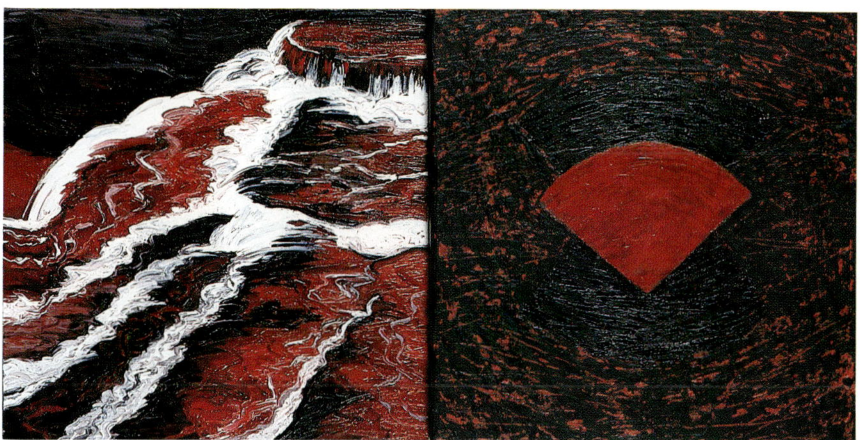

Kay WalkingStick, *The Abyss*
1989, acrylic and oil on canvas, 91.4 x 182.8 x 9.1 cm. Collection of the artist. Photograph by Jon Reiss, courtesy of the artist.

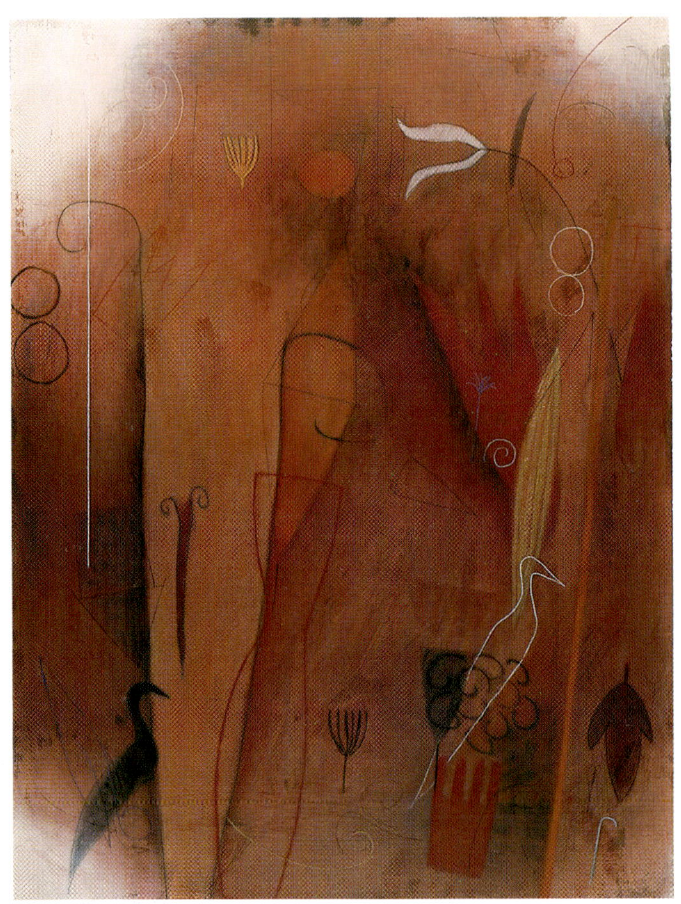

Emmi Whitehorse, *Untitled*
1991, oil on paper on canvas, 129.5 x 100.3 cm.
Collection of the Wheelwright Museum of the American Indian, Santa Fe, New Mexico. Photograph courtesy of the LewAllen Gallery, Santa Fe, New Mexico.

But I think that for contemporary art you have a double-edged sword. One is that galleries are going to show you, yes, but because they need to make money they might have a tendency to direct you. If you have something that is new, in the sense that it hasn't been exposed, then it's hard to get that opening. On the other hand, galleries can establish markets, by bringing back the use of natural materials in rug weaving, for example. They can promote a certain kind or level of art. But people themselves can get together and do that, and people sometimes do.

LA: You raise a point that you've written about in an essay, which is the importance of the bond between the traditional and the contemporary arts. How would you describe this bond or connection?

FL: I think that probably the best way for me to say that is, because I am a traditional singer and dancer, I can fall back on experience to draw some kind of symbolism or subject matter that is directly related to ceremonial activities or to activities which are cultural in nature. So in that sense the base is always natural, it's always real for me and it's not like someone looking back in history and trying to bring out a subject that is not relevant and living. So the connection and the validity of that connection is that immediacy and the living nature of the cultural reference.

LA: What I find interesting in that regard is that you're also an ethnographer. You wrote the section on the Wintu for the California volume of the Smithsonian's *Handbook of North American Indians*. Was that a difficult role, to step out of the living culture and objectively present it?

FL: Not really, because of what I had done in the late sixties and the early seventies. Early on the Wintu got reestablished by taking this land and organizing the tribe. I was one of the council members and we helped establish not only the rules but helped get the permit from the BIA after five years of struggling through the federal and state bureaucracies.[3] So in a way I had my foot in the history, my toes anyway, you might say, and I was interested in trying to put something down. I wanted to approach it much more creatively, start out with a myth, but that wasn't the way it could be done. The other part is that I had a lot of the references already because of my work on the council. So I didn't do that much original work. What I did was just reemphasize the historical material with more contemporary material.

You have to realize that I have a master's in ethnology and I've worked as an anthropologist. Also, I was working on my own tribe, so it wasn't that difficult in that sense. I had talked to many of the elders already, had been for a number of years, and what I found out by going into the research was that what they were saying was true. I had always had that feeling, anyway, but unless it's written down, the white society doesn't accept it. So my involvement in the research—historical society publications, unpublished manuscripts, the [John] Harrington papers, things in the Smithsonian—was enlightening in that it reinforced the oral tradition, and for me that was the greatest thing I could get out of it. Obviously there are a lot of other things that need to be said about our history, so in the back of my mind is a book I'd like to do.

LA: You were trained as an ethnographer. Were you also a painter?

FL: I was always a painter. In fact, when I was a little guy I always did art and was always involved in it. I remember when I was really young my mother colored a picture of a marine. I was probably five years old. She colored it and it was magic. When I went to Indian school in Stewart, Nevada, you had to do art, and I was good at that. When I started college I said that I was going to be an artist. I had from B to D in everything else, but had an A in art. I forgot most of the other stuff.

LA: But you're known, of course, as an artist, not as an ethnographer. Were you balancing the two fields?

FL: I sort of balanced. There's never been a question of choosing one over the other. I always chose art. I did the other because it was the most convenient way to get a Master's. I couldn't afford to go to art school for the M.F.A. I always learned on my own and just worked like a mad dog, and I think most artists, if they're real serious, they'll work morning, noon, and night. That's what I did while I was in school. It was something that I just wanted to do and had to do. In fact, when I was at Chico State in '56 we had painting classes in the Bidwell Mansion, way up on the top floor. At night I'd climb up the trellises and crawl up on the roof, shinny up and go into the studio and paint all night. Finally they figured it out and gave me a key. That was the kind of student I was in art. I needed to do it and I just did it.

LA: What were some of the influences on the evolution of your work?

FL: One of the important things was growing up in Northern California, with the mountains jutting up, huge, great big mountains. To the north of us is Mount Shasta in Dunsmuir, and when I stayed with my grandmother in Castella there was Castle Crags right outside our door. I remember that majesty and power and that difference of being down below and looking up at those great grand images of power. That was something. I had an affinity for landscape and for that connection, and at the same time understood the puniness of human beings compared to the majesty of those mountains. You have to realize that at that time in Northern California the streams were not polluted, they were not dammed. When I was a little boy we swam and fished the river. I think that had a bearing on my sense of what I wanted to do. And I'm sure this happens to most artists: you see certain things that you'd like to correct, or certain things that you'd like to emphasize that are not being done. Even as a young person you try to do those things, and if you're inclined artistically, that allows you to be yourself more naturally than something else that you're not inclined to. Another thing is when you're going to Indian school, you're all set in a great big dorm, and one of the things that made me unique was the fact that I did art and it allowed me to get out of school and do other stuff. And, of course, you're always learning. You have an individual vision, not so much in the spiritual sense because at that age you're not aware of that, but in a psychic sense of what is going on, a color sense. You're not even worrying about mechanical skills like you would if you got a formal education. You just do it.

Another part would have to be my family, like I was saying. I can remember different circumstances when people were putting down Indians. I knew that was not the truth. I lived part of the time with my granny, and granny was not anything like they said and granny was an Indian, so therefore when someone said something I knew wasn't true, there was no way they were going to make me believe it, and I think kids can realize that. I know I did. And I know a lot of people that have that sense of truth but maybe they're afraid to go back to their pasts. But I knew mine pretty firmly. At least some of it.

LA: Do you think that feeling of certainty about reality is still possible for youngsters, or has American society disrupted the traditional home too much?

FL: I think it's still possible to have that solid upbringing. But what you point out is the fact that today's society is so fractionalized and impacted by stimuli of all kinds and a misreading of what life is all about that it's very difficult. I've seen college students who have a skewed sense of reality because they have not been grounded in what life is really about. I'm not saying that I know what it's about, but I know that mass media does not tell you the truth. That means that there has to be another place where we can get it and it has to be from individuals we're close to and who can show by their lifestyle and their living on a day-to-day level what life means, by their living and doing and confronting.

But maybe you don't always get the best example of what a person can be, if they are drinking or running around or whatever. If you can wade through, though, and somehow get to the point where you have an opportunity to look back, then you can begin to understand the pressure and the situation that those people had to struggle through, and then you can also appreciate that they survived and maintained. I think there's a tendency to downgrade people without understanding their situation. I think of all the people I went to school with. Hey, these guys are all the medicine people, the healers, the singers, all the people who are up and working now. So as bad as you have it, you've got to maintain.

LA: Two major influences have been, then, the land of Northern California, and your family. Have any particular artists or other individuals been influential? I think some critics have mentioned Francis Bacon [the English painter, 1910–1992].

FL: No, no. I have no affinity to Bacon. I know who he is. What you're talking about is a piece, *Shaman*, I think, from 1974. It is a piece that superficially looks like it might have an affinity to Bacon. What I was doing in that painting was interpreting what medicine people told me about getting information, the idea of being able to relax and overcome your body and a number of levels of physical limits and go to another level. So what I was trying to do was get away from the clothing that the spirit wears and get to the base of the spiritual. So it reads that way. But if you look at my paintings you'll see that I don't follow one type of art or style.

LA: You've written in an essay that your work is more realistic than abstract. Would you say, though, that you're not depicting literal reality but that you're exploring a more spiritual type of reality?

FL: Painting is different in that sense. You have to realize that I've been showing professionally since about '58 or '59. My first solo show was in 1960. One of the things I find is that it's easy to do a realistic painting in the sense that it reflects reality in a documentation sort of way. When I do a painting I may in fact use that aspect of reality as a reference. But depending on what I'm trying to show, although it may have an element of or a reference to reality, it would have its own reality beyond the documentation. That doesn't say very much in words, but what I'm saying is that I transform the documentary or visual reality. See, I'm a traditional dancer, and if I do a painting of a dance it doesn't do too much for me as a painter to replicate the dance literally, because the reality of the dance is the participation in it. Therefore, I try to think about the purpose of the dance, like the color or the feeling of it, and I'll paint that. So the sense of reality I'm talking about is the conceptual reality of an event, and as I say, that's not to eliminate realism but to incorporate realism, and sometimes that can be very abstract. So what I do is paint the whole range from reality to the more abstract.

LA: You're a traditional dancer. How does that bear on your work?

FL: One of the things we were talking about was being young and having an influence as you were coming up. I learned about art and began to work at it and found that it was important to me. I first painted landscapes, because I was in it, I had a feeling for it, and I liked it. And as I became more and more involved in tradition, I started to incorporate more and more of that into the paintings. So there's a place where you are — and I'm sure that this happens to a lot of people — in time and space and what's going on around you, your environment, your circumstances, your situation, and it puts an imprint on you and on what you're doing. So when I write, I might write with reference to what's happening to me; when I paint I will make reference to some of the things around me, which might be a ceremony or beings in a ceremony or a dance. I might make reference to some words in a song. Experiencing the tradition is something that's very current with me.

LA: Do you have certain color motifs or uses of color?

FL: I make use of a predominant color or range of color that the viewer is not aware of until you look back at a number of works after several years. Sometimes I run through a series where I might like red and do a whole bunch of paintings that have red as the predominant tone of the painting. And then I might go through and have lots of things that are blue. And I've had things that are earth-toned. These colors often come out of an experience or a memory. I consider myself a colorist, basically, if I had to come down to one definition to explain my involvement with color. Whether I'm doing a painting with a predominant color scheme or doing something that's polychromatic in the best sense of the word, I always come back to areas of the painting and try to saturate them with an off-tone of the same color, or complement it with whatever it is, and then what happens is there begins to develop a richness that I like. And if I find that I need to tone it down, then I might start thinking, "What is this? What am I doing? What does this painting mean?" That thinking process might determine some colors, and the thrust of the painting may shift.

I did paintings of the four directions and started out with the idea that I'm going to do four triptychs of four feet by nine feet each. I finished one of the four and it never did anything for me. I was painting Mount Shasta, the North Spirit Place, and I thought, well, the natural format is four, so each painting became four feet by four feet, and the predominant colors were red, white, blue, and yellow and gold. Those colors were of the directions, so that concept of the symbolism of the four directions with the appropriate colors determined where I was going to go. It did not determine how I would work, just what I was going to work on. Doing one thing puts a limit on it. I'd rather just say I'm going to do a painting and see wherever it goes.

LA: It sounds like most of the time your painting is a discovery process.

FL: Again, that's one of those things that depend on the circumstances. About ninety-seven percent of my work has been done out of my imagination, and I like to work that way because what happens is that you're allowed the flexibility of creating on the run. It's more exciting, it's much more fun. It's a little scarier than planning something out, but at the same time you can deal with serendipity. You might want to put a wash on or take it off, and so something emerges. I'd say most of my stuff has gone that way. Other times, though, but not so much, I'll do something that I had in mind and that I had thought about. I did a painting one time that was about thirty by forty inches and I thought of that painting for maybe three and a half months, and I finished it in one day. I'm quite active; I can say that. I always have three or four paintings going and I always have a combination of techniques going. I'll work in pastel, collage, acrylics.

LA: And it came out pretty much as you expected?

FL: Yeah, but it was more of an abstract piece. What I did was I dealt with the idea. When you paint, you objectify as soon as you put on a stroke, whether it's a free thing or a wash; you have objectified it, so it's limited. That always happens when you put something down, but it will also allow you to take the concept and go back and do maybe ten paintings on the theme. You can never run out of things to do, but in that one instant you begin to discover where you're going on a new piece. On the four-directions pieces, I finished them and of course I've gone back and worked on that theme again.

LA: Do you conceive of works in a series, as a total experience of the subject, or is each painting separate in and of itself?

FL: That becomes a semantic thing; it explains but also doesn't explain the art experience. One of the things that happen, though, is when you're doing art you might find that the theme is so large or is of such a nature that one painting doesn't capture the complete reality that the subject expresses, so you must go back and do several. So in a way a theme results with the series or the grouping. On the other hand, in most instances I don't do a whole lot of subject matter, so if you look at my work you'll find that my work deals with nature; that still continues, the dance subjects continue, the sacred imagery continues, the specific beings in a ceremony continue. So I find that I'm not doing a wide breadth of topics, but I'm approaching them differently. I might be doing graphics, I might be doing collage, I might be doing engravings, and they're different. They are not so close to the other ones that they are copies of the same thing. They're different kinds of things, so in a way the theme—and there is a theme—would be something I'm aware of but I don't ever sit down and calculate it. For instance, if you were to take death as a theme important to you, what are you going to do with it? Are you going to talk about the burial aspect, the life after death, are you going to talk about the way that you relate to the spirit realm in tradition, that there is no death, or are you going to relate to the cessation of the life force in all things, which is the other side of it? So just analyzing it that way you can see the variables. And most people who do art probably have a number of things that they do. When I hear that an artist has dried up, that they don't want to do it, then what I think is that they need to just relax and they need to look back out.

LA: Not force things?

FL: Right, 'cause it's all there, everything's there. All you have to do is look out the window.

LA: N. Scott Momaday has talked about writing essentially one story, with each new work just continuing or extending that one story.[4]

FL: That's exactly what it is. You yourself are putting little pieces of the story together and then as you look at it, in time you find out it's there, that's who you are.

LA: You mentioned earlier the sense of space you experienced at Castle Crags, the feeling of loomingness and smallness. Does that come into your work at all? I had that feeling in the 1981 *Deer Rattle/Deer Dancer*, with the looming figure that dominates the frame.

FL: That's a good question, because it is something that I'm aware of, and there is a tendency for people who want to make an impact to do large pieces, and in a way I might have tried for that. But pure canvas size is not necessarily a determining factor in the power of a painting. Size is obviously going to catch your imagination by the power of presence, but a well-executed work is also going to draw you in close if it's small so you can relate to it, so I tend to think of that, too. But the other thing when I paint, regarding the idea of the composition and where the image fits on the plane of the canvas, and what I've done over a period of time, is that I've found that the images that carry the weight and have the best impact for me are the ones concentrated to a dominant form, no matter what the image is. So in thinking of that and doing that I just sort of naturally begin to compose the composition in the center of the frame and then fill up most of the space by having material around it. The painting done in that way can be very small or it can be very large. I feel most comfortable with a three-by-four-foot size. I can work with that; I don't have to try to fill it up or anything. It sort of feels real natural. Most of mine are that size, right around there. I like the smaller size.

LA: Your engravings are very small and precise.

FL: They are. They're eight-by-ten-inch wood engravings. I use maple wood and have settled on Japanese cold-press tools. They are the best. I tried all sorts of tools, but I found that I could get one about fourteen inches long with a very sharp cut on it, and with that size I could go through maple like butter.

LA: You've done a number of wood engravings, like *Mt. Shasta*, *Sacred Fire*, and *Big Head Spirit* [each 1987]. How closely does the physical existence of Mount Shasta, for example, connect with the spiritual?

FL: In this particular series, which came out of *The World Is a Gift* [a twenty-year retrospective at the Wheelwright Museum, Santa Fe, 1988], I thought of my relatives and I thought of the people who told me the different stories. I have been to all of the places I depict, and what was going through my mind was not only the experience of being there, but also the experience of what those places meant. All those places and things have relevance to the tribe as a whole, and then there are the individual relationships to those places. Mount Shasta was always important because as I found out later, my uncle — it's actually my great-uncle, but I always call him uncle — had painted Mount Shasta in 1905 and 1908, and you didn't have too many Indian painters at that time, and you don't have them in Northern California, because they just weren't part of society. But he painted, so it's real good. And I had already had a connection with Mount Shasta before I knew this. I used to do mountain climbing, and four of us set up the search and rescue for the sheriff's department in Butte County. We went to the mountain and came down with a dead person who had crashed into some rocks. We came down but had to go up again, but at that time I was packing seventy-five-pound bags, and I'm not really tall, about five feet three inches and at that time probably about 130 pounds, so seventy-five pounds is pretty heavy, and I ended up with bruises all over. It's one thing to see Shasta from a distance — it's very big and beautiful and has amazing presence — but to get up on it and trudge around emphasizes the largeness. When you get to around twelve thousand to thirteen thousand feet the thin air will slow you down. At twelve thousand people get sleepy and just sort of pass out along the side of the trail, or you'll hit Misery Ridge at thirteen thousand and lose your lunch or whatever. It's about a one-hundred-yard pitch at about a forty-degree angle and it's a real killer. So anyhow, knowing some stories about it and experiencing it in all weather and knowing the traditional aspect, visiting it for a sacred obligation, I was relating to the mountain on several levels.

LA: Casual viewers would not relate to many of these levels. They would just see a nice engraving of Mount Shasta.

FL: Well, yeah, not only that, but I remember there was a book that was published in 1990, *Sacred Mountains of the World*, and in it they pointed out that Mount Shasta was sacred to the tribes around it, but it's not sacred to them anymore because they've all been killed off or died off or they don't participate in the ceremonies. But I doubt that there was any effort to talk to any tribal groups. Our medicine woman has a specific ceremony that she does, and every year for years I have gone to the mountain in a sacred way. Since the early 1960s I have taken my boy there. Why don't people look at the material in my uncle's book, published in 1966 and compiled by Marcelle Masson, called *A Bag of Bones* [*Legends of the Wintu Indians of Northern California*], or *The Mt. Shasta Story*, by A. F. Eichorn, Sr., where my Uncle Grant makes reference to his dad in 1848? Too many people make frivolous claims and try to eliminate a part of the American Indian experience.

LA: How can the non-Indian viewer get a fuller appreciation about places, then?

FL: There's a real fundamental way and that is to go to the place that you have in mind and stay there, be of the place and listen to it and watch the seasons come over it and watch the sun come up and go down and watch the shifting shadows and listen to the snow crumple and roll. We vicariously read a book which talks about the thing but we don't really know what it is, so if you can go and actually feel that—and by doing that you're going to be cold, you're going to be in the wind, you'll have heat, you'll get thirsty, you will have tested your humanness, know your human qualities—then you will realize you have an affinity for the life force that the mountain is participating in.

I'm not saying that you live it twenty-four hours a day. Just experience the actual reality, that's all. Granted, I buy books like mad, that's my downfall, and I can appreciate paintings because I'm a painter. But I think that if you do certain things you'll get some affinity. I think that having done some mountain climbing, when I read about the Himalayas or Everest or wherever, I can appreciate it, and yet at the same time I don't need to be there to relate to it.

LA: Do you consider your paintings, in approach or final product, in any way a ceremony? You once wrote that art creates order through the use of symbols. Does your work create or maintain an orderly universe?

FL: Yeah, I think that what I mean is that there is a multilevel of experience in approaching a painting and giving a reality. Part of it has to do with objectifying a thing; whatever it is, you can now look at it in a different way. I think that that's one level of doing it. The other part has to do with defining an individual thought or feeling in a more personal way. The first thing has to do with social commentary kinds of stuff; the other has to do with clarification of what a person's choices or options are.

Then of course there's another level of painting. It's whatever we want to call it, a process or a solution, and I look at that level this way: visualizing, or looking, or searching. If I'm doing that kind of painting, it might be that I have in mind a person who is sick and I might try to paint something that relates to their healing. Those paintings are not done in the same way, even though they might look the same on the surface. The approach is much different, considerations are much different, the ideas behind them are much deeper. It's hard to sit around and talk about that aspect, because people will say that all Indian art is mystical and magical and religious, and it's not. But there is that element in some of the work, and I would say that if you were to try and explain that, people will put you in that category. Not every artist is a shaman or a magician, and people from the outside are all jumping up and down and putting you there.

LA: Your art has been referred to as shamanistic. Do you feel your works are connected to a shamanistic tradition?

FL: I would say that there are probably some elements in some of them but not a whole bunch. I think that more than anything I'm sensitive to and want to maintain the positive, and in order to do that you have to look at fundamental things of hope in lifestyles or feelings or thoughts, which in past instances have been taken and given between whites and the shamans. So there's a mutually shared concern there. An artist as an individual does what he does; it's his painting and his singing and his dancing and his traditional work or whatever. That is their experience and that is who they are, and if that also accommodates a healing and a striving for well-being and a centering and an affirming tradition within the culture, and if it helps to explain some things that other people are not aware of, that's fine. In other words, if you go through life and are not committed to it and are not involved in it, what you say will not have very much meaning. So you do art because you have a commitment to life, you have a feeling about things, you hate something or you love something, but you're never indifferent. You are always someone who is committed, and so what if no one likes what you do? If it's something that you are being honest about, that's the validity. But that needn't be shamanistic.

LA: So that's another misconception that people have about Native art, that it's all shamanistic or spiritual?

FL: Yeah, that's what I was talking about earlier. People who are involved in traditional activities may be involved in that aspect, but it's indirect; it gives them a foundation for life, but it's not necessarily in their paintings or other artwork. The spiritual is something that Indian people do all the time. I think that's something that white people don't do, so they have a hard time comprehending how a person can be in and part of a strong tradition and yet not be what the outsider says you have to be. No, no. The Indian people and other people under stress or threat have been able to accommodate a multiple level of things at the same time.

The non-Indian approaches things in a fractionalized way. They separate their jobs from their hobby, their hobbies and their jobs from their entertainment and whatever, so what you find is a person concentrating on that one thing, then switching to the other thing, then to the third or fourth thing, and none of it's unified, which creates all sorts of problems. It has to do with approaching life in a nonholistic way. So what I'm trying to say is that an Indian, even though he or she may not accomplish things for a lot of reasons, fundamentally has an awareness that a unified approach to life is much more satisfying than one that is fragmented.

LA: The course you're teaching has political ramifications, but I don't sense an overt political dimension to your artwork.

FL: There probably is some, but as a whole no, because I am involved as a tribal council person and in public lectures, so that's how I get my comments on society out. Right now I happen to be on the policymaking board on campus for burial repatriation, so I'm involved in the reality of political things and I don't need to do it in my art. I want to emphasize something more in my art, like ceremony, tradition, culture, other kinds of things like that.

Every once in a while I get off on a social commentary. I remember one I did in 1968 when an Eskimo settlement was made and they [the government] gave Eskimos and Aleuts 110 million acres and 89 million dollars or some such, and said, "That represents our benevolence." But then they turned around and took over one of the areas where they were drilling for oil and leased it for about 120 million. This just put the whole thing in perspective for me, the inequity. So I did a painting dealing with it and made reference back to treaties or agreements that the traditional people, the Aleut and Inuit people, had made, and then I painted about what was going on, wrote down the numbers. I was real unhappy with the situation because it was so basically unethical. So occasionally I will do some social commentaries. I don't remember the title of this particular piece but I traded it with Joe Sunugetuk for one of his prints.

LA: Could we discuss a 1991 work of yours, *New World Flower?* It seems to be more abstract than some of your other work. Could you talk about the genesis and development of that piece?

FL: I have always worked abstract and semirealistic, you know, that kind of imagery, but I don't always show all the stuff together. I don't show it consistently year after year, but I have shown a number of things that are totally abstract, with no reference to what we would call an Indian image. I was working on some collage pieces made out of old discarded monoprints, because I always use one hundred percent rag paper and good ink, so I thought, "Why throw this stuff away? I'll use it." So I had been saving a lot of assorted pieces of old monoprints. I was working on a number of different projects, as usual, but I got off on a tangent and started getting really excited about composition and form design, all the real fundamental things that get you excited when you're working, moving things around and manipulating things. So I began to lay down some monoprints that I had ripped up and started painting things out, and the result was that I did four images on paper which were very abstract. And in this sense, when I'm talking about a New World flower, I'm sort of thinking about the idea that the New World and the flower are the new nature. See, in the flower is the example of nature and then at the same time the theme of wildflowers, which are things that traditional people in Northern California relate to. And I'm sure that this must happen in other tribal areas, but in the north we named the women by the wildflowers, and we have a ceremony for the plants and the flowers that come up, and we wear them, so

I'm using the wildflower on a number of levels. I would say that the first level, though, was having fun in making a composition, having fun with forms, having fun with using gold leaf. And it's a real mixed-media piece.

LA: In regard to getting Indian art out there for people to see, is there a problem of getting into the mainstream and perhaps losing what is unique, and of being classified as just an ethnic artist? Is it a "damned if you do, damned if you don't" situation?

FL: I think it's both of those things. What happens is that no matter how good your art is, if you have that label there's going to be the tendency for that label to restrict you. Yet, at the same time, if Indian art shows can be at quality places, like the Heard, maybe people will start looking. So it's a mixed bag. Basically, though, I think that when you isolate people from the context of the field that they're in, their work does suffer from special treatment, and it tends to limit the exposure or the feeling or the value of that work. But Indian people have been in that bag for so long it's not going to make that much difference to us, and that's why I say we need to have the very best writing, the very best painting: because our validation as a people is ourselves. Then those who are lucky enough to see the work—and there are increasing numbers—will help expose the validity of all the Native American arts, whatever they are, whether it is traditional art, or clear down to playwriting and acting. All these arts carry an important message to the society at large, and that is in spite of all the negative that has happened to Indian people, they have survived, they have maintained, and have done it with quality and sensitivity and with a knowledge that other societies do not have. I think that's important.

SELECTED EXHIBITIONS

"Ancestral Memories" (1992), group exhibition, Falkirk Cultural Center, San Rafael, CA.

"Frank LaPena: A Retrospective" (1992), solo exhibition, C. N. Gorman Museum, University of California, Davis, CA.

"Light on the Subject" (1991), group exhibition, American Indian Contemporary Arts, San Francisco, CA.

"Our Land/Ourselves" (1991–93), group traveling exhibition, University Art Gallery, State University of New York, Albany, NY.

"Shared Visions" (1991–93), group traveling exhibition, Heard Museum, Phoenix, AZ.

"California Indian Shamanism" (1990), group exhibition, C. E. Smith Museum, California State University, Hayward, CA.

"Stars Swimming" (1989), solo exhibition, Galeria Posada, Sacramento, CA.

"Frank LaPena: A Twenty-Year Retrospective" (1988), solo exhibition, Wheelwright Museum of the American Indian, Santa Fe, NM.

"The Extension of Tradition" (1985), group traveling exhibition, Crocker Art Museum, Sacramento, CA.

SELECTED BIBLIOGRAPHY

"Frank LaPena." *Capital University Journal* [California State University, Sacramento], Fall 1992, pp. 12–13.

LaPena, Frank. "Dancing for the Earth." *Pacific Discovery* 45, 1 (Winter 1992): 42–47.

Frank LaPena: Wintu Artist and Traditionalist [videotape]. Fair Oaks, CA: Theo-Blount Productions, 1988.

LaPena, Frank. *The World Is a Gift*. Santa Fe, NM: Wheelwright Museum of the American Indian, 1988.

——, and Janice T. Driesbach, eds. *The Extension of Tradition: Contemporary Northern California Native American Art in Cultural Perspective*. Sacramento, CA: Crocker Art Museum, 1985.

LaPena, Frank. "A Native American's View of Rock Art." In *Ancient Images on Stone*, edited and compiled by Jo Anne Van Tilburg. Los Angeles, CA: Rock Art Archive, Institute of Archaeology, UCLA, 1983, pp. 25–27.

——. "Untitled," "I Am a Stone of Many Colors," "Wrapped Hair Bundles," "The Year of Winter," "Waiting for a Second Time." In *Songs from This Earth on Turtle's Back*, edited by Joseph Bruchac. Greenfield Center, NY: Greenfield Review Press, 1983, pp. 135–40.

Indian as Artist, Artist as Indian [videotape]. Ames, IA: Iowa State University, 1982.

LaPena, Frank. "Wintu." In *Handbook of North American Indians*. Vol. 8, *California*, edited by Robert Heizer. Washington, DC: Smithsonian Institution, 1978, pp. 324–40.

Carm Little Turtle

Apache-Tarahumara

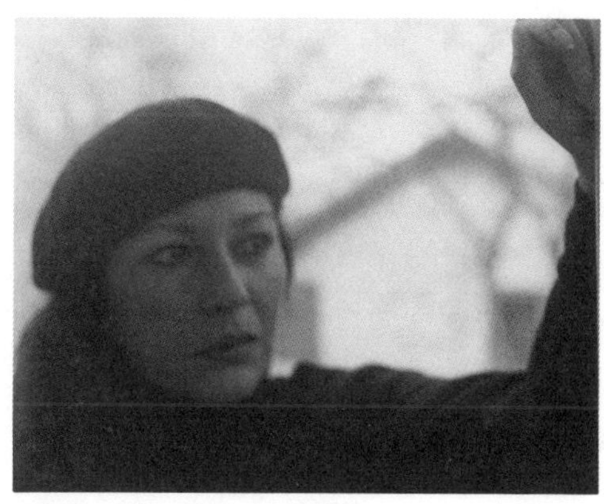

There is a deceptive sense of calm and stasis in Carm Little Turtle's photographs, where impossible moments are brought to life, brought to reality from the realm of the imagination. In many of her photographs time is stopped and laws of physics are disregarded. The world becomes light and image, and the act of seeing and perceiving unlooses the viewer from the everyday, from the expected. In *Daydreamer* (1984), for example, a figure is suspended in space halfway between the frame and what is beyond. Set in the characteristic Southwestern landscape of much of her work, this piece invites the viewer to consider the interplay between dream and reality. She invests the ordinary and mundane with deeper resonances of meaning. *Parasol* (1983) is a delicately understated photograph that presents a suggestive world within a world. Recognition of the dual images is an unsettling, eerie experience.

This duality is often central to Little Turtle's work. It is seen in terms of the images themselves, or in what the images represent, or in the tension between motion and stillness, between action and repose. This duality also functions on the level of male and female relationships. She writes that "the rugged terrain of northern Arizona or the mountains and clouds of northern New Mexico may serve as the backdrop to the politics played out, symbolically, between men and women. The frothy veil of sex, food and money is the symbolic coverlet rent by men and that [which] women continually amend. Areas [of the photographs] selectively handpainted only serve to heighten the schism."[1]

The way in which she uses light and manipulates color by painting on the image contributes to the overall atmosphere of her work. She is able to transform her subjects through careful structuring before shooting and by use of color after shooting. In this way she synthesizes the reality of the photograph with the personal connotations of color.

Many of Little Turtle's photographs are meditations on personal history, which can be in the form of memory, as in *Parasol*, or in the realm of fantasy, as in *Daydreamer*, or familial, as in *Iron Horse* (1990). Other works, like *Coming Soon* (1990) and *Grandmother Rodeo Spectator* (1991), depict scenes of life caught in action and have a spontaneous feel to them.

Carm Little Turtle was born in 1952 in Santa Maria, California, and is of Apache, Tarahumara, and Mexican heritage. In addition to being a still photographer, she has also worked as a producer and photographer for Shenandoah Films in Arcata, California. She is also an operating room nurse, having received her R.N. training from Navajo Community College, from which she graduated in 1978. She currently works in one of Albuquerque's major hospitals.

Little Turtle has been steadily exhibiting her work since 1981. Her work is held in the permanent collections of the Western Arts Americana Library of Princeton University, the Southwest Museum in Los Angeles, and the Southern Plains Indian Museum in Anadarko, Oklahoma.

We talked in her home in Albuquerque in July 1991.

LA: How would you describe your photographs?

CLT: My work has been described as "visual poems," and I think that puts it all together, because they are a dreamy, conceptual type of photograph. I always look for the aesthetic first, but if it also makes a statement, then I've been really successful. I try to create a dreamlike world where there are different props, where the faces of the models are not always noticeable. I try to use landscape behind the props and models, which is almost surrealistic, though. But I'll paint selectively on the work while other parts are left black and white, which adds to the surreal effect.

LA: They do have an ethereal look, like *Taos Still* [1982] and *Day Dreamer* [1985]. How do you go about structuring your imagery in terms of subject matter and in your use of light and color?

CLT: I structure my images very intentionally. I usually sketch out the basic positions of the models and the ideas. A title sometimes comes out at the same time as the sketching process. Then I'll pick a location and try several different positions of the models in the environment I want. There might be some improvisation by the models, but basically the shoot is based on the sketch I drew. I know what I want to accomplish, and when the painting comes about, that's very intentional, too. I have the colors in my mind, and I'll just mix and blend my palette until I get what I want. The painting is very deliberate. I've tried to get spontaneous, but, well, I'm basically direct and intentional. I usually only paint the textiles in the image; I don't paint the whole surface area. Some artists will paint on the whole image, but that strikes me as overdoing it at times, using neon colors, for example, to support a weak image. I leave the landscape itself and the skin color alone, but I do sepia-tone them.

LA: You mention that your work is highly planned, but do you ever discover a new way of approaching the image during a shoot? Do you do any other kinds of photography?

CLT: I do three different styles during a shoot. The most visible style, the one that gets exhibited most, is the one with the models and props in a chosen environment, but I also take shots of everyday life, people. I don't wear a camera around my neck all the time—I'm not that tight—but I go to events like rodeos, family gatherings, things like that, and take some photographs. Or, I could go to an event and not take any pictures because I don't see what I want. Then the landscapes I do aren't necessarily straight landscapes, like Ansel Adams's and so forth. There's always evidence of people around, relics, old cars, for example, so the human presence is very important. And if I do portraits, they're not really straight portraits. In fact, sometimes the person won't be in the image at all, just his belongings, but it will still be a portrait. They're not portraits that make the person in the photograph glamorous. I'm not out to make beautiful, pretty pictures. I'm out to capture the spirit of the person.

LA: In many of your works you have torsos of the models but no heads, like in *Bailerina y Terra* [1989] and *Wishing Well* [1982].

CLT: There are several reasons for this. One is that in my work, different meanings can continue to emerge. If you look at a piece for a long time and then look at it again, you'll see it in a different way. They're really open-ended; they're not closed, where everything is said for you. Although many of the props I use are objects that are typically Native American, they really transcend all cultures. A person of any race could look at those photographs and relate to them. If I reveal a face, the photograph belongs to that person, and that would be it. Everything would be closed. I want the viewer to play an important part in the work and have a chance to get involved in the photographs. The title is really important because it gives an idea to the viewer and he or she can take it where he or she wants to. If I put heads or faces in a picture, then the viewer will just concentrate on that person, not on the total image. The face in the image would claim the story.

And I don't do portraits of Indians, because lots of photographers think that if they take a photograph of an Indian that makes it art. Like the older Anglo male photographers who came through here — they made the people themselves, the Indians, into curios, instead of treating them like human beings. They become like trinkets. I'd like to go beyond that.

LA: This curio-making aspect of photography has had negative ramifications, yet there is a new interest in the medium as a fine art by Native artists. Why this growth over the last decade or so?

CLT: The negative aspect of photography is not limited to Native Americans. I think all cultures have that awe of the image maker. The camera is just very intimidating. The image of the photographer is one of intrusion. We just focus on the fact that we were abused by the camera and think that we were the only culture negatively affected. Among families, though, taking photographs was always acceptable. But I think that the main reason now that we see more Native photographers is that more money is available to use cameras. It's a very expensive medium, so a certain amount of money is needed to start and maintain a career. Plus, there's been such a technological revolution over the last ten years or so. Nowadays just about every household has a TV, a VCR, a camcorder. Equipment is much more easily obtainable now.

LA: Of course, some Pueblos, for examples, permit outsiders to take pictures, which has an economic impact. But I've seen tourists stand right next to a sign saying "No Photography" and merrily snap away.

CLT: People lack manners, and believe that they have to have a picture of Indians. There's a feeling in the United States that if it's not captured on TV or in a photograph, then it didn't happen. I mean, if someone sees an image on TV or in a photograph, it's more real and more permanent than if you actually experienced the event itself. People just *have* to get that picture of the dance, even though it's off-limits. I don't do that type of work myself. I don't need to rob people of their lives to make my work.

LA: Maybe we could talk equipment for a minute. What kind of camera do you use? Film?

CLT: There's a misconception that photographers need the best equipment in order to get the best photographs. Manuel Alvarez Bravo [photographer, b. Mexico City, 1904] once said that sometimes the technical gets in the way of the artistic. The camera is just a machine; you can get wonderful images with a pinhole if you have the time. I just use an old Minolta with a 55-mm. lens. I usually shoot outside, so I use a fast film, like Tri-X 400 or T-Max. I experiment within the Tri-X's or T-Max's range, and with infrared.

LA: How much do you manipulate in the darkroom?

CLT: Well, in *Iron Horse*, I did a double exposure, but usually I manipulate within the frame, with the models and props, and later with the paint and sepia. So I don't do that much in the darkroom. Most of the time I just use natural light. I generally make just three or four prints, so they're really all originals. And, my palette changes. Each time I paint on an image the palette is different. I don't paint exactly the same on all the prints of an image. I won't make five exact duplicates of one thing. It's too stressful.

LA: How do you come to decide on a particular subject?

CLT: Most of the time it just flows. I mean, it's just in my mind. My imagination just goes on working all the time. I just think of an idea. That comes from just living. I'm not someone who's been sheltered in the comforts of a living room. I've read a lot, experienced a lot, traveled a lot, and I listen closely to other people's stories, especially relatives, their histories. I have a real interest in women and their conflicts in society, in women's rights in marriage and reproduction. I'm aware of a lot of injustice. I'm also a registered nurse and work in the operating room of Northwest Presbyterian Hospital [in Albuquerque], so I see everything from extreme happiness to despair in a matter of hours.

LA: At first look there doesn't seem to be an overt political dimension to your work.

CLT: My politics deal with men and women, one on one. I believe everything starts from there, the relationship between men and women. However you relate to or think about the opposite sex in your personal life, it will carry over to more general worldly politics. All these conflicts about respect and choices start from that basic relationship. Any politician who has an outlook toward men or women which is not healthy or positive will carry that out in laws and social attitudes. All that is in the work; you just have to see it. There are a lot of things going on in the photographs, but they're pretty down to earth and stick with human relationships.

LA: When did you start doing photography?

CLT: Since around '79 or '80, professionally.

LA: Could you talk about your working methods? How many photographs might you do in a year?

CLT: This year has been really busy. Usually a group show will take five or so pieces, but it varies. I try to do one new work a month. Ideas come every day, though. Executing a piece depends on getting models, the right props, and if an event is happening. Then I'll develop a shooting schedule. I have to push myself to use film, because I'm really conservative with it unless it's a studio setup. I don't shoot wildly and hope something comes out of it. I do careful setups; I bracket. As I said, the structure of an image is very important to me. There may be only one chance to take a particular shot. You can't keep doing it over and over, especially out of the confines of the studio.

LA: One photograph that really struck me was *Parasol*, from 1982.

CLT: That's real nostalgic to me. It was during fall or winter; there were no leaves on the trees. Looking at it reminds me of looking at an old drawing when I was little, a very lonely feeling in a way. The eye is drawn first to the figure in the background, and then the veiled figure in the foreground sort of emerges and takes you aback. The face seems to come out of the shroud. I just wanted to paint on the umbrella and use the veiled woman in front as an image to represent a spirit or something that was on the mind of the other figure, a thought, like a wordless caption. It's a theme I work on a lot, the idea of the caption. Parasols, too, seem to recur. The way the landscape is incorporated into the image is very important, too. But you're never sure anything is going to work aesthetically until you develop it. Beyond technical problems, a shot may not work because of the sense of the design, or it's just too contrived.

LA: You mentioned *Iron Horse* and the use of double exposure.

CLT: I used superimposition on that one, which is something I rarely do. I remembered a story my mom told me about my grandparents traveling from New Mexico toward Colorado or California. They were hopping trains, like a lot of people were doing at that time, and there was a TB epidemic and people were dying left and right. The reason they didn't succumb, they believed, was the medicinal effects of their daily shot of whiskey. My grandfather had to carry a large trunk of their belongings on his back. They had a hard life. But I also wanted to bring up the whole idea of the train and its impact on Indian life out here. Without trains the West wouldn't have been settled and exploited the way it was. The scouts were paid by the railroads to clear out the Indians and the buffalo so the track could be put down. I bring this out by the use of petroglyph handprints. Indians at that time called trains "iron horses." Rays of light emanate out because of the way I've used yellow, red, and blue paint, but that's accidental. There are always happy accidents in art. Where did the image come from? There's magic in the darkroom.

LA: Use of color is a hallmark of your work, but you don't do color photography.

CLT: No, I don't. To me, the color photograph is very clean and sterile; the colors are saturated without the gradual variations in tone. In my work the use of black and white allows room for the surreal. The image itself can be manipulated, as I do a great percentage of the time with sepia tone and oil paint. With color photography you don't have that immediate control that you have with black and white. I apply paint to make the image come toward the viewer or to recede, using warm and cool tones. Like in *Cowboy Boots Con Pintura* [1990]. It was sort of like a pun, because "con pintura" means "with paint," but it can also mean a painting, which is there in the image. I incorporated a large painting by Ed Singer [Little Turtle's husband] called *Summer Storm*. What I wanted to focus in on was how sometimes we associate colors geographically, the colors we may be led to think of as the Southwest and the more festive colors associated with northern Mexico. But if a particular image doesn't warrant painting, I don't do it. I'll know that by looking. I'm not attempting the slickly colorful technical photographs of the Southwest landscape.

LA: What led you to photography? Were there any particular influences?

CLT: My mother bought me a camera when I was in seventh grade, a Polaroid Swinger. It was a cool thing to have. I don't know where in the world she got the money for it, or the film, but she did, and right then I started posing people. As far as going to school, in order to be in fine arts you have to try everything, like ceramics and printmaking, but I stuck with photography. My father always had a camera around his neck; he was always photographing. My mother was an artist, and when she wasn't doing her abstract painting on canvas, in her leisure time she would paint on photographs. I remember always looking to see what she was doing. She didn't paint on photographs in my style, but I watched what she did. I always remember the smell of paint and turpentine as a kid.

I've always hung around artists. I've always been around artists; all my friends were artists, going to school and so forth. As for influences, besides my mom, Barbara de Genevieve, who taught at the University of New Mexico, was a big influence. Manuel Alvarez Bravo is one of the main photographers I'm interested in; he was a great influence. He also posed his models; he had a favorite model and he brought in props. Ansel Adams and Edward Weston and people like that, not really at all. Of course, they're required reading, and you never know how much you absorb and then transcribe other artists into your own work.

I was born in California, but a lot of my relatives are from the Albuquerque area and southern New Mexico. I went to nursing school at Navajo Community College in northern Arizona. As far as art school, I studied in California and New Mexico [College of the Redwoods, Eureka, California, and the University of New Mexico]. I've been a registered nurse since 1979.

LA: How did the nursing career come about?

CLT: Being a single mother, I had to have something that brought some money in. Also, I don't like to be in the position where I think that I have to sell my work in order to survive, or change my style for the marketplace to be popular or commercial or whatever. This way I can do whatever I want whenever I want to, without being obliged to the business of selling art. I've never been that kind of woman. I've lived alone since I was sixteen and had to work in order to survive. I'm very independent. As far as the two worlds of art and nursing, I absorb what I can from everyday living. I see the conflicts and difficulties that people have to go through. For example, we were doing surgery on this fourteen-month-old child and I heard some screaming in the waiting room, and apparently the mother-in-law came in and blamed the baby's mother for not taking proper care of it. There's a lot of drama going on all the time. We're helping people, and each person or patient we're helping has his or her own story of how they ended up in surgery or waiting in the waiting room for their loved one. I keep my eyes open and I spend time with people, and I feel that I'm sensitive to their needs. I don't want to be an artist who's unapproachable or judgmental, or have people think that my work is mystical or reveals some kind of answer in a shamanistic way. My work has a down-to-earth, humorous side to it.

LA: Maybe the work is in some way a respite from an intense work life. They have that dreamy, almost detached look.

CLT: The work is intense in its way. They have to do with possible worlds. Like *Unborn Babe* [1981] could refer to a miscarriage, or an abortion, or a wish to be pregnant, or an idea that is not fulfilled. If I went around being morose and portraying that in my work, which could happen when your subject matter deals with the politics between men and women, it would be too limiting. There's more to life than that. But I also avoid the saccharine commercial photographic image.

LA: You're not drawn to using your work as a subject?

CLT: I'm not a photojournalist and I don't want to document things in that way. I know that a lot of people want to see that kind of document; that's all they can relate to as far as they think photography goes. They haven't seen my work, or understood the different styles of photography. The camera is just a machine and you do things with it. I'm trying to do something different, trying to expand people's minds. When some people first see my work it doesn't compute, because half of it is black and white, some is in color, it's sepia-toned, and they have no idea what medium it is. I'm not out to show something in the traditional way—in the sense of realistic documentation. Other photographers do that, and it's important to record things for people, to provide a record for the youth of the future. That's not what I do, though. I just do what I know. I use props that could be considered Indian, but there are some that are universal. I use props from people who bring me things, authentic things, or I might use stuff I pick up at a garage sale. I try to be intertribal, intercultural.

LA: You've used multiple images, the triptych form on occasion, like in *Desert Cowboy* [1985].

CLT: That three-part format has to do with the basic relationship between men and women, which deals with food, money, and sex. That particular work dealt with those three things. It's also the title of a poem I wrote which went along with it. I usually try to key a poem into a photograph, although I don't show the poem with the photograph. I enjoy doing sequential narrative pieces.

LA: Looking back over the ten years or so that you've been making photographs, is there anything that unifies all your work?

CLT: I try to make an image that the viewer can read as his or her own, and I tell the story of relationships between men and women. Every person is always going through some stage of a relationship, and those stages can be seen in the work. I can capture a lot in just one or two frames. Also, the way I use paint on my images. Overall, I think of my work as timeless stories frozen and captured in a frame.

SELECTED EXHIBITIONS

"We, the Human Beings" (1992), group exhibition, College of Wooster Art Museum, Wooster, OH.

"Counter Colón-Ialismo" (1991–93), group traveling exhibition, Centro Cultural de la Raza, San Diego, CA.

"Our Land/Ourselves" (1991–93), group traveling exhibition, University Art Gallery, State University of New York, Albany, NY.

"Compensating Imbalances: Native American Photography" (1990), group exhibition, C. N. Gorman Museum, Davis, CA.

"Ed Singer and Carm Little Turtle" (1990), two-person exhibition, Old Town Gallery, Flagstaff, AZ.

"Language of the Lens" (1990), group exhibition, Heard Museum, Phoenix, AZ.
"Personal Preferences: First Generation Native Photographers" (1989), group exhibition, American Indian Community Arts Gallery, San Francisco, CA.
"Women of Sweetgrass, Cedar, and Sage" (1988), group traveling exhibition, Gallery of the American Indian Community House, New York, NY.

SELECTED BIBLIOGRAPHY

Little Turtle, Carm. "Artist's Statement." In *Counter Colón-Ialismo*. San Diego, CA: Centro Cultural de la Raza, 1992, p. 68.
——. "Artist's Statement." In *We, the Human Beings*. Wooster, OH: College of Wooster Art Museum, 1992, p. 27.

Linda Lomahaftewa

Hopi-Choctaw

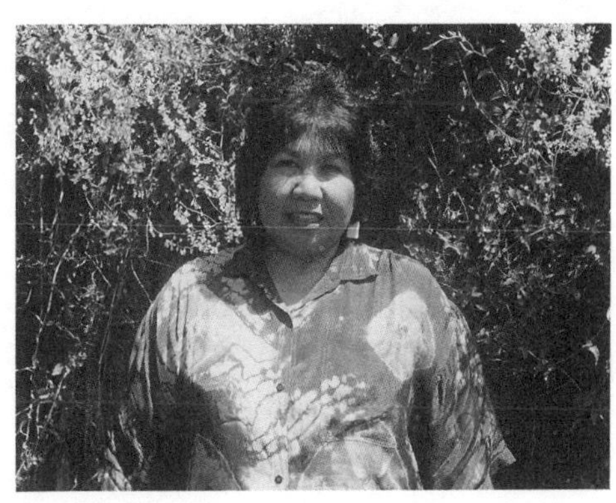

Linda Lomahaftewa's works are about knowledge and memory, the knowledge of the Hopi way and the persistence of individual and communal memory. Lomahaftewa intuitively draws on ancient sources to create her art, and combines contemporary processes and techniques with these sources to make her prints, paintings, and monotypes. She has written that her "imagery comes from being Hopi and remembering shapes and colors from ceremonies and from landscape. I associate a special power and respect, a sacredness, with these colors and shapes, and this carries over into my work."[1]

Lomahaftewa's art has not been static over the two decades or more that she's been an active artist. For example, Lloyd Oxendine, referring to *Snake and Animal Symbols* (1970), wrote: "Miss Lomahaftewa's art reduces natural forms to elements of design; to these she adds her own conformations in bold colors and organically unlikely juxtapositions."[2] This design orientation was maintained in the 1978 *New Mexico Sunset:* "The complex overlaying of designs and colors are reminiscent of patchwork quilts."[3]

But throughout the 1980s Lomahaftewa has drawn more on Hopi imagery and on personal memory. The *Cloud Maiden* series, ongoing since the mid-eighties, refers to Hopi cosmology, and *Awatovi Parrots* (1987), a monotype with oil pastel, comes out of her interest in the kiva mural paintings at Awatovi. As Lomahaftewa has noted about her own work: "These paintings that I'm using for my ideas come from the masters. The kiva mural paintings that were done, these were my masters. That's where I'm learning from."[4]

Yet she has also explored personal and family memory in such works as *Prayers from Marvin* and *Honanie* (both 1990), works which offer the viewer the opportunity to reflect on the connections between individual and cultural experience. What makes *Honanie*, for example, so compelling is the use of contemporary techniques, like *chine collé* and Xeroxing. Past and present are integrated in the very making of the work.

Linda Lomahaftewa was born in Phoenix in 1947 and spent part of her childhood in Los Angeles before returning to Arizona. She studied at the Institute of American Indian Arts (IAIA) while it was still a high school (it's now a two-year college), and then went on to receive her B.F.A. and M.F.A. from the San Francisco Art Institute. She taught at California State College in Sonoma and the University of California at Berkeley before returning to IAIA, where she has been a professor in foundation arts and drawing since 1976.

Lomahaftewa's work is in the collections of the American Indian Historical Society, San Francisco; the Millicent Rogers Museum in Taos; and the Southern Plains Indian Museum in Anadarko, Oklahoma.

We had the chance to talk one July afternoon in 1991 in Santa Fe and then to follow up a year later.

LA: Your imagery and style are very distinctive. Could you talk about how they developed and how they have evolved since you first started painting?

LL: I first started painting in my last year of high school when I was at the institute [IAIA in Santa Fe]. This was when it was still a high school. When I was a student there I was being trained to become a commercial artist, an industry-type commercial artist, but I went into painting in my senior year. After I graduated I went on to the San Francisco Art Institute [SFAI]. The work that I was doing there was just abstract, just putting down colors, working the movement of color and everything—there wasn't any type of imagery really going on. The first years of school in San Francisco we had typical training, painting from models and the still life setup and that kind of thing. We did a lot of that. It was actually toward the end of my fourth year at the SFAI that I started coming up with the imagery, you know, remembering different ceremonies and things. The city was such a new place for me that most of what I thought about was back home, the Southwest, Hopi.

LA: What years were you at SFAI?

LL: I started in the fall of 1965 and did the B.F.A. and then the M.F.A. and ended up in 1971.

LA: You spent some early time in Los Angeles?

LL: When I was about six to thirteen, and then we moved back to Arizona and I started going to boarding school. My family lived in Phoenix.

LA: Did you have any family or other influences on you in terms of art when you were growing up?

LL: When I was growing up, I was encouraged by my whole family. I was the artist of the family. I always drew, and I had pencils and crayons and paper and coloring books, and paints at Christmas, paint-by-number sets, that type of thing. I was just always creative in that way. But it's funny to say that now because my whole family are artists. My father carves kachina dolls, and I always watched him. My mom always did different types of crafts and now she makes different kinds of quilts and does ribbonwork appliqué. And my brother Dan went on to study art at Arizona State and got his degree. He's a painter and lives up in Utah. My sister does beadwork and my other two brothers dance. They did bead- and featherwork too, so the whole family always did something that was art related.

You can't really separate these activities from each other. They're all related. Like when my father is carving, he'd be singing a song. He always told us that whatever you do, always pray and sing a song because that's what makes your work good. You should always pray to the spirits to help you do your work.

LA: I guess your formal training began when you went to high school in Santa Fe?

LL: Yes, the IAIA, when it first started in 1962. I was one of the first to attend. It was a high school program and then a two-year postgrad.

LA: What was it like, that first year of the school?

LL: The whole thing was really new to me. I had gone to a mission boarding school and the Phoenix Indian School before, so that was my third year of going to a boarding school. The IAIA was just really neat because students came from all over the country and it was interesting to meet people and learn about each other's backgrounds.

It was a kind of "do your own thing" philosophy, but it really emphasized your particular tribal background. Lloyd Kiva New [former director of IAIA] was one of my teachers; so were Jim McGrath [former director of art, IAIA] and Fritz Scholder. There was a real creative atmosphere. Some of my classmates were, let's see, Earl Biss, T. C. Cannon, Karita Coffey, Alfred Young Man. There were a bunch of us.

LA: What led you to the San Francisco Art Institute?

LL: Actually my adviser, Jim McGrath, told me that I ought to go on to art school, and he mentioned places like the Chicago Art Institute, SFAI, the College of Arts and Crafts in Oakland. So I talked to my mom and dad about it and they said San Francisco, because it was closer to home in Arizona. So I applied and got accepted. It was scary but the good part about it was that a lot of us had come out from Santa Fe, so we more or less went as a group together, the ones I mentioned and also Kevin Red Star and Doug Hyde. They all made it easier because we hung out together; the ones who had been there a while showed us around the city.

I was out there during a pretty wild time, like the war protests, the peace movement, flower children. It's a wonder I ever survived! But my whole thing was to be there to go to school, and that's what I did.

LA: You didn't get involved with any of the political things?

LL: No. I could see doing it, but I also could see that that took time, and sure, I could go sit on Alcatraz Island and be part of that, but then what about my classes? To me, school was more important. I chose to be a student and to help in whatever way I could with my artwork.

LA: Maybe we could go back to your last year in the B.F.A. program and then your M.F.A. You mentioned that was a turning point in your move from purely abstract work to work that derives more directly from Hopi sources.

LL: I was doing really abstract work and using a lot of color and also painting the model and all that, and my critiques were not negative, but then I started adding my own thing to them, like corn would start popping up! And then, I didn't know how the teachers were taking it. One time I just did the painting the way I wanted to and that started leading to other things, using the Hopi symbols, and the teachers just sort of backed off and left me alone and said, "Okay, she's on her way."

LA: Were there particular stories or ceremonies that influenced your imagery in the early seventies?

LL: I guess more the totality of just remembering how it is at Hopi. I can't say that it was one specific thing, because life there involves everything, the cycle of the year, the ceremonies that go on, like the kachina dances.

LA: You've talked about your art education as a process of "unlearning European styles and techniques which predominate in art schools."[5] Could you expand on that process of unlearning?

LL: By European training, what I'm talking about, you have to learn perspective and have that dimension in your work if you paint realistically. But I don't paint that way, so I try not think about those concepts when I do my paintings, like "do I have depth?" I don't think about it in terms of perspective. So that's what I meant, trying not to be influenced by that whole tradition. Even drawing—it shouldn't have to be something in perspective or showing dimension. You should just paint color or line and not worry about showing that, because we know that perspective exists and lines exist and that's been done before, so why go over and over it?

LA: You've been teaching art since 1976 at the institute. Is there a conflict between the Euro-American artistic traditions and the way you approach your teaching?

LL: Yes. I do feel that it's a conflict and I explain to the students just what I said, but it's hard for them to understand, because many of them come from a high school where you have to learn in a particular way. You have to learn the basics, that line becomes three-dimensional with shading or with other lines, for example, and that's okay, but I don't think that you need to always follow that rule in drawing or painting. You need to know how to work your own style.

LA: One of the problems you probably see is that the art world or art market judges by those Euro-American standards, so if your students don't produce according to those standards, your work is devalued.

LL: Right. And a lot of the Indian art work I've seen, especially the earlier stuff, has been painted in the flat style, just with line and color, and I think that's fine; you don't have to show that dimension or perspective. But the problem comes when people say, "Well, Indians don't know how to paint." We're going to paint our own way anyway, no matter what anybody says. I mean, that's just like telling the potter, "Okay, you have nice designs with your pot, but let's see some depth in that or dimension." But the depth is already there because of the shape of the pot. It's actually like a painting on the pot.

LA: As a teacher at the institute you've certainly taught many, many students and from that vantage point have seen probably thousands of paintings and drawings. Have you seen any threads connecting all those works over time, any points of contact which would unify all of this tremendous body of work?

LL: How many days do we have? Really, though, that's hard to answer. There are so many different styles, and the content of a particular piece reflects the individual artist. The one factor I see is the determination a student has. You can always see that in a student, and as a teacher that's what you pick up on and try to direct so the person can become whatever kind of artist she wants. You encourage them to do that. That sense of determination links all of Indian art, I think.

LA: What about definitions of Indian art? Can it be defined?

LL: I can't speak for all Indian artists about what they may feel, but in speaking for myself, because I'm an Indian whatever I paint is Indian. Whether it's totally abstract or totally representational, it's Indian. It's like, you can see the artist's soul in the work. It's not just somebody who stopped by to paint for a few hours and go on. You can see and feel something, but I don't know how to explain it. I'd be interested to see what other artists say.

LA: You wrote in the catalog *After 5 P.M. . . . and on Weekends*, "I'm giving information to my viewers, information about who I am. My paintings tell stories about being Hopi and how I was taught."[6] Could you say what this information is? Do you think of yourself more as an individual creative artist or as a painter whose works embody Hopi culture?

LL: I'd say both. And what I mean by "giving information" is that in the things I paint a lot of the imagery comes from kiva mural ruins, but adding my own color and transforming things. That's how I give the information, because when I explain to people what those murals are, then I'm talking about my background, I'm talking about Hopi, and even where the murals come from, how they came to be, and how this particular village was destroyed during the Pueblo Revolt, that kind of thing. That's what I mean by "giving information," because my paintings contain the history of my people. Again, though, I use my own creativity to make the works, like combining different symbols or images together. And sometimes I'll develop my own. I still work within the Hopi culture but I put my own personal angle on it.

LA: It's like Mike Kabotie once said: "Tradition doesn't mean a loss of freedom." Could we talk about your working methods? Are you more spontaneous or more deliberate in your approach? How do you come to a subject?

LL: Both of those ways. Sometimes I'll plan a work out, while other times an idea will strike me and I'll just work on that. When I'm working on large canvases I usually start out with a color background and continue in layers of color and sometimes things will come out of that exploration. That's when I do the abstract work. But then symbols might start coming forward into a work and I just accent them, but I don't really plan it. Other times I'll have a dream about a design or something and I'll use that. I guess that's planning in a way, but it's not sketched out.

With my paintings I like to work in larger sizes and that lets me explore more and see what emerges. Lately I've been doing mostly monotypes and with those you do have to plan out ahead of time. I have to pay for working at the graphics studio and the studio space, so my time is valuable, so things have to be pretty clear.

LA: Have you shifted from painting to monotypes?

LL: At first I was doing both, but most recently it's leaned more toward monotypes. I'd like to get back to doing more paintings. Of course, I keep saying that. The reason I've been doing the monotypes is that it's a lot faster, and I've been doing more shows, so I have to have more work to exhibit. Lately I've been doing works with petroglyph imagery, so that's not too hard to do. You just have to figure out which images you're using for that day.

LA: Is that what you're working on now?

LL: Yes. And I guess I got interested in that because that's what my brother's been doing. I studied petroglyphs a long time ago but I never thought I'd use it in my work. That was our first art, so they were kind of in the back of my mind for a while. Since Dan was doing some in his work, I thought I'd try it and see how it would come out if I did them. His petroglyphs come out of Utah, where he lives, and mine are from around here, New Mexico and Arizona. Our work is real different, even though we're using the same basic images.

What I do is search out different areas with petroglyphs and draw or photograph them. Then I'll come back and study them and create different compositions. I studied them a long time ago and never thought that I'd use them in my work, but it's amazing how you can come around to things that you never thought you'd use. For the petroglyph works I'm doing, the composition and arrangement is just different figures, and sometimes I put them into a star scene, like in the *Star Gatherers* series. To me, the stars are just as important as the land, and the connection I was trying to make was that the figures or the images came from the rock, from the land. And there's that connection of space to the land. I was influenced a little, I guess, by Van Gogh's *Starry Night*, so I tried to get a feeling of swirling and spinning around. The eight works in this series were all monoprints, but since I wanted to get the idea of stars and space, I used black or a real dark purple-blue as the background.

LA: You've done a number of series, like the *Cloud Maiden* series from 1988. Do you usually conceive of works in a series, or are they more individual?

LL: Well, before the *Cloud Maiden* series I did a whole series of parrots because it was something I had to get out of my system. I painted parrots for about twelve years and I felt like I just had to keep doing them. I still add a parrot in there now and then. But with the *Cloud Maiden* series it was just that people wanted that particular image, so I did more than one cloud maiden, and that's how it became a series. I still work on that one and must have more than thirty by now.

Each new one is just a little different from the earlier one. They're monotypes, so after the ink dries I go back over them with oil pastel, and then in the background on some of them I use stencils of the stars or the dragonfly, which represents water, or other symbols. Sometimes I'll put a new moon in. So the imagery or the exact use of the oil pastel on the surface changes each one.

LA: Certain images tend to recur in your work, like parrots, petroglyphs, corn maidens, and lightning, cloud, and rainbow symbols. How does that recurrence of imagery structure your work?

LL: It's a ceremonial or cultural structure. Most of the rain symbols have to do with praying for rain to water the crops. Usually the men do the paintings of kachinas and the kiva murals. Women didn't generally paint, but because I'm a painter and I know all the symbols — well, probably not all of them, but I see them all the time — so that's what I painted. The lightning sticks, the rain cloud, and fertility symbols I see on the kachinas. I'm also from the Water clan, so that's why I use a lot of water symbols. Cloud maidens bring rain.

LA: I guess one thing that puzzles many non-Indians about Indian art is the referencing of the symbols. So if someone sees a cross in one of your paintings, say, they might make a Christian interpretation.

LL: That's what people always say to me: What are those crosses there for? They represent stars, and it's just another symbol used throughout Hopi painting. As far as the parrots are concerned, I just always liked birds and parrots. It was in San Francisco that I started painting the parrots. Actually, it was another bird, but I started looking through a book on kiva murals and I saw that there were parrots in the murals at Awatovi. That's where I took that parrot from and then I started using different colors and adding things.

LA: Were you trying to make a connection in your work to the kiva murals?

LL: Well, I just took one particular parrot shape that I liked and used it. But a long time ago we used to trade with Indians in Mexico for parrots and parrot feathers, so that's how they came up to Hopiland. I remember seeing paintings by Fred Kabotie of family scenes, home scenes, and there was always a parrot perched somewhere. People have told me that parrots come from the tropical forest and that they represent rain and growth. To this day parrot feathers are highly valued in the ceremonies.

LA: Your use of color is very striking. You've been quoted in a statement as saying, "I use designs and colors to represent my expressions of being Indian."[7] How important is the use of color to you, and what is its role in your work?

LL: The colors just come naturally, they just flow. I've been called a colorist, but it would be hard to teach someone how to do that. I can tell when I see my students that some have a natural way with color and others really struggle with it. I struggled a bit at first, when I changed mediums and painted in oils. I used to start out with muddy colors but eventually my color sense came through. Sometimes certain colors represent direction or the night sky, for example. I'll also use a pearlescence on the surface of work to give a shimmery or sparkle effect.

LA: *Prayers from Marvin* and *Mountain Lion Warrior* [both 1990] certainly look like departures from some of the works from the various series.

LL: Sometimes, like on *Prayers from Marvin*, I was working at the Institute using their press and I didn't have to worry about the pressure of time. I was experimenting with *chine collé* and just tried to do some abstract things, so I was a little freer with what I was able to do. And for some particular reason the imagery reminded me of a cousin of mine who had passed away. What's weird about it is when I showed it to my sister, she got the same feeling about our cousin, so that's why I titled it *Prayers from Marvin*—because we both felt that he was talking to us. When our relatives come to visit us like that, we call it a prayer and we know that they're praying for us.

LA: *Honanie* [1990] is an interesting piece.

LL: Honanie is my great-grandfather, and again I was trying to experiment. I used a black and white photograph and ran it through the Xerox machine and got it to where it was a highly textured gray, and then I Xeroxed it using rice paper and then *chine colléd* it onto the print as I was printing it. I had to work around that image for the background because I knew that it was going to be made into a collage as it's being printed. I was just experimenting to see what parts of the rice paper would go through the machine. It didn't take the very thin stuff.

The rice paper was collaged onto the printmaking paper as it was being printed, so I worked the plate and left room, you know, for that image to be placed on then and there. Everything is done all at once, the collaging and the printing onto the paper. It's hard to explain. I did another one of my father as a young boy. His Indian name was Qumaquaftewa. The ones using this technique are twenty-two by thirty inches. That's standard paper size.

LA: I guess a lot of people, myself included, aren't aware of the diversity of your work, in terms of content and technique. To me, you've been best known for the *Cloud Maiden* series and works similar to that.

LL: Yeah, those have been out more and have been reproduced in books, and that's what seems to be exhibited. But I guess that's only one aspect of my work.

LA: Do you have any specific projects planned for the next year or so?

LL: Not any really big projects. I talk to other artists all the time and we discuss collaborating on some things, but we haven't planned them out.

LA: One final question: what defines or what characterizes a Linda Lomahaftewa work?

LL: I think the use of the symbols and the color schemes. People seem to respond to my color schemes. They can tell my style. I don't know what that particular style is or how to explain it, but when other people see the work, they know it's mine.

SELECTED EXHIBITIONS

"Looking for Beauty in the Future" (1992), two-person exhibition, La Raza/Galeria Posada, Sacramento, CA.

"After 5 P.M. . . . and on Weekends: Art of the Faculty of the Institute of American Indian Arts" (1991), group exhibition, Institute of American Indian Arts, Santa Fe, NM.

"Our Land/Ourselves" (1991–93), group traveling exhibition, University Art Gallery, State University of New York, Albany, NY.

"Shared Visions" (1991–93), group traveling exhibition, Heard Museum, Phoenix, AZ.

"Native Proof: Contemporary American Indian Printmakers" (1990), group exhibition, American Indian Contemporary Arts, San Francisco, CA.

"Second Biennial Invitational" (1985), group exhibition, Heard Museum, Phoenix, AZ.

"Women of Sweetgrass, Cedar, and Sage" (1985), group traveling exhibition, Gallery of the American Indian Community House, New York, NY.

SELECTED BIBLIOGRAPHY

Lomahaftewa, Linda. "Artist's Statement." In *After 5 P.M. . . . and on Weekends: Art of the Faculty of the Institute of American Indian Arts*. Santa Fe, NM: Institute of American Indian Arts, 1991, p. 39.

——. "Artist's Statement." Quoted in "The Second Biennial Native American Fine Art Invitational," by Robert Breunig and Erin Younger, *American Indian Arts Magazine* 11, 2 (Spring 1986): 61.

George Longfish

Seneca-Tuscarora

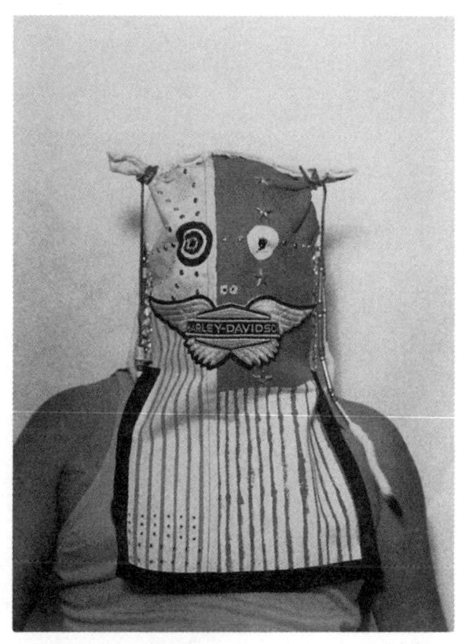

George Longfish was born in 1942 at Ohsweken on the Six Nations Reserve in Ontario, Canada, and studied at the School of the Art Institute of Chicago (SAIC), receiving his B.F.A. in painting and sculpture in 1970 and his M.F.A. in filmmaking in 1972. After his study at SAIC he directed the graduate program in American Indian arts at the University of Montana for a year before moving in 1973 to the University of California at Davis, where he is now a professor of Native American studies and director of the C. N. Gorman Museum. As a professor at Davis he has been a mentor to a number of artists, including Rick Glazer-Danay and Duane Slick, while as director of the Gorman he has curated numerous shows of contemporary Native art, bringing recognition to a whole generation of artists.

Longfish considers himself more a painter and sometime sculptor than a filmmaker, and has participated in nearly 170 group and solo exhibitions since 1967. His work has also been featured on the cover of *Wicazo Sa Review* (*Don't Mess Around with a Boy Named Sioux* and *Lightly Salted*—"in this instance, Land of Lakes butter is used in the creation of a mask").[1]

Longfish's work has steadily evolved in technique and imagery, and he points to his recognition a decade or so ago of Arshile Gorky's use of his Armenian "cultural information" as an influence on his own painting. In his early work Longfish "was working on aesthetic problems like an academician" and resisted the notion that he drew on his cultural heritage. "But I've found that when you are totally resistant to certain information, you create situations where you have to accept the information."[2] Longfish's work through the eighties and into the nineties has been an exploration of the various forms of this information and an investigation into, in Jimmie Durham's words, "who owns it, how it might be owned, and then, how one might use it."[3]

Such information includes both the personal and the cultural, and these often intersect. Some of Longfish's paintings deal with issues like personal relationships, healing, and one's search for the spirit. The imagery of *Spirit Guide/Spirit Healer* (1983), *The Contract* (1983), and *Groundings* (1986), for example, focuses on the dimensions of that search. Other paintings deal with the individual's relationship to society, as in *Goodbye Norma Jean, the Chief Is Dead* (1989), where the artist rejects the stereotype of "chief" as applied to Indians and takes a stand against the dominant culture's substitution of image for individual reality. The painting is a statement against the tendency to mythologize ("the vanishing Indian," "the defeated warrior") and raises questions about the process of destructively transforming the individual (Norma Jean Baker) to an icon (Marilyn Monroe).

Another type of information Longfish explores has to do with the warrior spirit. Some of the later warshirts, like *Golden Grass Warshirt* (1988) and *Mad Dog Warshirt* (1989) deal with the transformation of "the traditions by which people gave courage, morale, and integrity to each other in battle."[4] Frequently Longfish will attach small objects—Indian head nickels, toy planes, military medals, strips of reflective tape, buttons—to the canvas, as well as include text and messages. His piece for the "Submuloc Show/Columbus Wohs," *Born to Be Wild; or, We Are Damned Glad Columbus*

Wasn't Looking for Turkey, is an assemblage mask with numerous attachments, like dice, skulls, and miniature beer cans.

Longfish's use of common and pop culture objects and images takes on deeper resonances in the 1991 *Power Glove and Game Boy Meet with Kicking Bear on Their Journey Looking for the Yellow Brick Road*. First he recycles images from two 1984 paintings, portraits of his sons, really, entitled *He Cuts Leaves* and *Good Earth* (which are his sons' tribal names). In the 1991 piece these images of his sons are combined with his portrait of Kicking Bear into a large canvas (96 by 116 inches). Beneath the image of Kicking Bear are white and colored squares (the Yellow Brick Road?), some containing other small images, like Land o' Lakes butter wrappers and handprints. Longfish's sons were interested in video games and that became his entry into the painting. The painting meditates on the loss of Indian homelands and on the white man's capacity for destruction. Other recent work has become more explicitly political, in response to the Columbus quincentenary. *America 500 Years: "I" Is for Indian as "I" Is for Indigenous* (1991) and *The End of the Innocence* (1991), particularly the latter, focus on the necessity of change—change which leads to ownership of information. Longfish writes: "The more we are able to own our religious, spiritual, and survival information, and even language, the less we can be controlled. . . . The greatest lesson we can learn is that we can bring our spirituality and warrior information from the past and use it in the present and see that *it still works*."[5]

In addition to painting, teaching, and directing the Gorman Museum, Longfish (along with Joan Randall) has written a number of seminal essays on Native art. Their essays have been a voice against the usual stereotyping of Indian art and a call for artistic freedom. In "Contradictions in Indian Territory" they discuss how critics insist that Indian art look "Indian." They question, though, the real intent behind the critical "concern of recognizability": "It . . . has nothing to do with the quality of the art or whether or not the artist is truly an Indian. What appears to be the issue is the fact that the art historians, anthropologists, ethnologists and critics find themselves having to keep professional tabs on their growing and changing fields of study."[6] Other essays, such as "Made by Choice" and "Runners between the Tribes," also offer a corrective to restrictive views of Native art.

In "Contradictions in Indian Territory," Longfish and Randall write:

> Stand on the back of the Turtle, our mother, and look at the land and wonder what it would have been like if Columbus would have been successful in his pursuit of India and avoided the eastern shore of this continent. Wipe your Indian hands on your Levi jeans, get into your Toyota pick-up. Throw in a tape of Mozart, Led Zepplin [*sic*] or ceremonial Sioux songs; then throw your head back and laugh—you are a survivor of a colonized people. Paint what you see, sculpt what you feel, and stay amused.[7]

Throughout *his* career, George Longfish has stayed amused.

We talked in his office at the University of California, Davis in May, 1991, but due to the intervention of that inveterate doer of such things, Coyote, in the form of moribund tape recorder batteries, we followed up the initial interview by phone in April and October 1992.

LA: Could we start by talking about the piece you've just completed?

GL: I just completed it yesterday, and hopefully everything went well. It got shipped to Canada for the "Indigena" exhibition at the Canadian Museum of Civilization in Hull, Quebec. It's the largest piece I've done to date, and when it gets stretched and put up, it should be about ten feet by about twenty-five feet long. It's a triptych, and it's called *The End of the Innocence*. I took it from a song by Don Henley. I was interested in what was going on and what he was singing about, that whole thing, and it just kind of related to the culture. It also had to do with the whole concept of 1992 being an important year for not only Native Americans, but for all indigenous people. The people involved are not playing the game on the terms of the dominant cultures. Indians or Native Americans have to really get out of that space of being a victim and just take control of their own — I guess you could call it their own — business. And so the painting really looks at a lot of things. The center panel basically has to do with what happened in Canada and Oka, and where — to our knowledge, anyway — a white person was killed for all the wrong reasons, trying to take land away from the tribe for (it's our understanding) a golf course for recreation. But also looking at it for myself, it was a pool of information about their warrior information, which is, "We're ready to defend." You know, what is important to them and what it always keeps coming back to is land. I was trying to get across the idea that owning one's cultural information can have power.

So that's the center panel, which I painted first. The right panel I did second and it takes the characters from the Ninja Turtles' fighting positions. And they relate to our culture, for myself as Haudenosaunee and for the Iroquois, because the Turtle clan is the largest clan. The Ninja Turtles are in a city, but they're underground. It's really interesting. My kids got into it, and I got into it slowly. They're all named after artists; they're very creative. I find that extremely interesting because they're like seers, prophets of the future. All those things led me to begin the painting. It felt real good.

I found a photograph of a Pawnee who appeared in Washington, oh, I guess in the 1800s. He just appeared there. They didn't know why he was there. And what I realized was that the Americans used Indians against other Indians, like the Pawnee, who were the enemy of the Sioux. I saw that come out in the movie *Dances with Wolves*.

So anyway, there's this photograph of this Indian who's in Washington and he basically came and said, "Okay, I did my job. Where's our agreement? Where's my pay?" And they didn't know about the agreement. They just took his picture.

I also have all kinds of other things in that section, like the names of some tribes, words like "termination" and "assimilation," and other things that are happening. I like to pick a particular theme for it. There was a part that I had that was a rain forest. That's all written in stencil in the painting.

The last panel I did, the left one, had a Curtis photograph of Crow Medicine sitting in a chair.

And then I worked on that whole space about appropriate goods and inappropriate goods. For appropriate goods I stenciled in things like "Navajo Electronics," "Blackfeet Pencil Co," and "Apache Ski Resort," and then for the inappropriate goods I have what Oka was really about. It wasn't so much about the land; it was about bingo, cut-rate cigarettes, and gambling, and they wanted to get control of that.

Also, in the bottom and sitting on the side I kind of used the idea again of land, the shape of man, restoration — actually it has to do with toxic waste dumps. So it's really all about those things.

Looking at the whole scene, where I'm coming from, you don't have to play that game any more of being protected from society. First of all, we are spiritually moved. We have been. That's probably been our greatest survival information, and that's what I'm basically talking about.

LA: You seem to have integrated text into this painting, maybe more than in other work?

GL: Actually, I did, probably as I saw a couple changes as it got more political. It's going right to the heart of the matter. It's basically trying to make people really look at what some of the games are that have affected the culture. All the countries we fought wars against, like Germany and Japan, came out great economically. But the other side of it, what is America doing for its own people? They give us the worst education. We have the worst health problems, so we get the worst health care. The society doesn't allow people to heal themselves, so they've got everything going against them. Partly the idea is, well, "We'll take care of it. We'll take care of it." And then they totally isolate Indian people. The situation right now is that the government doesn't believe there is an Indian problem. The government may not have had the information about the problem, but they haven't had the desire to find out, either. Bush, or Reagan, says to somebody else, "Okay, here. Take care of the Indian problem," you know? I find that rather interesting.

LA: To the government, the only problem is you people won't go away.

GL: Well, yeah, and that's one of the things at the end of this painting. This last section is basically about survival . . . survival. We'll survive, and one of the things we need to be able to do is to find where our power is. Basically we are a spiritual people. We are able to heal ourselves that way and to have a reverence and a respect for the land, or to use it up. Predominantly the Indian people are the caretakers of the earth. But no one would have a tendency at all to talk to us a little bit about what that reverence is or how it works. We have a lot of information now, but no one has made an effort to come forward.

The new painting also has to do with how things get set up in this culture. It's like we're programmed in many ways ourselves; not having information, we're on the lowest level, we have very little self-esteem. Many times, in order to get out of that situation or that energy, we take up drinking. So we're programmed not to always offer our information. Once I realized I can do what I can, I don't so much offer it as I would become an observer, and then I make my artistic decisions from there.

LA: You mentioned that *The End of the Innocence* gradually became more political. Is it making a declaration for Native people's self-determination?

GL: There is that, but there's also something else. One of the things that I've been really aware of and working on, on many levels, in being an artist and working with a group, is that you tend to do what the group wants. You know, it's like one of the things I realized was that in this group dynamic you don't take yourself out and become an individual. You stay with the group. So when people ask you, "What do you do?" you talk about the group. And that's what has been done in the past. And now I'm in this place where I'm looking at myself, trying to figure what my beliefs are. Where am I? And it's like, you talk about self-determination; this is my own self-determination and where I want to be. And so one of the ideas is not living the lie anymore. And it doesn't bother me, and if people can't handle it, then it's really not my problem. But people say, you know, "Well, but. . . ." I'm not trying to say that I speak for Indian people, all right? What I'm saying is I speak for myself. This is where I am. I can't speak for everybody else. Other Indian people may be screaming at me, which is fine, but this is where I'm at.

LA: Another recent piece from '91 was *America 500 Years: "I" Is for Indian as "I" Is for Indigenous.*

GL: That was just before *The End of the Innocence*, but they were happening at the same time.

LA: Is that a big piece also?

GL: No, that's a very small piece. That's in the realm of about thirty by twenty inches. It just kind of happened. I started to work on that, and there was a show here in Sacramento called *America* at the new Center for Contemporary Art, which is the first time they've had that kind of institution here. The whole basis of that show was "America is always in the future." Actually I was giving up on the whole idea of what 1992 was going be about, but I realized that my work started to become more politically aware, and I started to clean away a lot of the garbage and really kind of look at what it was that I really wanted to say and get the true identity a lot clearer.

LA: You've talked about spirit and spirituality in your art. A lot of your past work seems to have a more overt spiritual dimension, like *Spirit Guide/Spirit Healer* from '83. Can you combine the spiritual aspect with the more political aspect, or does one seem to overtake the other?

GL: Well, my feeling is that they both exist at the same time. But we can talk about political things more easily because the whole idea of issues can be very real, very concrete, because, like what happened at Oka, you see it, it's on the news. But you don't get to see what's behind the scenes, the bigger issue, the concept of land and spirit. How do you validate spirit?

I find it rather interesting. When we had a conference here [University of California, Davis] in '90, one of the people that talked on the panel with us was Edgar Heap of Birds. Edgar basically participates in both politics and spiritual matters with tribal connections, and his rituals are planned with his own tribe. And people were really interested in what he does, but when he started to talk about it, he just left it at a point: "What I really do, in many regards, is I go through a renewal process," and that's all he would leave it as—a renewal process. By participating and owning one's cultural information, he completes the cycle and keeps going. But what I thought is, people wanted to know what that was. What specifically was that process? How do you do it? How do you get this living proof? That process and participation is very important for me and my tribe. I may have to talk about it to you very vaguely, but to me it's very concrete.

So I was really interested in what he said, because it is true. It's like America is always growing, it's always pushing, it's always out there. It never allows itself a renewal process. The government sets some goals up, and then it never validates them, and that creates so many problems. America doesn't look at what it creates, you know; the program is just over with, so let's move on to the next thing. There's no sense of continuation. And people always fall for the government's line.

But what I'm trying to do is give my sons a sense of meaning to their experience. What does it mean, "experiencing"? You forget about that, that whole aspect. You know, the dominant culture had that sense of meaning for a long time, but then they got so far away from it that they lost it. They put it into formal religion, which is concrete, like the state and government. But it more or less reaches a point where people aren't able to talk to the spirits. You may call it religion, but there is a spirit. I was taught at a very early age about the spirit. My mother said, "Be observant. See when people come in, who comes in with them. There's one person who came in; well, who are those other people that came in?"

LA: How do you work out ideas in a painting? How does your creative process connect to concepts or ideas you might have?

GL: I always start with a concept or idea, and I'm always amazed at the end. It's totally different than what I started off with. It may be close. It may have some resemblance, but inevitably it's different. But what I realized was that as an artist I'm in communication with my ideas. You're talking one concept basically, that everything has spirit. The Eskimo lives with a spirit stone and a communication is set up. Creation comes when the spirit in the stone emerges. You play with it, hold it and caress it. And just let it be. Finally it's your idea, it's the right time; the spirit is talking with you. It's that kind of agreement. So I look at that process, and the process with me is that I start off with ideas for the painting, and the space between the canvas and me is the place where I stand to do the painting, and where I move between the painting, back and forth, that's the space where I look at and create change. And in many regards I'm in communication with that canvas, and I'm beginning to create with that. That space allows me to grow and allows me to paint my steps, to move back and forth.

LA: How did that process work in *The End of the Innocence*?

GL: I first started talking with Gerald McMaster [curator of contemporary Indian art, Canadian Museum of Civilization, Hull, Quebec] in Canada last February [1991]. So it's the longest piece I've ever done, in terms of the time it took me to complete. I did have ideas about it, and I watched them change. I listened to the song quite a bit. The song got me into the concept of 1992. I started to process images onto the canvas. When I was drawing the two Indians, the Pawnee and the Crow, and really having a communication with them, I started to see how the dominant society uses Indians against Indians. The center panel set the energy in owning one's cultural information; it can be really powerful.

And that was a great process. When I started the panel with the Pawnee, I projected a slide of him onto the canvas and made an outline and a grid and then drew the image in by hand. That took almost two weeks. I was in communion with the Pawnee as a spirit; I had a conversation with him. He was stuck in his place. I made an agreement with him. "Do you want to complete the cycle as a spirit and come out of the photograph?" It's like I said, "I'm taking you now from a photograph into a painting, and the painting is going to be seen by a lot of people. Regardless of what you as person in your time have ended or committed, that is not the problem." It's a part of the game and allows you to look at the game yourself, and change it, and then take your step. There were two processes, myself and the canvas, and the communication with the photograph.

LA: Is that new for you to have that level of deliberation in the communication with your subject?

GL: I don't believe that it's new. I think it's always been there. It's just that I've been more aware of it and actually beginning to use it more. I can look at what to do from that point on. And that helps me get through a lot.

LA: After completing a piece like this, will you get right back into exploring those ideas further?

GL: Right now I'm just giving myself time. It was an incredible year for me and it's not quite done yet, but the year was intense because it was so involved with questions like Can you accomplish this? Can you get this done? And the museum had their deadlines. Most of them were by early September [1991], so I was painting away, you know, but finally I started to move. I got things done in December and I started the last panel. I was really working hard on it, but then it rained for about seventeen days straight, which really affected my canvas. The paint didn't go through its process because of the dampness. I use tape on the paint, and it would pull the paint right off the canvas.

LA: You've also been the director of the C. N. Gorman Museum at the University of California at Davis for twenty years. What have you seen in your time at the Gorman in terms of the development of Native art and artists? As a curator you've been instrumental in bringing the art to a wider audience.

GL: Over the years I've tried to turn around the perception that Indian art is a second-rate art, and change that around where people will come into the gallery and really see the art of Native Americans, wherever it's going. It's reached a point where people begin to look forward to what we are doing and come and explore the museum. And I've looked at the artists as they're beginning to take their own steps and go through their own changes. They are right there! I just had Jimmie Durham [Cherokee] in the gallery. James Luna [Luiseño-Diegueño] is one of the younger artists we featured who is getting tremendous recognition now. So we have a really good reputation about what we've been able to do to be in the forefront.

Another of the things I've seen is where the artists begin to question themselves. I mean that sometimes they don't stay in that basic role of "Okay, I'm just going to paint Indian art." We also did a twenty-year retrospective of Frank LaPena's work, and what I've seen for my satisfaction is his growth, where he originally started off doing paintings that had no relationship with our culture. They had a relationship with the land, but they didn't really have some of the culture, and I watched him grow. I watched Frank Tuttle, a very young and very committed artist, grow. And I guess for me, what I'm trying to say is, I'm watching these artists begin to reclaim their information, their cultural information, and begin to open up. That's probably been the greatest satisfaction for me.

Brian Tripp [Karok] is also doing very exciting stuff. I'm looking at that whole space and how that works for all the artists, and I find it really interesting where they begin to be in the culture and begin to get different perceptions, and how they perceive things in contrast to how a non-Native would perceive things. Then they begin to understand that difference and begin to look at it and see the lies that are said about their cultures. They begin to publicly talk about that, publicly talk about what happened to their cultures, what happened to their grandmothers and mothers and children, and the displacement and relocation of people. They talk about that, but they also talk about the aspect of that spirituality that gives them the strength to create. It is a cultural thing. They begin to look at it.

The other thing is that it's taken a long time for me to be able to say how I've been instrumental. I tend to say, "Well, I'm just a part of the group," rather than to take credit for something, for longevity, for a movement. So, essentially, within the last five minutes I've been able to say that I worked and helped things to happen. It's like Jaune [Quick-to-See Smith] said to me one time, "You know what we are? We're the elders." And I said, "What? What's that?" [laughs]. And then the last comment I had was, I was talking to a young artist who just graduated, Duane Slick [Mesquakie-Winnebago], and he mentioned that he talked to another artist. Duane told him, "Go talk to the godfather, Longfish" [laughs]. You know, I must be like Marlon Brando.

It's nice to be able to have that kind of respect, because I really like where they're at. By working at the Gorman I was able to have that kind of respect come back. The other satisfaction was, like I said, the idea where people would come and say, "We're really seeing some exciting things here, and some of the best art is being shown right now." And that's a validation of where the movement is and what the point of all this is.

LA: Would you say that's the one overarching factor, that sense of spirituality, or working with spiritual information, which links or unites Native art?

GL: Well, if you focus it on that you could say that they're all working on various levels of that information. They're making people aware. But also, on the level of materials, many people are doing installations. Jim Luna's right there, and he's aware that sometimes it takes a lot to get his point across. Also, though, he works with Indian students. He's involved as a counselor for an educational program [at Palomar College, San Marcos, California], so he knows firsthand some of the things that affect the culture, and he talks about that information. There's one installation [*The Artifact Piece*, 1987] where he talks about the idea of how Native American people are perceived through an anthropological or archaeological framework. They can't really deal with Native people unless they're dead, so in order for him to get your attention, he becomes that dead person. And in many ways it's done with a tremendous amount of humor.

You know, one of the things that puts the critics in a quandary is that we all aren't outrageous or mad or angry. Myself, I've been going through those phases, but I try to limit it within my heart.

Critics look at it differently and then they come to a different conclusion.

LA: One thing that's interesting about your work is the use of humor, and certainly these last two works have a humorous dimension. Would you say, though, that there's a subtext or an implicit sense of anger at the political situation of Native people in your recent work?

GL: I don't know if it's a sense of anger. It's a sense of looking at the information and making a decision. I believe in survival. I've been surviving for a long time, maintaining. But sometimes I find even if some work is angry, or if it comes across that way, people can still laugh at it.

LA: Maybe you could talk about how you come to title a work. Some of the titles seem to be intentionally humorous and have a sort of twist.

GL: Well, there is a time and a place where sometimes you don't have clarity or a sense of security about where your painting may be heading, and you say, "Well, okay, they may not like the painting, but they may like the title." But, really, some of the titles were just basically commenting on the dominant force today in art and trying to defuse it. You can't have fun because art is serious business—it's almost like a work ethic, okay? If your nose is not to the grindstone, if you're not very serious and committed, you eventually will be getting bullshit.

You know, I kind of look at that whole art world thing and try to say, "Okay." I remember talking to some people here at the university and they said, "If you had to give the graduates one thing, what would you tell them?" And I said, "Know that the game is to be an amusement." Because you can have that. See, the game is a Catch-22 game. If you're serious and you're in poverty, then you're an artist. If you're serious and you make it, then they don't consider you an artist because you're making money. Then you're not a true artist. I mean, they'll respect you from afar, but they don't want to really talk to you, like, for example, Frank Stella. And if they don't think you're serious, then they won't look at you at all.

And so I'm kind of looking at it right now and, yes, I can have those feelings. I can have those emotions in my paintings, but I can still be amused by it, and I find the amusement in the creative act. I look at what it is that I've created. You know, one of the things I have in the painting *End of the Innocence* is the Crow and the Pawnee, who were used by the United States and other tribes. My thing is, well, I may be angered at that, but it's not my problem.

And so I look at it, but then I relate it to coming to the future, coming to a more present time. You know, the government did the same thing in Vietnam and Cambodia. They were incredible fighters, and then we just left. And they were totally at the mercy of the Khmer Rouge, which is the same thing they did to Native Americans. Also like the thing that happened, where I talk of the whole idea of that ability to have renewal, or have the rites of passage. You know, in the Iraqi war, the generals knew that in order to be able to complete the cycle, to have complete victory, they have to say, "Go for it, let's get it over with." Bush comes in and says, "No, stop it." Well, he does, and he eliminates that process, eliminates that finality. You don't see it right away, but you begin to see a lot of it now happening in the country, a tremendous amount of anger and violence. It's right there because a cycle wasn't completed. No one will look at that. Why do we have people who won't even talk about it? The cycle hasn't been completed. It's not completed. The cycle that happened in Vietnam basically was not completed because we pulled out. We didn't say we lost. What it did, it affected all the soldiers in it. We never allowed them to deal with it. You know, the Native Americans, when they sent people over for the war, they had a ceremony for them, and when they came back, they had a ceremony. There was a healing process. The United States never had a healing process for the Vietnam War veterans. So there isn't a completion, and if you don't have the completion, you begin to kind of go to a survival level, and in total anger. You don't have that space to take that step.

LA: Can we jump back for a second to the idea of cultural information in terms of your own work. You mentioned that Ashile Gorky was an influence on you in the sense that he reclaimed his information.[8] Could you talk about that a bit?

GL: It's tragic for me the way he died, taking his own life. But then he was working on relationships. His studio had just burned down, he was in an auto accident, and he was incapacitated for a long time. So there was an overwhelming accumulation of situations that weren't working for him. But what's really interesting, before all that happened, he was trying all kinds of styles. He painted like Stuart Davis. He painted in many different media. Then he started looking at his own cultural information again, and he found his own color, and that's great. And when he used the information that he was brought up with, he could begin to create what he wanted to create. He began to reclaim his cultural information.

Right now it seems that a lot of people are up in arms about multiculturalism in the arts. People are accustomed to looking at familiar information, but now they're being presented with totally different information. So when Asians or Puerto Ricans or Native Americans come in and paint their information, there's a dilemma: is it good art? That becomes the whole question.

LA: You've written: "I believe that the observer brings his sensibilities to what he sees and interprets his own vision. I believe that painting must communicate. A finished piece is the first level where the observer and the artist meet and may then start a meaningful dialogue."[9] It seems to me that today there's more of a collision of information, more of a conflict.

GL: Well, that depends. Sometimes people go to a show and respond in a negative way to an artist's information. That is a connection in a sense because it's a dialogue. And in that dialogue, you begin to set your parameters. I mean, there's some stuff that I've done where people have looked at it and said, "This is what I see," and sometimes that's much better than what I see [laughs]. But you should try to experience the artist's information. So I never try to undermine what their thoughts are. I try to say, "Okay, let me look at this and see." There may be times that I won't be in agreement, but I allow that space so the viewer can have a reaction. I allow people the space not to like a work.

LA: There seem to be different levels of accessibility to the imagery and to the information. People might look at a more or less representational type of piece and say, "Oh, okay, I can see that that is a dancer." But then they might look at something of yours, like *The Contract* or *Groundings*, and say, "There are a lot of circles and turbine-looking things, and people's disembodied feet are up in the air," and not have that same sense of being able to respond.

GL: Well, in some ways it is a response to it. The response would be questioning the work. That also leads to a dialogue. Someone can say, "I'm confused. Is there something I should be looking at or something that I should know about?" "Okay, what is it you want to ask?" "Well, what are the dangling feet?" "Those dangling feet are how connections are made to the earth, how a person is grounded." "Well, yeah, okay! Oh! I see. I've had that kind of experience." That's the way to knock on the door, and sometimes the door opens. And that's where you begin to have a chance for dialogue and to begin to exchange information.

Let me give you an example. I remember when *The Contract* was hung in a gallery in the Southwest. It wasn't a great opening and very few people went through, but I remember this older person come through, a doctor. At that same time I was working on a level of psychic healing, and he was looking at *The Contract* and we began to just kind of talk about what his concept or idea was of what he was looking at. He was kind of hesitant, but as we began to talk, we began to open the door. I found out he had moved from Chicago. I had lived in Chicago. On that level we began to talk about different places in Chicago and so forth, but then finally we began talking about healing, and that opened another door. See, we start off with the idea of familiarity with a city or location and move on to talking about healing. So we take a step up to another level, where there are exchanges of information going on. It's not a one-way dialogue. It's the spirit of trading information . . .

LA: . . . between viewer and canvas.

GL: Well, between viewer and canvas, or between artist and audience. *Groundings* was actually about having a connection to the earth. I looked at the Native American who is grounded in his communication with and connection to the earth. One of the things I learned in doing psychic healing is that you're grounded into the center of the Earth and that the energy that comes from the Earth gets neutralized when you can let it go back to the Earth. Then there is a new energy to revitalize yourself. It's the whole process of rebirth, the way plants are. Plants actually start with death, then they go into gestation, germination, and then eventually they're reborn. It's a cycle. That's what I'm doing, creating a cycle, but I'm also asking the question, What is a cycle? Some of the things that I used in that piece kind of looked like block forms. Actually, a friend of mine said that if those shapes are there, go with it because eventually your answer will come to you. And when I started them, I never knew what that answer was. And finally it came to me about '81–'82. I finished a piece called *Great Blocks*, and what I realized with that piece was that the blocks were actually runes, which are again psychic tools.

LA: So you might use personal information in a broader way?

GL: Well, in some regards, it becomes universal . . . on a personal level. There have been times in my paintings where I have worked on personal information. In the early eighties I was in a relationship that was very involved, very tenuous at times, but it was still a long relationship, and it created a lot of problems. And in those works, I didn't see it at the time, but I guess I had a lot of anger. Then I'd go back and look at the work, and I'd see that what was going on in the relationship, on a very personal and intense level, was coming out in the paintings. Now I can look at it and say, "Wow, that is different!"

LA: You talked a little bit about how some of the work has a kind of universal appeal. Does it integrate the personal and cultural information to become universal? Is there some level where it can go beyond the specific references to one's cultural information?

GL: That's a question I have to think about.

LA: Spirituality may be universal. People have different ways of coming to it, but that's a universal thing.

GL: Well, if we take it out of the realm of formal religion and use the spirit, then it becomes universal and people can see that idea. Religion can be a communication with the spirit but it usually has more to do with performance and rituals. Now, ritual and performance don't necessarily mean that you're in communication with the spirit. That becomes dogma. I'm not sure of the context that you're referring to when you said my art was universal. That's what I'm trying to get to.

LA: I guess on the level of imagery. Many of the artists I've talked to have said that they sought a primal, universal chord in their work.

GL: There is a sense of that, I think. I remember talking to a young lady who liked my work. She said, "I always had this feeling that you were Indian, and it had to do with how you used color." I looked at the work and said, "Well, a lot of people use these colors." But it's the arrangement. Now, in a sense, color could be a universal concept. I think most people who really like my work are attracted by the colors. I'm probably considered, even by the contemporary art movement, as being an excellent colorist. Now that probably is a universal concept. I've heard that people are attracted to the color. So, in one sense, I could say that there is a universality. It would be interesting to see someone focus on the work that is happening now, see how that's functioning. Some of the comments that I've recently gotten . . . I've been in a couple shows right now that have to do with Columbus, like "Acknowledging Our Host" at the Richmond Art Center, and the only comment was that the critic thought that all the work had to be angry. Sometimes I have a tremendous amount of animosity towards critics [laughs]. Well, anyway, let's put it this way: for as long as I know, no one's really done an in-depth study of my work.

The thing is, I did these warshirts, and, for me, the work created parallels between the information they used from the Plains in a warrior society, and how they instill themselves with the power and the protection to go into battle. I drew that parallel between the U.S. Army and Native culture. One of them was called *Bright Wings* [1989–90], and I used this puzzle piece that had iridescent space tape kind of stuff on it. It was decorated down with beads, and the bottom had little airplanes and butterflies. The comment was that I was into resistance to the resources of the U.S. Army. The only thing that was validating was the use of my Kool-Aid colors (laughs). An observant person would look at the relationships and the parallels and the similarities involved, how they function. The other show I did was at the Triton Museum in Santa Clara. They had a piece called *Power Glove and Game Boy Meet with Kicking Bear on Their Journey Looking for the Yellow Brick Road* [1991; the catalog mistakenly deleted "*Glove*" from the title of the reproduction] and the only critical comment was that I used cheesy material. And I find that offensive and insulting, because I've been trying to adhere to the mainstream as an artist. I have a sensibility and I make a statement, and it's not taken in the context that it would be taken if maybe I was a white person. It's like, well, anybody else would've been given some credit for his use of material. But then I find that by being in it as long as I have, maybe I am doing something right because the response has been so negative.

LA: I get the sense that there are many different types of stories behind your work. Do you see your paintings as telling stories in some way?

GL: One of the things that's rather interesting is that even in

The End of the Innocence there is a connection to a kind of narration. Some of the artists, and I would include myself, are narrative abstractionists. That means we really have to search for what's going on.

LA: But in essence you're trying to tell a story.

GL: Well, regardless of whatever you're doing, it's not so much a story, but it's the way you're presenting information. You're allowing people to look at the information and make their own decisions and come to their own conclusions. Even though I say I'm a narrative abstractionist, I look at history, painting more and more from the concept of providing information, making people aware of the lies in history. A lot of artists are doing that, like the Spanish photographer Salgado. What he does is take photographs of what is happening in society. His work presents information. And Alfred Jaar, and Andre Serrano. Jimmie Durham is fully aware of what's going on. I find it very interesting to see all of this happening. From another angle you have Mapplethorpe. As much as some people claim to hate it, that's the area they enjoy.

But with my piece *The End of the Innocence*, the reviewers say, people say, "What's he doing? We can't relate to that." And that's where I see the problem. They don't make an effort to go beyond that. As artists we understand that reaction, but if viewers hold on to just one way of seeing and understanding, we're not going to transcend that limited response. It's like, the idea is to be accepted as a good painter, a good artist, a modern artist. Now that there's been a shift to postmodernism, we're still looked at as just Indian artists. We missed the boat again! Multiculturalism becomes another term to identify ethnic art. Maybe genuine multiculturalism is to have everybody working together regardless of all that.

LA: If "ethnic" artists give up their information, then they might risk diluting themselves in the mainstream, but if they keep discovering and encoding their cultural information, then the world at large can't understand their work.

GL: Yeah. It's the same thing, it's an old thing. I don't know if you've seen Calvin Reid's article in the January '91 *Art in America* ["Multi-Site Exhibitions: Inside/Outside"]. He makes the same statement. He says, "How long can these people last?" It's an interesting dilemma because it has to do with economics. One of the things that would be interesting to look at would be differences in perception, you know, how perception functions in the universe. Why not do a conference on perception and invite medicine men in so you could get a sense of who we are? The view others have of us doesn't always meet our reality. But by having that presentation, then you begin to change the perception and you begin to trade information. You begin to share information, and then maybe, on that level, change. In art, I think the basis for different perceptions is different information. Audiences need to begin to look at the artist's information, but people are afraid to look.

And one of the things that's real interesting is that the artists have gotten to where they are because of their own information, their survival. Now they present it and it's not in line with what they've been taught. They take the rules and then apply them to their information so it gives them a concept. I don't believe in exclusivity. There are some aspects of the art that are cultural, like symbols and so forth, but that's what you get to know as you start to get involved as a viewer; you become more aware of the information.

LA: Let's close with one final question. You wrote an essay called "Runners between the Tribes" [1987] and you developed the idea of artists carrying information back and forth. I'm wondering if, in the five years since that article, the message that the runners are carrying has changed at all?

GL: Well, let's put it this way: there will always be a change. In that essay I was looking at the heart of what culture is. In talking to [Tuscarora photographer] Jolene Rickard about it, in the Iroquois culture there are those people that become runners who go out and they come back, bringing information back. That information is looked at, studied, watched, and if it creates something that the tribe allows to happen, the runner goes out again. So, in many ways, from where I am and where my culture is, I look at myself as a runner, because I wanted to go out and understand the world. So I'm always in change. One of the things that has been very important to me is to understand that aspect of culture. There are those who preserve this aspect of the culture, what I call the grass-roots people and the traditionalists, because it's an important aspect of the community and the tribe. It is an aspect, really, of the spirit. But there are also those who are the hardliners, where the culture owns them. It's like, "this is the way it's got to be; no changes."

Well, the other aspect was to look at the whole thing about, "Do I own culture, or does culture own me?" Now, if culture owns me, I don't doubt that I would've been something within the tribe, maybe a leader. But because I was a runner, I brought information into the culture, and that allowed me to change and therefore to grow. If it doesn't have that capacity, then the culture becomes stagnant and can die. So, in one sense, when I was looking at it, the whole space was basically the culture: "Okay, ha-ha, you're stuck. We got you!" And so it was a battle for me at that time, but I just see, right now, that it's changed so much. As we begin to understand the game, we bring more and more information back to the culture and allow the culture to grow. And that in itself is change.

SELECTED EXHIBITIONS

"500 Years Since Columbus" (1992), group exhibition, Triton Museum of Art, Santa Clara, CA.

"Haudenosaunee Artists: A Common Heritage" (1992), group exhibition, Tower Fine Arts Gallery, State University of New York, Brockport, NY.

"Indigena: Contemporary Native Perspectives" (1992), group exhibition, Canadian Museum of Civilization, Hull, Quebec.

"The Submuloc Show/Columbus Wohs" (1992–94), group traveling exhibition, Atlatl, Phoenix, AZ.

"We, The Human Beings/27 Contemporary Native American Artists" (1992–93), group traveling exhibition, College of Wooster Art Museum, Wooster, OH.

"Acknowledging Our Host: Communal Sources" (1991–92), group exhibition, Richmond Art Center, Richmond, CA.

"America" (1991), group exhibition, Center for Contemporary Art, Sacramento, CA.

"Our Land/Ourselves" (1991–93), group traveling exhibition, University Art Gallery, State University of New York, Albany, NY.

"Shared Visions" (1991–93), group traveling exhibition, Heard Museum, Phoenix, AZ.

"The Decade Show" (1990), group exhibition, New Museum of Contemporary Art, New York, NY.

"George Longfish" (1989), solo exhibition, Jennifer Pauls Gallery, Sacramento, CA.

"George Longfish Paintings" (1989), solo exhibition, LRC Gallery, College of the Siskiyous, Weed, CA.

"Eight Native American Artists" (1987–88), group exhibition, Fort Wayne Museum of Art, Fort Wayne, IN.

"Common Ground: New Works by George Longfish" (1986), solo exhibition, Bernice Steinbaum Gallery, New York, NY.

"The Extension of Tradition" (1985–86), group traveling exhibition, Crocker Art Museum, Sacramento, CA.

"Paintings by George Longfish" (1984), solo exhibition, Museum of the Plains Indian and Crafts Center, Browning, MT.

"Contemporary Native American Art" (1983), group exhibition, Gardiner Art Gallery, Oklahoma State University, Stillwater, OK.

SELECTED BIBLIOGRAPHY

Longfish, George. Untitled essay. In *Indigena: Contemporary Native Perspectives*. Hull, Quebec: Canadian Museum of Civilization, 1992, pp. 150–51.

WalkingStick, Kay. "Like a Longfish Out of Water" [interview]. *Northeast Indian Quarterly* 7, 3 (Fall 1989): 16–23.

Longfish, George. "Artist's Statement." In *Eight Native American Artists*. Fort Wayne, IN: Fort Wayne Museum of Art, 1987, pp. 36–37.

——, and Joan Randall. "Runners between the Tribes." In *New Directi ons Northwest: Contemporary Native American Art*. Portland, OR: Portland Art Museum, and Olympia, WA: Evergreen State College, 1987, pp. 14–19.

——, and Joan Randall. "Runners between the Tribes." In *New Directions Contemporary Northern California Native American Art in Cultural Perspective*, edited by Frank LaPena and Janice Driesbach. Sacramento, CA: Crocker Art Museum, 1985, pp. 44–47.

——, and Joan Randall. "Contradictions in Indian Territory." In *Contemporary Native American Art*. Stillwater, OK: Gardiner Art Gallery, Oklahoma State University, 1983. Reprinted with minor revision in the *Journal of Arts Management and Law* 18, 2 (Summer 1988): 20–24.

——, and Joan Randall. "New Ways of Old Visions: The Evolution of Contemporary Native American Art." *Artspace: Southwestern Contemporary Arts Quarterly* 6, 3 (Summer 1982): 24–27.

——. "Artist's Statement." In *The Sweet Grass Lives On*, by Jamake Highwater. New York: Lippincott and Crowell, 1980, pp. 144–45.

Mario Martinez

Yaqui

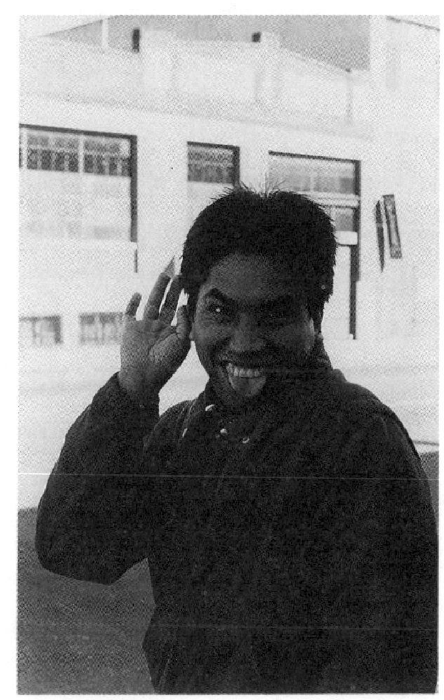

Although Mario Martinez has lived in San Francisco for nearly ten years, he has maintained a strong connection to the Arizona desert and to his Yaqui heritage through the color and composition of his work. There is a dynamic movement and feeling of density in many of his paintings which bring forth the essence of Yaqui ceremonialism. *Earth Stick* (1990), for example, focuses some elements of the Yaqui Easter celebration on the sword used in dancing during Holy Week, the end of the ceremonial year.

Although other works have different references, they also show an underlay of traditional Yaqui imagery with Martinez' characteristic colors. *Bleeding Earth* (1990) suggests an ecological nightmare, while the structure of the 1986 *Desert* reminds the viewer of Gauguin's French landscapes. Still other pieces seek a political dialogue, as *For Nelson Mandela* (1990) shows. Although he is not a political activist and prefers to let his paintings and works on paper carry his ideas, Martinez is involved in curatorial work that gains exposure for artists of color. But in what could be called a political act in America in the 1990s, Martinez has dedicated *To My Lavender Siblings* (1991) to other members of the Yaqui community who are homosexual. This work, mixed media and acrylic on paper, embeds a photograph of traditional deer dancers within a bell-shaped form, and is more figurative than most of his other work.

This range of concern may well spring from the various worlds of Martinez's childhood and adolescence. Born in 1953, he really considers himself tricultural, having grown up in Phoenix in an urban Yaqui community in the midst of surrounding Anglo and Mexican cultures, an environment that allowed him to draw on a wide spectrum of sources for his life and art.

Martinez received his B.F.A. from Arizona State University in 1979 and an M.F.A. from the San Francisco Art Institute in 1985. His formal art education thoroughly grounded him in European modernism, and he has acknowledged Monet, Kandinsky, and Picasso as instrumental in the evolution of his vision.

But coming to an understanding of the growth of Martinez's work involves seeing the synthesizing power of his art, seeing the boldness of Kandinsky, for example, along with the sense of color and symbolic form derived from Yaqui culture. As Martinez has written about the evolution of his painting:

> For many years my work has been a synthesis of Western modernist visual traditions and concepts with images rooted in my Yaqui Indian heritage. Now my creative quest has expanded to include not only concepts and images from my specific cultural background but also materials used by Yaquis in ceremonial traditions and ceremonial regalia. . . . because I was born a member of a great indigenous culture situated within the world's most technologically advanced nation, I hope my work captures a contemporary cultural dynamic, specifically some of the emotional, spiritual, and psychological dimensions I experience when observing Yaqui cultural traditions.[1]

We talked in San Francisco in May 1991 while looking at paintings and works in progress lining the walls and hallway of his studio.

LA: To start with, could you talk about your art education background? When did you start drawing and painting, and what were some of the influences on you?

MM: I guess I've always identified as an artist since I was very young. I even remember painting in kindergarten with tempera paints. It was just an involvement with color, and it had a really profound effect on me. I knew I was an artist! I just felt an inner connection to color and paint. I remember in my second grade class, Mrs. Cawkin's class, that I learned what the term "artist" meant, because everybody would say to me, "You're such a terrific artist." So I identified the action of painting or drawing, art projects in class, that type of thing, as part of the artistic and creative process. I remember clearly that that's what I thought of myself. Of course, I didn't really know how that was going to be in later life, and of course I didn't have a totally concrete idea of what an artist's life was, but I *knew* that I was an artist. That feeling and belief went all through grade school, high school, through the good times and the bad times. I had slack periods constantly, but that identification with art was there all the time.

I graduated from high school in 1972 and started at a community college. I went for a year, dropped out in 1973 for two years, and then went on to Arizona State [ASU] from '75 to '79 and got my B.F.A. At ASU I was introduced to the whole realm of modernism and to art history, in the Western sense, and that has always had an effect on me, whatever I do. Painting from the nineteenth century on has had a profound effect on me.

LA: How much do you think artists like Monet and Picasso and other modernists have influenced you?

MM: Well, to be honest, they've influenced my work a lot, and yet at the same time I'm doing a big turnaround at this point in that before, I always knew that my specific cultural experience was part of me and part of my identity, and therefore was part of my art, even if it wasn't all that clear in the art. But now I think that I have to go back to explore that cultural aspect. I mean, I have to continue learning how to paint and how my work fits into the contemporary scene and the modernist tradition. But I also have my specific culture to look at; that was the first source of my experience, so I want to see how that information can be presented in an artistic context.

I mean, artists like George Longfish — he puts it right on the line, he's got it down. It's true that we as Native Americans have something of another dimension of cultural experience than the general population. The Euro-American has a different source, but Native people have had lots of different experiences. So modernists have been very influential on my approach and my thinking, but now I'm going back to the deeper or more underlying sense of the basis of it all, and that's been my culture, my heritage.

LA: How would you characterize what George calls "cultural information"? What would that be in the Yaqui world?

MM: It would be everything. But more specifically, it would have to do with the true and basic essence of one's identity. With any contemporary individual there are so many sources in your identity, but like I said, the one thing that makes Native Americans very different is that they do have that cultural information or background which is unique; they will never be able to get away from it. Not that one would want to, but it's so powerful and has such a profound effect that it alters and dominates your world-view for your whole life. This to me is cultural information—not just facts, but the totality of the meanings within the culture and the interconnections of the meanings.

LA: What were some of the other influences in your upbringing? Were you also influenced by the other cultures in Phoenix, and the so-called dominant culture?

MM: Yeah, I guess you could say it was dominant, in the sense that when it comes to politics, economics, and the media, there is broad control of information. I grew up basically in three worlds: the Yaqui culture, the Mexican-American culture, and the Anglo culture. The Anglo culture has also always been there. When I go back to my first images of childhood, besides those from my Yaqui culture, the cultural tradition was TV. It's very strange, but we grew up on that, and my first really enjoyable recollection was Dick Clark and "American Bandstand" and all the music from the fifties on. Music is a real pleasure, and I've always been a rock-and-roll fan. People wouldn't think that, but it's true; it's a part of my experience.

LA: That's interesting, because you wrote in the catalog for "Talking Drum," "My work is a visual revelation of a dual cultural identity."

MM: It's really tricultural, but go ahead.

LA: You continue: "I believe my work is abstract because abstract reasoning is primary to the mythic qualities of Yaqui songs, dances, ceremonial rituals and religion, as well as to the essence of the western European modernist tradition. My works are my visual interpretations of Yaqui ceremonial regalia designs."[2] How do you embed in your painting these aspects of Yaqui culture? I'm thinking of the painting *Earth Stick* [1990], which looked to me like a Chapayeka's stick.

MM: The sword work? The ceremonial work? Did you see that? Nobody else can get it, you know. I'm glad you got it. That's the sword used in the Yaqui Easter ceremonies, so I just took the shape and the form of the design from the ceremonial wooden swords. So in the sense that somebody didn't know that information, they wouldn't understand the cultural reference.

LA: How much more abstraction or symbolization of Yaqui culture is in that painting, or in others generally?

MM: I give more information in some paintings than others. I think that although I have literal or figurative elements in my work at times, and sometimes these elements are more apparent than at other times, I am still very geared toward abstraction in the sense of an emotional quality, a psychological quality, and a quote "spiritual" unquote quality that comes about when you partake of and know certain things about your culture that are not interpreted visually, in a work of art. I've always felt that what goes on in ceremonies in my culture, our cultural traditions, and even what goes on in everyday life—in any culture—is identified with in a literal way, and maybe less often, not in a way that understands the essence. I try to present the essence in a visual way, in an abstract way. Like, how do you really know what anything is? That's the realm that I'm interested in. Some people pick it up and some people don't, some people care and some people don't.

LA: How much do you as an artist think about that, that is, people not understanding a particular work? Somebody could look at *Earth Stick*, for example, and say, "That's a nice color and a nice shape," but they don't relate to the totality of the meaning of the work.

MM: Well, I think it comes down to one's life and cultural experience and one's personality. I'm just geared toward what I do, and don't worry about people's responses in terms of the style and structure and content of a work.

In that sense, I guess I'm on the side of quote "contemporary Native American visual expression," unquote, in that my work tends to be less recognizable as Indian art, whatever that is, however people define that. I mean, those images are not so apparent or graspable, perhaps, but I also believe that in any kind of cultural expression there is a realm of creation that is in and of itself. That's just the creative part of it.

For me there is a psychological and emotional reality to the creative experience. And that means that there is a part of life, and certainly part of art, if not all of it, that's undefinable and very mysterious and very beautiful, and it doesn't have to be explained the whole time. I think if people look at my work and say, "Well, it's not identifiable as Native American," they can still respond to it on many other levels and, I hate to say this—dimensions—because it sounds so corny, but they can experience it visually even if they don't have a clue into the culture.

This is not to say that you totally ignore the audience, because you're attempting to communicate; that's the basis of it all. Now, you may be communicating something, but on the other end, you have no control over what a viewer is getting. The larger problem seems to me to be that out there in America people seem to have this need to define us and our art in a certain way, and when we don't fit into that mold, then we're in the mainstream or we're not Indians or something. This says to me that people believe that all Indian cultural experience is the same, which obviously it's not. So as an abstract artist, people say to me, "Your images aren't specific enough, you're not being literal enough, you're not presenting Indian imagery," which is the imagery that they want to see. They tell us our experience and then how to paint it and draw it.

I know what my experiences are. It's very offensive when people lay that on me. I mean, I'm in tune precisely with my culture, what it is and what I get out of it, but I'm also in tune with and have correlations with many other artists from many different cultural backgrounds. I've had critics tell me that my painting has no recognizable cultural symbolism or that I have nothing to say in the work.

It's funny to me, and quite maddening really, that people who have never really given a damn about Indian culture and Indian people, not in the least concerned about what really happened to the Native cultures in their own land, are all of a sudden trying to set boundaries about our art. At this moment in my life I am very happy with the term "Native American artist" in the sense that while nobody wants to be pegged and get secondary or tertiary status in the art world, the labels are *their* doing, not my doing. Labels are tied in with economics and all the rest, but it also has to do with miscommunication or noncommunication and ignorance about what Native culture is and is not. So for me to say that I'm a Native American, a Yaqui, is very important, because if I don't say it's all right, then it's never going to be all right. As a Native person, a Native artist, if I don't say it's all right to be who I am, then it's almost like saying that, yes, I am playing a role, I do have secondary status in society. Until you say it's all right to be Indian, or black, or a woman, or gay, it's not. So for me, I'm owning the label.

LA: You mentioned earlier, and sort of bring it up again, your multicultural upbringing and your correlations with other artists. You did a painting in 1990 titled *For Nelson Mandela*. How did that come about?

MM: What happened was that that weekend, I think on a Friday, I heard that Mandela was going to be released, and I really didn't believe it because I thought, yeah, right, another disappointment. On that Sunday I started the painting. It was an old painting, a small painting, and I scraped all the paint off and started painting on the canvas again. He did get released and I finished the painting in about eight hours. I was taken by the fact that this really amazing person, an extraordinary person, was alive right now. In the painting I made him a symbol for what human beings can be, against all odds, to be who you are. It's like, who are you and what do you hold onto? What is really crucial to you as a person? I mean, he has done everything that is morally and ethically right, and he's gotten so much contention from his stand, that to me he is a hero in the human sense. So I thought, in my own little way, that I'd make a painting. It was like a psychological and emotional tribute to him.

LA: You touch a bit here on your working methods, at least with that work. Do you have a particular way of approaching a canvas?

MM: I work in lots of ways. Sometimes I'll work on two at a time because there's not enough money to go to four. I have at times worked on four or five at the same time, though. But one always wins; one takes your interest and you go with it. It holds you for a while until you finish it, or almost finish it. I take anywhere from a couple of weeks to six months to finish a painting.

So in six months I could make a lot, or only one or two, depending on the situation and what's happening with the painting.

I'm very nonanalytical, intuitive, so I don't really think about what it is that's going to be done or how it's going to be done. I just begin. I do have ideas about how I feel about certain things, in that I'm very aware of what's going on here in the city. I'm here by myself and I've never been more aware of my culture than when I'm painting. For me, painting takes me down to the real essence of things and to the core of my very being, which is always in doubt anyway and is always being questioned in our culture.

I mean, how many critics have said that there's no genuine human experience anymore, so trying to do a painting or make any other form of art is useless? But they don't know Indians; they really don't. If you lost all identity, if you've gone through the whole homogenizing process, if you lost your identity and your heritage, if you lost community, if you move away from your family, if you've done all that, then that is all dead for you. But Indians don't do that, and even when we do—it may happen sometime, I don't really know—but even when we do, we can never forget community, that group we came from. We can never let go of that emotional, psychological, and spiritual attachment that we have. I think the difference is that Native Americans are always aware of that real sense of being human within a group. I think mainstream America has lost all that. And that attitude is reinforced by the media and by consumerism, for example, and while I partake in that somewhat, I know the difference. At least I feel like I do, even if that feeling might be an illusion.

LA: You've been in San Francisco about eight and a half years, but much of your work seems to be concerned with nature and even the Arizona landscape.

MM: Really? Go ahead.

LA: Like the 1986 painting *Desert*. How much does memory come into play in your paintings? Are you still influenced by the land in Arizona, the desert?

MM: Well, I'll tell you something: Arizona is still home. My father died two weeks ago and I went back for what would be considered a more traditional Yaqui funeral and burial, and it made me realize that no matter how urban one gets, meaning me, and how much I'm in this culture leading a contemporary life, there is really no comparison. This contemporary life is nothing to what I sensed back home where everything was going on.

It was very intense. The Yaqui priest and the *cantoras* came to pray. The Yaqui Matachines came to dance because they were his friends. The sense of family and community was so intense that it shifted my focus and my eyes again, meaning that no experience that I've had in this modern setting in San Francisco can match it. I didn't expect that. It kind of threw me for a loop because I knew it was always there and I'm always pulling on it, my — how would I put it? I guess my cultural sources — that the specific cultural sources have been with me all my life and that's what I've been drawing on, but I really didn't realize, or I had forgotten. I still go back once a year for the ceremonies. What a pity it is to lose all that if one chooses to go away from the group forever.

LA: Do you think that in your art you maintain that connection to the group?

MM: Well, in my art I'm always pretty lonely, meaning that it's such an individual, loner experience. It's not collaborative at all. In that sense, time and time again when I am painting, especially here in San Francisco, I realize how I left the group — a feeling of loss, you know, like, why am I here and not with the group? The question is always there because, like I say, when I paint is when I'm really most aware of who I am in terms of my original experience. It's getting to the core of being Indian and human. My Indian cultural identity is so powerful that I'm reminded that I'm basically alone and so there's a longing there. I guess I just had to see that there were other things, that there was a big, wide world out there.

Related to that, though, is the fact that in the Yaqui culture there is a big element of individualism. It's a myth that all Indians are the same, or that even in the tribe all are the same. You can do what you need to do when you need to do it, whether it follows group beliefs or not, and you don't have to believe exactly the way everyone else does, you know, totally accepting everything because everybody else is acting, being, and doing the same way. I got a formal education, so that was big part of taking me away.

LA: Maybe we can shift gears here a minute. Looking at a number of your works here in the studio it struck me that many patterns and shapes seem to recur, and colors certainly recur. You use a lot of yellows and reds and browns.

MM: Blues, everything. You haven't seen them all. But I feel that at this moment these paintings are my very loose interpretations of what design feels to be to me. A lot of the imagery has to do with cultural designs, like the ceremonial swords we talked about, but also essential designs from nature, like sticks, shapes of trees, branches. Now that I'm getting into mixed media more and more, I'm using the materials that my tribe would use in ceremonies, like ceremonial clothing. But certain forms are in much of my work, even if they aren't so apparent to people. Somehow or other that obsessiveness with design should spell it out, what I'm doing, but I guess it doesn't.

LA: Red is an important color in Yaqui.

MM: Yeah, and I already forgot the interpretation. I mean I always use it and I say, "What is it?" The definitions are escaping me right now. But it has to do with the flower world, and the deer dancer wears a red sash or cloth that's just a flower or maybe flower pollen. It could be all kinds of stuff.

Color for me, though, is more just my personality. I'm very attracted to brighter colors, and I can think of it, I guess, as what my culture likes in color, how we interpret color in our culture and in our traditions, and what the average Yaqui person would find aesthetically beautiful. I think that a lot of indigenous people go toward that very festive or very bright color.

But I was also influenced by Kandinsky and a few other modernists. I mean, really, you are who you are and you're attracted to do certain things because of your personality. So the use of color in my work is very personal; it might make some people throw up, while others will find it attractive.

LA: How much was Kandinsky an influence?

MM: Well, all I remember is when I saw Kandinsky's work I was floored, because even though I didn't know the meaning of the shapes and stuff, I didn't need to. Whatever he was doing with the shapes, if it was figurative or nonfigurative, it was the way he was using color and texture and movement that hit me. I understood his work on that level. I really did. I was so attracted to it that I thought, man, this is too much. I think I maybe got caught in it too deeply. Picasso, too. I think he was probably the major influence. He's very controversial right now, being that he was imperfect and inhumane and an ogre at times. But I think what he left and what you can see in his work is amazing. There is a life force there, sometimes a negative life force, but certainly a powerful force.

LA: Your painting *Bleeding Earth* [1990] is a commanding piece, pretty large, about six feet by six feet. Could you talk about that work? How did it develop for you? Would you start with colors or with shapes?

MM: I generally work medium to large, but not over six by six because my studio is too small. Well, I was having a show at the C. N. Gorman Museum, George's place over at Davis [George Longfish, director of the museum], and he was very nice to let me have a show there. I needed a big painting because there was a lot of wall space; actually, I needed a lot of paintings. I had always worked sort of large but that space was something else. I finished all the paintings for that show in six months, but the last two months were the clincher. I finished *Bleeding Earth* in two weeks.

But I'm not an artist who starts with a plan and just paints it in. On this one I just started putting paint on and the ideas or images develop as I go. It's always apparent to me that I'm involved in natural forms, the branches and sticks, the connections between them, the visual connections of the design element and the natural form. I'm trying to bring out the idea that we're more connected to nature than we realize. We're like the tree and the air and the earth. We're interdependent. I'm reading this Buddhist, a Vietnamese Buddhist, Thich Nhat Hanh, and he says that paper you're reading, that paper is you, you are connected with it. And like the tree from which that paper is made, you're connected to the tree and everything else because the tree provides air for you to breathe. Without the system that's got it all going, which is the natural system of the Earth, none of us is going to be. So whether you realize it or not, in a way you are the paper.

This painting, and my paintings generally, are about my reality and about nature. Maybe my work can help us to see just a little bit into the future, to see some of the choices in front of us, in terms of the environment. My involvement in the creative arts is one way to promote something positive.

LA: When you were back in Arizona for your father's funeral, did you think about moving back there? Or is being here part of the whole process of being a painter, a sort of momentum that comes from living in San Francisco?

MM: I think that maybe one day, when it feels right to be there, I won't hesitate to go back, because it is home. I mean, home is the world, Mother Earth, and as a human being I'm a pretty contemporary citizen of the world, not just an American or a Native American. I work for the whole world in the broad multicultural sense. It's a "world you," so to speak. So I think that I could probably live anywhere, but if it felt right, and if it ever does, then I'll know then that I could move back to Arizona.

I moved to San Francisco for graduate school at the Art Institute, that was first and foremost. But when I was in high school, in the late sixties, I was a young hippie. Now I'm going on thirty-eight. But I had this idea back then that San Francisco was *the* place to be, that it was the happening place. Little did I know; I mean it was over before it started, but I still had this thing. So I thought, if I'm going to move somewhere, it has to be San Francisco. So there was that, plus school. Then the other part of it was that San Francisco became a real big gay community, and part of the reason that I didn't fit into my culture at the time is that being gay wasn't totally socially acceptable. It still isn't, but I think my Yaqui community is very cool about it. So the combination of the three reasons led me to coming out here. Still, I'm not a real full-fledged member of the gay community; I hardly know any gay people in San Francisco and I'm just not interested in Madonna (that's a joke), but just to know that there is a community as large as this feels comfortable to me.

LA: In addition to your painting, you also curate shows and work in various multicultural projects. Do you feel that your work has a political dimension on some level?

MM: Well, the political aspects of it would be the way that I approach my view of where we are as a culture, or cultures, in this nation, and how I speak the truth about my being in the world. But certainly it is not so evident ever in the art. But it is unfortunate—or maybe it's really not unfortunate—that if you're a Native American and speak the truth about your heritage and your history, then all of a sudden you become a political bad guy, you know. The other side never wants to know the truth. So I don't know if I'm very comfortable with that, because we're not the bad guys and never were. I don't want to make anybody feel guilty, but nobody's really wanted to know the real history of America. So that creates a lot of ignorance, intolerance, and the human ills we see toward Native Americans and everybody else.

Are we supposed to see some sort of changes in the nineties, because of '92? Everybody keeps saying that the decade of the nineties is going to be this and that and all of the above and focused on Native cultures and the Americas. I don't know; I really don't know. I've heard before from people who have lived longer than I have that we come into fashion every twenty years, so this might be our little fifteen minutes.

All I know is that all I can do is to become more aware of myself constantly as a person who is Native American and lives in the United States. But all that other stuff, it's just superficial. Even politics is superficial. It's all special interest, it's all economics. Basically I'm hopeful, but I've always been a cynic. And so I don't expect too much to come out of it, but if something does, then I'll be the first person to be really happy about it. All these things come along, *Dances with Wolves*, stuff like that can happen culturally, but I don't know if they are going to stay around for any length of time and have a more permanent effect on society.

LA: So you get your Warholian fifteen minutes and the society at large then goes on to something else.

MM: Can real lasting change even happen if people don't have a desire to learn about us? We don't even know the history of Native peoples in this country, so how much change can really take root? How much is going to happen if most people don't even want to learn the fact that Indians were slaughtered like crazy? To get to the point where a large majority of people have to accept that their forefathers were part and parcel of that . . . I just don't see where any change can hold.

LA: What about in terms of art? Can Native art be an agent for change?

MM: For the last five years the people most responsive to my work have been Native people, like George Longfish and Jaune Quick-to-See Smith, and people from different cultures. They seem to understand it and feel that we're all in this together, that it's all right that we're not in the mainstream and all that kind of stuff. But we're going along. It's almost like many different streams, and the mainstream is the dominant one that has all the political power and all the economic power, but there are all these other streams that have at times crisscrossed, like the Latino or the Chicano or the Native American or the Asian. We're all existing in the same moment and going along and nobody's turning to us and saying, "Oh, you are the artists of our culture and this generation." They're not saying that.

But that doesn't mean that one doesn't live the life of the artist, as a creative person, as a human being, that one just gives up and says, "Well, they're not paying attention to us, so we'd better stop being creative individuals." It's never been like that. If the mainstream cultural institutions and galleries did suddenly recognize us and legitimize us in a way as Native American or Asian-American or African-American artists, that would be just one level. Sure, it would be great and would mean a lot monetarily for artists, and for influencing other artists, and for communicating to a broader quote unquote "world." I mean, if you're not in a magazine or in the media you're not going to communicate with too many people. But at the same time I think that most of us are aware that that probably will not happen in our lifetimes. But why would that stop us? Why would we stop creating, or learning, or teaching?

SELECTED EXHIBITIONS

"Hot Native Art" (1992), group exhibition, Gallery of the American Indian Community House, New York, NY.

"We, the Human Beings" (1992), group traveling exhibition, College of Wooster Art Museum, Wooster, OH.

"Portfolio III: Ten Native American Artists" (1991), group exhibition, American Indian Contemporary Arts, San Francisco, CA.

"Our Land/Ourselves" (1991) group traveling exhibition, University Art Gallery, State University of New York, Albany, NY.

"The New Genre: In the Dissidence of Tradition" (1989), group exhibition, Berkeley Art Center, Berkeley, CA.

"Four Sacred Mountains: Color, Form, and Abstraction" (1988), group traveling exhibition, Arizona Arts Commission, Phoenix, AZ.

"Introductions '86" (1986), group exhibition, Gallery Paule Anglim, San Francisco, CA.

SELECTED BIBLIOGRAPHY

Martinez, Mario. "Artist's Statement." In *We, the Human Beings*. Wooster, OH: College of Wooster Art Museum, 1992, p. 30.

——. "Artist's Statement." In *Portfolio III: Ten Native American Artists*. San Francisco, CA: American Indian Contemporary Arts, 1991, p. 22.

——. "Artist's Statement." In *Talking Drum: Connected Vision*. Oakland, CA: Koncepts Cultural Gallery, 1990, unp.

Nora Naranjo-Morse

Santa Clara

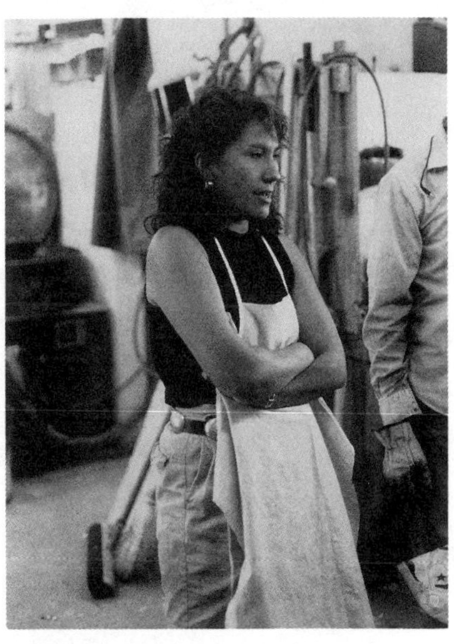

Nora Naranjo-Morse's studio is home to spirits in the process of birth. Bits of clay, moist coils, nascent forms, and finished pieces, standing and hung, are spread throughout her workspace, which is in front of her home in the Santa Clara Pueblo, less than an hour north of Santa Fe.

The studio is a microcosm of her work in clay, mirroring the stages that she follows in developing a piece, and is a clear instance of what Stephen Trimble meant when he wrote: "Potters live in the present; they don't hoard the past."[1] Decidedly contemporary sculptures, fetishes, masks, and clay hangings stand on the floor and adorn the walls and corners of the studio. But even though the imagery is not what comes to mind when Santa Clara pottery is mentioned, Naranjo-Morse still maintains a strong connection to tradition, from digging her clay to filtering it, fashioning it, and firing it. It is her relationship to the clay which places her squarely in the Santa Clara tradition.

Naranjo-Morse was born in Espanola, New Mexico, in 1953, but spent her early life at Taos, where her father, Michael Naranjo, served as a Baptist missionary for nearly three decades. She left Taos at sixteen, but her time there has much to do with the unique look of her work and her use of micaceous clay. Earlier pieces, like *A*

Christmas Scene (1986) and a 1987 untitled sculpture of a Pueblo village, utilize "images of ladders from the multi-storied pueblo and of clowns not seen at Santa Clara for years."[2]

She has studied at the College of Santa Fe, but the understanding of and respect for clay came from watching and experimenting and, after she returned to Santa Clara in her twenties, following her own lead. "Holding that clay was the first time I ever felt a connection with something greater than myself. . . . I had come home."[3]

But the key to appreciating the vitality of Naranjo-Morse's work is to recognize its diversity and its evolution. Throughout the 1980s her work included Pueblo scenes and clowns; other sculptures, like *Wheat Girl,* originally done in 1988; and the reflective, meditative *My Favorite Time of Night/The Bird Is Transformed When She Comes Home* (1986),[4] and the *Pearlene* series, for which she is best known. The satirical edge to these pieces, and their gentle but pointed humor, provide her comment on contemporary Pueblo life.

With the close of the *Pearlene* series Naranjo-Morse has not stopped exploring new directions. She continues to find different ways of expressing her vision and reflecting the changes she experiences. Her most recent work, like the *Mask of Singer* series and *We kwee na muu* (both 1991), show her openness to fresh influences. The latter piece, the delicate suggestion of a female form in repose, reveals a new level of accomplishment in her handling of clay. She has written: "I'm stretching the boundaries of what the clay has been asked to do so far. . . . The pieces just represent who I am and what I go through at particular stages in my life. I think that is what art is."[5]

In 1992 Naranjo-Morse's book of poems, *Mud Woman,* was published by the University of Arizona Press. Like her work in clay, the poems explore different facets of her art and her life, from the character of Pearlene to her family to her role as a modern Pueblo woman.

We talked one afternoon in late July 1991 in her studio while she took a break from work on some new figures, and then again a year later when she was working on some new bronzes at a foundry outside of Santa Fe.

LA: How did you begin in clay, and how did your early work develop and evolve?

NNM: My mother and most of my six sisters do pottery. When I started, everyone was doing symmetrical bowls, perfectly shaped. But that was the hardest thing for me to do, and I thought that something must be wrong with me. Not being able to make those kind of pots represented to me that I wasn't part of this group of women who make pottery. But I wanted to work with clay, so I started making things. That's what happened. I just picked the clay up, and instead of worrying about what turned out, I started making forms and figures. I knew that something was happening because I could feel it. Do you know when something is right? I had never had that "so right" feeling so strongly before, so I kept on making the figures. That's how they began.

LA: When was this?

NNM: About fifteen or sixteen years ago, in the 1970s.

LA: Some of the figures and scenes are humorous, even satiric, like *The Intellectual from Tuba City* [1988] and the Pearlene pieces, like *The All American Woman (Someone Take That Credit Card Away from Pearlene)* [1988] and *Pearlene Teaching Her Cousins Poker* [1987].

NNM: I think that Pueblo people have a great sense of humor, but it's often lost in the translation. But it's very basic, raw, and sharp. When I go to, say, Las Vegas, where I went for the first time, how could I not leave there without saying something about it? The statement in clay which involved Pearlene teaching her cousins how to play poker, I mean the idea of this modern Pueblo woman teaching her traditional cousins the art of the game, verged on the ridiculous. I combined what I had done while visiting Las Vegas with who I am in the Pueblo. So that's how some of those pieces came about. And, yes, the humor is on purpose, but that's the way it comes out on its own. I don't dare manipulate it, because it could become contrived. When it is humorous it's because it should be that way.

LA: How did Pearlene as a character develop?

NNM: I don't make Pearlene anymore; she was a phase that's now over. She started maybe ten years ago when I was trying to figure out my place and, being a modern Pueblo woman, trying to find out where I belonged. And I was trying to say things that I was not ready to say, or was afraid to say. It was easy for me to make these sculptures that said those things, like, "Hey, I went to

Vegas and had an incredible time and I want to tell you about it." Or the Pearlene that's shopping [*The All American Woman*]. So she evolved that way because of circumstances I experience on a daily basis. What was so magical about her was that once I did her, people immediately started to relate to her and see reflections of themselves or their relatives or their friends in her. She has a universal appeal. That's also why I stopped making her. The last of Pearlene came about because some businessman from California wanted me to make a mold so we could mass-produce her. She had been such an important part of who I was that to mass-produce her would reduce her message and make her less meaningful for me. Pearlene was a real turning point in what I was trying to do as a human being and as an artist that I couldn't just let her become ordinary or overdone. I wanted her to be special. So one day I came in the studio and made the last one. That was it. People still call me all the time about her. We're talking about her now. Sometimes I miss her and wonder what it would have been like to keep making her. But something would have been stunted in who I am and who I'm trying to be, if I kept making her because of market demands.

LA: She sounds like she was an alter ego.

NNM: She was an alter ego who honestly told me the way things were. She represents the soul or the source of us as a good, kind, creative, conscious, and often mischievous people. That's why so many people related to her.

LA: As much as you created her, she created you.

NNM: Exactly. That was such a wild thing because I had never experienced that before and it was great. I could come into the studio and just look at her for hours and think about her and her next move. It was good to know her.

LA: It sounds like when a style turns into a formula it prevents an artist from following a new direction. You're sort of caught by success.

NNM: Marketing of Indian art is very popular and has been a strong creative and monetary influence in the Pueblos for a long time. My mother even talks about the traders who would come in and ask her to make the same bowl over and over again. The tourists like things that are identifiably Southwestern. The talk has become more sophisticated, but it's really the same basic message about which direction you should go. That goes against my grain and what I want to accomplish. I'm here in this life for such a short time that I want it to be real for me. I understand that whatever decisions others make are fine for them, but for me I wanted to try it my way. I think that's really reflected in what I do.

LA: An artist might get well-known for a particular thing, but then if she goes on to something else, people will only relate to the past work.

NNM: And people want that because it's easiest and most comfortable. I think it's hard for a lot of people to see and accept new work. It's hard for *me* to accept new things, because after Pearlene I was really nervous and didn't know what to do. I was afraid, but I see that also in people who are collectors. They generally have to be told what is good or what's not so good, what the criteria are, instead of just seeing something and saying, "Yes, that's it!" One simply has to trust that part of the self that feels, allowing the choices one makes, whether it's to purchase a new form from an artist, or for the artist to create something new and exciting. I want my life to be that way, so it's probably hard for people who collect my work. There are some things I'm really certain about, but at the same time I'm not ever sure where I'm going.

LA: It sounds like there are some perils to success.

NNM: I used to worry about it, but now I just do what I want. I'm getting ready to do life-sized sculptures out of adobe and metal. That's always been in the back of my mind, but I've never had enough confidence. Success has given me the confidence. But that's a difference type of success that comes from learning. The other kind of success I have a hard time relating to. Somebody will want to interview me, and I get nervous, because the way I see myself is, I'm the person who, after you leave, will go to the house and cook and clean. That's who I am. Going to the Smithsonian or a gallery opening for a cocktail party is something I have to acclimate myself to. Traditional Pueblo women don't know about that. Five o'clock cocktails? I have to get used to all that. The cooking and cleaning I've got down, though.

LA: You once wrote, "It makes sense that whatever emotion I bring into the studio is released into the clay. You're touching it. It's a circle, the connection between me and the finished product. People that react to my work enter the circle. They are involved in the experience. That's what pottery is all about for me."[6] Could you talk about how that connection process works?

NNM: That has a real strong traditional base, because every

spring my mother, sometimes my sisters, the children, cousins, we put our picks and shovels in the truck and go out to get clay. From the moment we make the decision to do this it becomes the start of a coil; digging the clay out of the earth becomes an involvement in a real powerful thing. In the larger society everything is fast-moving, but what clay does for me is slow everything down. The whole process is long and can be difficult, especially if you're carrying out wet mud from the side of a mountain and dragging it to the truck. You're giving yourself. It's a commitment and I really love that; it nurtures me, does something to me, it does something to my mother. And that's why I say it probably comes from a traditional base. And once I start on this process, all that I am, Indian woman, wife, mother, and all the things I do, like baking cookies, making chili, eating sushi, visiting Hawaii, everything I am or have done, gets released into this clay, this material, because I feel very close to it and I allow myself to be comfortable with it. I build a rapport and commit myself to it. That creative channel is opened and there's a feeling of tremendous freedom.

And if you work with clay on a daily basis you appreciate it more, it becomes more symbolic. I believe in my heart that the Indian people where I'm from feel that, too, because they have the connection to the earth. Many talk about their connection to the earth, and this is how I get it for myself. Clay teaches me the wild, wonderful, precious things that come from creating, but also all kinds of other things about life. That's why it's such a powerful thing.

LA: There's a whole dimension of touching, of hauling, of carrying, the physical labor, that people don't realize.

NNM: Yeah, it's not just what you see at the end. In fact, the final, finished product is only a small part of the entire creative process.

LA: Although your work is not traditional, in the sense of bowls and the like, you are still sustained by pottery-making traditions.

NNM: It's a basic feeling, very primal. I become so involved that I feel that the more clay that's all over me, the better. I can be covered in it. It's very sensual. For the Pueblo people, it was originally spiritual and utilitarian. Those things are really basic to human life and growth, and it is no different for me, living in this time period.

LA: Could we talk about how you go about conceptualizing and executing a piece? What are your working methods?

NNM: Well, I can give you an example, using those masks I was showing you. I have twins. They are very connected. If you live with twins you really know how connected they are! Sometimes they'll finish each other's sentences. So I was thinking about that one day and how special that is, and I started making a form. Then somebody called me up, the phone company or something, and I wasn't listening to them; I was looking at the form. And it hits me: cut it in half and make twins. It wasn't really a voice in my head, but a whole picture just snapped. Like I was saying, I've become so comfortable that I feel connected to this creative will. What happens, if I allow myself to be immersed in that creative will, is that I could be talking on the phone and have an idea by the way somebody says something, or by looking at how a line in your shirt goes a certain way. All that just gets absorbed into who I am, so that when I come to the studio I often don't draw a picture or plan anything out. It's almost as if I'm ready to release, and I feel very lucky for that. I just release what I've absorbed.

LA: We've talked a little already about the amount of work that goes into making the finished piece.

NNM: The whole process involves getting the clay and bringing it home. I'll dig out about one hundred gallons, and after I bring the wet clay back, I lay it out in the sun to dry into small, hard nuggets. Then I put the dried clay in a barrel, water it down into a soup, and sift it through an old door screen, which purifies the clay from rocks and other impurities. I pour the mud into a pillow sack and let the extra water drip out. Then I put it on a large plastic sheet and add volcanic ash, mixing them together with my feet for about three hours, constantly mixing, until the mud becomes a supple, workable clay. It takes a month until the clay is ready to be used. That's when a whole other part of who I am comes out.

I use the coiling method, so if I'm going to make a form I start doing coils, like snakes, one after another. The snakelike coils are layered one on top of the other until a basic shape starts forming. I allow that source of creativity to envelop me and to direct the growth of each piece. The coils are different because I'm different everyday. When I go into the studio and start making a coil, whatever I'm feeling and whatever is happening to me that day gets coiled into the piece I'm doing. So it's always changing, and the way I'm looking at things is always changing. But after the coiling is done, I let it sit and dry slowly, carefully packing the surface of the piece with a knife to make it smooth. After the piece is dry I sand it with sandpaper and smooth the surface again with a wet cloth.

After I sand the form I fire it, and if I fire it outside in the pit, I chop wood and put it all around the container I made out of corrugated tin. And I place the piece inside the tin box, light the fire, and if it doesn't explode, the piece is pretty much done. Then I'll bring it back in to see if it needs anything else, like a necklace or whatever.

LA: Do you paint on the piece after firing?

NNM: Yes, I do, and I've used from coffee to paint, whatever it takes that will balance the piece. I think about ways to enhance it at that point. If Pearlene had just been done with a natural matte she wouldn't have had the same voice she does. I had to use paint with lots of colors to make her look a certain way. But I shouldn't get too much credit for making these things. They basically tell me; I'm just ready to play, I just listen to that part of me.

LA: You do a lot of different types of work — fetishes, masks, sculpture like *Wheat Girl* [1991]. Even the fetishes, like *Moon Fetish on the Half Shell* [1991] are unique.

NNM: This one's a TV fetish; here's the antenna. The bear fetish is more traditional. I was throwing clay on the floor and getting different textures from the way the floor is uneven. Each fetish liberates me even more. This piece here represents a small spirit, like a baby spirit, and it needed lines. Why it needed lines I don't know and so, on intuition, I cut a stencil and sprayed a coating of sealer over it, so the colors are sort of muted, not garish. But this is a more subtle statement than Pearlene. You have to hold her down sometimes.

LA: *Pueblo Traveler* [1986] is a striking piece.

NNM: I like that piece. I did a series of about twenty of those, and they were all very different and exciting. I like color very much, and I guess we're so used to seeing Santa Clara pottery on a table in a certain perspective that I kept thinking to myself, Why couldn't you hang clay, frame it, do all sorts of things with this earth? That's where that idea came from. I wanted to see how clay looked on the wall and that was the beginning of what I'm doing now. And when I first did that series, I took some of them into a gallery and they just weren't accepted, nobody wanted them. That response was interesting because I was so excited about them. I felt that I had gone another step in exploring clay. And it's not like I'm being disrespectful or anything, but my work is done with my sincerest intentions. That shows in the work. So that goes back to the marketing response. Santa Clara women are supposed to be making highly polished jars and wedding vases and I wasn't. I haven't been doing that. So that collision with the market was strange. I thought that all I had to do was walk in and say, "Here I am." But there was that whole aspect of selling and what would and wouldn't move. I had to wake up to that. I just thought that if you did art, it would be accepted. Little did I know.

LA: Has the market and gallery response changed in the five years or so since that happened?

NNM: I don't know. Now I don't have much to do with the people who didn't accept my pieces then, probably because they would still be uninterested in my work. They have their own paths to go. I'm not going to stop what I'm doing, and the people who are somewhat interested in what I do understand that.

LA: Do you consider yourself a potter, a sculptor?

NNM: I'm just a woman having a good time in the studio and trying to learn all the time. I can't be identified in that sense, and I really don't want to be. A hundred years ago there wasn't that separation or labeling. People were farmers, potters, builders, herbalists, medicine women, all sorts of things. Lives just flowed; there wasn't compartmentalization. That's happening with me. My husband and I built our own home, we have children, I cook, bake, can food, read, build coyote fences, not just work with clay. What's wonderful about that is, when I'm with my children, they feed me on many levels, so when I come to the studio I've been nurtured. When I'm here working, I'm here, then I'm ready to be a good mother. There's no breaking off—it's a continuous flow, like the flow in making a pot; it's seamless. That's why I like clay, because it reflects what I'm doing, and I like that.

LA: Are the masks a new direction?

NNM: I do masks every now and then, when I get the urge. They're becoming more simplified. Once they were a caricature with a lot of detail. Now the masks are straightforward and simple, like what's happening to me. They are very stylistic from the design point of view, though. There's an interplay of paint and natural colors, which represents the blending of living in a more organic environment with the rush of living in the dominant society.

LA: Did anything influence you in the particular design you use in the *Mask of Singer* [1991] pieces?

NNM: I'm sure. I think I had been looking at a book on African tribes. They use a lot of adobe and their buildings are incredible. If I see something like that, how can I not be influenced? And I think that's the purpose of art, in a way. You see things and then express them in your own way.

LA: What were the influences on you growing up?

NNM: Clay was always there; it wasn't a foreign thing. I had a lot of interesting times with my mother. You know, when you're close to someone and there's something you don't understand about that person—the times that we've been most emotionally together were when we were involved with clay. So she's been an influence. I played with clay as a kid; I learned the process of clay when I was quite young. I remember walking to where my mother was working, at two in the morning, and I'll never forget the way she looked, so involved and happy, as she worked on a large storage jar. That's how Indians traditionally learned, through observation and example. It's not linear like in Western societies. I remember the contrast, too, of going out to sell the work. That was a completely different arena. I was really impressionable and those things stuck in my mind. Besides my mother and my husband, my children are a big influence today. They teach me how to be a better potter. I draw from traditional and contemporary experiences. It's very inspiring to be alive.

LA: Your book came out from the University of Arizona Press in early '92. How did it come about?

NNM: It's called *Mud Woman*. Have you ever had an idea that wouldn't leave you alone? I thought to myself, Why is it that most of the books done about Pueblo pottery are done by anthropologists or non-Indians? That's fine, and I'm glad. It needs to be recorded. But it's always been once removed from the experience, by someone who's an observer. I wanted to talk about the direct experience, like when a piece breaks after you've spent six months on it, or how it feels to go sell a form you've spent months working on and caring for. I wanted to talk about those things. I started putting poems together that I had written, and I started realizing that the poems and the clay figures were very closely related, and that I was writing about Pearlene and making her at the same time. It never dawned on me until I got this idea in the middle of the night that something was happening, a creative volley between words and clay, clay and words, and it needed to be looked at. The book shows my creative process in simple form.

I present some poems, and each poem is more or less related to the overall subject. It's been really interesting and has taught me a lot about putting a book together. It's a dream. I've written poetry since I was fifteen — I'm now thirty-eight — and to have this happen is pretty major. It makes me think that some ideas in the back of my mind should be looked at more carefully, too.

LA: How do you balance writing with your other work?

NNM: I take all sorts of approaches. I'll be driving down Cerrillos Road in Santa Fe, a very busy street, and I'll have an idea, these words in my head, and I'm trying to maneuver through the traffic, and I'll write down as much as I can. Or I'll spend time sitting down and just let the words come. My father was in the hospital and I wrote about that while waiting for the doctor to tell us about his operation. Everything has equal time, and I try giving as much thought as I can to each part of who I am and what I'm doing as a human being. I want to be conscious while I'm living.

LA: Is there a connection between the physicality and the tactility of clay and the more abstract nature of words? Both can be manipulated in their own ways.

NNM: For me, in my own vision, there is a connection, and I need that connection; I really do. If you see Pearlene you think, "I wonder what she's saying," and then you see a poem about what she's saying, that she's talking about Indians, actually human beings in general, even though she looks like the American consumer. That all helps make the whole picture for me. The more I add and blend color, form, and written word to my work, the more each creative endeavor has to offer in the way of communicating and inviting the balance I'm striving for. The possibilities really astound me.

LA: Are you writing new poems?

NNM: Yes, and they're very different from the *Mud Woman* poems. Once I finished the book it was as if I'd closed a chapter in my life. What I'm doing now is very different. I had to go through *Mud Woman* and make the things in *Mud Woman* and write of the things in *Mud Woman* in order to get to where I am now. What will come next will be new chapters in my life, exciting, difficult, continually confusing, and constantly enriching. But my responsibility to myself is to keep recording what is happening.

LA: Could we look at some of the newer clay pieces? *Seasons of the Fetish* is fairly large. What led you to the larger works?

NNM: The larger bronzes are a new direction which evolved

from my experiences in building our home. If you work on building a structure that requires five thousand adobe bricks, with seventeen-foot-high walls, then it's not too difficult to think of making larger sculptures. That's how it works for me. Inside the house the walls are uncluttered, so that one can see and feel the uneven surfaces that bend and curve from one room to the next. It's very sensual, very sculptural. I'd like to make those same textures and feelings of movement in my sculptures. I want to share these exciting revelations, no matter how simple, with others, because I think that's how my people, the Pueblos, really thrived — through feeling, by taking the time to become conscious of their surroundings, of the textures and the lines. One aspect of life was fuel for the next, and so on.

The newer pieces evolved in size and materials. What's appealing to me about them is that from whatever angle you look at them, they have very simple lines. The way I'll place them, one line will lead you down here and another line will lead you another way. I like that feeling, when a simple line can lead you here and there, collectively telling a story, or in the case of *Seasons of the Fetish*, showing the connection between men and women, even though we are very separate species. We are connected by simple lines in our bodies, even if our lines are not visible all the time.

SELECTED EXHIBITIONS

"Earning Her Place under the Willow" (1992), solo exhibition, Maxwell Museum of Anthropology, University of New Mexico, Albuquerque, NM.

"Portfolio III: Ten Native American Artists" (1991), group exhibition, American Indian Contemporary Arts, San Francisco, CA.

"Separate Visions" (1991), group traveling exhibition, Smithsonian Institution, Washington, DC.

"Artifacts for the Seventh Generation" (1990), group exhibition, American Indian Contemporary Arts, San Francisco, CA.

"Earth, Earth Life" (1988), group exhibition, Heard Museum, Phoenix, AZ.

SELECTED BIBLIOGRAPHY

Naranjo-Morse, Nora. *Mud Woman*. Tucson, AZ: University of Arizona Press, 1992.

——. "Artist's Statement." *Portfolio III*. San Francisco, CA: American Indian Contemporary Arts, 1991, p. 25.

Jaune Quick-to-See Smith

Flathead-Cree-Shoshone

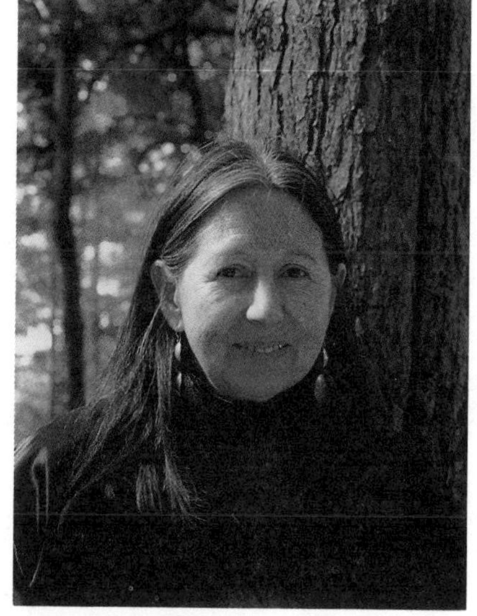

Jaune Quick-to-See Smith's work encompasses both the lyrical and the political. Some of her earlier series, like the *Red Lake* series (1979–80), are delicate landscape abstractions, often in pastel, with such recurrent imagery as horses, buffalos, and petroglyphs. In 1986 Smith completed a set of drawings on paper entitled *Horses Make a Landscape Look More Beautiful*, which spoke about aspects of her childhood and her view of the land.

Environmental concerns and perceptions of the land have informed and continue to inform Smith's work. The series *A View of Western Lands* (1990) appears to be abstract landscapes, but on another level it deals with the preservation of the environment. In this series Smith "includes vessels traditionally used to store or save life-giving things. It is her plea to save the environment. The paintings are composed of layers of pigment, scraped expanses and pictoforms—the vocabulary in which she attempts to portray a reverent view of the land."[1] The *Chief Seattle* series (1991) continues this plea, with each work focusing on a different aspect of the environment, such as *Chief Seattle Series: The Colorado* and *Chief Seattle Series: Prince William Sound*. In these works, some of which are pastels and others mixed-media collages, she embeds words and messages to the viewer.

In *Chief Seattle Series: The Spotted Owl* she writes on the canvas: "The rivers are our brothers / They quench our / thirst. The rivers carry our canoes / and feed our children C.S. 1854." In other cases Smith invokes the figure and ideas of Chief Seattle as a counterpoint to the imagery. In *Rain* (1990), for example, she hangs silver-plated spoons on a canvas dripping with the dark detritus of industrial apocalypse. Next to the piece is a small plaque that reads "C.S. 1854."

Some other recent series more explicitly challenge the hegemony and view of history of the dominant culture, especially as its perspective of "discovery" emerged during the Columbus quincentennial year. Her two-person exhibition with Emmi Whitehorse at the LewAllen Gallery in Santa Fe in August 1992 included the piece *Indigenous*, which combines a variety of imagery with hand-lettered words and fragments from found texts. One of the images is a hand-drawn picture of the last Flathead chief, Charlo, juxtaposed with a spotted red smallpox suit cut-out that "fits all sizes." The smallpox suit reappears in other works as well.

The October 1992 exhibition at the Steinbaum Krauss Gallery in New York City featured the 60-by-170-inch triptych entitled *Trade (Gifts for Trading Land with White People)*. Again, this piece contains text, drawings, and photographs, with the outline of a canoe running nearly the length of the work. Above the work, hanging down from the wall on a chain, are the trade gifts: pennants, team caps, plastic dolls, and the like. In both of these works Smith layers irony upon irony but at base is making a statement about the relationship of America to her indigenous peoples.

One series of her works which has traveled to numerous shows in the United States and abroad is the 1991–92 *Paper Dolls for a Post-Columbian World with Ensembles Contributed by the U.S. Government*. Containing various eleven-by-seventeen-inch drawings, it presents Ken, Barbie, and Bruce Plenty Horses as a way of telling the story of the Flathead people after contact. The dolls come with a variety of clothes, including a "boarding school outfit," a "capote for traveling on forced removal after 1891 Garfield treaty," and "matching smallpox suits for all our Indian families after U.S. gov't. sent wagon loads of smallpox infected blankets to keep our families warm." In this group of mixed-media pieces the juxtaposition of text and image, playing off the reference to the innocuous Barbie and Ken, heightens the impact of the artist's statement.

Smith has also written poetry to accompany some of her work. She wrote "Spring 1979 Moon of the Buttercups," in seven sections, to accompany her 1979 *Ronan Robe* series (reprinted in *That's What She Said*). The series is named after the town of Ronan (about sixty miles north of Missoula) on the Flathead Reservation in the northwestern part of Montana, and the poem reflects the creative process of the artist in making the visual work. In the poem she moves from a "family history" of her people and her relations to the gradual isolation of visual imagery, from the artist's mind to its appearance on the canvas. History, family, self, dreams, art become interconnected, "And she senses the past and present sealed in / the wax." Images become shapes; color appears, then design, then the fire to smoke the canvas. Recurring throughout the final two sections of the poem is "Heads to the left / Tails to the right / Stripes going round," referring to the way a buffalo robe would be worn.

Smith sees her artistic process as similar to that of the poet, and in a way echoes Emily Dickinson's poem 1129: "Tell all the Truth but tell it slant—." This affinity has led Smith to illustrate the work of poets Joy Harjo (*In Mad Love and War*, 1990), Elizabeth Woody (*Hand into Stone*, 1989), Luci Tapahonso (*A Breeze Swept Through*, 1987), and Charlotte DeClue (*Without Warning*, 1985).

Smith was born in Montana in 1940 in the town of St. Ignatius on the Flathead Reservation. She received her B.A. degree in art education from Framingham State College in Massachusetts in 1976, and her M.A. in art from the University of New Mexico in 1980. She has been exhibiting her work since 1976 in the United States and abroad, and has lectured about both Native art and her own work at universities throughout the United States. In 1987 she lectured in Warsaw, Lodz, and Krakow as part of a cultural exchange program sponsored by the United States Information Agency. Most recently Smith curated "The Submuloc Show/Columbus Wohs" and "Our Land/Ourselves." She has done public art under commission for the Denver airport, the Salt River Utilities headquarters in Phoenix, and the Washington State Arts Commission. Her work is in numerous permanent collections, including those of the National Museum of American Art (Washington, D.C.), the American Medical Association, the Heard Museum, and the Museum of Mankind in Vienna. Additionally, Smith received an honorary doctorate from the Minneapolis College of Art and Design in 1991 and the Arts Service Award from the Association of American Cultures in 1990 and held the Beaumont Chair as an honorary professor at Washington University in 1989. Smith also serves on the board of the College Art Association. She now lives in Corrales, New Mexico, just north of Albuquerque.

About her painting she has written: "My work comes right from a visceral place—deep, deep—as though my roots extend beyond the soles of my feet into sacred soils. Can I take these feelings and attach them to the passerby? To my dying breath, and my last tube of burnt sienna, I will try."[2]

We talked by phone for two nights in April 1992 and then again for a night in December.

LA: Could we start off by talking about the ways your work has evolved through the mid-1970s and '80s?

JQTSS: My work has always been concerned with the landscape—an inhabited landscape of plants and animals. You could go through all the series and find an inhabited landscape in everything I've done. And there has always been a concern with political and environmental issues. Progressively, I think, my work has become more blatantly political and at the same time more accessible.

In the mid-1970s I painted on unstretched canvases based

loosely on hide shapes. These were called the *Ronan Robe* series, named after a town on my reservation. They were muted in color, minimal, and distanced from the viewer. I spent 1978 and 1979 drawing in pastels to develop ideas for other paintings. I titled them the *Wallowa Waterhole* series and exhibited them at the Clarke-Benton Gallery [Santa Fe] and the Kornblee Gallery [New York].

I had done a lot of reading about Chief Joseph and his intelligent and sensitive leadership. His trek into Canada with women and children while under siege by the U.S. Cavalry and his amazing maneuvers back into the Wallowa country [northeastern Oregon] inspired this series. It was a haven of peace and safety, if only for a short while. Since the Nez Perce had been friendly with the Flatheads far back in history, this was a way to recognize that, to pay homage to Chief Joseph and to sustain the goodness of that place. Perhaps in my own way I was reconnoitering at this waterhole. Out of this series I developed a language that has sustained me to this day. Picto figures of humans and animals emerged. I wove drying racks and tipis through these stories that had no beginning and no end.

Then, at the beginning of the eighties, I moved to a series called *Red Lake*, which were shown at the Marilyn Butler Gallery in Scottsdale. These pieces were split in the middle like the Rockies splice the eastern Montana plains from the wooded slopes and prairies of western Montana. My own nomad yearning wells up and is urged on by a shift in seasons.

On paper and canvas I journeyed across the land recording moose, beaver, and other forms of wildlife, as though these were diaries of our thousands of years of migrations between summer and winter homes and I could suspend them in time. Many of my images were already focusing on endangered species. In a prayerful way, like the cave painters, I wanted to bring them into reality.

LA: The *Site* series [1981] was an important set of paintings.

JQTSS: The *Site* series were exhibited for the first time at the Bernice Steinbaum Gallery in New York City. I created landscapes by crosshatching thick and thin paint with collage that rippled and stopped with blotches of color. These paintings were based on researching Indian sites throughout the West, so there were hand-rendered picto forms of tools and artifacts along with a horse or two. My horse Cheyenne, who is my constant companion at the studio door, was depicted as though he traveled to these places with me or as a stand-in for me. I wanted to bring attention to the fact that many cultures and societies existed here long before the arrival of Columbus. I commemorated each place by entitling individual paintings with names such as *Blackwater Draw*, *Newspaper Rock*, *Yellow Bay*, *Aztec Ruins*, *Salmon River*, and *Wild Horse Island*.

In the mid-'80s, around 1986 and '87, I developed another series about the pictographs on the seventeen-mile lava escarpment along the west side of Albuquerque. There may be as many as ten thousand petroglyphs there, and they were being ravaged by housing development. Many people were going up there and chipping them out, putting them in gardens or selling them to gift shops. That became the impetus for the work. I joined the Friends of the Petroglyphs, an advocacy group determined to save the escarpment as a historic monument. After hiking the area repeatedly, creating a portfolio of black and white photographs, and collecting newspaper articles, I slowly entered a new phase of work which was intent on bringing attention to the plight of this thousand-year-old site. Not through my work, but through that of many other dedicated people, foremost Ike Eastvold, this area is now a national park and is protected.

For example, in terms of the work in this series, one of the developers had put a large rock with petroglyphs in a crate and dumped it on the steps of the courthouse downtown and said that he was going to do that until we gave up our fight. They didn't do that, of course, but the developers got some publicity. So one of the paintings in the series is named *The Courthouse Steps*, and one is called *Sunset on the Escarpment*. The sun *does* set on the escarpment because it lies on the west side of Albuquerque, but it has a dual meaning. Sometimes my titles have that.

LA: It struck me that other paintings from that series, like *Moonrise*, *Sandia Sunset*, and *Sandia Sunrise*, have a feeling of vibrancy and movement in the pastels.

JQTSS: I moved into big shapes, Paul Klee kind of shapes, but using the pictographs. Some of the work pointed to the fact that the Sandia Mountains here have arms and munitions stored in them, so there's an eerie light, sort of a nuclear bluish-white light, in the paintings, which referred to those storage areas.

LA: Many of your images echo or resonate with other pieces you've done, especially the pastels from the late eighties, like *Tule Huts*, *Scented Chants*, and *Tiger Moth* [all 1988].

JQTSS: About the *Moth* pieces, I had been doing a lot of research on bugs and plants and wild animals to incorporate them into the paintings and drawings, and *Tule Huts* and *Scented Chants* are from Elizabeth Woody's writing [Warm Springs–Navajo poet]. I had done illustrations for her book *Hand into Stone.* After that I used imagery from her poetry and incorporated it into the paintings.

LA: You've illustrated a number of other books, too, like *Without Warning* [Charlotte DeClue] and *A Breeze Swept Through* [Luci Tapahonso]. Does your work have an affinity with poetry? Do you feel that your work is a kind of visual poetry?

JQTSS: I feel that there is a connection, because I put my images into the canvas or into the drawing metaphorically, like a poet does with words. When a poet is telling you something, she isn't using language like a journalist. It's more metaphorical or symbolic. I obtain and convey messages in my work that same way. So that's why the writers and poets have a great appeal for me. And I know a lot of the writers and have worked with them over the years.

LA: How would you develop the images to accompany their writing?

JQTSS: I read and reread their manuscripts, think about them, dream on them, make some sketches, then do the finished work. It's the same process that I use in my own work. There's an interaction going on with something besides the act of drawing.

LA: Some of your own paintings connect to your concern for the environment.

JQTSS: The appearance of butterflies and moths in the 1988 paintings was in direct concern for their diminishing populations, among many other natural populations. I had been doing a lot of research on plants and insects. I live in a flyway for sandhill and whooping cranes. They appeared in my work in the early eighties. Again, it was a commemoration of these disappearing populations. No text appeared in the work at that time, but they were meant to be political. I think I developed political text in my work out of sheer frustration in having to explain the work in written statements.

In 1989 I used writings from Chief Sealth's [Seattle's] environmental speech of 1854. There are arguments pro and con as to whether he actually said these words. But Duwamish Tribal Chairman Cecile Maxwell told me that she stands behind these words. I wrote Chief Sealth's words on the canvas and attached objects. These paintings were dense oil and wax with somber colors. They felt like the Pacific Northwest environment to me. I imagined that I smelled thickets of fallen damp cedars, wet salt air, and that I was standing in the greenish twilight of day there. But they were truly about the waning existence of an environment that I knew as a child and that in my half century of life has awesomely changed. At the exhibit in New York at the Bernice Steinbaum Gallery, we mounted the text of Chief Seattle's speech on the wall and provided copies for visitors to take with them. People were openly moved by his words.

LA: To shift gears a little, could you talk about your art education?

JQTSS: In 1976 I came to Albuquerque to go to graduate school at the University of New Mexico because of their comprehensive Native American studies program. I knew I would have to teach to support myself and my children. I particularly wanted to teach at the Institute of American Indian Arts in Santa Fe. But as they say: "Best-laid plans. . . ." I applied three times to the graduate school of fine arts and was turned down each time. I continued to take classes, kept making art and exhibiting. I was encouraged to enroll in the art education department, where the majority of Indians were sent if they had a hint of Indian imagery in their work. After I had a review in *Art in America* from my exhibit at the Kornblee Gallery in New York, I was finally accepted into the fine arts department.

From the time that I started taking college art classes in 1958 to the time I finished college with a master's degree in 1980, twenty-two years, it wasn't acceptable to show any ethnicity in my work. My professors taught from a perspective that was all white, Euro-centric, and male. I worked many years developing a painting surface based on my academic training.

LA: When did you start using text in your work?

JQTSS: Toward the end of the eighties I began to throw caution to the winds and experiment with more materials and mixed media. I also began to see that what I had to say was equally as important as the painting surface. Perhaps more so.

LA: In the *Shared Visions* exhibition you have a piece called *Rain* [1990] where you have embedded things into the painting. How did that come about?

JQTSS: That would be like another journal entry. In that painting I attached silver—really, stainless steel—iced tea spoons to the oil and wax surface. This painting was a direct result of my three-day journey in upstate New York with my Seneca friend Peter Jemison. After we visited at the Seneca site and museum he directs, we traveled to St. Lawrence University in Canton, where we lectured, and then we drove to the Akwesasne Reservation to visit friends. Along the way Peter pointed out many things to me, but the most poignant fact that kept going round in my head in the studio after I returned was the demise of the maple trees. They were dying because of acid-rain from the steel mills. Of course, Reagan was saying that we didn't have an acid rain problem and that we needed more studies.

Iroquois people taught whites the process of tapping maple trees and boiling sap into sugar and syrup. More importantly, this is medicine for the Iroquois. My problem was how to boil off and distill this story. Iced tea spoons, with the handles up and bowls down, represented the acid rain. Corporate and government heads have a silver spoon in their mouths. Plus the spoons were made of steel.

That same year, I had been to a snake dance at Hopi with my friends Karita Coffey [Comanche] and Linda Lomahaftewa. I tried to visualize these two diverse images of rain, one bringing death, one bringing life. I framed a sketchy ink drawing of Indian rain dancers to hang beside the painting illuminating a good aspect of rain. A small plaque hung below which said "C.S. 1854"—Chief Seattle 1854—as a reminder. *Rain* reflected the long process of having gone up to Akwesasne and meeting with the people there and traveling across that country and thinking and reading about what was going on. Then that painting came into being.

LA: There are pieces similar to *Rain*, like *Forest* and *Starry, Starry Sky* [both 1990] where you've embedded things in the canvas like handsaws and bullet casings.

JQTSS: I scavenged the bullet casings in some open sagebrush land here. I got the idea for *Starry, Starry Sky* when things were going on in Nicaragua, and later Desert Storm came along, so it became a viable painting for my message, although I don't know if people got it at the beginning. The title was taken from van Gogh's work, which had a more pastoral vision, while mine was, with the bullet casings, very clearly about the evil of war and what it does to the environment, although it was more metaphorical. There's no beginning and no ending to that story.

LA: Do you feel that your work, even though it's metaphorical or symbolic, is on some level a narrative, or is telling a story?

JQTSS: Well, I think that my paintings are expressing my feelings about particular things. They are not generic works. In some recent work, in addition to writing words in the canvas, I'm cutting words out of magazines and newspapers and burying them in the paint, hiding them here and there so they crop up, although you wouldn't discover the words until you came up close. Each painting is a kind of story about something that I'm thinking about. And if I can't relate to it personally, if it doesn't have meaning for me, if I'm not feeling pressured about a particular issue, if I don't feel the pain of it, then how can I make a painting about it? My work is very concrete in that way.

Euro-Americans have a linear form of time and their stories have a beginning and an end, but we have a horizontal sense of time which compresses history and present reality. My paintings have no beginning and no end to their stories. They describe the dichotomy of life between the Indian and the white world: AIDS, hunger, sobriety, education, health, and the Catch-22 world we live in today. For instance, the depiction of the canoe in the work *Trade* [1992] carries a load of serious information, but it also has a humorous backtwist, Coyote-style, with a line of trade goods hanging above the canoe, with the offer to trade these trinkets with white people for land. The trinkets are Washington Redskins, Cleveland Indians, and Kansas City Chiefs caps, T-shirts, plastic tomahawks, feathered drums—items that are made in Taiwan that non-Indians buy. It has to be provocative in order to bridge the gap in understanding between Indian issues and the mainstream.

LA: What is your process of developing a painting?

JQTSS: Charles Garabedian, a California painter, said in an interview that his process was a lot like walking around in a fog knowing that the cliff is nearby. That's a fairly apt description of my process most of the time. I sort through all the memorabilia in my head, condense my travels into a knowable form, research natural phenomena, and mull over Indian politics patchworked from my reservation to the pan-Indian world—all make rich resource material, too rich sometimes. I have things that just don't form up and don't reveal themselves to me. Eventually I have to cut that canvas up because it's just beyond hope. Or the canvas just sits there for years and then I'll pull it out and try to make something of that, or I'll collage over it or recycle it. When I do a painting I'll have some notes that I've written down on things I'm thinking about. My paintings usually take me months, but I don't work on them every day, but I'll do a part. I do have the piece conceptualized — it's lucid; it's in my head and at the tips of my fingers and I can feel it.

Although as I age I can see with hindsight that I cling to certain patterns in my work. Over the years my art walks in SoHo and conversations with my friends Paul Brach, Miriam Schapiro, Lise and Harvey Hoshour, and Bernice Steinbaum have sharpened my vision and given me more clarity in my direction.

LA: When does a sense of completion come about?

JQTSS: A piece may sit in the studio for a few weeks, and I'll go in there every day and look at it. Then I might go on a trip and I'll come back and look at it again. It may need something dark over in this corner, or need something light in that corner, or a section may need to be repainted. And then I'll go on another trip, look at the piece again, and say to myself, "This is as much as I can do." It's balanced in the right way, meaning that it's unbalanced and tipping. It has to tilt a little this way, tilt a little that way, and then I can leave it alone. But it takes time; I can't just do it and then get it out to you tomorrow. I have to live with it before I know it's done. And sometimes I'll take it out of the studio and bring it into the house and hang it up and then take it back out to the studio so I can see it in a different place.

LA: Do you worry about your work being accessible to the viewer?

JQTSS: When I'm wandering around here in my sandbox, my acre of desert land, I'm not really thinking about how to be accessible but rather how to communicate to the viewer in layers. I really strive to reverse the old adage that what you see is what you get. If I can be Coyote and practice my sneak-up, I can engage the viewers from a distance with one image and lure them in for exposure to another layer, which changes the initial view into quite a different reality. After all, this is what ethnic culture is all about — or even an ongoing relationship. What you see on the surface is never the same again once you begin to plumb the depths. I think I'm more surefooted as I follow this path.

LA: You're not only a very active painter, but you also find time to curate major exhibitions of Native art.

JQTSS: For the past seventeen years I've been organizing Native American art exhibits, approximately one a year, in order to help younger Indian artists. And I'm blessed with dealers who support my activism as well as my work. The show I curated most recently is "We, the Human Beings" [1992–93]. I wanted to deal with the issue of naming ourselves. I worked with Thalia Gouma-Peterson and Kitty Zurko at the College of Wooster Art Museum in Ohio. The show features twenty-seven contemporary Native American artists. I wrote about how we've been manufactured by colonial painters and writers, anthropologists, Hollywood, and the media.

Even our tribes have been externally named. For instance, we Flatheads, *Têtes Plattes*, were named by French traders who mistakenly identified us as the Indians who flattened their heads. We *never* flattened our heads, but this misnomer remains. We call ourselves the Sqelix'u — We, the Human Beings, or Salish (our language). Some tribes have reverted back to their original names and I believe we'll see more of this, like the Papago in Arizona [Tohóno Óodam] and the Navajo [Diné].

But going back to the mid-seventies: I organized a group of Native artists here in Albuquerque, including Emmi Whitehorse, my first friend in New Mexico. We called ourselves the Grey Canyon artists, which described the cement canyons of the city. We did exhibits in churches and banks, and in the later seventies, with the help of Laurel Reuter, director of the North Dakota State Museum, we toured Grey Canyon in the U.S. and eventually to Europe. In the early eighties I organized a group on my reservation called Coup Marks and traveled their work to the American Indian Community House Gallery [AICH] in New York with the help of Peter Jemison, who was director at that time. After New York, Retha Gambaro, a Cherokee sculptor, generously brought the show to her gallery in Washington, D.C.

Around this same time I discovered Jesse Cooday's [Tlingit] photography at the AICH in New York and started a search for more Indian photographers. That search took three years to locate fifteen photographers. Then I couldn't find a gallery or museum that would exhibit the work. Rosemary Ellison, director of the Southern Plains Indian Museum, took the exhibit and added other photographers from her region. She also created a beautiful black and white brochure. Peter Jemison booked it at the Community House and held it over an extra month because it was so well attended in New York. In Seattle, Joe Feddersen [Colville painter and printmaker] convinced the Silver Image Gallery to take the show. Erin Younger, who was director of Atlatl at that time, helped us get the exhibit into the Heard Museum for the summer. By this time "The People's Show" had sixty American Indian photographers.

The next exhibit, "Women of Sweetgrass, Cedar and Sage," was composed of thirty women artists ranging in age from their early twenties to their mid seventies. The work included beadwork and quilts as well as photography and painting. That show opened in New York at the Community House with a performance by Spiderwoman Theater. It then traveled to museums across the U.S. with a catalog that had essays by art critic Lucy Lippard, Erin Younger, and myself. Touring museums with a catalog and a New York writer put this exhibit into the big time. The days of scraping pocket money together and begging people for an exhibit space and Xeroxing announcements became part of our history.

In 1989 Nancy Liddle, director of the University Art Gallery, SUNY at Albany, flew to Albuquerque to see me about doing an Indian exhibit. I had been thinking about a landscape exhibit since we are uniquely land-based people. She liked the proposal and the exhibit "Our Land/Ourselves" was formed from that initial meeting. At the end of its tour in 1994, this exhibit will have traveled the U.S. for four years with a full-color catalog and articles by Paul Brach, Rick Hill, and Lucy Lippard. During this time I was a board member of ATLATL and MICA [Montana Indian Contemporary Art] and I began thinking about doing an exhibit as a response to Columbus. I called a meeting at my cousin Jerry Slater's house on the Flathead Reservation. Corky Clairmont [Flathead-Kootenai artist] was doodling with a pencil and wrote Columbus backwards and created "Submuloc." "The Submuloc Show/Columbus Wohs" exhibit was born. I also had the idea that some interesting things would develop if I asked some of the artists to work together in collaborations.

LA: Who were some of the collaborators in this exhibit?

JQTSS: Joe Feddersen and Elizabeth Woody created a spare, elegant funereal installation with text [*Histories Are Open to Interpretation*]. They liked working together and have since collaborated on some other projects. I asked Jesse Cooday, who does still photography, if he would collaborate with Vira and Hortensia Colorado [Chichimec actresses] on a short video. Jesse asked

Steve Thurston to join the group and they made a really wonderful video [*Diablo Te Escupo*]. They also are now working on some other projects together. Robert Houle from Canada [Salteaux-Ojibwe painter and conceptual artist] collaborated with the Mohawk photographer Greg Staats. They did an incredible coyote appropriation from a German artist who appropriates Native language to decorate museum walls [*Extinct/Distinct*]. This way of working actually comes right out of our tribal roots, but I think with our Euro-American art training we have separated high-art functions from tribalness. There are craftworkers who work tribally; sometimes whole families collaborate together. I'm also hoping to see tribal collaborative efforts develop in our fine art communities. I think this is certainly a good beginning.

It's funny to me that when you look up the word "tribe" in the dictionary, the Greeks and Romans are used as examples. Yet I haven't heard any Greek or Italian people refer to themselves that way. Indian artists refer to themselves as tribal people. We are tribal within our individual tribes and tribal as we network intertribally. Since the late seventies I've networked on projects with Peter Jemison, Jolene Rickard [Tuscarora photographer], and George Longfish. In Seattle I've networked with Joe Feddersen and Gail Tremblay [Onondaga-Micmac] and in Portland with Lillian Pitt [Warm Springs–Yakima] on Indian projects.

LA: Why is the idea of process so important to Native artists?

JQTSS: Part of our two-language or two-culture world is our commitment to making sense of—or seeing through the glibness of—our Eurocentric education. Understanding is part of our process, and actually this process is more important to us than the product. Process probably takes the place of ceremonial function. We are still bound to that in our artmaking. We have a hard time with art that is so removed from personal connections that it becomes a veneer, a facade, an empty product. Our artmaking has to be an extension of who we are and what our life experiences are—that's a time-tested process going back thousands of years.

LA: How would you define Indian art?

JQTSS: You see, this is a point of contention I have with anthropologists who want to keep us in categories or who develop new labels for us so we can be accountable to them. They want us to be static, or mimic convenient categories, so their slow-moving science can fit us into their boxes and compartments. Unfortunately, their science hasn't kept up with the times, and further, they do a Eurocentric number on who's valid, a "real Indian," and what's valid, a copy of the past, and write off everybody else as the vanishing American. They totally separate human beings from their cultures—changing, evolving, developing, living cultures.

I must say at this point that there is one anthropologist who is breaking down barriers in his field, and that is Dr. Jack Weatherford from Macalester College. He writes with a bicultural view in recovering and discovering Indian America. He doesn't neatly categorize, but he approaches our cultures in a holistic way. He's been warmly received in Indian America and we're hoping that others will follow his lead.

But American Indians who make fine art have found themselves in a real dilemma. Both anthropologists and art historians look for easy references to Indianness—Indian designs, pictographs, or feathers—and dismiss the work for not being Indian enough. On the other hand, fine art critics will look for easy references—Indian designs, pictographs, or feathers—and negate the work for being too Indian. Therefore they claim that they can't write about our art because it's out of their arena.

European and American white artists have appropriated or borrowed from all ethnic peoples and that seems to be sanctioned by another standard. Also, when historians write about contemporary white artists they do research on their backgrounds, interview them, and follow their work, all of which gives them in-depth information. The solution, I feel, is to develop writers from within our ethnic communities. That's not an easy task. Our institutions, composed of and controlled by a white elite, somehow feel their charge is to maintain the Eurocentric canon. When many of us have put out a plea for them to recruit through our twenty-six tribal colleges or offer scholarships in their departments, they disappear into the woodwork of their institutions.

LA: At the same time, many Native artists have been strongly influenced by European modernists.

JQTSS: In my Euro-American art training, Kandinsky, Klee, Miro, Dubuffet, cubism, and constructivism have had an influence on me. These artists and movements were all influenced by so-called primitive art. When I'm in a museum, I do a compare-and-contrast kind of looking, going back and forth between modern art and Indian art, as well as other ethnic art. A lot of the Plains geometric design on parfleches and in beadwork has a symbiotic feeling with cubism and constructivism. After all, cubism was a derivation of African art. And there are commonalities with African and American Indian art. I saw a buffalo robe in the Denver Art Museum that had lines of blue beads which made me think of an Agnes Martin painting.

I find that not only do I teach myself this way, but that many of my other Indian artist friends are doing the same thing. We simply don't get this education in our university training. The connections to the ethnic worlds have been severed. Eurocentrism would have us believe that there is an abrupt "aha!" at which time white artists invented cubism, color theory, and abstract art. It's just not so.

LA: You've also organized some site-specific works with groups of artists.

JQTSS: In 1991 Corky Clairmont and I organized a site-specific environmental art symposium at Salish-Kootenai College on our reservation, the Flathead Reservation in western Montana. I'd had this idea rumbling around in my head for a long time after seeing art by Michelle Stuart which referenced our old medicine wheels, and other white artists who dug big holes in the desert or rearranged boulders. I felt sure that Indian people would do this in a different way, but it was totally experimental. We brought contemporary and traditional artists together for a weekend, like Neil Parsons [Blackfeet], Ernie Pepion [Blackfeet], and Joe Feddersen. We ate our meals together, listened to Victor Charlo, a Flathead poet, read to us during our meals, and spent our evenings sharing our work with each other. We divided into two groups—half slept at Corky's house and half on the floor at my cousin Jerry Slater's house. During the day we worked on our projects either singly or in groups on the campus or in the fields behind the campus. Our elders came and watched, so the site was a very busy place. Totally spontaneous things were happening. One of the most exciting things was Ernie's piece. He made a medicine wheel out of blocks of ice and red paint and dirt. As the sun melted the ice, the red was revealed through the dirt, a metaphorical description of the fragility of Indian life. James Luna [Luiseño-Diegueño] worked with videographer Roy Big Crane [Flathead] and they created a film, which James humorously narrated.

When another grant turned up for the Cattaraugus Seneca Reservation in upstate New York, I took Donna House, a Navajo botanist who was also at Flathead, with me and we did another site-specific workshop there. We ate our meals together, slept on the floor together in an old church, and talked into the wee hours of the night. Donna and I believe that this process of artmaking is a tribally revitalizing process and takes the emphasis off product, sales, and critical review, thus allowing tribal bonding, intertribal bonding, and traditional acknowledgment of the land to take place. Of course, the land there was very different to work on and there were different tribes than we had at Flathead. Some artists made altar pieces. One artist made a ceremonial circle with red ochre. Brook Maroldi singlehandedly videotaped the site pieces and Donna and I narrated. Jolene Rickard took photographs.

LA: You also collaborate with other artists of color. What are some of the connections you see between Native art and African-American, Asian-American, and Hispanic arts?

JQTSS: My first response would be passion, passion for our political thought, for our ethnic group, a passion for our art and for one another. I think also that when you face resistance, which all these peoples have, you push harder, so that's an important key to what's going on for us in this country right now.

Another connection is the sense of story. A while back I was thinking about this idea of story, particularly oral story, and I was talking to my dealer in New York, Bernice Steinbaum, about the thing that we have in common—African-American people, Jewish people, Asian people, those of us from an ethnic background—and that is stories. We're all committed to narrative work on some level. I think that one of the real differences between people of color and Euro-American people is that we're such storytellers and we get it firsthand. We get stories from our parents or grandparents as though they happened today or yesterday, not five hundred years ago. They're that real. These stories are passed down from parent to child, all the way down, and they stay real.

There is also a strong sense of survival which bonds us. For people of color who come from a background like mine, which was strictly on a survival basis, a struggle for food to feed my kids, and when you start in that mode from early on, it stays with you.

LA: Scott Momaday has written about the ways literature, language, and the imagination create the self. You've also stated that Indian people are "here to stay." Is art a means of survival and endurance?

JQTSS: Absolutely. Native people have something like three thousand languages from Patagonia to Point Barrow, with no word for art in the Western sense, yet art is deeply integrated in daily life. There is an integration of art with life. It's such a natural process, all part of that sense of art in daily life. On the reservation you'll be working in the kitchen, cooking, you've got a child on your hip, and you're doing beadwork at the same time. It's part of your life.

And it's a way of praising the Creator. Art is a way of expressing that and using a creative part of yourself. In essence this is true for all people, not just Indians. If you've lost that creative piece of yourself there's something missing in your life. So I see creativity as part of our survival. Granted, we have to have food, we have to have a roof over our heads, we have to stay warm, but I see the creative spirit as a basic part of life.

LA: Your work, and your idea of art, is clearly not bound to the studio. You've had a very peripatetic upbringing and have traveled quite a bit. What sorts of work have come out of this?

JQTSS: In my family, my great-great-grandmother, great-grandmother, grandmother, and my father were all involved in trading as a family unit. They all spoke Salish and some Shoshone and Kootenai. My father, who was a horse trader, was raised by these women in the old ways and I was raised by my father. As I paint, travel, go between two worlds and carry messages interactively, I believe I'm an extension of this age-old process. My cousin Jerry Slater, who is a founder and the vice president of our tribal college [Salish-Kootenai], is trading information and networking with the other tribal colleges around Montana. We are both carrying on our family and tribal tradition, whether it's trading goods or networking information and education. The journey of my work follows the journey of my life as I move through public art projects, collaborations, printmaking, traveling, curating, lecturing, and tribal activities.

LA: Your sense of trading information also involves doing public art projects?

JQTSS: In 1991 I was hired by the City of San Francisco to create a three-dimensional piece in the Yerba Buena Park on top of the Moscone Center. It is to honor the First People in that area, the Ohlone tribes. I brought James Luna into the project with me because I felt that, one, there should be a California Indian working on the project, and two, I wanted to bring more Indian artists into public art. We've designed a circular seating area of handcut limestone rocks partly encircled by a reflection pond and a low wood wall with basket designs. It can be used for small performances, picnics, family gatherings, poetry readings, or children's play — a living site for living peoples.

Also in 1991 I was hired by the City of Denver to collaborate with Ken Iwamasa on a large granite floor, 300 by 150 feet, for the main terminal of the new Denver airport. It will be on top of an old Arapaho hunting ground, which has been excavated. The floor is filled with colorful designs loosely based on old parfleche designs, as well as fifty pictographs which encircle Doug Hollis's large water piece and under Anna Murch's light work in the ceiling, which slowly revolves across the area using colors from the floor.

In Seattle I was hired by the King County Arts Commission to do a piece which honors Seattle's original people for 1992. There were five Indian artists hired to do individual projects which would sit near the Boeing plant on the Duwamish River bike trail. I specifically asked if I could collaborate with the Duwamish tribe and was told that there were no artists in the tribe. That statement was a challenge to me.

The Duwamish tribe has a treaty which has not been honored and I felt this was a way to bring attention to that issue. They were supposed to receive fishing rights, government recognition, and reservation land. In 1970 Judge Boldt ruled against their plea. Over sixty of their long houses had been destroyed by the government, and with no land they can't build a long house, which is the center of the community. They have asked the City of Seattle for five acres of land at the end of the two-mile bike trail. It's an insignificant amount compared to the thousands of acres they signed over in the treaty. I felt we could address the issues of fishing rights, land, long house, and the tribe's lack of recognition with this work.

Because of time constraints I couldn't fly there, and so day after day by telephone with the Tribal Chairman Cecile Maxwell, Culture Committee Director Frank Fowler, and other tribal members, we worked out a plan. I wanted to be the conduit and have them take ownership in the project. We received a King County Arts Commission grant in order to execute the work.

One hundred years ago their fishing wheels were destroyed along with the longhouses, so I wrote the proposal for the large grant and suggested we mount a six-foot fishing wheel on a pedestal near the bank of the Duwamish River, their traditional fishing grounds. I wanted it on the Parks Department land they were requesting instead of the Boeing site. I also requested a cedar canoe for racing and fishing and a canoe rack with a roof to place it on. I called it functional sculpture. After all, other artists make sculpture with swings, seating areas, and other functions.

We received the smaller grant. So this meant the tribe can build the fish wheel and canoe rack . . . but no canoe. This describes their plight better than any words. The tribe has taken ownership of the project with their own timetable, including filming of the project with elders teaching young carvers.

Another project I've just started is to construct an art building on the Salish-Kootenai College campus on my reservation. We have forty-seven different tribes going to school there and presently use computer and science classrooms for beadwork, drum making, and other arts. In non-Indian schools art is considered irrelevant to a good education. But for Indian people traditional arts are interwoven with beliefs that affect their well-being. Pam King, owner of the Buffalo Gallery in Alexandria, Virginia, and Larry Garfinkel of Vancouver, B.C., have kindly offered to help raise funds. Depending on our fund-raising, we may do the building in increments, but we are slated to see a groundbreaking by the end of 1993.

In a circular way, these projects and activities stretch and inform me so that I bring ideas and information back into the studio to incorporate into my work.

LA: How would that process work?

JQTSS: Well, for example, the *Nomad* pieces developed from all my travels and from researching parfleches for the Denver airport. I taped fifteen-by-fifteen-inch squares together in different combinations which carry messages about the environment and Indian life. These became *The Nomad Art Manifesto:*

"Nomad Art is made with biodegradable materials."

"Nomad Art can be folded and sent as a small parcel to save shipping costs."

"Nomad Art can be stored on a bookshelf, which saves space."

"Nomad Art does not need to be framed."

"Nomad Art can be recycled."

One *Nomad* piece was called "Decent." It had two squares

across and four down. It was based on a quote from Thoreau: "What good is a house if you don't have a decent planet to put it on?" Another one was called "Learn English." That one had three panels down and three across. In "Manifest Destiny" I used words like "consume," "obliterate," "conquer," "damage," "fraud" to make a statement about the environment and the impact of Reaganomics. These were like vignettes, juxtapositions of thoughts that go in different directions. I leave it up to the viewers to make their own connections, their own associations, to these "sound bites."

LA: How were these pieces done?

JQTSS: They were mixed-media drawings and collages in paint and charcoal on rice paper. I used hide paints from Japan with rice glue. These pieces can be folded and easily shipped and don't require any storage space. It was my response to the budget cuts in galleries and museums.

LA: The *Paper Dolls* are similar to the *Nomad* pieces?

JQTSS: *Paper Dolls for a Post-Columbian World with Ensembles Contributed by the U.S. Government* was a piece created in response to the Quincentennial of Columbus in 1992. I did them in the fall of '91, into '92. They were small, too, eleven by seventeen inches. There were thirteen in the set, actually Xeroxed sets. I made a story through the placement of each panel and the sayings. Ken and Barbie Plenty Horses were used to tell the story of my tribe and its forced march from the Bitterroot Valley to our present location. I gave them ensembles for cleaning houses of white people and smallpox suits which fit the whole family. I Xeroxed and hand painted them for museum exhibits as far away as Europe. Some people liked my irony and others were offended. In October 1992 the U.S. Forest Service in Hamilton, Montana, removed them from an exhibit because they were too offensive.

The *Nomad* series led me to the work I had at the LewAllen Gallery [Santa Fe, 1992] and at the Bernice Steinbaum Gallery [New York, 1992]. I broke the blocks apart and made much bigger work, using large outlined images. My art, my life experiences, and my tribal ties are totally enmeshed in that most recent series at the Bernice Steinbaum Gallery. I literally described Indian life today through the use of large icons meaningful to my tribe, like a buffalo, a horse, and a warshirt, laid over a mottled background of paint and bits of collage composed of articles from my reservation's newspaper, *Char-Koosta*; magazine articles; fabric; and photocopies of photographs. I just gleaned things from the media and juxtaposed words and images.

LA: What is it that links together the diversity of your work?

JQTSS: There are essentially two driving forces for me — working in my studio and spending time on my reservation with my family. These two things keep me healthy and balanced. But in between I feel a commitment to actively participate on boards, at conferences, to lecture and organize exhibits. But probably the central link is the idea of giving back. That's an innate responsibility placed on you when you are born a tribal person.

SELECTED EXHIBITIONS

"Jaune Quick-to-See Smith" (1993), solo exhibition, Parameters Galleries, Chrysler Museum, Norfolk, VA.

"Jaune Quick-to-See Smith and Emmi Whitehorse" (1992), two-person exhibition, LewAllen Gallery, Santa Fe, NM.

"The Quincentenary Non-Celebration" (1992), solo exhibition, Steinbaum Krauss Gallery, New York, NY.

"Counter Colón-Ialismo" (1991–93), group traveling exhibition, Centro Cultural de la Raza, San Diego, CA.

"Other Voices: Mediating between Ethnic Traditions and the Modernist Mainstream" (1991), group exhibition, Baxter Gallery, Portland School of Art, Portland, ME.

"Portfolio III" (1991), group exhibition, American Indian Contemporary Arts, San Francisco, CA.

"Shared Visions" (1991–93), group traveling exhibition, Heard Museum, Phoenix, AZ.

"Without Boundaries: Contemporary Native American Art" (1991), group exhibition, Jan Cicero Gallery, Chicago, IL.

"A View of Western Lands" (1990), solo exhibition, Steinbaum Krauss Gallery, New York, NY.

"Beyond Survival: Old Frontiers/New Visions" (1989), group exhibition, Ceres Gallery, New York, NY.

"The Soaring Spirit" (1987), group exhibition, Morris Museum, Morristown, NJ.

"Women of Sweetgrass, Cedar, and Sage" (1985), group traveling exhibition, Gallery of the American Indian Community House, New York, NY.

SELECTED BIBLIOGRAPHY

Smith, Jaune Quick-to-See. "Artist's Statement." In *Counter Colón-Ialismo*. San Diego, CA: Centro Cultural de la Raza, 1992, p. 82.

———. "Curator's Statement." In *The Submuloc Show/Columbus Wohs*. Phoenix, AZ: Atlatl, 1992, p. iii.

——. "Give Back." Keynote Address. Women's Caucus for Art National Conference, Chicago, 1992.

——. "We, the Human Beings." In *We, the Human Beings*. Wooster, OH: College of Wooster Art Museum, 1992, pp. 9–12.

——. "Artist's Statement." In *Portfolio III*. San Francisco, CA: American Indian Contemporary Arts, 1991, p. 31.

——. "Curator's Statement." In *Our Land/Ourselves: American Indian Contemporary Artists*. Albany, NY: University Art Gallery, State University of New York, 1990, pp. vi–vii.

——. *Charlo 84-4* [1984; cover art], *Untitled* [three works, each 1984], and *Arrowhead* [1988]. In *I Become Part of It*, edited by D. M. Dooling and Paul Jordan-Smith. New York: Parabola Books, 1989, pp. 17, 168, 257, 269.

——. "Women of Sweetgrass, Cedar, and Sage." *Women's Studies Quarterly* 15, 1 and 2 (Spring–Summer 1987): 35–41.

——. From the *Charlo Series* [1983; cover art] and the *Ronan Robe Series* [poetry]. In *That's What She Said*, edited by Rayna Green. Bloomington: Indiana University Press, 1984, pp. xvii–xix.

——. "Artist's Statement." In *The Sweet Grass Lives On*, by Jamake Highwater. New York: Lippincott and Crowell, 1980, p. 180.

Susan Stewart

Crow-Blackfeet

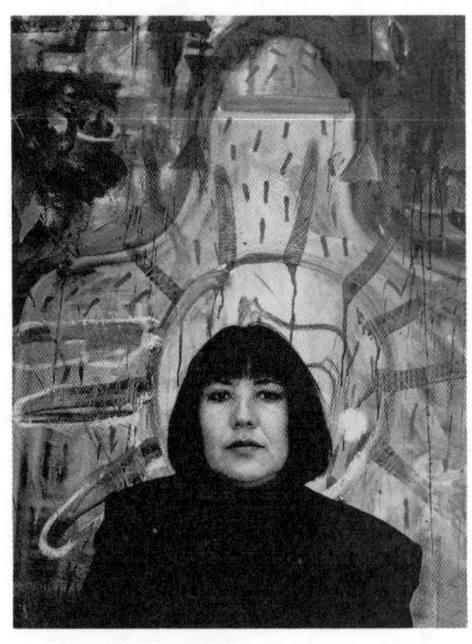

Susan Stewart was born in Livermore, California, in May 1953 and lived there and in Nevada while she was growing up, completing high school in Reno. She studied painting at the California College of Arts and Crafts in Oakland from 1971 to 1975, and after graduation taught beading and weaving in Concord, California, and silkscreen and painting in Oakland. When she went back to Montana she resided in Lodge Grass on the Crow Reservation before moving to Bozeman, where she now lives. She received her B.A. degree in fine arts from Montana State University in 1981.

Stewart's imagery has steadily evolved over the last two decades, and her use of media has ranged from watercolors and pastels to oils and monoprints. She has lately expanded to performance and installation pieces and videotape, but the one constant has been the exploration of her tribal roots. About her early work she wrote: "My paintings are a reflection of my inner visions. I combine color, spontaneity, and the free flowing medium of watercolor and draw on the inspiration of my background which I try to reflect in a contemporary manner."[1] Her focus on the land is evident in such early works as *Adoption Lodge* (1977) and *Morning Prayer* (1979) and is a focus that continues in the recent *Awé* series (1990).

Stewart is also active in the development of the arts in Montana and has served as the coordinator of Montana Indian Contemporary Arts. Her work is in the collections of the Museum of the Plains Indian in Browning, Montana, and the North Dakota Museum of Art in Grand Forks.

We talked in her studio in Bozeman in August 1991.

LA: Perhaps we could start off with a little bit about your art and family background and the influences on the development of your work.

SS: My father had been relocated to Livermore, California. I was born there and spent twelve years there before moving back home to the reservation. After I moved back he passed away. Then I lived in various western states for a time. When I was eighteen I returned to California and started attending CCAC [California College of Arts and Crafts]. I studied there for five years. That's where I met Frank [LaPena], George [Longfish], and Jean [LaMarr, printmaker of Pit River–Paiute heritage]. They were my biggest influences. I also was drawn to Kandinsky and Klee. Ultimately the major influence was my grandmother and my link to the Crow community.

LA: Why do you think so many Native artists have been influenced by Kandinsky?

SS: For me, primarily, it was his attitude about spirituality and, secondarily, color. His sense of color was quite inspiring, and one of the most important aspects of my work is color and what it means.

LA: How did you go about integrating these influences?

SS: It's my feeling about the land. Living in Montana, which is so immense and so spectacular and vast, and which is such an immense part of my life, I can't help but be enmeshed in the landscape. And the essence of the land is always prevailing. There's not a day that I'm not touched by what I see, especially here in Bozeman, because historically and traditionally this is Blackfeet and Crow land. So that plays a real big part in how I feel and how I respond.

LA: You mentioned the importance of color in your work. How much of your color is derived from the land, from the environment?

SS: I would say quite a bit. The sunsets, you know, are so

incredible that I derive a lot of my color sense from that intensity, or from the mountains. There's such a subtlety of color. What I see strikes me in such a way that I use color for an emotional-type response. It's an emotional and spiritual response to nature. My work is not literal; it's a feeling, it's an essence. I'm trying to pull from a place that's deep within me. I'm having a dialogue with nature.

LA: You mention the influence of your grandmother. Your sister [Kathryn Stewart] is also an active artist. Were you always artistically inclined?

SS: Well, I'll say it this way. When I was five and she was seven — she's two years older than I am — we were doing a mural with crayons behind the couch in our house, and no one knew this. The family thought we were back there playing with dolls or whatever. For months we would go back there and create the mural. One day our mother discovered it and it was incredible; it was the size of the couch. You know, she was mortified. I think that from that point on we were artists. I mean, that's kind of a silly tale, but I always felt in my soul that I could never do anything else. It's kind of a curse in a way. You know, what else would I do? I certainly don't think that there's anything else in the world that I'd rather do.

LA: Did you focus on any one medium at CCAC?

SS: I went there thinking I was going to go into sculpture, because my sister was the painter. But I went right into painting because that's what I really wanted to do. But I also studied sculpture and printmaking. Painting seemed to be the one medium that really drew me in, though, so I continued with that.

LA: Maybe we could discuss your approach to painting.

SS: I walk into a piece with an idea, a set idea, and once in a while there is a series of paintings, which I sometimes call sisters, but when I start painting it's like I become possessed. The imagery might come from a dream consciousness where I'll wake right up and think that I have do a painting *now* — you know, level the room, everyone out of my way type of thing. It's a feeling of possession. But at other times I just go into the studio and it's work, work, work, and a piece might come out of it. I was always told, sometimes you're inspired and sometimes you have to work until the inspiration comes. I go both ways.

LA: You seem to frequently work in series, like the recent *Awé* series [1990].

SS: Yes, yes. I work something to death and then it's gone. I just have to get whatever it is out. I worked in watercolors for many years, but I don't think I could go back to them because I worked them to death. But I think that also helped me with my painting in oil for some reason. I haven't quite figured out how, but it seemed to have helped.

I haven't gone back to that series for some time and I don't know if I ever will, but that series was based on the earth. *Awé* actually means "land" or "earth" in the Crow language. That series is about my feeling about the land and a celebration of our home, the land. We feel connected to it. Living here in Montana in the ancestral home of my people, I wanted to honor that land and the people. There's also a whimsical feeling to those pieces, about how I feel kind of utterly small in the context of the land and the powers of the earth.

LA: Were they based on direct observation of particular places, or did you just try to communicate a general sense of the land?

SS: I was drawing on several places in Montana. I got inspiration around Bozeman, but also from my family's home and the reservation, drawing on the memories of the land and the landscape, the way it looks to me and the way in which I relate to it. The pieces sort of combined memory and the present.

LA: Could you talk about the imagery in the *Ceremony* series from 1989?

SS: I would say that, to date, there are maybe twenty-five to thirty pieces in that series on ceremony, and the imagery still pops up here and there. It's lingering. Once in a while I'll do a piece and I'll say, "That's a *Ceremony* piece." How they come about, it's an idea that will hit me and the imagery will fit together and it will be something that I'm obsessed with. I work on it until it resolves itself. I did a series called *Sacred Lands*. That one is still ongoing; I don't think I totally exhausted that one. The imagery seems to float in and out until I work it through. I get a very intense focus. I guess that's why I work in series.

LA: What links the works in a series, any common factors?

SS: Imagery, color, there will be a certain symbolism that I use for a particular series. There's a lot of imagery that creates a connection from one piece to the next. And that imagery will change, it will become transformed, it will become something else, and then the transition piece will happen. I'll see the transition piece and I'll say to myself, "Okay, that series is beginning to change and go into something else." And then a new series will be born.

LA: In a way, it seems like your work could be one extended series.

SS: Yes. *Long*. And it's really interesting to me, but also quite rare, that a person will come along who understands my work well enough to see the transition pieces and say, "Where are you headed?" And they'll wait until the series starts, and come back. "Oh, yeah, I see where this is going."

LA: You have a number of recurrent images in your work, like handprints and swirls and some petroglyphs.

SS: To me, those are all very ancient symbols and they appear in many cultures, not just Crow culture or Native culture, but human culture. I think that you see swirls and handprints throughout many cultures, and I want to create a sense of connectedness between cultures. Although we're all very different, we're still all the same, and I think that's what those images are all about. They're unconscious types of things that come through.

LA: Red is a recurrent color, too.

SS: I always come back to that. I tend to go toward certain colors that were used a lot in beadwork designs and I always notice that they seem to come through. I guess if I weren't a painter I'd be a beader. And I'd be beading Crow designs and using those particular colors, like the reds and some particular blues.

LA: How has your work evolved over the 1980s?

SS: The first thing I'd say is the maturity and clarity of my ideas. My sense of merging with the land has become stronger — the self with the land. I think that's been a part of maturity and clarity. I've gained direction and focus in my work, or at least I've come to understand what those things are.

I've had lots of good influences and encouragement. I have to mention Jaune Quick-to-See Smith as a mentor because she was very encouraging about my work.

LA: You're known mostly as an abstract painter, but you also do more figurative work, like the spirit horses. How do you balance the two types of imagery?

SS: Both are important to me, but I think that sometimes you need the figurative in order to convey something that is very important and closer to the vision that you may be trying to get out. And the spirit horses just started to develop a short time ago.

They're more symbolic to me in the sense that they're about transformation. There's a lot of transformation in my work right now, and when they came out they also spoke about the transformation of a culture, like when the horse came to North America and arrived on the Plains. The horse made our culture more mobile and faster and quicker. It transformed us as a culture. So to me that's a real symbol of transformation, and the horse is like the connecting of the two worlds, and how something can happen that radically changes a whole culture.

LA: What are the transitions going on in your work now?

SS: It's dealing with a spiritual world and how this world comes into the physical. I have figures, spirit beings. And within and without them are floating symbols, like there may be one central figure with two figures superimposed on it, or a horse superimposed on the figure. I'm working through some ideas about how I see myself in a spiritual sense and in the physical world. Death has something to do with this, and rebirth, of course, because my sister went through an illness, coming close to death. I also wanted to deal with the thought of losing someone so close to me. We're always kind of on that edge, anyway. I want to identify for myself that I'm in the physical world but I'm also connected to the spiritual.

LA: It sounds like there is a very strong personal dimension to your work. Do you work out these types of questions and experiences in your art?

SS: Yes. I've also done a series of paintings concentrating on a red woman, an earth mother. It's called *Red Women*. She's something very personal, and I wouldn't necessarily show those pieces. They're real personal. I'm not interested in putting them out there. Some works are just meant for me to learn from, for my eyes mainly, and maybe for a few people who come to the studio. It's funny, if people come to the studio and I have one of those pieces up on the wall, I'll make a note mentally of who responds. I've had several men that come in and become very drawn to it, and say, "Oh, that's just such a powerful piece. What is this? What's going on?" On the other hand, many of the women who see the same piece may not say anything.

LA: What do you make of that?

SS: I don't know. Maybe it's the earth mother imagery, the mother icon, that they relate to in a kind of nurturing way. It's the mother within, or the nurturing notion of women. And to have this powerful figure standing there emits that idea of a nurturing mother.

LA: Looking around your studio at some of the pieces you're doing now, a lot of them seem to be pretty big. Do you prefer to work on large canvases?

SS: That one over there, the one 60 by 110 inches, is a diptych. But, yes, I like working big. I like big things. You can see that I have to have big spaces, like these twenty-foot ceilings. I have a dream of doing larger site works in the future. I'm working toward that. On the other hand, I work very tiny, too. I did something that I called the *Medicine Wheel* series from '87 and it went from real large to very small five-by-seven-inch pieces. It was an interesting series. Some Japanese collectors bought some of the very small ones. So I do work small but it's pretty rare.

LA: Could you talk about your working methods for painting?

SS: I like working on the floor as opposed to the easel. There is something really comforting about having the piece in front of you on the floor, bending over it. Maybe it dates back to some kind of genetic memory of scraping hides, I don't know. That sounds pretty weird but I feel most comfortable bending over a piece. It's just something I've unconsciously done, so I don't really think about it. I don't feel so good when I hang something up and start working. It doesn't make me feel comfortable to do it that way. My monoprints and the slate works are done horizontal on the floor or on a table. It's just my process of doing things, I guess. And I like rubbing and scraping. Sometimes I sew my work down.

When I'm on the floor, I can work all around a piece. I've always worked like that. I also like to work in twos, so I always have my sisters. I mean, not always, but there is a real good portion of my work where I'll have sisters, or I'll call them sisters, or a diptych, and they have to get together.

LA: Do you apply the colors by hand?

SS: Yes, and I'll use a scraper or whatever is at hand. I'm like a madwoman. "Well, hell, this looks interesting." I'll throw that on there and see what it does. I'll use a brush only when I have to. I'm not a traditional painter in that sense, no. I just do whatever it takes to get a piece out. I'll use anything. Somebody convinced me to buy an easel once, and it's nice to put a work on it to look at, but I feel very uncomfortable. So I end up putting the work back on the floor. Sometimes I think that I should try to use brushes or something, but I find myself squishing up the paint and grabbing it and mushing it around with my hands. I can never keep my hands clean when I'm in the studio.

LA: Do you ever return to a finished piece and try to change something about it?

SS: I don't think so. Once in a while I might dot an "i," you might say. But it feels redundant for me to return to a finished piece. I'm more interested in the process and not the product. I'll go through a lot of stages in the creation of a work and I get the product out and then I go on. If I go back that product is only like a page in a journal.

LA: You've mentioned that you create patterns like songs in your work, and that energy is like music. Could you talk about those connections?

SS: When I get started on a piece all of a sudden I see a pattern start to develop. It's like a spontaneous dialogue that goes back and forth between me and the piece, and it becomes like a song or a dance. There is some kind of a musical pattern I hear and I go back and forth with it. It tells me, I tell it. It's like jamming with the work. There's a certain kind of underlying direction and then there is a melody that goes on around it. So there would be a foundation, like a drum, and all of a sudden the lyrical or melodic part starts to emerge, and then the whole song is formed.

LA: How did you come to use oil paints on slate?

SS: I was really interested in the Italian painters who used to paint on slate, and I saw a really wonderful piece and was inspired by the whole idea. I do a lot of collaborations with other artists, and I had been working with an artist friend of mine from Utah, Phillip Bell, and he got me going. I was working on a piece of slate, carving into it, and I said, "I've always wanted to paint on slate." It has a quality of being very dark, and there's a richness in that, a darkness with luminous colors. When I started working on it I got very excited about it because it's a very laborious process. It takes a long time to come to some sort of resolution with it. That's different than my monoprinting, which is very spontaneous, very fast, an instant-gratification kind of thing. Working on the slate is very slow and you have to wait for a while for things to come together. I kind of bounce the two things off. I'll do very quick monoprints and then I'll work on my oil paintings, which are very slow. I'll work on them for a year sometimes before they'll ever come to some kind of resolve. And I'll live with them, and they actually become very good friends to me. I guess it's a dichotomy in myself, but I need to have things that take a long, long time and then things that are right there.

LA: How do you reach that point of resolution?

SS: When it's whole, when it feels whole. Some pieces never reach that stage of having that quality of completeness.

LA: The slate pieces are interesting because the slate does make a darker image. That's different from a lot of your other works, which are brighter.

SS: That's my dark side, I guess. I've always believed that human beings have the dark and the light. There is definitely a dark side to mankind. Maybe that's something I'm dealing with symbolically by using the slate. I don't know. There are different ways of looking at it.

LA: Where do you get the slate from?

SS: It's a quest. I go around hunting for it. This piece here was from a school chalkboard, and sometimes I've gotten pieces from pool tables. It's kind of funny. I don't do very many of them, because it does take so long. When I do want to start one I just ask people, "Hey, have you seen any slate around?" You make certain connections, rock places, and they think I'm crazy at the rock stores. "What do you do with this stuff? We want to see what you're doing." I've never taken anything back because I'm sure they wouldn't know what the hell I was doing.

I've got this thing about rocks anyway. I've always been interested in geology. I've always loved rocks. I think it's a way of literally bringing rock into my work. Anywhere I go I always end up getting something, and I might even take some with me, like when I went to Argentina. I'll pick up a rock and take it with me. Rocks are part of the way I communicate.

LA: What was that trip about?

SS: Argentina was a real interesting thing that just kind of happened. It started with a vision I had over two years ago. It's really hard to explain, this dream, but I was taken above the Medicine Wheel and the Big Horn Mountains and was given directions by a woman to look south. And sometime after that I was contacted by a woman from a group who said that we would be interested in taking you to the south. It was coincidence, or synchronicity, or something. I had been thinking about the southern part of the U.S., but she says, "Well, would you like to go to Argentina?" Sure. Who wouldn't? So she said, "A group of us are going and we have a ticket for you as part of the group." Then the group thing got canceled, but she still had the ticket for me. An organization called Partners of America was facilitating the whole thing. We do projects together, and people from Argentina come to Montana and we go down there.

So the next thing I know I'm on a plane to Argentina and I'm going to be on a cultural and artistic exchange with the Mapuche people and with the Patagonian and Namancura people. I was to go down there and participate in a sacred ceremony called the Nguillatun. And I believe that I was the first North American Indian to do so. It was a very intense situation for me and the experience transformed me, it just literally transformed me as a human being, spending time with these people. We did not speak each other's language—we had no form of verbal communication—but yet there was an incredible form of communication that was underneath the language. We had to communicate through gestures and through our eyes. Spanish was their language of colonization, while mine was English. It was very interesting to be in their company, and when you remove that layer of colonization, underneath were Indian people. It was natural. It was as if I were home and I felt so connected, a real north-south, Americas connection. It was incredible.

LA: Did that trip have an immediate effect on your work?

SS: Oh, yeah. It was like I came back and I had all these feelings about what I wanted to say in my heart, so I started on my *Mapuche* series. I was given a drum when I was there. I was taught women's songs, which were quite different from the north, so I have a strong feeling about the drum and what the drum means to me as a North American Indian. It's the heartbeat. It has a real spiritual feeling for me. So to be given a drum is almost like being given the heart of the people—that's the way I see it. It was a healing process in itself.

I came back and started doing some performance work and installations that have to do with wholeness, using symbols and objects and placing them in a ritual form. I'm continuing to do this on small scales, large scales, it doesn't matter. I'm designing these pieces constantly in my head, and when I have the opportunity then I go find some land and stick this stuff down there and put it in the landscape and let it be there for a day and then I take it up and then it's gone.

LA: Do you do a lot of cross-cultural art?

SS: Well, I just did an installation called *Survival* [1991] which was about indigenous people and how we interact, not just indigenous people from the Americas. This particular exchange was with the Maoris. We worked together and discussed issues and ideas about colonization. There were a lot of parallels and comparisons between the two cultures. One of the Maoris was an installation artist and the work she does is incredible. She deals with the spirituality of the land and ceremony. This is very apparent to me in her art.

LA: Do you see any global connections between the people you met in Argentina, the Maoris, and Native artists here?

SS: Yes, many. I think that being indigenous people, living on a land base, on our ancestral lands, for one, and how we relate to history, the history of thousands of years that can't be taken away. That's all just a part of who we are and how we live in the world. So I think that it doesn't matter if you're in New Zealand or Africa or Argentina or in Montana. They have a very rich sense of connection to their cultures and how they perceive themselves. There are a lot of underlying similarities.

Art to me is a language that most people can relate to; it's like a universal language.

LA: This question may be related to that. You mentioned that there's a tradition of visioning and dreaming in Crow culture. Has that been an influence on you or had an impact on your work?

SS: Yes, I really think it does. I think that we have a tradition of seeking visions. The last chief of our tribe had visions when he was eight years old that came to pass. So it's a very strong part of our culture. That's a part of our reality. So it's second nature to me that dreams are very important. If you have a particular dream that seems very important or is trying to convey a certain message, you might go to someone and say, "I had this dream and I don't know what it means." You would ask someone who could interpret that dream or give you some insight about what that dream might mean. And that could become a source of art. For example, the whole exchange with the Argentineans and the Indians and my trip down there came out of a vision that happened two years before I went. I was being told that there was something that I needed to seek out and to follow. It took me some time to get to that point of actually going, but I was using that dream as a base to search out and find the information about going there, and by which I would come back and eventually create the piece *Without Words* [performance, Portland Art Museum, 1992], which was dedicated to the Crow and Mapuche people. But I'm always working on something that comes from a dream source.

LA: You do a lot of different types of work, like gallery installations, performances, and earth works. Could you talk about the development of those forms?

SS: I think that after a while painting or printmaking is a solitary type of process. You go into a studio and you paint. I really feel the need to do work that is more community-oriented, in the sense that when I went over to my reservation and did these works, the biggest reward for me was that my people were able to participate in the piece. They watched it, became a part of it. The audience becomes important. People help me implement the piece. So having my brothers and my sisters and my cousins and other Crow people witness this work being made gave me a real strong sense of community. It was like I was giving back something to honor them. So now it's become a major part of the creative process for me to do this work to honor my people. I have a real high regard for where I come from and I wish to honor that.

LA: Could you talk about the "Hammer, Nail and Brush" show from October '90 [Centro Cultural de la Raza, San Diego]? That sounded pretty interesting.

SS: That show was put together with two other artists. There was a non-Native woman named Debra Mitchell and Corky Clairmont, a Salish-Kootenai man from Montana. I knew Corky pretty well, but Debra I didn't know at all, really, just in a limited kind of way in a professional setting. I thought it was very interesting that the organizers had chosen two Natives as well as two women.

We were put together in a room with a lot of different objects that we each got. We were locked in a space that was totally empty and told that we had three days — three twenty-four-hour periods — to complete an installation of our choosing. So, to me, it was like creating a very small sense of community through the collaboration of the artists. At the beginning of our time we decided not to create separately. We put all our duplicate items into one pile and created the installation collectively. At the beginning I felt like I was being put into jail, art jail, and then being forced to create, but in the end we became really close with each other and a sense of bonding came out of the process.

The installation dealt with what confinement means, about when you are confined and forced to do something. Some of the imagery had to do with flying birds, and there were altar pieces, and on the wall, portraits of each other and how we felt and how we linked up to each other. We also documented the time in there, like having a piece that would go around the room, so there was a strong sense of time in the art and a sense of being in a room together trying to create cooperatively.

LA: Do you think that the experience has had a long-lasting effect on your work?

SS: What it did for me was give me the chance to work on some issues in isolation. It did transform me in a way because it started me thinking about space, confinement and space. Basically, though, I've been doing installation work and performances. I did a piece called *Luna, Luna* [performance-installation, Montana State University, 1992], which dealt with bonding between women. I did another piece about the land and technology using neon and things like that. But that was natural to me because gases are part of the earth, but it's the way that they're used that raises questions about technology.

I'm working on a piece called *White Girl*. It was a performance installation, a performance piece actually. It was about stereotypes, and about how Native women don stereotypes, and the images that are presented to us in the media, and about how we feel about that. When I was growing up, looking at *Vogue* magazine, for example, all you'd see were white girls. There was no one in those magazines that I could relate to. I never really felt connected to the mainstream culture. It was very much of a struggle for me to relate to it, because there was nothing there for me to relate to. But the piece focuses on how one can put on certain aspects of the dominant culture, and how we don stereotypes but are never comfortable with them. Beyond that, it also talks about how we always come back to who we are, how we come back and feel most comfortable when we're in our own community. It's about who I am when I'm within the culture. I can speak the language that you speak, but that doesn't necessarily mean I see things that way.

LA: You've moved into video work also, producing a piece on one of your installations.

SS: Well, yes, I'm quite interested and excited about the video and film work. These are whole new media for me and it's addictive and expensive. You can reach a much wider audience, so your work becomes more accessible. You can address issues, and we are in a media age. I try to say a lot in my paintings, but they are not all that accessible to a broader audience. The audience I'd like to reach I can only reach through video work. Some of the projects that I'd like to do concern issues about the land and the environment.

LA: Is there a split between your political orientations and the imagery in your work?

SS: I think my paintings and monoprints are probably less political, and that's where I see video fill in the void where my activist type of work is concerned. Working in video will fill that particular activist need, while painting to me is more emotional and spiritual in its content. But I found that my video came out more on the aesthetic side as a result of my input to the director. I think that as I work more with him there might be more of an emergence of political themes, or an integration of the two. But that's projection. I really don't know how it will turn out.

LA: You're the director of MICA [Montana Indian Contemporary Arts]. Could you talk about the work you do?

SS: What we are trying to do is to locate and document contemporary Native artists and to encourage them to participate in exhibitions. We are looking for artists who don't have the usual avenues for exhibiting their work, perhaps because their work is coming from a place that is unique. It may not be fashioned for a particular market in Montana, or even nationwide. There is no real market for Indian art unless you're doing Western art. The state is so large that we have to do a lot of networking. Recently we had Jean LaMarr come over for a symposium, and her concept was to use the earth as a medium and to do site works, performance pieces, installation works. We try to encourage this type of art in this region. That's my first hope. And then we want to find the young people who are in high school and create role models for them and show that art is not just one set way; there are many ways of expression.

LA: To finish up, is there any one theme that links or connects all your work?

SS: I'd have to say, first and foremost, the earth. That's the biggest inspiration, the earth and the way I see the land. That's very strong. And I'd have to add community — where I come from, my perception of that community and my connection to it, and ultimately what I give back to the community. I'd have to say that my art is a way of giving back, and I really dedicate my work to my people. Everything I do is a dedication to honoring my people, the Crows.

SELECTED EXHIBITIONS

"The Submuloc Show/Columbus Wohs" (1992–94), group traveling exhibition, Atlatl, Phoenix, AZ [collaborative piece with Kathryn Stewart].

"Our Land/Ourselves" (1991–93), group traveling exhibition, University Art Gallery, State University of New York, Albany, NY.

"Hammer, Nail and Brush" (1990), group installation, Centro Cultural de la Raza, San Diego, CA.

"Native Proof: Contemporary American Indian Printmakers" (1989), group exhibition, American Indian Contemporary Arts, San Francisco, CA.

"Montana Dream Reflections" (1988), solo exhibition, American Indian Contemporary Arts, San Francisco, CA.

"Portfolio II: Eleven American Indian Artists" (1988), group exhibition, American Indian Contemporary Arts, San Francisco, CA.

"Our Contemporary Visions" (1986), group exhibition, Sierra Nevada Museum, Reno, NV.

Frank Tuttle

Yuki–Wailaki–Koncow Maidu

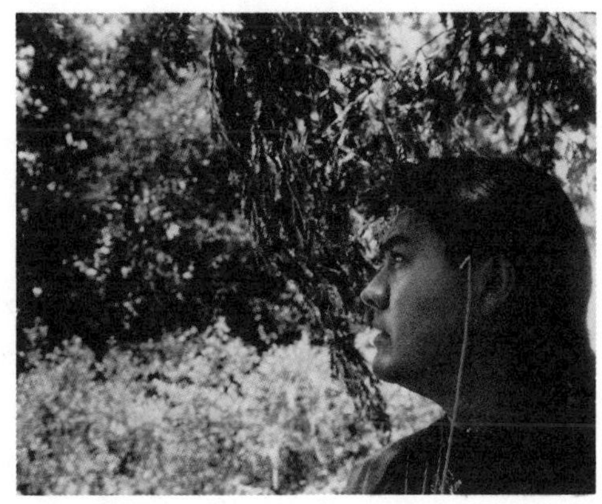

Frank Tuttle is a thoroughly modern painter whose work is as shaped by tradition as it is constantly seeking new ways of expression. Not reluctant to experiment with imagery and materials, Tuttle explores the meaning of tradition in contemporary social and artistic contexts. He has written: "I enjoy a particular thrill in being able to contrast and compare fragments of the old and new order. There exists a continuum of the tradition of the vision quest in which the new visions, as works of art, are informed by both Indian traditions and the modern art traditions."[1]

Tuttle's work searches for the essences of the traditions and ceremonies of the people from Northern and central California. Paintings like *Shaking All 'Round* and *The Abundance of Things* (both 1983), for example, with a delicacy of execution and sense of color and movement, are visual analogues of Tuttle's experience of ceremony and ritual. About *The Abundance of Things* he has said: "This image reminds me of the time when our people should gather together in appointed places to offer prayers, to give dances for a world in constant motion. Such events mark time and celebrate the abundance of things."[2] Tuttle's personal memory intersects with communal memory. Newer works like *In Good Faith* (1989) and *Life Is at the Mov-*

ing Center I and *II* (both 1990) continue in this direction. Although some of the materials may have changed (*Loren's Cap* [1989] uses glass for "canvas"), Tuttle's essential focus has not.

Frank Tuttle was born in Oroville, California, about sixty miles north of Sacramento, in 1957, and was raised there and in Ukiah, where he now lives and teaches. At Mendocino College he is a lecturer in both Native American art and Native American studies. He received his B.A. degree in fine arts, with a special emphasis in Native American studies, in 1981 from Humboldt State University and has been exhibiting his work since then.

Although Tuttle is strongly influenced by the richness of his heritage, he does not find it to be a constraint on his art, nor does he expect it to limit his audience's response. In fact, as George Longfish has pointed out: "Frank Tuttle does not concern himself about whether or not viewers understand his Konkow Maidu or Yuki-Wailaki themes; rather, he works with color and texture in abstract motifs, creating paintings that elicit emotional responses. The cultural tag others ascribe to these feelings does not appear to be a problem for him."[3]

Frank Tuttle's art has steadily grown in form and content since 1981. In addition to works on canvas, paper, and wood, he experiments with adding cloth and netting to his surfaces. As he has written about his art: "It is not reinterpretation but an evolvement of my own personal symbols."[4]

I talked with Frank Tuttle in Ukiah in May 1991.

LA: Could we start off with a little bit about your personal background and art education?

FT: Okay. First of all, my tribal affiliation on my mother's side is Konkow Maidu and on my father's side is Yuki-Wailaki. Those are north-central California tribes. As far as my art background, I feel that it goes back a long time. I've been drawing, consciously drawing, since I was very young, and in my own mind drawing with intention and a real purpose. I've always had a creative sense and the best part is that there is no end to it.

Regarding my academic background, I have a bachelor's degree in painting. I also have a special emphasis in Native American studies. Presently, I teach beginning through advanced painting courses, a sociology course concerning the cultural dynamics and political history of Northern California Native peoples, and an introductory Native American art history course.

LA: You're a practicing painter and a teacher of art history, painting, and political science. Can you combine all of these endeavors in any of your classes?

FT: In my classes I attempt to do just that — to expose history through art or vice versa. The Native American art history course is a general survey course covering topics in prehistory right up to what I've been working on, on my own easel. We journey from the East Coast to Alaska, with stops at various places in between. I like to contrast traditional California art and culture with contemporary art movements. All this provides a valuable background for students regarding Native cultures. From my perspective, everything derives from a visual perception basis. Art, as well as Native peoples, does not exist in a vacuum. It's very much a part of our daily lives and religious philosophies. So my courses cover the art and the social-political aspects. I slip all of it in.

LA: Do you think Native art has a political message, or at least can you discuss political issues through the arts?

FT: Oh, sure I do. Art, artmaking, can serve many applications. When contemporary art is on public view and is open to critical assessment, and as far as those works come out of a contemporary social context, then often the imagery has a political foundation from both the artist's motivation and from the viewer's perception brought to the image — simply by the fact that the piece was created by a Native American. The message is that Native Americans are alive, potent, creating, not an idle curio from the country's dim frontier. From a particular standpoint, ethnological or anthropological material collected from the late 1800s regarding Native peoples can be seen as revealing a standard ethnocentric bias, a bias not complimentary to the people under scrutiny. The accommodations that came out of that clash and conflict are clearly shown in much of the art.

And I certainly think that contemporary work is a vehicle for political discussion. At times Native artists created art to interject their own viewpoints and that level of thinking is evident today. Certainly that's evident in my own work. Today's artists may consider those accommodations made as a result of the drastic changes, clashes, and conflicts between Indian and non-Indian people, and see the frustrations and the energy of those clashes as opportunities to make art. In one of my recent works, *Coloma* [1989], that political dimension subtly comes through. It is a small "devotional icon" piece which refers to the conflict between the California Native world-view and the European-American world-view and value system. Social change was social fragmentation and destruction for thousands of Native people of California, beginning with the process of Spanish missionization. I ask myself and others, "What happened to all of those tens of thousands of Indian people in the decades following California statehood? What forces were at work which left only a small percentage of Indians left to struggle for survival at the turn of the century?" These questions, and the answers, especially, ignite waves of imagery within me. That work *Coloma* relates to those questions. A small number of California Indian artists address these issues; a smaller number of our own people are aware of the history. Consequently, I use my art to bring forth an awareness.

Individuals who frequent galleries and museums are predominantly non-Indian and, we can probably say, unaware of California cultures. They are also probably unfamiliar with their own social and political situation. So much of my work raises questions for the viewer, both silently and loudly: "What am I looking at? How do I relate to these images? Why *don't* I relate to these images?" So if the viewer hangs around long enough, he or she may get a little bit of information.

My work brings forth a dark and frightening time hidden behind a beautiful array of color and image. Indian and non-Indian people need to be aware of what happened in the places where they choose to live.

LA: Hopefully, your work might be a spur for people to look further into the history of Native people in California. People just don't know what they are supposed to be seeing.

FT: The reason why people out here don't see Indians is that the public image of Indians, insofar as there are public images of Indians, is for the most part derived from the Plains or the Southwest. These become our immediate images of Indians, but in California it's always been different, politically, socially, culturally. Our traditions and our art reflect that difference. I take a great deal of pride in the fact that some communities in California have strong traditional ties that have survived and continue to flourish.

LA: There seem to be many tribal groups up in Northern California which maintain an active ceremonial and religious life. Were these groups less impacted by missionization than communities in the south?

FT: You know, missionization did come up into Sonoma and the mission itself is in the neighboring fringes of it. But in order to get the labor forces needed for that mission they took people out of Lake County and went into Round Valley all around there for a hundred miles. People were brought out of our area here [Ukiah] and taken into the Central Valley and Southern California, and so it did have an effect. Those tribal units which weren't impacted by the missionization are those that were from the Klamath River area and from northeastern California.

LA: I guess that the attitude toward Father Serra and the missionization process couldn't be more opposite between Native and non-Native people?

FT: That was an impetus for my personal devotional images, especially after that whole issue of the church honoring him and the drive to raise him to sainthood.[5] So in those little personal icons I've done recently you see references to church architecture. You can also see references to the jeweled covers of sacred texts out of the Middle Ages. Those are aspects of the different worldviews and everything. Those founding tenets that were brought to California caused the destruction of the Native people here. I needed to deal with these issues, like the lack of a land base and the trauma that was felt only several generations ago, in my art.

I've seen the results of those problems, having worked for years in nonprofit Indian organizations in housing and employment. Some of our communities aren't as politically astute as other Indian communities are, and that has a lot to do with the lack of land bases and, which is unique to California, a lack of treaties. Northern California is also different in a cultural sense. It is really different. My own opinion is that it derives from that fragmentation, that social trauma.

LA: Whereas the Southwest, for example, has had more time and space to deal with those kinds of changes.

FT: It's amazing to me that the Navajo have so many acres. I can't imagine that. Here in California the land bases are less than two hundred acres; in Mendocino County the land bases are less than fifty acres. People on individual tribal areas number less than three hundred. They are all small, separate political entities. Traditionally, they were separate entities, small villages, extended-families types of groups. All that has to with the way they react today to acculturation, assimilation, to taking part in the larger society. That is all part of my work. That is why you see traditional dancers or traditional people in my paintings. I want to put them into a western context, at least as far as a museum exhibition goes, so that viewers will have some questions about the people in the paintings: "Who are these people? Where did they live? How am I supposed to relate to this?" These are questions which I hope to raise as I am making images, and questions I hope people think about. It makes me feel good to create images that come out of the very long history that still unifies our communities.

LA: Do you feel that you are a California artist?

FT: Yes, that is how I would describe myself. And I certainly do identify myself that way, as do others who are Native artists, like George Longfish, for example. He's been here for so long that he has got to be one of us! And what that description means to me is, first, that I am a California Indian, and second, that I am an artist whose primary concerns at this moment focus on imagery strongly derived from my ethnic background. This focus is a personal choice. I choose to work with this type of imagery not because I am a California Indian but because I make the decisions regarding my imagery. When my imagery is not immediately identifiable as a traditional California Indian image, it will still remain California Indian because I am the source and I choose to always work from that angle of vision. I am the artist and I am not giving up that claim.

LA: Even though you are doing totally different work, you are still linked as California artists, or even Northern California artists. Is that a good thing?

FT: Yeah, definitely. And we are linked on a more personal level. We are all friends. George Blake [Hupa-Yurok] is the same, or Jean LaMarr [Pit River–Paiute]. We are all from California and we are all friends. We are all artists, so that makes us a very unique group, and at the same time, within our communities, with what we do, we are a diverse group. So I always take a little bit of comfort in that when our work goes out to the Southwest or to the Plains or back east or even to Europe; it is still California work. For the most part we all still deal with imagery that is identifiable as California and I have to say that that is the way it is always going to be. All of my work is going to be that way. Revealing and sharing a California world-view with others is important to me. I've been somewhat fortunate, too, in that many of my pieces are able to cross over, that is, to be exhibited in shows that are not strictly organized around California art. But that's great with me.

LA: That brings up the question of regionalism and the larger problem of ethnic labeling of art. Some people just want to be known as artists, not Indian artists or Southwestern artists or Navajo artists. At the same time, there are special or distinctive qualities that Indian artists draw on and which are brought forth, sometimes symbolically, in any particular work. Then of course there are the expectations that people have about Indian art, and viewers seem to get confused if contemporary work doesn't fit into those expectations. How do you respond to the question of ethnic labeling, and that the art market might affect people's work or the way people present their work?

FT: Labeling is one of those unavoidable issues for Indian artists or black artists or Hispanic artists or women artists and, fortunately or unfortunately, is here to stay. But if you think about it, labels can make you feel comfortable. Labels have a lot to do with expectations from the outside, and even from the inside. First of all I consider myself to be just a human being and the way that I relate to the world is very visual, so I am an artist, and that itself is a label other people have put on me and it is a label that I have grown into. It has become an expectation I have of myself and how I choose to live my life. And after a lot of years of doing other types of jobs and occupations and what have you, the label "artist" becomes more true for me. The entire question is: Is it Indian art because an artist of Indian descent creates it or because the piece exhibits Native American imagery? Well, my work fits both labels. Perhaps, on initial glance, my abstract images have little recognizable Indian imagery when you walk in and see them on a gallery wall. Oh, there are colors, forms, and shapes to see, but these colors, forms, and shapes are Northern California to me. They have to do with living on this land and with the physical and emotional features of the landscape. Colors and forms may relate to the Klamath and Trinity rivers joining together at Weitchpec or the river bar near the jump dance ground. To me, painting and living in this place is a series of world renewals. So I try to express a certain moment in the culture and what that moment represents. I don't take living here for granted and neither should anyone else.

But in the context of an Indian art show, a casual viewer might say: "I don't see beads, Appaloosa horses, war bonnets, or baskets. I just see red and black and all kinds of shapes. Where is the Indian art"? But the viewer has to ask him- or herself: "What *don't* I know about this artist, this moment, or what they're trying to represent? What culture do they come from and what are they trying to say about that culture?" So I use the exhibition context, that total environment, to make people question. I use it to make other Indian people ask questions of themselves. This will bring our tribal groups closer together. Plains people may not understand people from the Northeast, so I use it in that way. I push that label "California Indian artist." And given the larger issue of establishing oneself, having a unique label may provide a niche that didn't exist before. It is nice to already have a niche. So I take it upon myself to use it to my advantage. But then again it is also nice to be among people who are just creative people and who see you just as a painter or as someone who works in oils as opposed to acrylics or something else. The labeling thing becomes monotonous and redundant after a while, but it is a real fact of life. The bottom line, of course, is that we primarily recognize ourselves as actively creative individuals.

I get really bothered by the fact that many people still relegate much of Indian artistic production to the notion of crafts — a safe, passive, and impotent label for what could be vital and progressive artmaking. This tendency clings to the anthropological or ethnological perspective whereby Native aesthetics are considered to be less developed. It seems that people believe that when you have a Native person of Native descent making art it somehow lacks the aesthetic value that other art has. This work is just as aesthetic as any other people's. It seems that the anthropologists see all our art from the perspective of the Dorothy Dunn Studio in the 1930s. Most of that was done just in terms of documentation and recording.[6]

Don't get me wrong. Visual record making is an important tool for understanding peoples different than our own — it's a way of bridging gaps. I continue to document visually many important aspects of my life because of their personal importance, not because it is something observed of Indian people. I document for myself, for my community, and for people to understand my culture. If others are unfamiliar with my culture, then I am doing them a service making them aware of it. Then they create frames in their own minds for something that wasn't there a moment ago. But for all of the creative work by Indian artists to be pushed into that realm to where it somehow has lesser value, to be relegated to glorified crafts, is a disservice and constitutes yet another struggle. I have been speaking largely of realistic imagery; now, nonrealistic, abstract work is another issue. I think most people just go blank when confronted with an image and not a picture.

LA: You mentioned this point in regard to a piece of yours, *Down River Prayers* [1984]. A casual viewer could look at that painting and see a nice image and a nice use of colors and get a sense of perspective and depth, but there is another level to the imagery that isn't apparent in that there is a reference to a specific ceremony. But it is not a literal or documentary reference.

FT: Yeah. Like some of my other abstract pieces — for example, *Shaking All 'Round* [1983]. That one has collage cloth pieces on the top and netting in the front, and it's about the livingness, the life energy, that is present in Northern and central California traditional Indian dancing. To my eyes and ears, I can read and listen to those shapes displayed across the surface of the work. But for others, what they'll look at are the linear aspect, the three-dimensionality of the netting that I made and attached to the surface of the cloth pieces, the feathers that are on the top. But there are also little tiny marks here and there that have always been present in my work. I orchestrate my marks to represent particular sounds, delineate movements and rhythms and cadences which carry the dance. The piece is my emotional-sensory response to the dance. I become very involved with that painting, in particular, in that way. I also know that it works that way for other people, people who are unfamiliar with things. They will look at the structure of a piece and somehow pick up on that sense of patterning. So my hope, then, is if they come to a dance, they will see the dance's pattern and structure. Our world is perceived every day through all these senses. To me, those same senses reveal the spirit found in our environments: the life of trees or rock or a splash of light. It's not something in the realm of science in terms of physics. It is the experience and perception and understanding of nature and I just interpret it, transfer that real-world information to a canvas using color and line.

LA: So your work has been very strongly influenced by dance, song, music, and ceremony?

FT: A great deal of it, yes. Most of what I show professionally has been influenced by dancing and ceremonial aspects of my culture because, to me, that is what the people are about, that is the heart of the California Indian. But my work is also very individual in that it shows my reaction to song, dance, and to the dream process, for example. I'm an individual but I'm within a group, a community. A dance can never happen, you know—it's like art—in a vacuum. The dances are done nonpublicly, sometimes in very small groups, but when I'm there and I'm dancing and I see all the old folks and I eat with them and hear these songs that are very old, and I suddenly remember that we're nearly in the twenty-first century, all that helps me understand why I'm here and why I didn't exist before, why I don't exist later than now. I'm here for something and so the whole wonderment and amazement of just being here, in the world today, is exciting.

LA: You've written, "I find myself in the position of repossessing the past to resolve the old into a new emerging self."[7] Do you feel that in your work you are a sort of translator of tradition and that you seek a continuity of past and present?

FT: Well, we all come from a past of one sort or another and for some of us it is more specific than for others. Fortunately, I think that I know a great deal about my past, in terms of both culture and tradition. That knowledge is important to my artistic perception. I understand how they work, how they are revealed to me and how I reveal that part of myself to tradition. I think that we all do that and we all know ourselves by looking at who we were in the past. I work on revealing that past, coming to grips with it both personally and culturally. It helps us become who we are and I use my art that way. I am like a translator, because my work is about my life. Conscious and unconscious imagery can tell me what is happening, how I am responding to and sorting through information. I think that the same occurs for traditional people, dancers or singers or medicine people. I think that a long time ago someone might have sat around on a hillside and things happened to him, a vision or an idea, and they translated these experiences for the people. That is how translation works. But in my work the translation may not always be pretty. Light and dark, internal and external, good and bad, always trying to seek a balance.

LA: Do you use color in any particular way? You mentioned lights and darks, and some of the pieces from the mid-1980s have a lot of red and white. In the more recent paintings do you have light and dark parts that would reflect this conceptual split?

FT: In terms of symbolic use of color, I don't have a rigid scheme. Some artists have a much more direct use of color. Mine is much more subtle and indirect and sometimes I'm amazed at what does occur. Colors that continually reappear just happen to be the colors I use for those symbols or images. I guess you could say that my working method is largely intuitive and emotional. Most of my reds, for example, have to do with maleness—maleness as it corresponds to woodpecker and its mythological associations. Woodpecker feathers hold great value, something akin to currency. For me, green has to do with humans and healing, life and growth. Blue is always the sky or celestial types of things. Black, like red, is powerful and individual; it exerts itself and is elemental. Lines are important, whether they're singular or massed, defining boundaries or cryptically evoking sounds. I prefer colors that are within my reach, colors that can be found close by. When colors are common they need to be made special and personal.

LA: So you draw colors from the natural world?

FT: It is not a direct connection to specific kinds of things, but I sort of have boundaries that I know I can't push the color beyond and then I use that color, but as I said, it is subtle. Even in the realistic things, the reds, the darks, there is always a fire. There is always a dark spot somewhere in the images. There is also a sense of closure in terms of a circle. Something else that I always have in my work is a connection, a vertical connection between heaven and earth. That is usually a pole or a line or a direct vertical movement in some way. It is always there. And so there is a division of spaces on the canvas. I have found that there are quadrants or thirds, and there is this movement upward, always this connection. To me this is a real space, a parabolic space, a womblike space.

LA: In *Down River Prayers* you have groupings of items in threes. There are groupings in the foreground and then some recede, creating a sense of depth.

FT: I do utilize groupings. You will find them in other pieces, too. The groupings are, well, there is nothing if there is no order, nothing is isolate. It belongs to something else. Things are associated in some way. So if I have a group, whether it be many things or a few, I am trying to make a connection, or like there's safety in numbers. At the same time it is like the helpingness of things, a kind of support.

LA: Do you think that the traditional people who made baskets or pottery sought the same type of ordering through their work that contemporary artists seek?

FT: Oh yes. I make baskets myself, and I've spent a lot of time with some of the well-known older folks and with some contemporary basketmakers. There is a certain attitude which comes about with the whole process of making baskets. Like when I sit down to paint, I just become intensely focused on what I'm doing, the moving around of paint and putting one color against another, say, or the viscosity of one color versus the looseness of another. Basketmakers have the same sensibility. There is a certain mental place that you find and you set yourself in that place and things just happen from there. I don't know that much about pottery, but I've always thought that the basket people were the beginning. You say prayers when you start a basket and you let it know that it is going to be started, to be created, and when you are finished you end with prayers to let it know that its birth is complete.

And then there is always the escape, the path out from beginning to end. A lot of my marks are those paths out, because in my art the viewer is looking in upon the work while at the same time I feel, I hope, that he or she is a part of what is going on. It is sort of a confrontational thing, although I don't mean that in a negative way. The viewer is not peeping at something or getting a quick glimpse of something, but is becoming grounded in the reality of the image. It's the same process of grounding, whether the piece is realistic or abstract, or if it's a basket or a pot.

As an artist, you have to ground yourself and become part of the process and the materials and the act of creating. It is not a mechanical thing, stitch after stitch. A basket whirl will talk to you. Songs will come, designs will come. We are always told that when you make baskets you never, never think of it as a chore or you'll become hunched over. And that's true. Resentments do do that to your back, twist it and bend it. I'd rather go to the flip side of that and take the pleasure in thc basketmaking itself. That makes the basket live. It's the same thing when I make regalia or work with feathers. If you have a good heart, if you are in the right place, then it will come in its own time. When I'm ready for it or when it's ready to come, it will come. Paintings will do that. Some will incubate or gestate for a long time in my mind, while at other times they are ready almost immediately. They will come out in like a couple of hours. I just sit back and let it happen and then sort of rejoice in the wonder of what the mind can do. To me it's like, "Wow! How did this happen?" A painting is something that occurs that was not there before, or it went from a nontangible image to a tangible thing. That's what dances are. Dances are nontangible to begin with, they become tangible in the performance, and then they become memory and finally an emotional part of ourselves to be kept. All of this type of activity helps me to understand the totality of our culture, the interconnectedness.

LA: Frank LaPena wrote about your art that it is a journey, and that your perception and comprehension define your imagery and that your paintings encompass the full dimension of that journey.[8] Could you talk about that journey process and how it leads to a painting?

FT: I've explained it to Frank as if I'm entering a house. A house has rooms, and the image that comes to my mind is that this house has a variety of rooms with hallways, a traffic flow. And what I do is begin. All my experience is like a house, like your home, my home, it's filled with experiences. It's representative; it manifests who lives there. When you walk into it you are able to perceive or pick up on things and then make an interpretation. Then you formulate opinions about that. I do the same thing. I have a blank canvas and I bring my experiences to that and then I begin. I will usually get a real strong sense of where I'm going and I'll work out, in a general sense, the technical aspect of things like volumes and color sense. I never carry that too far, though. I never preplan too strictly; the painting needs to work those things out on its own. And then I begin. And the painting will change, but not so that I have to rub off or scrape down an image. The process just happens. Somehow I just have a really clear and distinct vision of where the image needs to go. There will be all sorts of little nuances that come out, because as I'm working I think of places I've been or people I've been around that have something to do with the image. I bring all of that in, so sometimes when heads are tilted or hand gestures are a certain way, it is reminiscent of something that I've seen, certain actions of certain individuals which bring that painting alive. I can look at it and know that it's based in reality or on a real truth.

LA: Your paintings are based on real experiences?

FT: Yeah. They make the painting real and the painting will live in that way; it gestures out by itself. Or when I see colors in certain ways, like colors from around a real small fire at night, or the way shells will shine in a certain way. Large abstract shadow shapes or those flashes of color, they are all true so I try to put those things in my work. It is because I understand that type of experience of color or shape, and whatever is in my painting comes out of my experience. Of course, these types of perceptual experiences are not confined to individuals but are shared by groups of people, creating a common reality.

LA: How so?

FT: I think Frank tries to interconnect all his work, bring it all together. But for me, each piece is a completely new piece. Even in this whole series of twenty-seven, each one is different. My desire was to have a total of twenty-seven but I had no idea what they were going to be. That's why they're all so unique. To me, that is part of the uniqueness of them, their irregularity. I don't put a lot of formal constraints upon myself. Of those twenty-seven, a lot are just irregular shapes; they're not perfect in that way. It drives some people crazy but for me that's fine. That's what I had to paint on. What I want to do is paint. I'm not concerned whether one side is a quarter-inch higher than the other side — that's someone else's problem. I would find a way to hang it, no problem to me.

LA: You mentioned earlier that you teach and have studied art history, especially the northern Italian Renaissance. Did that have any influence on your work?

FT: Oh, yes. I remember that just from early on, when I was in high school, there were no texts of Native art, there weren't catalogs, there weren't references to Native art other than archaeological artifact images and that sort of thing. I was interested in the painting process, like how people paint and what they were capable of painting and how they rendered images. That was what I was really interested in. If I can understand that, then I can render the images that I want to render, so in the time that I was formulating my painting process, what better place to look than the Old Masters? I began a self-guided study of them. I had, and still have, a great desire to understand their roles, their artistic production, their muses. Also, in high school, the American expressionists, like Franz Kline and Jasper Johns, and I spent a lot of time together. There were books on them that I could find in libraries, so I took those. Later I could get catalogs for the European biennial shows, American and South American shows, and natural history collections. I would find those catalogs and look through them. I wasn't restricting myself. In order for me to understand what I was doing as an artist, and not knowing that a tradition of Indian easel painting existed, the next place to go was to Western art traditions. That has always fascinated me and I found that line of Western artists very appealing. I needed to understand the ins and outs of that tradition. It allows me to gain a perspective on the Native American creative experience.

I also studied Chinese art and Pacific Island art for a couple of years, plus, of course, anything I could find on American Indian art. Those other traditions just allow me to put into perspective what I'm doing and what can be done in terms of a contemporary Native American art history. It is important to me as a Native artist to be knowledgeable about the total context of the arts. I need to know what other people are thinking about art in general and that informs me about their responses, positive or negative, to Native art. For me, this broad study is the only way to go.

LA: You mentioned making ceremonial regalia. Are you involved in dance or any other ceremonial activities?

FT: Yes. That is something I've always had an interest in. My grandmother and great-grandmother have been involved, my whole family really, even in things like traditional healing. In Northern and central California you have a real strong history of dreaming that informs the religious and social community, and that was a powerful experience. I was brought up immersed in that tradition through the extended family. That was the way to perceive how people behaved. Dreamers could find lost things. I understood how people could use dream imagery to see what was yet to come or to bring things back from the past. I observed how people used these faculties to resolve problems, faculties which I don't think other people use.

LA: You seem to approach art and ceremonialism, the making of regalia, participation in dance, in the same way. Is there a similarity or unity of approach?

FT: Yes, I approach my art in the same way as I approach dance. For example, I abstain from certain things and ground myself in a certain way to keep focused on my task. That's the only way to approach art for me, because that's the way the image needs to be created. I can't separate a painting from other real-life experiences. But then there are other things, like I push my boundaries, because as a person who works with traditional things and as an artist working with traditional images I have to find my own margins, and so I push them and I'll work right up to them and see what happens. So in a way I work in three dimensions, the way a dance is three-dimensional. It's not sculpture per se, but I'm a firm believer in manipulating three-dimensional materials and understanding three-dimensional space in order to do two-dimensional work. That's important for my work, especially for the abstract kinds of things. Three-dimensional work brings in not only the visual sense but also a tactile sense and a feeling of being able to go around and through and behind objects to feel weight and volume. Then I tie in those kinds of aesthetic and formalistic notions to traditional dance. Although the dance makers probably aren't thinking of it that way, I see it that way and I can create paintings using this completely other set of rules. So the approach to these two activities is quite similar, and very satisfying to me.

LA: Can we talk about the evolution of your work? In the early to mid-1980s you did a series of abstract images, although they were very bound to nature and the environment. Can you link those to the new work, the series of twenty-seven panels?

FT: The older work was done on sheets of rag paper, while the new series is done on small wood panels. These panels I had made were all pretty much a standard size, like eight by ten or ten by twelve inches, and I prepared them for painting. This transition from paper was out of necessity—I didn't have any left to work with! As I did the abstract work in the eighties I was always drawing in my sketchbook, but making more realistic images. And now, as I work more realistically, I develop abstract images in my sketchbooks. This allows me a great deal of freedom and gives me a balance that I need. I've always done that, two parallel types of images. The realistic images were considered a private part of my work, kept within a small circle of family and friends, who saw them and collected them over the years. But the public never saw these pieces, only the abstractions. So I needed images and materials for new work, and I just thought to myself, those realistic images were just piling up and I needed to get them out of my head. So I started painting them and they evolved into this series that eventually took up three years, which is a new thing for me to work in that way. When I ran out of the paper, I decided to work with different imagery.

But actually now I'm going back to larger pieces because, for one thing, people are expecting the smaller realistic kinds of things and I don't always do what's expected of me. So I'm going back to the abstract things and I'm doing more on unframed canvas, you know, just pin it on the wall, or I'll combine realistic and abstract imagery. My notion is that I'll stay there for a while and watch the images that come that way. But I don't set out any goals for myself, any formal goals that I'm going to do this or that. I don't work on aesthetic problems or things like that with a real conscious effort; I just do whatever I want to do.

LA: You've mentioned that the twenty-seven panels were split in half, with the extra one based on male and female and the lunar calendar.

FT: Yes. They represent a ceremonial year. It has to do with my family and friends here in Northern California. I've painted images from Maidu country to downriver in Yurok country. This series is a celebration of living as Indian people, a celebration of family and friends. I loosely based the series on a lunar year, each painting having a male and female aspect. That makes twenty-six, so I made a self-portrait, which is the twenty-seventh image.

Within the body of work there is a range of specific images. There are straightforward images, like *Thursday Night, Brush Dance* [1990], a Yurok dance image. The brush dance is a communal event to set an infant on the good path of life and to respect the Creator and all that the Creator puts forth for Indian people. It's a three-day dance. Friday is a rest day. They gamble that day, and then on Saturday, late afternoon or early evening, the dances start up. They dance all night and the sun comes up Sunday morning, at which time a lot of this beautiful, really stunning regalia comes out. It is just unbelievable to take part. For me, a lot of the images I've seen that deal with the brush dance have to do with the prettiness and opulence of the regalia. But there's another aspect to the dance that's just the rolled-up jeans and the headbands and the willow. To me, that's the pretty part of the dance. I want that as one of my basic tenets for doing things, the beauty in the simplicity, the beauty of the people.

LA: Could you talk about *The CenterMan* [1990]?

FT: Oh, *The CenterMan*, sure. That one was done at a time when the Yurok, Karok, Tolowa, and Hupa peoples were struggling with the government about issues of American Indian religious freedom. Eventually they argued their case before the Supreme Court, and so I did this painting to focus my energy and to lend support to those individuals carrying this struggle. I wanted to draw energy to those people and let them know that we support them in our hard struggle to validate our own beliefs in a system that has no idea about Indian people. The system thinks that our religions are like craft religions, something just a little more advanced than the Boy Scouts. It was so frustrating to experience this denial of our rights, especially when we're a very religious people. I did this painting because it was the only thing I could give of myself.

About the painting itself, the centerman is in the Yurok jump dance. It's a ten-day dance held in September, and the weather is hot and dry. It is a hard dance requiring a strong sense of concentration. The centerman is chosen from among the dance people and he's the timekeeper. He's in the middle among a long line of dancers. The dance is a healing dance for the entire community, and is very profound and serious. This dance pushes sickness away from the community, pushes it back upriver so it is away from the center of the world. A unique basket is used only in this dance. It's interesting because it seems to me that when we dance we forget that we're in a whole group; we become the center of the world. And when you're dancing in the jump dance then the centerman becomes the follower. The singers are on either side of him and singing. He keeps time with a long, rhythmic stomping with one foot. You stomp and you push away the evil. The spirit people are there on their side watching and the spectators are on their side. The people watching see the necklaces or clay gods that are in their family, and you dance to let the spirit people know that you are still spiritual people and that you believe in them. To me, all that resides in the centerman.

I believe the painting measures close to ten by twelve inches. The image is depicted differently than the actual setting. I parted the trees in the background to reveal the mountaintops where the individual might travel to pray and be closest to the heavens and at the same time be near the heart of the community alongside the river. It's quite a distance from the top of the mountain down to the river, physically and spiritually. In the painting the eagle feather reaches up to touch the top of the mountain in the background to connect the centerman in the foreground to the fire and the people.

LA: Do you feel that your works connect to a shamanistic tradition, as some critics say about Frank LaPena's work?

FT: I happen to think that all artmaking is shamanistic. Perhaps I'd say that my work is a product of a personal shamanistic process. You know Frank is a dance maker, so he understands that aspect of his tradition and I'm sure that that forms his work in some way. I don't have that background. In my work I extract images from my personal experiences and from the environment. Like many Indian people, I feel a closeness to the Indian way, the way our people thought of this place, the way one must develop a trust with the world. What we know about the world is personally felt or told to us or shown to us. So I learn about and explore my own culture; that's what we all need to do, I think. When we as Indian people dance, that is how the world knows that we are thankful to be here and to look out upon the earth. By dancing and painting I can take part in the creation.

LA: How do you see your work as contributing to that learning and growing process, both for yourself and for others?

FT: Well, when I do my work, I think about all that I have and all that I would like to share, so I try to include some of that desire in my work. I use my paintings, beyond the economic sense, by simply giving them as gifts. In this way they are akin to baskets and take on a feeling of community and ritual. In that way they're sort of shamanistic. And I really believe that everybody is an artist on some level, but for some of us it's more obvious. When individuals or communities allow that artistic self to rise to the surface, the world is never quite the same again. As I gain more painting experience, I try to share with others the absolute wonder of just painting—it's magical and it's a powerful thing. That's how medicine people and dancers work. They know how life is just by experiencing more and more. So in my work, each time that I paint, I know a little bit more about painting and I realize what I don't know, and I think about how wonderful it is just to be able to do that. It's kind of a neat thing, but it's not a shamanistic venture for me in a formal sense. It's just on a personal level; it's a way of reaffirming our own world. For me it's really powerful.

LA: Let's finish with one question. Your style has evolved; you paint both figuratively and abstractly. Looking back over your career, is there one thread that connects all of your work, even if they may look different on the surface?

FT: Yeah. I did them all and to me that's the thread. No matter what I do, no matter what the images look like, I did them. I can make my images any way I want to. My time and place is here and now. I can make any kind of image and it is acceptable.

SELECTED EXHIBITIONS

"The One Looking Back" (1993), solo exhibition, Meridian Gallery, San Francisco, CA.

"Ancestral Memories: A Tribute to Native Survival" (1992), group exhibition, Falkirk Cultural Center, San Rafael, CA.

"From the Source" (1991), group exhibition, Ink People Gallery, Eureka, CA.

"Sacred Spaces, Spirit Places" (1991), group exhibition, Memorial Union Art Gallery, University of California, Davis, CA.

"Recent Work by Five Northern California Indian Artists" (1990), group exhibition, Gallery Route One, Point Reyes Station, CA.

"Healing That Way" (1987), group exhibition, Humboldt State University, Arcata, CA.

"Signs and Messengers of the Earth" (1984), group exhibition, Union Gallery, California State University, Sacramento, CA.

"Innovations: New Expressions in Native American Painting" (1983), group exhibition, Heard Museum, Phoenix, AZ.

SELECTED BIBLIOGRAPHY

Tuttle, Frank. "Artist's Statement." In *Ancestral Memories: A Tribute to Native Survival*. San Rafael, CA: Falkirk Cultural Center, 1992, p. 10.

——. "Frank Tuttle." In *Recent Work by Five Northern California Indian Artists*. Point Reyes Station, CA: Gallery Route One, 1990, unp.

——. "Artist's Statement." In *Innovations: New Expressions in Native American Painting*. Phoenix, AZ: Heard Museum, 1983, unp.

Kay WalkingStick

Cherokee

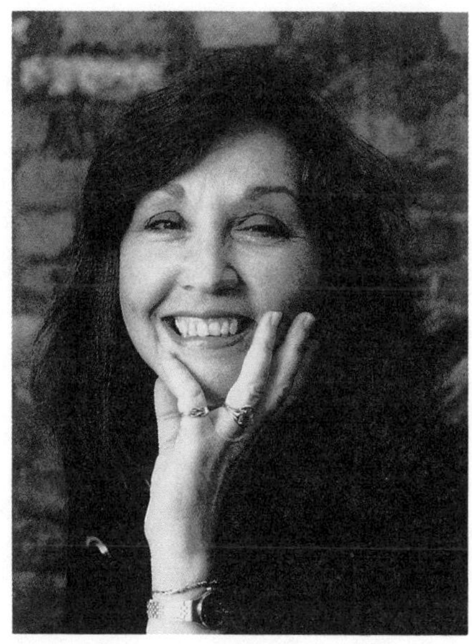

Kay WalkingStick's work seems to pull in two directions at once. On one level, the images are precisely balanced, reinforced by the diptych form and canvas sizes measured down to eighths of inches. On the other, her technique is very intense and physical, involving a layering of paint and saponified beeswax. She does not use a brush, but applies this mixture with her hands. The heavily layered side of the diptych is then cut and gouged with razor blades and scissors, revealing depths beneath the surface. The viewer is drawn into a counterpoint of action and stasis.

The figurative side of the canvas teems with movement, often turbulent, even violent. The image on the abstract side is perfectly placed in the center of the frame. As she has said about her work: "The abstract, often centered shape in the non-representational side, is found in a hypnogogic or intuitive manner. The two portions of the work relate in a mythic way—the natural is made fuller, more concrete by the abstract. One is not the abstraction of the other, one is the extension of the other. I want the two portions to resonate with one another like stanzas of a poem."[1]

WalkingStick's work has evolved markedly since the mid-1970s, from single-panel abstractions to the diptych form she uses today.

This form not only embodies aspects of her personal journey but also reflects her conception of and affinity for the land. At the same time, she says, "it is through abstraction that I perceive transcendence, and in that sense, I am, perhaps, not a landscape painter at all."[2] Nevertheless, there is a powerful spiritual quality to her work which is centered in the land.

Born in Syracuse, New York, in 1935, WalkingStick received her B.F.A. degree from Beaver College in Glenside, Pennsylvania, and her M.F.A. from Pratt Institute in Brooklyn, New York. She has had over a dozen solo and museum exhibitions, and her work is in a number of permanent and corporate collections. She has lectured on art throughout the United States and has been artist-in-residence at Fort Lewis College. She is currently an assistant professor of art at Cornell University.

We talked one May morning in 1991 in Phoenix before she drove out into the desert to take some photographs.

LA: Your work seems to have gone through a number of different styles or representations. Could you discuss the evolution of your painting?

KW: How long do I have? I always thought of myself as an artist. I grew up thinking of myself as an Indian and an artist. And to talk about the evolution of my work is really a lengthy subject, but I got out of college in 1959 and started painting in a rather hard-edged, realistic way. I continued in that way for about ten years while teaching and exhibiting. I saw myself as a working artist, although I was also trying to run a home and enjoy my family, too. I was also teaching. At one point I decided that I had taken those paintings as far as I could, and I also felt that I wanted a better teaching job than I had. So I decided to return to school and I went back to get a master's degree at Pratt. At that time one of the primary movements in American art was minimalism, so that interested me most when I was at Pratt.

At the same time I was going through a period in which I was trying to discern just how Indian I really am. And that may sound strange, but I was raised to think of myself as an artist and as a

Cherokee. But I was raised in Syracuse, New York, by a white mother—my father was not around by that time—and so although my siblings had been raised with him, I was not. My view of myself as an Indian was based on idea alone; I was not raised in a Native culture. And consequently, I had some questions about myself as a Native person, and so I decided to investigate that part of myself. I came to realize that I was my father's daughter after all, whether I had lived with him or not. And in many ways I realized that I'm very much like him. I started reading Native American history and trying to, through painting, find out about myself. I've always seen painting, good painting, great painting—I don't mean decorative painting—as investigatory painting. I mean, I see Rothko as an investigator. Creativity is an investigation for me. So this was a way to investigate my Indianness.

LA: For you, painting as a form of investigation worked on a number of different levels?

KW: Yes, about myself and also about the painting process itself and the ideas that are inherent in contemporary painting. I did a series of paintings based on the tragic history of Chief Joseph. In fact, in my retrospective which is coming to the Heard Museum in August [1991] I have some of that series in there. They are very minimal in their components, but they're not minimal in content at all. When some minimalists work, the art is the content. In mine, the content was the art, but the content was a whole lot more, too. I was looking at primal art, a lot of tribal art, and I realized that the spirituality that I saw in this work was conveyed through the formal aspects of it, especially the materials used. I became more and more involved with the material aspect of the painting itself. The medium that I was using was acrylic. I was mixing it with wax to get a very dense quality, and I was layering the paint. I started about that time putting the paint on with my hands because I felt a lot of the energy of that tribal work came through the fact that the artists made these pieces with their hands rather than with tools. I did thirty-six of the *Chief Joseph* pieces and they're all based on complementary colors. First there was a layer of acrylic stain and then the second layer was a complement of that color; for instance, it would be a red ink, then a green paint, and then it would be covered with a black that had one of those complements mixed into it. But I painted with a knife, and as I said, sometimes with my hands, and used a razor blade to cut a line. There are four arcs, two small, two large, in a rectangular format, with two cut lines by a slightly recessed rectangle. That's all. I was looking for archetypal imagery.

You see, I feel that we are all primal people in our souls; in our deepest selves, we are all primal peoples, whether we're Native American or whether we're English. I wanted an archetypal image that spoke to our primal selves, to everyone. I found an arc shape that derived from the series of paintings I made of my work aprons and also some paintings I had done based on a tepee I built. It is a festooned shape: it's a draped hide, draped skin, draped fabric shape.

I made a tepee called *Messages to Papa*. It's just a one-person tepee; it's just big enough for me. I made it out of standard art supplies—you know, one-by-twos, canvas, paint, and staples—and I hung pieces of a cut-up letter to my father in it. I said in the letter that I understood a lot of what had happened and I forgave him and I hope he forgave me, forgave me for hating him all those years. Of course, I hated him because he wasn't there when I needed him; on the other hand, I no longer blamed him for that. He was dead by this time. I also copied out the Lord's Prayer in Cherokee because this was the only thing I had then that was written in Cherokee. He had spoken Cherokee as a child and I knew he could read it. He had a Christian background, so the prayer seemed appropriate.

At any rate, I was going to burn the tepee and never did. I thought it would be a wonderful image to see it go up into smoke, you know, but it didn't happen. I am not a destroyer and I couldn't do it. I still have it. But that tepee really had a big influence on what I've done for the rest of my life. The Cherokees never had tepees—they lived in permanent dwellings—but the tepee is kind of a symbol of Indianness to a white world. I was making this tepee for my father, you know, from a white view, my white view, the white side of myself.

At the time I was told by a professor that the paintings based on this shape were too ethnic, which I thought was funny—but in a sense I knew what he meant. I didn't want to be a painter of feathers and tepees, either. I agreed with him in a way; I thought it was kind of a dumb thing to say, but I knew what he meant. Anyway, I made a long series of paintings relating to those *Chief Joseph* pieces, relating to those tepees, and as I worked I continued making paintings that were very dense, and the paintings became more and more layered. I stopped using any tools at all other than my hands. The paintings became huge. They're very heavy, the big ones. I used to swing them around — I can barely lift them anymore. I worked flat, on a table, and I had to put them up and put them down, so I moved them a lot. Many of them had as many as thirty layers of paint, which is why they're so heavy.

And the paintings became more and more about the earth, the landscape, and they looked, many of them, like seeing the earth from many miles away, or like a cutaway of the earth in the geological diagrams one sees of the different-layered remains of the various eons of the history of the earth. The paintings had this feeling of accruing the way the earth has accrued with layers of rock and sediment. The surface itself sometimes looked very much like limestone. But it also sometimes looks very much like skin, pachyderm skin or something. And it has, because of the wax, a very organic quality, so that it related to the earth itself, to the ancient earth, to the earth as seen from thousands of miles up. But also living things on the earth. It was not a picture of the earth so much as it was about the earth.

In 1984 I was asked to do a work for a show called "Homage to the American Elm," and I told them that I didn't paint realistically and the curator said that was all right. And then she said, well, she knew that I was Indian and she knew that some of the Senecas venerated the elm. I said, "I'm not a Seneca; I'm a Cherokee." She said, "That's all right; it doesn't matter. To most people all Indians are the same anyway." I have been asked, for instance, to say something in Indian, as if there was one Indian language. Incredible! But what is incredible to me is that there are still those stereotypes after five hundred years.

Anyway, back to paintings. I thought, if I'm ever going to do realism again — and I'd been trained in realism — I would do it with my hands, paint with my hands, because I was making all my paintings completely with my hands. Some of them were very colorful and some of them were not. I had gone from a very flat paint to a very manipulated color. And as soon as you manipulate color you're manipulating atmosphere; you see space. And so they were taking on more and more of not a landscape abstraction but a look of real landscape because they were becoming atmospheric. I had been scratching the surface for years to activate the surface. It gives it a lot of life to manipulate the surface physically, although that action also conveys a certain anger. That manipulation, those cuts and scratches, were becoming almost like drawing. They're gouges, but they appear to come forward on the picture plane. I realized that there was no reason not to do real landscape if I felt like it, because I had in a sense been doing landscape for many years. One painting was called *Satyr's Garden* [1982]; another one of them was called *Genesis, Violent Garden* [1981]. Eden I saw as a violent garden. And a lot of the paintings had garden titles, so that obviously it was in my head all along that I was doing landscapes. So I did the painting of an elm tree and put it with the abstraction that I had done for the show. I decided that there was a kind of a symbiosis there that was quite remarkable, that I would not have predicted. They spoke to one another. They became more than what they were alone. So basically, that's how I started doing the diptychs, and I have been dealing with a diptych format ever since.

LA: This began to develop in the mid-1980s?

KW: '84, '85. In '84 I went to Durango, Colorado, after I'd just experimented with a few of the diptychs, and continued working in the format on images of the Colorado landscape. The paintings have changed over the five years. One thing that has changed is that now it's important for me that they are not specific places. Originally I was doing specific views of landscape. I painted *Canyon de Chelly* [1984–87] and also I painted the Cliff Palace at Mesa Verde. The painting is all about the color of Mesa Verde—sort of creamy white—and there are bits of stone from Mesa Verde embedded in it, and Anasazi pottery shards embedded in the paint.

LA: Are the stones and shards visible?

KW: No, but it makes the surface lumpy and a bit rough. Very often I have embedded something from a place, like an interior rhyme—it's almost like some of the spirit of the place is in it physically. But the paintings have become more and more nonspecific, and the reason was that I felt that people were looking at these paintings as if they were only landscapes. In truth they are not landscapes in the sense that Thomas Cole or Church painted landscapes. They are paintings that are about landscapes, they are about the land. The subject is land, the earthscape, but it is not pictures of a place.

LA: There can be a major difference between the two.

KW: And that's sometimes a hard distinction for viewers to make, but I think it's an important one for me because I want the idea to be dominant. Now it may be that that is because I was raised with the idea of Indianness, and ideas are very powerful.

LA: You mentioned Thomas Cole and Frederic Church. They are often thought of as *the* American landscape tradition. Have you seen the recent Bierstadt show at the Brooklyn Museum [1991]?

KW: I did. The best pieces there were the oil sketches. Great little sketches; they were wonderful, done very quickly, from observation.

LA: He might be best known for the massive *Storm in the Rockies*. It's unbelievably detailed.

KW: He never left anything out. Indians, rainbows, birds, animals, everything is in there.

LA: But he and Church and Cole, the Hudson River School generally, do you think they had that same sense of an idea of the land, or were they more dramatists in a way, makers of "big pictures" and the stunning scene? They painted with an audience and way of exhibiting in mind.

KW: I think that they were so much part of their era, of trying to tell people about something that they, the viewers, would never see, that they were almost like cinematographers. I think that they were the filmmakers of their day. If they were alive today, they probably would have worked for PBS doing, you know, Himalayan photo descriptions.

LA: Their paintings are very dramatic.

KW: Very dramatic. I think there's something very theatrical about the whole thing. I don't think that the issues that concern me were part of their era, much less part of their own personal thinking. But, you know, for me the idea of people seeing the earth as sacred is really important because we are really destroying it; an idea like that never entered their heads. These artists bought into the notion of Manifest Destiny and that the earth is there to be exploited for mankind's use, which is one of the things that has destroyed our United States. Not just the aboriginal inhabitants, but the earth itself. Although I can certainly admire Bierstadt's or Church's skills, they were men totally of their era.

LA: In that sense they erected an analogous aesthetic structure for the dominant culture's political and economic system. Their paintings encoded those systems through their imagery.

KW: Oh yes. Sure.

LA: Were you influenced at all by the Cherokee holy land or homeland in North Carolina or Oklahoma?

KW: My father was born in Indian Territory, Tahlequah, Oklahoma, and I've been there as an adult. I was not part of that culture, as I said, as a child, and I regret that. I would really love to learn Cherokee because I think it would help me. You know, people are very much defined by their own language, by the way they speak their language, by the kinds of sounds it makes. A language describes people—we are, in a sense, our tongue. And the notion of breath is very much a part of the spirituality of Native peoples. You know, that's who we are, our language, and we are so much a product of that breath of language that it seems to me that it would be a way to key into some of the spirituality of the Cherokee. But there are so few speakers today, and you find that more anthropologists speak Cherokee than anybody else. As children my brothers and sisters had more of a Native culture than I did, although I've heard all their Indian stories. It's unfortunate that I missed that. On the other hand, I was born during the Depression, my father was an alcoholic, and my mother left Oklahoma because her other children were starving and she had another one on the way—me! I probably also missed a great deal of pain. So perhaps I was actually fortunate, because I have been able to, as an adult, find out about my Indianness; and my mother talked constantly about our being proud to be Indians. On the other hand, I don't have the hang-ups that I think I would have had if I'd been raised with my father. I find a lot of young Indians who don't even want to talk about being Indian.

LA: Right. But do you have any regrets about what you might have missed?

KW: You know, what is, is, and I'm happy with myself as I am. I see my biraciality as a blessing.

LA: You can draw on two cultures, and as an artist you've been influenced by both cultures. Who have been the artists who most influenced you? About your recent work, one critic said that "the images owe something to Jasper Johns."[3] You've also mentioned Rothko. The modernists have been influential?

KW: I was educated in twentieth-century art, you know, mainstream art, and I have a master's degree from a major American art school, so of course.

LA: Couldn't escape them.

KW: One can't escape that in contemporary art education, and on one level that's what my work is about. It's a synthesis of who I am as a Native person and who I am as a mainstream artist. I think that a lot of things that I've done have been influenced by the ideas of Johns and Rothko and early Stella. They say so much to me. They speak of things that cannot be verbalized. The writer who said that was primarily referring to the use of wax. There is a definite reductive quality in much of my work, even the work today, which seems so complex. I reduce the image to the essence, and then reduce the color to the essence.

LA: The image is reduced, embedded in the layers of paint?

KW: Yes. I still think that there is this underlying reductiveness, and I think it has to do with my own kind of intelligence, like the way my head works. Rothko said that—how did he put it?—all great art has content and the content is transcendent. Something like that. Anyway, that notion of art being transcendent is certainly a large part of what I'm doing. I think the spiritual quality in my work—if one is tuned in at all—is picked up. And I think that spirituality is also seen in abstract expressionism. At least in the theories behind abstract expression, if not the work itself. A lot of them didn't succeed, but people like Rothko certainly did. And these artists very often started with primal forms, forms that come directly out of Native American petroglyphs.

LA: Pollock was also greatly influenced by Native forms, which many people don't realize. Your works, to me, have a strong presence.

KW: Part of that comes out of the totality of the piece and the density of the paint. But I think that all strong work does have presence. I think art is not only a visual language, but I think it's almost a visual personality. It's like dealing with another person. The work takes on a life of its own. It has its own internal essence.

But one of the things I would want to say about the painting I do now is that I've come to realize that the two different portions are about two different kinds of memory. The one is a short-term, sort of snapshot memory, which is done very quickly, and the other represents a long-term memory of our earth. I see our lives as part of the continuum of life that reaches back into history to the beginning of time, but also stretches forward to the unknown future. And I see the earth that way. The abstract portions of the paintings are about that quality of the earth, that continuum of the earth, that long-term memory, that memory that goes back eons but forward eons as well. Also, they have a very mythic relationship, those two portions. Myth is the way we understand that which we cannot understand. It is that which explains the great mysteries. And if that is how we comprehend myth, then we see my paintings as relating in a mythic way, because one, in a way, explains the other. In the deepest sense, it's a way to understand our life on earth.

LA: I'm seeing, if I'm reading some of the paintings correctly, that the representational side and the abstract side are related also in terms of color.

KW: Oh yes. They really need that color relationship to create a unified whole, and in order to get that unity, you have to have something repeated, and it's usually color.

LA: And is the image on the abstract side drawn from the representational side, like in *The Abyss* [1989], for example?

KW: Well, in *The Abyss*, the attempt was not to do that, rather than to do that. Of course, the rational, linear, the Euro-American way to connect them would be to repeat abstract shapes. I have tried to get beyond that to reach some kind of gestalt connections.

LA: It looked to me like one of the forms in the abstract portion was drawn from the representational portion.

KW: You could see that.

LA: But that's more in the viewer's perception?

KW: Yes. You could find repeated abstract shapes, but the goal is to have it relate in a mythic way, in a deeper way, rather than what I see as a rather superficial abstract relationship.

LA: Critics have talked about duality as it applies to your work, and said that this duality exists on a number of levels.

KW: Yes, it does, and I think that unifying two—to most people's minds—totally dissimilar viewpoints in painting, that unity of the total dissimilar, is important to my psyche.

LA: And then it becomes a higher-level unity.

KW: Yes. Exactly. And it's a very difficult thing to talk about, especially with very conventional people who are really closed-minded about abstraction, which must be specifically defined, and about realism, which also must be specifically defined. To me, there is little difference between the two. I don't think they can be so specifically defined.

LA: Critics or viewers say these two approaches can't be unified, but you clearly attempt such unity in your work. You've also talked a bit about your works being conceived as poetic stanzas?

KW: Oh, well, yes, I think that the portions of the paintings relate in that way, the way poetry relates in stanzas, meaning they have thematic or structural development. But the stanzas themselves can stand alone very often also, and the theme is the thread through them, rather than a rope.

LA: Right. It connects rather than constricts. You talk about duality and balance — your canvas size is very precisely measured and exacting, even down to eighths of inches, it seems. Is that an important consideration for you in constructing a work?

KW: Yes, that's kind of critical. I think that comes out of that minimalist thing. What you see now as usually a central static image in the abstraction has not always been centered but was always related in size to the size of the canvas as a whole. They all have a geometric relationship, not only with the image itself but with the object, the painted object itself. So that if the arc is ten inches long, the painting would be four times that on each side. There is an underlying, implied grid, which shapes the overall sense of balance.

LA: Do you create a sort of a grid structure on the canvas?

KW: Yes, and the long sides of the frame are exactly double the shorter.

LA: And the abstract side is raised?

KW: The abstract side is raised because I wanted to maintain that sense of it being an object, of it being concrete: it is real. The abstraction is a real thing.

LA: So to remove it from the other picture plane or to create a new plane is crucial?

KW: Well, perhaps not crucial, but it creates an interesting perceptual experience. Because the other plane is an illusionistic plane — I mean it's real in that it's also a painting, of course, but it has that illusion of space, not a real space. The abstraction has real space. Lately I have been making the two portions the same depth and the perceptual dilemma remains. The abstraction is still very object-like.

LA: You mentioned this a little, about your work as very tactile. You work with wax and paint and with your hands, and you've talked about the importance of the tactile feeling. It sounds almost sculptural.

KW: Yes. In fact, when I talk to people who obviously are not accustomed to looking at new art, I always ask them, "Well, look at it as if it were a sculpture." It seems to help people's understanding.

LA: To follow up on that, in a recent interview with George Longfish, "Like a Longfish Out of Water" [in *Northeast Indian Quarterly* 7, 3, Fall, 1989, pp. 16–23], you asked him how he felt about people reading symbolic imagery in his work and perhaps misinterpreting it. How do you reconcile—if it's a problem at all—intention and interpretation? Is it part of the artist's job to even care about how the work is interpreted? Many artists prefer not to discuss their work, for one reason or another.

KW: I think it's important that we do that, at least until our biographers take over. I think that it's part of our job. I mean, art is a visual language, but sometimes people don't speak that language, so it is our job to tell people what is going on. I would hope, though, that there is more to my work than just what I tell. You know, I hope people get a whole lot more out of it. Any kind of artwork, whether it's visual, verbal, musical, or kinesthetic, should have layers of meaning that even the artist is not aware of. So my comments are not meant to restrict an individual's looking at my work. You know, often people insist upon seeing tepees and feathers, but on the other hand, if I can provide a key for someone to look at the work—you know, if I can correct any misconceptions—then maybe it's okay. Viewers need something to clue into a work; I try to provide more accurate keys.

LA: But I guess there's a balance between the artist not saying anything about the work versus overstating something and then closing out possible interpretations.

KW: Yes, well, but it's more my style to try to balance statement and silence. But one of the things that I find is a problem in the galleries is that people want to know where the feathers are. They think my work is not sufficiently Indian. As a matter of fact, I don't show in the Southwest, primarily because my work is not Indian enough for most of the galleries, despite the fact that I'm an Indian. I simply make art, art that is meaningful to me.

LA: I guess that one of the major areas of discussion in the arts today is the problem of mainstream labels and ethnic labels; Indian art must look Indian, must have recognizable Indian imagery, as derived perhaps from the Plains or from the Southwest. How do you negotiate those perilous waters, if at all? You've just had a solo show at C. W. Post College [Brookville, New York, spring 1991], and you'll be exhibiting at the Heard Museum [Phoenix] in the fall of 1991. Is that a problem for you in general, or for Indian art, that to relate to works by Native Americans the viewer must have a certain stereotype in mind or a set of expectations about what constitutes Indian art?

KW: I think stereotypes are dangerous anyway because they limit what you can find out about people, and if one expects a person to behave in a certain way, it limits the way that person is seen. The implied limitations are what I resent about viewers who haven't experienced a great deal of contemporary Native art: as soon as they see my name, I have to do feathers. It limits one's expectations of a person and his or her work. So, sure, I think it's dangerous, and I think part of the thing that is done by getting up and talking about one's work is that it helps people overcome those stereotypes.

LA: Has the pervasiveness of the Southwestern image, the Santa Fe style of the 1930s, constrained artists because one feels an implicit comparison or judgment being made?

KW: I don't know. I'm not a Southwestern Indian; I'm a Western Cherokee, and I'm not, you know, a Santa Fe artist. I don't live there; I live in New York City [now Ithaca, New York]. But there's a museum director who I know in the East who has said something about this issue. He was talking about another artist, and I said, "Well, I'm as much Indian as that artist," and he said, "Well, you don't look it." That is another stereotype: one has to look a certain way. There is a Southwestern and Plains Indian look that's acceptable, but people know so little about eastern Indians anyway that the way they look doesn't seem right. Isn't that absurd! Even sophisticated people, knowledgeable people like museum directors, get caught up in that. There are a number of people who think that authentic Indian art only comes from the Southwest. Pete Jemison, I think, may suffer from the same problem, because he's a Seneca from New York State. Somehow, if you don't come from the Southwest, you're not really an Indian, you know.

LA: Pete has a painting about that, *All Indians Don't Live West of the Mississippi*. Somehow, maybe from movies and TV, there is a very restricted sense of who Indian people are in contemporary society.

KW: I think that slowly the public is changing. But you know, in a way it doesn't matter. I'm an artist, I happen to be an Indian, and I try to sell my art as art. Period. I'm not interested in getting into the so-called Indian market. That really doesn't matter to me because I think that my work should be seen as art first. I don't want people to buy my paintings because I happen to be an Indian. I don't think that's a valid reason to buy art—or even look at art, to tell you the truth.

LA: We'll finish up with one final question. In *Mixed Blessings*, by Lucy Lippard, you're quoted as saying, "No doubt, the diptych form is interesting to me because I am biracial, two sides singing in concert, each very different from the other, yet united as a whole. I like that."[4] This sounds like the Indian and Anglo worlds are more balanced and harmonious than they are in opposition.

KW: Well, I think within my own life they are. And I think that they have the potential to be in our culture also.

LA: And that the paintings sort of mediate or are mediatory . . .

KW: On a number of levels I think the paintings are expressing that mediation, but what I think I have found is that painting is an investigatory process. I think what I've found in that investigation is my own center, my own sense of wholeness. I think that this sense of wholeness is something many people never find, and so I'm very fortunate to find that. Lucy's book, by the way, has such a perfect title because those of us who are biracial are really very blessed people. I feel it's been a blessing in my life; being able to call upon those cultural resources and making art out of it has gotten me through a lot of difficulties. Artmaking is a positive act.

SELECTED EXHIBITIONS

"'For the Seventh Generation: Native American Artists Counter the Quincentenary, Columbus, New York'" (1992), group exhibition, Chenango County Council of the Arts, Norwich, NY, and Golden Artist Colors Gallery, Columbus, NY.

"The Submuloc Show/Columbus Wohs" (1992–94), group traveling exhibition, Atlatl, Phoenix, AZ.

"Vision Quest" (1992), group exhibition, Art Gallery, Cleveland State University, Cleveland, OH.

"We, the Human Beings" (1992), group traveling exhibition, College of Wooster Art Museum, Wooster, OH.

"Kay WalkingStick: Paintings, 1974–90" (1991), solo exhibition, Hillwood Art Museum, Long Island University, C. W. Post Campus, Brookville, NY.

"Light on the Subject" (1991), group exhibition, American Indian Contemporary Arts, San Francisco, CA.

"Our Land/Ourselves" (1991–93), group traveling exhibition, University Art Gallery, State University of New York, Albany, NY.

"Shared Visions" (1991–93), group traveling exhibition, Heard Museum, Phoenix, AZ.
"The Decade Show: Framework of Identity in the 1980's" (1990), group exhibition, New Museum of Contemporary Art, New York, NY.
"Soaring Spirit: Contemporary Native American Arts" (1987), group exhibition, Morris Museum, Morristown, NJ.
"We the People" (1987), group exhibition, Artists' Space, New York, NY.

SELECTED BIBLIOGRAPHY

WalkingStick, Kay. "Native American Art in the Postmodern Era." *Art Journal* 51, 3 (Fall 1992): 15–17.
——. "Democracy, Inc.: Kay WalkingStick on Indian Law." *Artforum* 30, 3 (November 1991): 20–21.
——. "Contemporary Native American Art: A View from the Inside." Lecture. College Art Association Convention, New York City, 1990.
——. "On Spirituality in Landscape." Slide and lecture presentation. Women's Caucus for Art Annual Convention, San Francisco, CA, 1989.
——. "Like a Longfish Out of Water." *Northeast Indian Quarterly* 7, 3 (Fall 1989): 16–23.

Emmi Whitehorse

Navajo

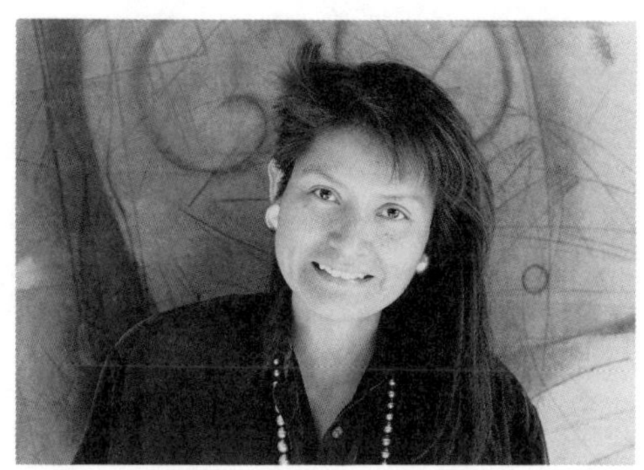

A sense of quiet and calm exists in the fields of Emmi Whitehorse's complex and interactive images. The viewer is drawn beyond the surface of the painting into the layers and depths of color and form. Her technique of layering materials by hand and transforming common objects and personal experiences creates, for Lucy Lippard, "the overall impression . . . of lightness, openness, and activity."[1] Yellows, blues, and reds dominate, creating the horizon for her recurrent images: triangles, leaf- and comb-like shapes, birds, White Shell Woman, floating men's trousers. All these and more constitute the personal iconography of Emmi Whitehorse.

These images derive from the specifics of her life, but are not literal presentations of facts. She frees the images and memories from their personal associations in order to recombine and reformulate them and place them in a new context. Recent works like *The Black Cup* (1989), *Musical Dialogue* (1990), *Composition for Scott* (1990), and *Water's Edge* (1990), for example, use many of the same forms but in different pictorial spaces. Because Whitehorse does not work on an easel, such terms as "top" and "bottom" become fluid, undefined, creating her characteristically ethereal look. About her work, and Native art generally, she has said: "It's hard for them [viewers] to accept the contemporary aspect. . . . They are always looking for the past in your work somewhere. They're trying to make something ritualistic and ceremonial out of it. . . . There's a lot of humor in what contemporary painters are doing. They are also very environmentally aware."[2]

Whitehorse was born in Crownpoint, New Mexico, in 1956. Her early education was at a boarding school, and she completed high school in Page, Arizona. She went on to study at the University of New Mexico in Albuquerque, receiving her B.A. degree in painting in 1980 and her M.A. in printmaking, with an art history minor, in 1982. She has been exhibiting nationally and internationally since 1978, and her work is in a number of collections, including those of the Heard Museum, the Wheelwright Museum, IBM, and Prudential Insurance.

We talked in August 1991 at the LewAllen Gallery in Santa Fe while her show with Jaune Quick-to-See Smith was being installed.

LA: To start with, Lucy Lippard writes in the introduction to your recent retrospective at the Wheelwright in Santa Fe, "Two worlds are revealed in Emmi Whitehorse's art. Her paintings are consummate abstractions welcome in the world of art for art's sake for their finely balanced forms and colors. They are also metaphysical views of the Navajo world. As such they offer to viewers from both worlds a glimpse of what art can mean."[3] Do you feel that her statement is accurate? How do you go about revealing these two worlds?

EW: I think Lucy's statement is true. It is the only comment or written criticism that I have liked so far. I thought that it was accurate in my case because usually I am being compared to Paul Klee and the like, and I have no real association with—what's the word I'm looking for?—I have no real sense of commonality with such artists as Klee or Kandinsky. She is right when she says that two worlds are revealed. You can't help but see that in my work. I have the Navajo aspect, but I also make use of Western methods and approaches in terms of modernist techniques. There are a lot of ethnographic items that I use from my culture to make up the imagery in my work. At the same time, my imagery is very personal—extremely personal. I work very loosely and everything is intuitive. Nothing is ever preplanned; in fact, I work against that Western tendency to schematize. For example, I work with no top or bottom to the canvas. I work flat on the floor or on a table top, whereas another painter might work standing at an easel, using a brush, in a rigid fashion. I have never used a paintbrush in my life.

LA: How do you go about applying materials to the canvas?

EW: I don't use canvas, except to mount the paper; it's all paper pieces. I've always worked on paper. I do a drawing first, and then it's glued onto the canvas with an acrylic medium so it becomes like a plastic glue. Once it's set, that's it; you can't get it off. It's all a mixed process. It's a layering of pastels on the bottom, an application of a plastic spray, then turpentine over the top of that, a wash with oil sticks, and then more chalk and more oil sticks, so by the end it is mostly oil sticks with pencil or graphite.

LA: So you don't use a paintbrush but would apply the color by oil sticks?

EW: It's all by hand. All the paint is applied by hand. People say that I waste so much time, you know, taking the paint off the paint sticks with my fingers and then reapplying it on the paper, but that's the way I work.

LA: Kay WalkingStick also applies paint directly. Is there an added dimension for you in the tactile application of the paint, as opposed to the distancing from the work you might feel by using a brush?

EW: Yes, definitely. The work becomes more personal for me and to me because of that hands-on technique. I think the work would suffer if I approached it with a brush.

LA: You did a B.A. in painting and an M.A. in printmaking. Do you draw techniques or approaches from one to the other? You're best known, though, for your painting.

EW: I think I feel more of a printmaker person in the sense that I still work very much like a printmaker. I like the quality of paper and appreciate it very much. I've always worked with paper and I tend to be graphic. I draw more in my work than a painter might. I have a hard time calling myself a painter because of that, because the drawing is very strong in the work. I had my own print shop and a press, and I worked on lithographic stones. Somebody pointed out to me once, too, that my working process is very similar to an artist doing a print. It's the sense of layering, the running through the press, that layering process that is uniquely planographic.

LA: Maybe we could talk about the influences critics have remarked about. Not a few have written about connections to Rothko, Kandinsky, Klee, Chagall, and so forth. As you just mentioned, do you think these critics are misreading your work?

EW: Oh, I don't know. Some of the time the artist is inept in discussing his or her work. And critics sometimes pride themselves on being the people who are able to translate what the artist is doing to the public. In my case I've been disappointed in modern reviews because I've often thought that there was a misunderstanding about what I was doing or where I was coming from. And then I say to myself, "Am I not translating the work for the viewer? Am I not clear enough in putting out my ideas?" That's why I think it helps if I have a statement at a show for people to read. Then I can guide them exactly in a particular direction. Of course, that can be helpful in some ways and detrimental in others. They can become tunnel-visioned, restricted to a certain view, and do not feel free to go beyond what is said by the artist or what is put in front of them. I don't want to spoonfeed the viewer. That's not my duty. The work should ultimately speak for itself.

LA: You've mentioned the influence of your grandmother on your work. You've written: "I'm intrigued by the casual equating of nature and geometry in her weaving. It's like putting nature and high tech together."[4] Do you try to do the same in your work in some way?

EW: Well, I think "high tech" is a misspoken word there in my case. It is the equating of nature and geometry, true, in her weaving that fascinates me. The patterns are highly abstract, or sometimes they are very complicated geometrically. I was always very intrigued with that, and the way she worked at the loom was also very interesting. I make the comparison between how an artist works at an easel and how she worked at the loom. To me, both were in the same manner. I saw her weaving like she was actually painting, because the loom was upright in the way an easel would be set up.

I guess I always identified with her. I sort of align myself with her in some of her working process. I don't know what I'm going to be painting and I don't know what the finished product is going to end up looking like, you know. I don't know what it's going to look like, and my grandmother worked in that same fashion. She had nothing to go by when she worked at her loom. The bottom part would have a pattern, but the top part would just be all open space, so everything had to be figured out immediately as she worked. That's the same way that I work. Everything is done intuitively. It just flows and I don't know what to expect when I start out.

Of course, once in a while it can get out of hand. In her case sometimes the patterning wouldn't make sense and didn't fall together correctly in the measured spaces the way she anticipated, and in the end she would just unravel the whole thing, line by line, you know, yarn by yarn. I've also ended up in that same box because I've had to erase or clean out a whole canvas, or a section at least, and start all over again. It's like the same unraveling of a whole piece. I like to think that I share that process of working with her.

LA: Both of you use a layering of levels. Weaving is a layering up, while you layer out.

EW: Right. Exactly.

LA: You mention false starts. The viewer only sees the finished piece on the wall. How many times do you just reach a point where you say something's not going to work?

EW: Oh, let's see. When I work, I start out with about ten paintings. I like the chaos. I make myself work in this crazy sort of confusion. I like to think of it like that. I see things flying by in my head and out of that group of ten at least two paintings end up hitting the dust or being ripped apart, and in some cases I've cut up works where half of a whole piece might not work and I'll tear that off and throw it away and make a smaller piece out of the good half. I've done that to fairly large pieces, too, where they have been reduced down to like twenty-eight by thirty inches from fifty by thirty-nine and a half.

On the other hand, I'll put two separate pieces of paper together to form a larger work. I have a hard time finding paper that is long and wide enough. Usually the paper comes very thick and is difficult to uncurl and it always reacts differently. I have to know how much it will shrink when I put two sections together. It's gotten easier. I can calculate how much shrinkage there'll be on the ends. During the mounting and drying process all the moisture is sucked out of the paper, so it has to be strong enough to withstand those changes. And in some cases, if the paper is too thin, it will rip apart in the drying process.

LA: What makes a piece work for you? Can you explain that intuitive sense that tells you something is working or tells you to cut it up?

EW: Oh, let's see. I have to go by an innate visual feel, if there is a balance. I arrive at a point where the work just feels finished; it feels balanced everywhere. If I turn it one way it feels right and if I turn it another way it feels right; in every which way the color, line, spatialness, all feel balanced. Then I think to myself the piece is finished. It's very hard for an artist to answer a question like this because I, for example, never know when the process is complete.

LA: It's not a quantifiable type of thing.

EW: No. I might see one of my paintings again four months later and I think, oh, my God, that's an awfully unfinished work, and I'll run and go home with it and paint on it again. Or I might see another painting again and realize that it's such a terrible piece of work that I'll go home with it and destroy it and make another in its place.

LA: You recently had a ten-year retrospective at the Wheelwright. That must have sent shivers up your spine. But do you look back at work done over that time period and say, "Well, that's just half done or three-quarters done?" Or would you not send certain pieces out into the world?

EW: Actually, I called it a survey, "Ten Years." I didn't want it to be called a retrospective. I was rather self-conscious about terming it a retrospective, so to get around that we just called it "Ten Years," *Neeznáá,* which means ten in Navajo. I was very lucky in getting that show, because I was given free rein. I designed the whole exhibition space. I designed the catalog. I decided on every painting that was in the show. And because of all that, I was very happy with everything. I really liked seeing the older, earlier pieces again from the early eighties, '80 through '82. There were some in there that were very geometric, with sharp lines, that I truly loved and wished I had kept for my own collection. It made me realize that it might be more important for me to keep a lot of my best pieces for myself rather than give them away.

I was very happy with the whole result of that show. Yes, I enjoyed seeing a lot of the older pieces. It felt like they had come home, you know, and it just felt really wonderful. I do get attached to my work as though they are human. They are inanimate, of course, but you give them life. And in my thinking that's usually what I end up doing.

LA: Did looking back at the work from the early eighties surprise you at all?

EW: Yes, because when you first do them, you're very insecure and you always think that it's the worst work you've ever done. But ten years later, I saw them again and I thought that they were actually the best pieces I've ever done because they were highly abstract and nonfigurative, nonnarrative, just pretty much free from a lot of translating or storytelling. They didn't need to be explained.

LA: You wrote in the catalog for a 1989 show called *Six from Santa Fe:* "At this point in my work everything revolves solely on the axis of personal experiences, but my aim is not to present the viewer with literal images but to act as a narrator or gossiper. I may change or bend what I reveal about my personal life so it becomes ambiguous and I'm interested in this process of narrative that might be embedded in the art in some way."[5] Could you talk about this process of being a transformational narrator? Do you present narratives in a symbolic or figurative way?

EW: That statement is true and always has been, I confess. The work that I do and the work that I have done has always been very personal. The first paintings that I did were about landscape, but the landscape was the place where my summer home was, Kin-náh' zin', and then beyond that I painted in different areas of the U.S., and this variety of surroundings has affected my work, in terms of color and imagery. My personal surroundings have highly influenced my work. I'm now moving into work that is sometimes figurative and sometimes symbolic, but that's not really my intention. I'm interested in the shape of the bird, for example, not in the symbolic meaning of the bird. Somebody else might see it symbolically, but I use the bird shape because it is a puzzle to me and it remains a mystery in the painting. I like the idea of using the bird as a recurrent image. Actually, the bird figure came off a label of a Belgian beer, so that tells you how important a symbol that bird is. In most cases, I bend or alter or translate the images that you see in the paintings and that are based on real or exact things. Some of the women figures I picked up from stories that I remember my grandmother told me, the Navajo creation and myth stories. I plucked visual images from these stories and then made the female up, gave them a form. For example, there's a story about White Shell Woman. I made her up to look like the bell-shaped, pinch-waisted woman that you see in some of the paintings. So in that sense, yes, I feel very much like a gossiper, because I'm intensifying or enlarging a story beyond its actuality, beyond its true form.

Also, I think in a way it makes it easier for any viewer to approach the work by doing this, because then you don't have that heavy, heavy cultural baggage that's attached to these symbols which oftentimes bar the person from truly getting involved with the work or flowing with the work. The door is left open for the viewer so that he or she could make of the imagery whatever he or she wants to make of it. On the other hand, there is a sense of Navajo culture in each piece and the viewer can see and sense this, but it's not so closed, or copied from an actual image, that he or she feels like he or she's treading on private ground or private space.

LA: So the work does exist on two levels: on one, it embodies aspects of the Navajo world, especially shown through your titles, and on the other, it makes reference to the non-Navajo world?

EW: Right. I'm very much intrigued by the ambiguity of these things.

LA: That brings up the question of just what is narrative art. When people think of Native narrative art, what might come to mind is the literal art of the 1930s, the works from the Santa Fe Studio that more or less document dances and ceremonies and regalia and the like, or the works of the Kiowa Five.[6] People say, well, that's narrative art because it tells a story and the images aren't abstract. Then they look at your work, for example, and say that it can't be narrative art because it's abstract. You can't be telling a story because there is no clear referencing of the imagery. What intrigues me about your work, and much of Native art generally, is that there is a narrative behind the imagery even though it may not be literally embodied in it. I was thinking about the *Mt. Taylor* series, where on one level it's about Mount Taylor as an environment which anyone can appreciate, and on another, it's about the sacred dimension of the mountain, which is more culturally specific.

EW: Actually, we had two sheep camps that we went to. My grandmother had land in one place which was called White Horse Lake, and then my mother and father had another place out by

Cabezon Peak, almost in the middle between Cabezon Peak and Mount Taylor, and I always felt that we looked at Mount Taylor from the back side, because you usually drive by Mount Taylor on the south side and you have the impression that it's the front side. So that was where the winter sheep camp was, the back side of Mount Taylor.

The *Mt. Taylor* series came out of my living in Connecticut for five years [1982–87]. The greenery out there, the leaves, the trees, it was just like a canopy over you all the time. In a sense it became very oppressive for me, you know. I hated the trees and that dark green, the pine trees, all the hedges and the vines. I hated it so much that I ended up painting trees and leaves but in Southwest colors. I used yellows and reds instead of the dark green. I guess it was a lonely time for me because I had spent so much time inside dark houses and I really felt lost, mentally and physically. I had a sense that I had lost my sense of direction because I never could tell which way was south or east or north from living under that canopy of trees. And I think the work reflected that lost sense of direction. Actually, I didn't like a whole lot of the paintings that I did during that time. But you had thought they had more to do with a broader narrative?

LA: Right. Because people might, seeing the title and the imagery, if they are familiar with Navajo cosmology, interpret the works to be visual extensions or visual narratives, to be your perception of the sacred mountain.

EW: Well, as I said before, all my work is very personal, so these, too, reflect a very harrowing personal experience of the time. Now that I remember, though, I did title some of the work with mythological titles, like *Yei's Divisive Manner* [1985], because they had something to do with the stories, the stories of how *Yei* used to live on top of Mount Taylor, how the Navajo twins came up and slew Yei. When Yei died all his blood ran down the sides of Mount Taylor and it hardened, and that's the lava you can still see today. So I guess in some of the works I actually did visualize in my own mind Yei, not what he looked like but what his sense of being was like and what the landscape might have looked like surrounding him at that time. But the largest measure of the series reflected my sense of dislocation back in Connecticut.

LA: What lead you to Connecticut?

EW: I met a printmaker from Connecticut who came to study at the University of New Mexico, so I moved back there with him and lived with an Italian family. But it also meant access to New York City without having to live there. I didn't even try to live in the city, but could go to all the museums and openings. But at the same time there was a claustrophobic feeling from the trees I was talking about, there was also stimulation from what was going on in the arts in New York.

LA: Much of your work is in series. Do you generally conceive works that way, where they all relate to a larger theme?

EW: They accidentally come about. They're not planned. They just so happen to work out in that way where I end up titling a whole year or two years' worth of work as a series after they're all done. The *Kin-náh' zin'* series, for example, which took about two years, was about my home and the landscape. Also the *Mt. Taylor* series. We had a visitor from Belgium who stayed with us for a month, and after he left, I did a half year's work dedicated to him about his stay in the U.S. with us. This was *The Visitor and the Lovers* from '87 and '88. As I think over what I've done in four years since I returned to New Mexico from back east there are series that do exist. 1989–90 has to do with accepting one's self, accepting my background, my being a Navajo. Much of the work over this time has Navajo titles, with English subtitles. These new works have been like a celebration of accepting my-self, just being proud of my ethnic background, finally! And it's been a big relief. This has come about since 1987.

LA: Has there been a qualitative change in your approach or imagery since then? Has your work become more Navajo, what-ever that is?

EW: I think so. There's more cultural baggage. There's a lot more of my background exposed. There are ethnographic items that I use in the work, such as the Navajo wedding basket. The bottom of the basket has an arch, and that's the arch you see in some of my paintings; people assume that they're rainbows, but they're not. It's the arch from the wedding basket. The bowls you see in the paintings are the utilitarian bowls that are used at home that Navajo women have a great affinity with. There's an impor-tant first lesson in teaching young women growing up the care of dishes. It sounds ridiculous, I know, but that's why I took the bowl and used it in the work. Also, the comb you see in my work looks like a fork, but it's actually the comb, in a simplified design, that my grandmother used. Weavers used a comblike object to batten down the yarn, to tighten the weave. The woman figure that I was speaking about, the woman that I made up to be White Shell Woman or White Bead Woman, that is all pretty much cultural baggage.

LA: When you say "cultural baggage," it sounds like a negative thing.

EW: No, not for me. I don't see it as detrimental or restrictive. I welcome it. I have more to draw from, a much bigger source to draw from.

LA: You mentioned once that your work is not "strictly Native American" because you felt that that would alienate viewers who would not be able to relate to the work.

EW: What I meant, like I was talking about before, was that I use an image from Navajo, for example, but I turn that around to mean something else, or else I strip the total image down to a simplistic shape or an abstracted shape, and it becomes less narrow, it becomes a more universal language. I don't want the image to be so specific and so literal that it would become what I think of as "strictly Native American."

I don't know, but I think I have a problem with the term "Native American artist." I guess you can say that there are Jewish artists and black artists, but I have never liked to be called or labeled Native American artist. I just want to be known as a woman artist. Even if I say Navajo woman artist, then I'm saying Native American. So I just really would prefer woman artist.

LA: That's the focus of the debate right now: does ethnic labeling help or restrict the understanding and appreciation of work?

EW: Yes, I think with Native American work, it does close certain doors because people automatically start looking for feathers and beads rather than approaching the work on a more sophisticated level. Of course, our distinct cultures influence how we see or respond to art. But the underlying basis is always the same. The ideals and methods of modern art are evident in much of Native work, myself included. I think work made by ethnic artists or women is wrongly seen as not abstract, not theoretical, not conceptual enough.

LA: Do the terms "Indian art" or "Native American art" create an expectation in the mind of the viewer about what that work will look like?

EW: Yes, I think they do. Generally, I think, images of pots and beaded hides flash in people's minds when the term "Indian art" is used. But again, people are failing to see that other cultures are keeping abreast of the mainstream culture. Our young kids go to school just like their young kids go to school. All cultures grow and develop. So I think people get thrown off by seeing educated artists who have learned to use their talents and minds to transcend some of the limitations placed on them, in terms of their lives and the art they make. Conservative thinking about what Indian art is or what Indian artists should do sets the stage or creates the climate for the putting down of newer work. I guess the basic problem is that people assume that if you're culturally different, you don't have the same intelligence as everybody else.

LA: Can you say how many paintings you would do in a year, or how many you're satisfied with?

EW: Let's see, we actually counted one time and it was between fifty-five and sixty-five that I completed in one year. Out of that I would probably be very happy with thirty-five to forty. And then maybe half or a little more than half of those would be, to me, extremely good. Sometimes I end up rushing so much that I don't give all of them the total concentration or the extra time that's needed.

LA: In the course of a year do you work toward a show, so you have to produce a number of new works? Or are you more internally driven?

EW: It helps to have self-discipline, where you make yourself go into the studio every day and have work on hand to do. That would be the ideal approach or working condition. But in my case I'll work feverishly for a month and then do nothing for two weeks, and then work feverishly for two weeks and then take a week off. That's best for me because by working in that fashion I force myself to use up the ideas and imagery that are floating around in my head. And by working at a breakneck speed a lot of imagery that I'm harboring sort of falls out and I can explore it. I discover things that I really like and can work with. Yes, there's always the need to work for a show or to complete a set of paintings. There is always that pressure. But again, I like that pressure, I almost prefer that; otherwise I probably wouldn't paint.

LA: Many artists seem to work that way. In your off periods, does a lot of imagery build up in your mind?

EW: I think so. I mean, all of a sudden it has to be forced out. Because most times we are absorbing everything—at least I do. I take in everything visually and I'm like a sponge. I soak up everything and eventually all that has to be wrung out in my work. That's why I work fast. Otherwise I forget and lose the point, I lose the direction that I had imagined, so I have to work the way I do. I have to work fast.

LA: How many pieces would you do in that two- or four-week burst?

EW: Maybe four to six. Each one takes me about a week to do, maybe a little less, and after that comes the other process, where you have to clean it up, you have to mount it, you have to stare at it all day long because you have to title it. That's usually the hardest part for me, to sit down and look at a piece and title it. Then, finally, they all have to get catalogued.

LA: Do you ever come up with a title before you do a particular piece?

EW: No, no. Never, never. The work suggests the title to me. I can't work the other way around.

LA: One thing I've noticed about your most recent work at the LewAllen Gallery [Santa Fe, summer 1991] is the sense of depth, that layering we were talking about. The work really draws you in visually. How does color and light and space function in your work? Do you start out with a basic color and work out from that?

EW: Well, the sense of space, that atmospheric quality, is very important in my work, as is a certain kind of light and a feeling of graphicness, of drawing. I begin creating that atmospheric space by starting out with chalk—any color is fine—and I lay that down and spread it out. Actually, I just pick out colors, a whole mass of colors, put them down on the paper with my hand, just line every single color up no matter which is which, and spread out the whole thing and mix the colors and dirty up the paper as fast as I can because I can't stand this white, clean sheet of paper staring at me. So I dirty up the paper as fast as I can, and after I do that I spread out the chalk dust by hand and rub that all into the paper so it becomes softer and the colors get evenly mixed. And then finally I'll finish with a paper towel, rubbing some colors in or taking some out. After that, the drawing begins. Then that one is put aside and I go to the next one and do the same thing and then the next one after that.

So I'm layering and then also stacking up the paintings as I'm working on two or more at a time. The drawings might have more chalk added to them, and they are sprayed so the chalk dust doesn't fly off. Then that is hit with a clear acrylic gel and set aside to dry. After they dry, I come along with an old stump of a brush and pour turpentine on the paper sheets and just soak the whole thing. Then the oil colors go on and are washed over all the paper, and if it's too strong a color I'll take rags and wipe the oils off, wiping it clean so I can keep the transparency. And I work in this fashion with the chalk and the oil until I get spatial depth, and as I'm doing that I'm also layering the lines, the imagery, the bird shapes, the triangles—all are thrown in there at the same time. Because of that process some of the images end up overlapping and some are upside down; like I said, I work in all directions. So most of the upside-down figures are not preplanned, they happen out of chance. I'll decide later how I want to hang the work, so some images will happen to be upside down.

So this layering process goes on and on and on until the whole picture is just loaded with lines and imagery and the paper feels like it's saturated, it can't take any more. I sense that saturation and feel that the work is finished.

LA: I also felt that your work has a calming effect.

EW: Yes, yes there is. There is that very calming sense in the work. That probably has to do with my personality. I am the kind of person who prefers nonviolence. I can't stand loudness. I can't stand being in a crowd of people. I'm always hiding away from people. Because of that I prefer to be with animals. I guess it has to do with growing up where I did at Kin-náh' zin', with just silence, with just space, with just listening to what was there in nature, the songs of birds, the wind blowing through the trees. I grew up with that calmness and I'm used to that and that comes out in the work. Even though there may be a lot of images and colors in a work, they don't clash. I would like to think that the works have a steadiness and are grounded and balanced.

LA: These new works are also quite large, about four feet by three feet.

EW: I go even bigger. These are small, these are tiny. These are small to me. I particularly like working on the bigger pieces because I feel that I have more room to work. I have trouble working on the smaller ones because I don't feel that I have enough space. It's much harder for me to do smaller work than it is to do the bigger pieces.

LA: Your work is often shown or discussed with Jaune Quick-to-See Smith. You are paired at this show at the LewAllen Gallery. Your work seems very different. Jaune's paintings have a very active surface, while yours seem to be . . .

EW: . . . retreating.

LA: Yeah. You were both in the Grey Canyon group. Was there a mutual influence on your work? What lead to this pairing?

EW: We've actually known each other since around 1978 because we both went to the University of New Mexico. We were in the same painting class and we both did our graduate work there, so we became friends. And as buddies, we helped each other out. She helped me get into galleries because her career took off much sooner and she was more well-known than I was, so in certain ways we went up the ladder together, one behind the other. And that's why we are in the same gallery here and why we show every year at Indian Market [in Santa Fe in August]. We have also been in a lot of group shows together and in a lot of touring shows across the continent. But I think this one here is the only one we've done together for a while, because it has become expected. We have each become very busy and hardly have time to sit down and talk. And you see in this exhibit the personality of each artist. Jaune has much more movement in her work and the images are more overt. She is more outspoken. She is more politically conscious. As for me, I'm more retreating, more internal. I have a hard time being verbal, expressing my ideas. So seeing our work together is a real contrast.

LA: It's interesting to see them together, about a dozen or so each, because they are at first glance polar opposites. But she draws from her past and from petroglyphs and from nature in the same way that you draw from many of the same sources. So you're both using in your own ways the same materials. Each of you translates those materials through your own individual personalities.

EW: Very much so.

LA: You've talked about your artistic process as stepping through doors into other rooms. Can you expand on what you meant by that?

EW: Oh, I think that comment had more to do with me living in two worlds. My parents still live on the reservation, so in going home I have to close the door on the contemporary world in Santa Fe and open the door of the Navajo world. The pace slows down, the language changes, and I have to switch to a different mode of thinking and talking.

LA: Does that have an impact on your career?

EW: Yes, I think it does. I'm not aware of it but it manifests itself everywhere, in the way I live and the way I paint. It's a luxury to have dual worlds, to have the ease of function in both worlds. I tend to be very modest about whatever successes I've had. I am a very harsh critic of my own work. I always think that the work is not good enough — it's terrible, it's this, it's that. There's always a big insecurity about putting forth the works. But I think that just being stubborn and going ahead slowly and steadily I will probably end up being more accepted in the mainstream art world. But I don't see that, even if it happens, as a final step or level, or even as a comfortable place.

I'm thinking that I'm just a kid. I have just begun; I have more things to do. I'm very much interested in exploring glass sculpture. It's very exciting. Glass is a very hard, unforgiving material to work with and I like that aspect of it.

LA: How did you get into glass? Do you see any connections between that and your painting?

EW: Maybe a little. Actually, I had done sculptures before, and they were very minimalist steel sculptures. They were almost like paintings, but they were these huge six-feet-by-five-feet- or seven-feet-by-six-feet pieces of metal that would just lean against the wall, like you would lean a painting against the wall. The materials were very expensive and I ended up selling my torches and cutting equipment because I couldn't afford to keep them or to store the finished sculptures. I was a student then, but I said to myself that I'll just put that work on hold until I have a little money and then I'll go back to it. So I see this now as the time to return to sculpture, but I've chosen not to use steel but to work with glass.

I guess it's the luminosity that draws me to the glass. My grandmother once gave me a fetish animal that I've been intrigued with, not so much the fetish itself but with the material it was carved out of. It's like glass you'd find on the beach, and that has just been in my head. I want to work with something like that same material. So I'm really looking forward to working with glass. I'm having molds made now so that I can start casting small things, just to see how the material reacts and how it looks. If it comes together, I want to do pieces that would be about six feet tall, sort of humanoid figures, a being, a faceless and armless figure. I don't want to do a fetish, but a primal being is what I'm after. It would be a figurative piece.

LA: Could we talk about one of your new works, *Where Animals Thrive* [1991]?

EW: I started working on that immediately after I came back from Europe. I started doing this tremendously bright red piece and I was thinking that I didn't want it to be so flaming red, but I ended up doing it that way anyway because in the red there was this nice comfortable feeling of being home again, and I felt like flaunting it. I think some of the mystic-like quality in the work comes from some of the things I saw in the south of France. Somehow I associated the Roman ruins there with Anasazi ruins here. I felt alienated when I saw the ruins and I had the same feeling growing up in the Chaco Canyon area because there are nothing but ruins there, and I sensed that same ancientness. I tried to bring that out in this piece.

LA: There are a lot of recurrent images in your work, like birds, fish, leaves, the weaver's comb, which appear in *Where Animals Thrive*.

EW: All these things suggest that ancient feeling. The leaves remind me of the fossils that you find in slate or limestone. Other things have something to do with the growth of the vineyards and the olive trees I saw in France. The urn-shaped things are another ancient form. It's an ancient utilitarian object, and it could translate as a woman's shape, a female shape. It could be a vessel to hold something. The house is something familiar to me from my reservation.

LA: Do you strive for that feeling of ancientness generally in your work?

EW: Not necessarily in the other works, but for some reason it came out and presented itself in this one.

LA: Looking back over the ten-year survey at the Wheelwright, are there any threads or links which connect your work over this time?

EW: Oh, I think it's the highly personal aspect of it that connects them all. It seems like all the work is about one idea, the same idea, even though that idea evolved and changed over the years. You can see the progression very slowly. Something else that unifies everything is that I work consistently, evenly, very slowly. What I mean by that is I change very slowly when it comes to saying my ideas and executing them on paper, expressing them. It takes me a very long time. I think that those are the two things that unify the work.

SELECTED EXHIBITIONS

"Jaune Quick-to-See Smith and Emmi Whitehorse" (1992), two-person exhibition, LewAllen Gallery, Santa Fe, NM.

"Neeznáá" (1991), solo exhibition, Wheelwright Museum of the American Indian, Santa Fe, NM.

"Presswork: The Art of Women Printmakers" (1991), group exhibition, National Museum of Women in the Arts, Washington, DC.

"Emmi Whitehorse" (1990), solo exhibition, Hartje Gallery, Frankfurt, Germany.

"Primavera" (1990), group exhibition, Tucson Museum of Art, Tucson, AZ.

"Six from Santa Fe" (1989), group exhibition, Gibbes Museum of Art, Charleston, SC.

"Emmi Whitehorse" (1988), solo exhibition, Yuma Arts Center, Yuma, AZ.

"Eight Native American Artists" (1987), group exhibition, Fort Wayne Museum of Art, Fort Wayne, IN.

"Women of Sweetgrass, Cedar, and Sage" (1985), group traveling exhibition, Gallery of the American Indian Community House, New York, NY.

"Emmi Whitehorse" (1984), solo exhibition, Galleria del Cavallino, Venice, Italy.

SELECTED BIBLIOGRAPHY

Whitehorse, Emmi. "Artist's Statement." In *Six from Santa Fe: Contemporary Native American Art from Santa Fe*. Charleston, SC: Gibbes Museum of Art, 1989, unp.

——. "Artist's Statement." In *Eight Native American Artists*. Fort Wayne, IN: Fort Wayne Museum of Art, 1987, p. 44.

Notes

INTRODUCTION

1 Two brochures are available from the post office. Each provides a brief history of the murals, with titles and descriptions, and one has black and white reproductions. An interesting exhibition of earlier murals, executed in 1929 by Spencer Asah, Jack Hokeah, Stephen Mopope, and James Auchiah, was held at the Southern Plains Indian Museum and Crafts Center in Anadarko, Oklahoma, in 1991

2 George Longfish, quoted in Margaret Archuleta and Rennard Strickland, eds., *Shared Visions* (Phoenix, AZ: Heard Museum, 1991), p. 94.

3 Paula Gunn Allen, *The Sacred Hoop* (Boston: Beacon Press, 1986), p. 69.

4 Paul Zolbrod, "White Shell Woman and Other Mysteries: Poetry and Painting in the Wheelwright Gallery," lecture presented at the Wheelwright Museum of the American Indian, Santa Fe, New Mexico, April, 1991 (p. 24 in printed text of lecture). Focusing on the connections between Navajo verbal and visual art, Zolbrod discusses in some detail the ways that each art form shapes the other.

5 Paula Gunn Allen, *Spider Woman's Granddaughters: Traditional Tales and Contemporary Writing by Native American Women* (New York: Fawcett Columbine, 1989), p. 8.

6 Henry Louis Gates, Jr., " 'Ethnic and Minority' Studies," in *Introduction to Scholarship in Modern Languages and Literatures,* ed. Joseph Gibaldi, 2d ed. (New York: Modern Language Association of America, 1992), pp. 298–99.

7 Paula Gunn Allen, " 'Border' Studies: The Intersection of Gender and Color," ibid., p. 309.

8 Rick Hill, *Creativity Is Our Tradition: Three Decades of Contemporary Indian Art at the Institute of American Indian Arts* (Santa Fe, NM: Institute of American Indian and Alaska Native Culture and Arts Development, 1992), p. 15

9 George Longfish and Joan Randall, "Made by Choice," in *The Extension of Tradition: Contemporary Northern California Native American Art in Cultural Perspective*, ed. Frank LaPena and Janice Driesbach (Sacramento, CA: Crocker Art Museum 1985), p. 45.

10 Eugene Odum, *Fundamentals of Ecology,* 3d ed. (Philadelphia: W. B. Saunders, 1971), pp. 157–58.

11 Gerald McMaster, statement in Native American Artists Resource Collection, Heard Museum, Phoenix, AZ.
12 Jimmie Durham, "Ni' Go Tlunh A Doh Ka," in *We Are Always Turning Around . . . on Purpose* (Old Westbury, NY: Amelie A. Wallace Gallery, State University of New York, 1986), p. 1.

RICK GLAZER-DANAY

1 Susan Shedd, "Contemporary Iroquois Art as a Cultural Border," *Northeast Indian Quarterly* 3, 2 (Summer 1986): 8.
2 Gene Grey, "Roberson bans painting in Indian exhibit," *Binghamton* [New York] *Press and Sun-Bulletin,* May 9, 1986, pp. 1A, 12A.
3 Rick Glazer-Danay, in an unpublished interview with David K. Morgan, November 30, 1991, p. 6.
4 Rick Glazer-Danay, unpublished artist's statement, August 12, 1992.
5 Gerald Vizenor, "Trickster Discourse," *American Indian Quarterly* 14, 3 (Summer 1990): 285.
6 Rick Glazer-Danay, "Artist's Statement," in *Eight Native American Artists* (Fort Wayne, IN: Fort Wayne Museum of Art, 1987), p. 30.
7 Rick Glazer-Danay, "Artist's Statement," in *Contemporary Native American Art* (Stillwater, OK: Gardiner Art Gallery, Oklahoma State University, 1983), unp.
8 Glazer-Danay is quoted in the *Eight Native American Artists* exhibition catalog as calling his construction helmets "a modern day Mohawk headdress" (p. 16). He mentioned to me, however, that the phrase was "first coined by Dr. [William] Sturtevant in *The Arts of the North American Indian,* by Wade, but if I remember correctly it was Rennard [Strickland] who *first* used it in a talk in March 1982." In his caption to the reproduction of Glazer-Danay's painted hard hat entitled *Mohawk Headdress* in *The Arts of the North American Indian,* Sturtevant refers to the work as a "headdress" (p. 43).
9 Glazer-Danay, "Artist's Statement," in *Contemporary Native American Art.*
10 Rick Glazer-Danay, statement in Native American Artists Resource Collection, Heard Museum, Phoenix, AZ.

SHAN GOSHORN

1 Shan Goshorn, *Moontime: The Cycles of Life* (Anadarko, OK: Southern Plains Indian Museum and Crafts Center, 1987), unp.
2 Ibid.

HACHIVI EDGAR HEAP OF BIRDS

1 N. Scott Momaday, *The Way to Rainy Mountain* (Albuquerque, NM: University of New Mexico Press, 1969), p. 5.
2 Hachivi Edgar Heap of Birds, "Introduction," in *Modern Native American Abstraction* (Philadelphia: Philadelphia Art Alliance 1982), unp.
3 Hachivi Edgar Heap of Birds, "My Past, My People," in *Sharp Rocks;* reprinted in *Blasted Allegories,* ed. Brian Wallis (New York: New Museum of Contemporary Art; Cambridge, MA: MIT Press, 1987), p. 171.
4 Lowery Stokes Sims, "Words into Vision: The Art of Hachivi Edgar Heap of Birds," in *Claim Your Color* (New York: Exit Art, 1990), p. 12.
5 Hachivi Edgar Heap of Birds, "My Past, My People," pp. 170–71.

6 The Fort Marion artists were a group of Plains Indians who were held prisoner in Saint Augustine, Florida, from 1875 to 1878. As Heap of Birds himself has written in one of his "Insurgent Messages for America" (on the exhibition announcement for the 1987 opening of "Sharp Rocks" at the Artculture Resource Center in Toronto): "Because of these actions in 1874 [Native raids to recapture traditional lands], seventy-three defiant warriors and chiefs from the southern plains were arrested by U.S. troops. They were exiled to Fort Marion, St. Augustine, Florida, and imprisoned. These seventy-two men and one woman were taken from their families without a trial and charged with the vague term of 'ring leaders.' While suffering through the sad prison life many warriors created artworks by drawing. The colorful drawings became the messages that the warriors could relay about their captivity, the damaging interaction with the whiteman, and their personal expressions of Native freedom." See also Moira Harris, *Between Two Cultures: Kiowa Art from Fort Marion* (St. Paul, MN: Pogo Press, 1989) and Karen Daniels Petersen, *Plains Indian Art from Fort Marion, Florida* (Norman, OK: University of Oklahoma Press, 1971).

7 Edgar Heap of Birds, printed announcement flyer for December 5, 1986, lecture entitled "Insurgent Messages for America" to accompany "Sharp Rocks" exhibition opening at 911 Contemporary Arts Center, Seattle, Washington.

RICK HILL

1 Rick Hill, "Along the Flowered Path," in *Silver Drum: Five Native Photographers* (Hamilton, Ontario: NIIPA, 1986), p. 28.

2 Rick Hill, "Photography's Next Era," ibid., p. 21.

3 Rick Hill, "Transformation," ibid., p. 27.

4 Rick Hill, "The Whiteman in North America," in *Portraits: Paintings and Photographs by Rick Hill* (Thunder Bay, Ontario: Thunder Bay Art Gallery, 1986), p. 9.

5 Rick Hill, "Art as a Sovereign Act," in an untitled brochure for a symposium on American Indian Law sponsored by the American Indian Law Students Association, Columbia University, October 24–26, 1986.

6 Hill, "Photography's Next Era," p. 20.

7 Carol Podedworny, in *Portraits: Paintings and Photographs by Rick Hill,* p. 3.

8 Robert Frank, *The Americans* (Millerton, NY: Aperture, 1978). See especially "U.S. 91, leaving Blackfoot, Idaho" (p. 75) and "Bar—Las Vegas, Nevada" (p. 59).

9 Hill, in *Silver Drum,* pp. 24–25.

10 Hill, "Photography's Next Era," p. 22.

G. PETER JEMISON

1 *G. Peter Jemison: Mid-Career Retrospective* (Browning, MT: Museum of the Plains Indian, 1987), unp.

2 G. Peter Jemison, "The Paper Bag Works," in *We Are Always Turning Around . . . on Purpose* (Old Westbury, NY: Amelie A. Wallace Gallery, State University of New York, 1986), p. 22; Jimmie Durham, "Ni' Go Tlunk A Doh Ka," ibid., p. 4.

3 Jemison, "The Paper Bag Works," p. 22.

4 "Peter Jemison, Seneca Painter," in *This Song Remembers: Self-Portraits of*

Native Americans in the Arts, ed. Jane Katz (Boston: Houghton Mifflin, 1980), p. 46.

5 Ibid., p. 50.

6 Durham, "Ni' Go Tlunh A Doh Ka," p. 4.

MIKE KABOTIE

1 Patricia Broder, *Hopi Painting: The World of the Hopi* (New York: E. P. Dutton, 1978), p. 280.

2 Tryntje Van Ness Seymour, *When the Rainbow Touches Down* (Phoenix, AZ: Heard Museum, 1988), p. 239.

3 For a discussion of Herrera and some of his work, see Seymour, *When the Rainbow Touches Down,* especially pp. 149–52 and 171–75. W. Jackson Rushing also discusses the importance of Herrera in "Authenticity and Subjectivity in Post-War Painting: Concerning Herrera, Scholder, and Cannon," in *Shared Visions* (Phoenix, AZ: Heard Museum, 1991), pp. 12–19.

4 In addition to Mike Kabotie, the other organizing members of Artist Hopid were Neil David, Sr., and Terrance Honvantewa. (Talaswaima legally changed his name to Honvantewa, his adult Hopi name). Other members included Delbridge Honanie and Milland Lomakema. Tyler Polelonema also exhibited with the group. See Broder, *Hopi Painting,* pp. 299–304.

5 Seymour, *When the Rainbow Touches Down,* p. 258.

6 Quoted in Jamake, Highwater, *The Sweet Grass Lives On: Fifty Contemporary North American Indian Artists* (New York: Lippincott and Crowell, 1980), p. 142.

7 Kabotie attended the Southwest Indian Art Project at the University of Arizona, held during the summers of 1960 and 1961. The basic aim of the project was to offer young Native artists exposure to less traditional and more modernist approaches to art. For a brief discussion of the project and its underlying philosophy, see Joy L. Gritton, "The Institute of American Indian Arts: A Convergence of Ideologies," in *Shared Visions,* p. 23.

8 Joe Herrera of Cochiti Pueblo was one of the instructors at the summer program in 1960. He brought his enthusiasm and excitement for the Awatovi kiva murals, excavated in Arizona in the 1930s, to his students, one of whom was Michael Kabotie. See Seymour, *When the Rainbow Touches Down,* pp. 149–52. The murals, dating from c. 900 A.D., depict religious symbols and such figures as Ahula, the Germinator. For a discussion of the murals, with reproductions, see Broder, *Hopi Painting,* esp. pp. 201–30.

9 Quoted in Seymour, *When the Rainbow Touches Down,* p. 239.

10 See note 4 above.

11 Mike Kabotie, statement in Native American Artists Resource Collection, Heard Museum, Phoenix, AZ.

FRANK LAPENA

1 Christopher Brown, "Contemporary Indian Art: A Critic's View," in *The Extension of Tradition: Contemporary Northern California Native American Art in Cultural Perspective,* ed. Frank LaPena and Janice Driesbach (Sacramento, CA: Crocker Art Museum, 1985), p. 16.

2 Frank LaPena, "My World Is a Gift of My Teachers," in *The Extension of Tradition,* p. 13.

3 A pan-Indian group including a number of Wintu people occupied a construction worker housing site left idle after the completion of the Shasta Dam

project north of Redding, California. The group gained occupancy, quite legally, by the takeover of unused government land. However, the Bureau of Indian Affairs bulldozed the area in the mid-1980s and the group lost its claim on the land.

4 Momaday discusses this idea of the single continuous story in an interview with Joseph Bruchac in *Survival This Way* (Tucson, AZ: University of Arizona Press, 1987); see especially p. 187. In his introduction to *Ancestral Voice: Conversations with N. Scott Momaday* (Lincoln, NE: University of Nebraska Press, 1989), Charles Woodard refers to the Bruchac interview and also notes: "It is important to understand that Momaday means to tell one long story, as he has said on several occasions" (p. x).

CARM LITTLE TURTLE

1 Carm Little Turtle, "Reflections in Time," unpublished artist's statement, n.d.

LINDA LOMAHAFTEWA

1 Linda Lomahaftewa, "Artist's Statement," in *After 5 P.M. . . . and on Weekends: Art of the Faculty of the Institute of American Indian Arts* (Santa Fe, NM: Institute of American Indian Arts, 1991), p. 39.

2 Lloyd Oxendine, "Twenty-three Contemporary Indian Artists," *Art in America* 60, 4 (July–August 1972): 60.

3 Margaret Archuleta and Rennard Strickland, eds., *Shared Visions* (Phoenix, AZ: Heard Museum, 1991), p. 94.

4 Quoted in Robert Breunig and Erin Younger, "The Second Biennial Native American Fine Art Invitational," *American Indian Art Magazine* 11, 2 (Spring 1986): 61.

5 Lomahaftewa, "Artist's Statement," in *After 5 P.M. . . . and on Weekends,* p. 39.

6 Ibid.

7 Quoted in Jamake Highwater, *The Sweet Grass Lives On* (New York: Lippincott and Crowell, 1980), p. 138.

GEORGE LONGFISH

1 See *Wicazo Sa Review* 7, 1 (Spring 1991) and 7, 2 (Fall 1991), respectively.

2 Quoted by Kay WalkingStick, "Like a Longfish Out of Water," *Northeast Indian Quarterly* 7, 3 (Fall 1989): 20.

3 Jimmie Durham, "A Central Margin," in *The Decade Show* (New York: Museum of Contemporary Hispanic Art, New Museum of Contemporary Art, and Studio Museum of Harlem, 1990), p. 174.

4 Ibid., p. 174.

5 George Longfish, in *Indigena: Contemporary Native Perspectives* (Hull, Quebec: Canadian Museum of Civilization, 1992), p. 151.

6 George Longfish and Joan Randall, "Contradictions in Indian Territory," in *Contemporary Native American Art* (Stillwater, OK: Gardiner Art Gallery, Oklahoma State University, 1983), unp.; reprinted with minor revisions in the *Journal of Arts Management and Law* 18, 2 (Summer 1988): 20–24.

7 Ibid. (p. 24 in the *Journal of Arts Management and Law*).

8 WalkingStick, "Like a Longfish Out of Water," pp. 18–19.

9 "George Longfish" [artist's statement], in *Contemporary Native American Art,* unp.

MARIO MARTINEZ

1 "Mario Martinez," in *Portfolio III: Ten Native American Artists* (San Francisco, CA: American Indian Contemporary Arts, 1991), p. 22.
2 Mario Martinez, "Artist's Statement," in *Talking Drum: Connected Vision* (Oakland, CA: Koncepts Cultural Gallery, 1990), unp.

NORA NARANJO-MORSE

1 Stephen Trimble, *Talking with the Clay* (Santa Fe, NM: School of American Research Press, 1987), p. 105.
2 Stephen Trimble, "Brown Earth and Laughter: The Clay People of Nora Naranjo-Morse," *American Indian Art Magazine* 12, 4 (Autumn 1987): 60; see also Linda B. Eaton, "Nora Naranjo-Morse," in *A Separate Vision* (Flagstaff, AZ: Museum of Northern Arizona, 1989), p. 14.
3 Trimble, *Talking with the Clay,* p. 50.
4 This piece has been reproduced under both titles. Naranjo-Morse told me that each is correct. The circumstances of its production, and even the process of giving titles, provide an insight into her work: "I did this particular piece very late one night, when all living things seemed to be sleeping, [and] there was a certain density to the early morning air that filled the studio with peace and utter silence. . . . The messages I receive from a magical night of creating rest on a certain level inside my memory bank, and the memories will surface and feed me when I then try to make sense of these other worlds I live in. When I left the studio that night, I made preparation to leave for . . . New York City, for business. When I returned home, I arrived very late at night [and] got out of the car and just stood in the freezing cold. . . . I was home. I was being transformed. . . . I get tired telling this all the time to people, so I just say the titles; funny, but they just keep getting longer and more often [a work will have] two or three titles" (personal communication, February 26, 1992).
5 "Nora Naranjo-Morse," in *Portfolio III: Ten Native American Artists* (San Francisco, CA: American Indian Contemporary Arts, 1991), p. 25.
6 Trimble, *Talking with the Clay,* p. 50.

JAUNE QUICK-TO-SEE SMITH

1 *New Paintings by Jaune Quick-to-See Smith: A View of Western Lands,* exhibition brochure, Bernice Steinbaum Gallery, New York, NY, 1990.
2 "Jaune Quick-to-See Smith," in *Portfolio III: Ten Native American Artists* (San Francisco: American Indian Contemporary Arts, 1991), p. 31.

SUSAN STEWART

1 Susan Stewart, *Paintings by Kathryn and Susan Stewart* (Browning, MT: Museum of the Plains Indian and Crafts Center, 1979), unp.

FRANK TUTTLE

1 Frank Tuttle, "Artist's Statement," in *Innovations: New Expressions in Native American Painting* (Phoenix, AZ: Heard Museum, 1983), unp.
2 Frank Tuttle, "Artist's Statement," in *The Extension of Tradition: Contemporary Northern California Native American Art in Cultural Perspective,* ed.

Frank LaPena and Janice Driesbach (Sacramento, CA: Crocker Art Museum, 1985), p. 71.

3 George Longfish and Joan Randall, "Made by Choice," ibid., p. 47.

4 Frank Tuttle, "Artist's Statement," ibid., p. 70.

5 Junipero Serra (1713–84), a Spanish Franciscan priest, led the Spanish missionary efforts at present-day San Diego from 1769 until his death, a period during which members of his order established nine missions in California. In the 1980s the church's desire to canonize him met with opposition because of the cruelty and racism of the mission system and its near-genocidal effect on Indian communities, and the plan was dropped. See Robert L. Schuyler, "Indian-Euro-American Interaction: Archaeological Evidence from Non-Indian Sites," and Edward D. Castillo, "The Impact of Euro-American Exploration and Settlement," in *Handbook of North American Indians,* Vol. 8, edited by Robert Heizer (Washington, DC: Smithsonian Institution, 1978).

6 Dorothy Dunn (1903–92) founded a painting studio for Native artists in Santa Fe and operated it from 1932 to 1937. She encouraged a flat, two-dimensional style in the work of her students (who included Allan Houser, Fred Kabotie, and Pablita Velarde) which became known as "traditional Indian art." See Dorothy Dunn, *American Indian Painting of the Southwest and the Plains Areas* (Albuquerque, NM: University of New Mexico Press, 1968) and "America's First Painters," *National Geographic* 108, 3 (March 1955): 349–77.

7 Tuttle, "Artist's Statement," in *Innovations: New Expressions in Native American Painting.*

8 Frank LaPena, "My World Is a Gift of My Teachers," in *The Extension of Tradition,* p. 13.

KAY WALKINGSTICK

1 Kay WalkingStick, "On Spirituality in Landscape," slide and lecture presentation, Women's Caucus for Art Annual Convention, San Francisco, CA, January 1989.

2 Ibid.

3 Vivien Raynor, "The Male Figure, Dual Images and Landscapes," *New York Times,* March 26, 1989, p. 17.

4 Lucy Lippard, *Mixed Blessings: New Art in a Multicultural America* (New York: Pantheon Books, 1990), p. 186.

EMMI WHITEHORSE

1 Lucy Lippard, "Shimá: The Paintings of Emmi Whitehorse," in *Neeznáá* (Santa Fe, NM: Wheelwright Museum of the American Indian, 1991), unp.

2 Emmi Whitehorse, quoted in Jan Best, "Indian Museums Combine the Old and the New," *Bienvenidos* [Santa Fe, NM], Summer 1992, p. 30.

3 Lippard, "Shimá: The Paintings of Emmi Whitehorse."

4 Emmi Whitehorse, "Artist's Statement," in *Eight Native American Artists* (For Wayne, IN: Fort Wayne Museum of Art, 1987), p. 44.

5 Emmi Whitehorse, "Artist's Statement," in *Six From Santa Fe: Contemporary Native American Art from Santa Fe* (Charleston, SC: Gibbes Museum of Art, 1989), unp.

6 Regarding the Santa Fe Studio of Dorothy Dunn, see Frank Tuttle, note 6, above. The Kiowa Five (actually six) were a group of artists who studied at the University of Oklahoma around the same time as Dunn's group was

active in Santa Fe. For a discussion of the Kiowa Five, see David M. Fawcett and Lee A. Callander, *Native American Painting: Selections from the Museum of the American Indian* (New York: Museum of the American Indian, 1982) and Jean Sherrod Williams, *American Indian Artists: The Avery Collection and the McNay Permanent Collection* (San Antonio, TX: Marion Koogler McNay Art Museum, 1990).

Photo Credits

Rick Glazer-Danay photographed by Gayle Glazer, courtesy of the artist.

Shan Goshorn photographed by Shan Goshorn, courtesy of the artist.

Hachivi Edgar Heap of Birds photographed by Hachivi Edgar Heap of Birds, courtesy of the artist.

Rick Hill photographed by Bob Wartell, © 1991, used by permission of the Institute of American Indian Arts.

G. Peter Jemison photographed by Jolene Rickard.

Michael Kabotie photographed by Helga Teiwes, used by permission.

Frank LaPena photographed by Carla Hills, courtesy of the artist.

Carm Little Turtle photographed by Carm Little Turtle, courtesy of the artist.

Linda Lomahaftewa photographed by Lawrence Abbott.

George Longfish photographed by Samuel W. Woo, courtesy of the artist.

Mario Martinez photographed by Stephen Hawthorne.

Nora Naranjo-Morse photographed by Lawrence Abbott.

Jaune Quick-to-See Smith photographed by Jolene Rickard, used by permission.

Susan Stewart photographed by Terry Macy, courtesy of the artist.

Frank Tuttle photographed by Cheryl Tuttle, courtesy of the artist.

Kay WalkingStick photographed by Peter Tilgner, courtesy of the artist.

Emmi Whitehorse photographed by Dirk DeBruycker, courtesy of the artist.

In the American Indian Lives series

I Stand in the Center of the Good: Interviews with Contemporary Native American Artists
Edited by Lawrence Abbott

Chainbreaker: The Revolutionary War Memoir of Governor Blacksnake As told to Benjamin Williams
Edited by Thomas S. Abler

Chief: The Life History of Eugene Delorme, Imprisoned Santee Sioux
Edited by Inéz Cardozo-Freeman

Winged Words: Contemporary American Indian Writers Speak
Edited by Laura Coltelli

Life Lived Like a Story: Life Stories of Three Yukon Native Elders
By Julie Cruikshank in collaboration with Angela Sidney, Kitty Smith, and Annie Ned

Alex Posey: Creek Poet, Journalist, and Humorist
By Daniel F. Littlefield, Jr.

Mourning Dove: A Salishan Autobiography
Edited by Jay Miller

John Rollin Ridge: His Life and Works
By James W. Parins

Singing an Indian Song: A Biography of D'Arcy McNickle
By Dorothy R. Parker

Sacred Feathers: The Reverend Peter Jones (Kahkewaquonaby) and the Mississauga Indians
By Donald B. Smith

I Tell You Now: Autobiographical Essays by Native American Writers
Edited by Brian Swann and Arnold Krupat

Standing in the Light: A Lakota Way of Seeing
By Severt Young Bear and R. D. Theisz